PERSONALIZED DEEPER LEARNING

Blueprints for Teaching Complex Cognitive, Social-Emotional, and Digital Skills

JAMES A. BELLANCA

Solution Tree | Press

Copyright © 2021 by Solution Tree Press

Materials appearing here are copyrighted. With one exception, all rights are reserved. Readers may reproduce only those pages marked "Reproducible." Otherwise, no part of this book may be reproduced or transmitted in any form or by any means (electronic, photocopying, recording, or otherwise) without prior written permission of the publisher.

555 North Morton Street
Bloomington, IN 47404
800.733.6786 (toll free) / 812.336.7700
FAX: 812.336.7790

email: info@SolutionTree.com
SolutionTree.com

Visit **go.SolutionTree.com/instruction** to download the free reproducibles in this book.

Printed in the United States of America

Library of Congress Cataloging-in-Publication Data

Names: Bellanca, James A., 1937- author.
Title: Personalized deeper learning : blueprints for teaching complex
   cognitive, social-emotional, and digital skills / James A. Bellanca.
Description: Bloomington, IN : Solution Tree Press, [2020] | Includes
   bibliographical references and index.
Identifiers: LCCN 2020025264 (print) | LCCN 2020025265 (ebook) | ISBN
   9781951075415 (paperback) | ISBN 9781951075422 (ebook)
Subjects: LCSH: Individualized instruction. | Self-managed learning. |
   Machine learning.
Classification: LCC LB1031 .B435 2020 (print) | LCC LB1031 (ebook) | DDC
   371.39/4--dc23
LC record available at https://lccn.loc.gov/2020025264
LC ebook record available at https://lccn.loc.gov/2020025265

Solution Tree

Jeffrey C. Jones, CEO
Edmund M. Ackerman, President

Solution Tree Press

President and Publisher: Douglas M. Rife
Associate Publisher: Sarah Payne-Mills
Art Director: Rian Anderson
Managing Production Editor: Kendra Slayton
Senior Production Editor: Tonya Maddox Cupp
Content Development Specialist: Amy Rubenstein
Copy Editor: Kate St. Ives
Proofreader: Elisabeth Abrams
Text and Cover Designer: Abigail Bowen
Editorial Assistants: Sarah Ludwig and Elijah Oates

Acknowledgments

From our first partnership writing *Blueprints for Thinking in the Cooperative Classroom* in 1997, Robin Fogarty has inspired my thinking about professional development. Together, we stepped outside the box, not only with our determination to focus our efforts on cognitive-collaborative learning theory practices, but to make what we taught practical for preK–12 educators. Our work together over these decades has thrived. Our early collaborations, later reinforced by research that supported our intuition, seeded the many ideas published in the first *Blueprints* to this *Blueprints*. Every book of our many celebrates Robin's creative spirit and dedication to best practice.

For their experience, encouragement, wisdom, and collaboration, I celebrate the expert voices of the Solution Tree staff, with special kudos to Tonya Cupp and Amy Rubenstein, editors par excellence, to Abby Bowen and Rian Anderson for reader-friendly design inside and outside the book, and to president and publisher Douglas Rife for his many years of support for my work.

I also want to acknowledge the influence and mentoring of those who have contributed to the ideas advanced in this book: Roger and David Johnson, Ron Brandt, Reuven Feuerstein, Eleanor Renée Rodriguez, Art Costa, Carolyn Chapman, Kay Burke, Brian Pete, Howard Gardner, Linda Darling-Hammond, Howie and Barbara Kirschbaum, Craig Maki, Elliott Masie, Joel and Margie Goodman, Terry Stirling, Rod Napier, and my youngest daughter, Kate Bellanca.

For their patience and support, I hail my other grown children—Carla, Mary Jo, and Jamie—and my wife, Gerry. I especially have to appreciate my children's children for their sometimes brutal but appreciated comments from a teenage perspective.

For their contributions to the design of the personalized learning template, I thank parents and colleagues Kerry Berger Trigg, Gwen Lavert, Arline Paul, and Sue Segal for their outside-the-classroom perspectives. Lastly, I give hearty shoutouts to the many teachers and school administrators with whom I have collaborated over the years. I value their from-the-field perspectives as much as the formal research I rely on to guide my writing and consulting endeavors.

Solution Tree Press would like to thank the following reviewers:

Louis Lim
Vice Principal
Richmond Green Secondary School
Richmond Hill, Ontario, Canada

Rosemarie Swallow (Olsen)
Social Studies and Reading Teacher
Lava Ridge Intermediate
Santa Clara, Utah

Andrea Paulakovich
Director for Learning Services
Olathe Public Schools
Olathe, Kansas

Bruce Preston
Assistant Superintendent of Curriculum and Personnel
Howell Township Public Schools
Howell, New Jersey

Visit **go.SolutionTree.com/instruction** to download the free reproducibles in this book.

TABLE OF CONTENTS

Reproducible pages are in italics.

About the Author xi

Introduction 1
    How This Idea Began 2
    How the Idea Works in This Book 5
        Focusing on How-To 6
        Digging Deeper Into Theories 6
    How the Idea Works in Your Classroom 8
    How the Chapters Are Organized 9
    Takeaways 10

CHAPTER 1
Personalized Learning Plans 11
    What Is Personalized Learning? 12
    What Evidence Supports Personalized Learning? 13
    What Does a Personalized Learning Plan Look Like? 13
    What Are the Personalized Learning Plan Processes? 18
    How Do I Launch Personalized Learning Plans, and What Should I Include? 20
    What Does Personalized Learning Look and Sound Like in a K–12 Classroom? . . 23
    What Is the Potential for Personalized Learning in My Classroom? 23
    How Will Personalized Learning Plans Help My Remote Learning Instruction? . . . 24
    How Do I Ready My Class for Personalized Learning? 25
    How Can I Address What Students Need to Know With
Personalized Learning Plans? 27
    How Do I Ensure I Cover My Standards During Personalized Learning? 27
    What New Skill Sets Will I Need to Teach? 30
        The Complex Cognitive Skill Set 30

The Social-Emotional Skill Set 32

　　　The Digital Skill Set 32

　Takeaways 34

CHAPTER 2

Engagement and Trust 35

　What Is Engagement? 35

　What Conditions Promote Deeper Engagement? 36

　Where Do Communication and Collaboration Come In? 36

　How Can I Gauge the Level of Mutual Respect and Trust in My Classroom? 37

　How Do I Engage Students in Peer Interviews? 39

　How Do I Promote Reflection? 39

　What Activities Are Best for Building and Maintaining Trust? 41

　　　Prompt Circle 43

　　　Shapes Made Perfect 43

　　　Science Scavenger Search 43

　　　Engineering Feats 44

　　　Collaborative Class Puzzle 44

　　　By Any Other Name 44

　How Do Cooperative Learning and Team Problem Solving Maintain Trust? 44

　What Does Research Say About Cooperative Learning? 45

　　　Informal Cooperative Learning 45

　　　Formal Cooperative Learning 46

　What Activities Are Best for Transferring Team Skills to Decision-Making Scenarios? . . . 46

　　　Tight Problem Solving 46

　　　Loose Problem Solving 50

　Takeaways 52

CHAPTER 3

Outcome-Driven Instruction and Assessment 53

　What Is Outcome-Driven Instruction? 53

　How Do I Apply Design Thinking to Personalized Learning Plans? 57

　How Do I Plan for Deeper Learning Outcomes? 57

　How Do I Make Deeper Learning Competency My First Priority? 58

　How Do I Create My Personalized Teaching Plan? 60

　Do I Help Students Construct *Authentic* Outcomes in a
　Personalized Learning Plan? 65

　What Is Outcome-Driven Assessment? 65

　What Outcomes Can I Assess With a Personalized Learning Plan? 67

What Do Outcome-Driven Assessments Look or Sound Like? 68
What Tools Work Best When Assessing Personalized Learning Plan Outcomes?. . . 69
    What Is a Guiding Rubric? 70
    How Is a *Guiding* Rubric Different From a *Grading* Rubric? 71
    What Does a Guiding Rubric Look Like?. 72
How Do I Assess My Personalized Teaching Plan? 77
What Are My Responsibilities in a Personalized Learning Plan Assessment? 78
    Identify Outcomes 79
    Select, Create, or Co-Create Guiding Rubrics 80
    Set Up a Record Storage System 80
    Schedule Personal Feedback Time 80
    Dialogue With Students 80
    Ask for and Listen to Students' Feedback 80
    Capture Need-to-Know Teachable Moments. 80
    Communicate With Parents and Guardians 81
    Prepare Playbooks 81
    Prepare Playlists. 81
How Do I Keep Personalized Learning Plan Playbooks, Playlists,
Rubrics, and Artifacts Organized? 82
What Logistics Are Necessary for a Personalized Learning Plan Assessment?. . . 83
Takeaways 85

CHAPTER 4
Student Agency 87

What Is Student Agency? 87
What Does Research Say About Promoting Student Agency?. 88
What Does Agency Look and Sound Like in a Classroom? 89
How Do I Determine the Degree of Agency Appropriate for My Students? 91
How Do I Encourage and Develop Student Agency? 95
How Do I Promote Agency With Two-Way Feedback? 97
How Do I Assess How My Feedback Impacts Student Agency? 98
How Do I Provide Agency-Enhancing Feedback?. 99
    Set Feedback Criteria. 99
    Establish Norms for Respectful Two-Way Feedback. 99
    Encourage Peer Feedback. 100
    Build Teamwork Skills 100
    Guide the Feedback Process 100
    Develop Feedback Skills 101
    Save All Feedback 102
How Do I Find the Time and Place to Give and Get Two-Way Feedback? 103
Takeaways 104

CHAPTER 5
Skill Transfer 105

- What Is Learning Transfer? 105
  - Proximity Transfer—Near and Far 106
  - Depth Transfer—Shallow and Deep 107
  - Directional Transfer—Backward and Forward 107
- Why Should I Focus on Learning Transfer? 110
- How Do I Plan for Transfer? 110
  - Elementary School Example 112
  - High School Example 112
- What Do Far and Near Learning Transfer Look and Sound Like? 113
- How Do I Assess Transfer? 115
- Takeaways 118

CHAPTER 6
The Complex Cognitive Skill Set 119

- What Is Complex Cognition? 120
- What Skills Make Up the Complex Cognitive Skill Set? 121
- What Is Critical Thinking? 122
- What Is the Relationship Between Content and Thinking Skills? 122
- How Are Educators Responding to the Need for Students to Know How to Think? ...123
- How Do I Create a Guiding Rubric for a Critical-Thinking Skill? 123
- What Strategies and Activities Promote Critical-Thinking Skills? 126
  - Elementary School 126
  - Middle School 127
  - High School 127
- What Is Creative Thinking? 128
  - What Is Visualizing? 129
  - What Strategies and Activities Promote Visualization? 130
  - How Do I Create a Guiding Rubric for Visualizing? 132
  - What Is Ideating? 132
  - How Do I Construct a Personalized Learning Plan That Promotes Ideation Skills? 133
  - What Strategies and Activities Promote Ideation? 135
  - How Do I Create a Guiding Rubric for Formal Brainstorming? ... 139
  - What Is Synthesizing? 139
  - How Do I Construct a Lesson or Project That Promotes Synthesis Skills? ... 140
  - What Strategies and Activities Promote Synthesis? 140
  - How Do I Create a Guiding Rubric for Synthesis? 143

What Is Accessing the Future?......................................143
How Do I Construct a Lesson or Project That Promotes Predicting Skills?...144
What Strategies and Activities Promote Predicting Skills?..............145
How Do I Create a Guiding Rubric for Predicting?...................147
Takeaways..148

CHAPTER 7
The Social-Emotional Skill Set 149

What Is Social-Emotional Learning?...................................150
What Skills Make Up the Social-Emotional Skill Set?..................150
What Is Emotion Self-Management?...................................150
   How Do I Construct a Lesson or Project That Promotes Emotion Self-Management?..............................151
   What Prompts Encourage Emotion Self-Management?...............153
   What Strategies and Activities Promote Emotion Self-Management?......153
   How Do I Create a Rubric for Monitoring Emotions?..................156
What Is Empathy?..156
   How Do I Construct a Lesson or Project That Promotes Empathy?........158
   What Prompts Encourage Empathy?................................158
   What Strategies and Activities Promote Empathy?...................159
   How Do I Create a Rubric for Building Empathy?...................161
What Are Interpersonal Relationship Skills?...........................161
   How Do I Construct a Lesson or Project That Promotes Interpersonal Skills?...162
   What Prompts Encourage Interpersonal Skills?.......................163
   What Strategies and Activities Promote Interpersonal Skills?...........163
   How Do I Create a Rubric for Interpersonal Relationship Skills?.........165
What Is Goal Setting?...167
   How Do I Construct a Lesson or Project That Promotes Goal Setting?.....167
   What Prompts Promote Goal Setting?...............................167
   What Strategies and Activities Encourage Goal Setting?...............169
   How Do I Create a Rubric for Goal Setting?........................172
How Do I Best Develop Students' Social-Emotional Skills During Remote Learning?...172
   Collaboration..172
   Student Agency, Self-Direction, and Self-Management................173
Takeaways..174

CHAPTER 8
The Digital Skill Set 175

What Are Digital Skills?...176
What Skills Make Up the Digital Skill Set?............................176

How Do I Determine What Digital Skills Students Need to Learn?..............178
How Do I Construct a Lesson or Project That Promotes Digital Skills?..........179
    Elementary School..180
    Middle School...182
What Strategies and Activities Promote Digital Skills?......................192
How Do I Create a Guiding Rubric for Digital Skills?........................193
How Do I Assess My Implementation Plan?..................................194
What Are the Most Helpful Digital Tools for Enhancing
Personalized Learning Plans?...195
    Tool Categories..196
    Learning Management System...................................197
    Digital Portfolios..198
    Playlists...199
    Playbooks..200
    Rubrics Bank...203
    Templates..203
    Reflection Journals..203
    Social Media Networks.......................................203
    Free Websites..205
What Digital Tools Facilitate Remote Learning?............................205
Takeaways...207

CONCLUSION
Personalized Deeper Learning for a Lifetime 209

APPENDIX
Templates 211

Personalized Learning Plan 212
Starter Personalized Learning Plan 215
Interview Questions 217
Personalized Teaching Plan 219
Rated Checklist—PreK–3 222
Improvement Rating Scale—Grades 3–12 224
Single-Point Guiding Rubric—Grades 3–12 226
Multi-Point Guiding Rubric—Grades 3–12 228
Open-Ended Self-Assessment Rubric—Grades 3–12 231

References and Resources .... .233

Index... .249

About the Author

James A. Bellanca is internationally recognized as a practical innovator who provides teachers and administrators with the how-to knowledge to make abstract ideas concrete and ready to go on the next school day. He is a senior fellow with the Partnership for 21st Century Learning and was founding editor of its innovative online publication *P21 Blogazine*. He is the 2013 recipient of the Malcolm Knowles Award for lifetime contributions to the field of self-directed learning from the International Society for Self-Directed Learning.

With his extensive experience as a classroom English and language arts teacher, alternative school director, professional developer, intermediate service center director, business owner, and not-for-profit executive, Jim has developed expertise for transforming mandates, such as the Common Core State Standards, into practical classroom tools that enrich instruction and engage students.

He is past president of the Illinois Consortium for 21st Century Schools and lead trainer for MindQuest: Project-Based Learning in the 21st Century Classroom, which helps schools with large English learner populations and students of color and poverty adopt the project-based learning model of instruction. Jim has worked with educational leaders in the United States, Australia, New Zealand, Norway, and Israel. His specialty is the application of group investigation and inquiry models of learning as the primary methods for helping school leaders and teachers adopt 21st century models of instruction. His aim is to help school districts design, implement, and assess programs that promote 21st century skills to increase academic performance among all students, including high-risk populations.

Jim works closely with Solution Tree Press to identify emerging authors who address the themes and practices that define and describe 21st century learning. He has authored or coauthored multiple Solution Tree Press how-to books about thinking in the Common Core, enriched learning projects, and leadership for the Common Core. He coedited the *Leading Edge*™ series title *21st Century Skills: Rethinking How Students Learn* with Ron Brandt and edited *Deeper Learning: Beyond 21st Century Skills* and *Connecting the Dots: Teacher Effectiveness and Deeper Professional Learning*.

To book James A. Bellanca for professional development, contact pd@SolutionTree.com.

INTRODUCTION

> [Artificial intelligence] will be a great tool for teachers and educational institutions, as it will help educators figure out how to personalize curriculum based on each student's competence, progress, aptitude, and temperament. However, teaching will still need to be oriented around helping students figure out their interests, teaching students to learn independently, and providing one-on-one mentorship.
>
> —Kai-Fu Lee

In summers during my novice teaching years, I instructed young campers to qualify as Junior Maine Guides in the camp where I was a counselor. I did this by readying each camper to pass a rigorous survival test. These pre-adolescents had to prove their mettle over the course of three tough days. The test included a solo camping trip in which each camper was equipped with only a multi-tooled Swiss Army knife. Giving lectures or showing videos was insufficient preparation for the solo trip. So too were pep talks. Single-answer quizzes had no value. These eager kids needed to learn hands-on and demonstrate what they could do.

When I was hired as an instructional guide, I was told my role was to model, show, coach, and mentor. This was my introduction to the challenges inherent in wearing an instructional guide's hat. In the years that followed as I worked as a teacher, school leader, and professional developer, I learned much more about how to help young people develop competence, whether in the classroom or camping in the woods. When I was growing up, my mother had a favorite saying, "Don't be a smart aleck; your head is more than a hat rack." And she would add, "Any dope can wear a hat. People will know you are doing it the right way when you wear it the smart way." Although I had heard my mother say this all my life, I didn't start to truly think about what it meant until I gained experience as a school leader, teacher, and guide. I realized that my job was not just to give the Junior Maine Guides their own guide hats; it was to teach them how to be smart when they wore the hat. Likewise, my job as an educator is not simply to impart knowledge but to help students know how to find and use knowledge to learn and continually grow.

Years after I first heard my mother's phrase, and even years after I began to think about what it meant, my mentor, psychologist Reuven Feuerstein, gave me another sound piece of advice. At the end of a tutorial session, I said, "Dr. Feuerstein, I am puzzled. I hear you talk all the time about modifiability of intelligence and the *no-limits mind*. I never hear you mention the heart and emotions. Surely, feelings play a part in learning?"

Raising and wagging his index finger, he looked intently into my eyes, a twinkle in his own. "Jim," he said softly, "It is your heart that keeps your brain alive. Without feelings, you do not think. There are no limits on either. They work together."

I was silent. As I thought, "He must be a smart man to be so wise," he finished by saying, "I am only as smart as my heart is big."

Teachers who see learning not as reception of knowledge into empty containers of set capacity but rather see and foster learning as the construction of meaning by both thinking and feeling beings are the *smart* guides.

In this book, I share what I learned over the years about facilitating the processes of learning as construction of meaning by thinking *and* feeling beings. I articulate my ideas through a context that includes the use of digital tools in the learning process. I see these digital tools as resources similar to the expandable Junior Guide's Swiss Army knife. But first, what prompted my idea of using digital tools to further comprehensive learning that engages the mind and heart?

How This Idea Began

I am part of a group that began as a neighborhood coffee klatch informally discussing local school issues. One day, during a discussion with this group—colleagues and friends that include a grade-school instructional coach, a retired auto mechanic, an art teacher, and a university professor of adult learning, among others—someone shared a chart comparing the predicted hours workers will spend in jobs. Figure I.1 shows the top-three growth areas in those hours workers spend on their jobs: (1) complex cognitive, (2) social-emotional, and (3) digital.

My coffee klatch pal and colleague noted how the figure groups skills into sets that differentiate memory from thinking, and it includes social-emotional and digital skill sets, making it more specific and perhaps more representative of true-to-life learning than the widely accepted Partnership for 21st Century Learning's (P21; 2019) four Cs of (1) communication, (2) collaboration, (3) creativity, and (4) critical thinking. Our colleague

Complex Cognitive	Social-Emotional	Digital

• Critical thinking:
   • Analyzing
   • Comparing
   • Differentiating
   • Evaluating
   • Reasoning
   • Problem solving
• Creative thinking:
   • Generating
   • Associating
   • Hypothesizing
   • Inferring
   • Synthesizing
   • Transferring
   • Designing
	• Collaboration
	• Cooperation
	• Conflict resolution
	• Cross-cultural communication
	• Self-management
	• Empathy
	• Caring
	• Mutual trust and respect
	• Decision making
		• Coding
		• Programming
		• Analytics
		• Managing social media
		• Multi-platform user experience (UX)
		• Video sales design
		• Cybersecurity
		• Instructional technology (IT)
		• Design
		• Technology teaching
		• Engineering robotics

Source: Adapted from Bellanca, Fogarty, & Pete, 2020; New York State Department of Education, 2018; Organisation for Economic Co-operation and Development (OECD), 2019; World Economic Forum, 2020.

Figure I.1: Preferred job skills.

explained that considering content along with any of these skills presents a big challenge for teachers—especially with the emphasis on content standards and higher test scores. He said, "Test prep is about remembering content. I think if they had an easy way to personalize learning that considers the 21st century skills and complex cognition, social-emotional learning (SEL), and digital learning, our teachers would be ready" (R. Barnhardt, personal communication, March 2017). Ready for deeper learning, I thought, ready to help students engage in deeper learning.

Hewlett Foundation (2013) offers a definition of deeper learning that supports my perceptions of what it is. They define *deeper learning* as:

> an umbrella term for the skills and knowledge that students must possess to succeed in 21st century jobs and civic life. At its heart is a set of competencies students must master in order to develop a keen understanding of academic content and apply their knowledge to problems in the classroom and on the job.

The foundation's list targets six desired competencies as evidence of high levels of proficiency. In short, the foundation's definition makes clear that deeper learning advances skills both inside *and* outside established academic content areas; it considers the whole student, in his or her present and future.

Prior to this conversation with my friends and colleagues, I had already been reviewing ideas about deeper learning and how to make it more accessible to teachers. Many teachers talk about how they believe in teaching complex thinking skills like cause and effect and compare and contrast so students better understand the information they are studying. They accept the definition of deeper learning and view this form of learning as valuable, but they aren't always certain how to achieve deeper learning. The most common question that arises from discussions about deeper learning is "How?" Teachers ask, "How do I help students become more efficient as critical and creative thinkers? How do I enable them to transfer those skills through all their coursework? How do they learn how to use what they learn wherever they are?" Some ask about transfer into lifelong learning but want to know how to recognize authentic transfer.

I had also been thinking about the fact that digital skills have grown increasingly important since the four Cs were chosen, and how most teachers I've worked with worry about missing content they think will be measured if they take up the four Cs. Yet, I understood well that there are increasing numbers of schools that show positive results from whole-school efforts to produce deeper learning outcomes, not just among the gifted and talented honor students in affluent white suburban English-speaking districts or selective charter schools, public or private, but among students from disadvantaged socioeconomic backgrounds and in schools with limited resources. The American Institutes for Research's (AIR) seminal study of deeper learning outcomes (Vander Ark & Schneider, 2014) presages a slow movement of more schools into deeper learning.

"Even with the research," an instructional coach from the klatch noted, "what's happened is only one small step for mankind. No big steps yet." Another colleague added that while he and his peers would love to move into deeper learning, there are obstacles:

> There are two obstacles. Like most schools, ours isn't ready. Our board wants better test scores, not better thinking. Second, while some of us have adopted project-based learning and seen results like the best of those in the American Institutes for Research (Huberman, Bitter, Anthony, & O'Day, 2014) report, most of our colleagues think all the planning is too much. What we need is a simple, flexible tool that edges teachers just a little out of their comfort zones. Project-based learning overwhelms a lot of our teachers. (R. Barnhardt, personal communication, March 2017)

The art teacher listened and then proposed a visual that addressed Richard's concerns. "Look, teachers have always looked to the how-to. We don't have to make a mountain from a molehill. Let's think about connections, not divisions," and she drew something and showed it to us. "Look at this pyramid. I think it shows a way for everyone to get the *how-do-I* questions answered without everyone needing to walk the same straight line." (See figure I.2, page 4.)

"Wow," Richard responded. "Your pyramid visually clarifies everything that goes into deeper learning. It shows how the separate skill sets that we're talking about interconnect."

"Yes," said the art teacher, "and it shows how you can link different skills from the different sets to fit one outcome."

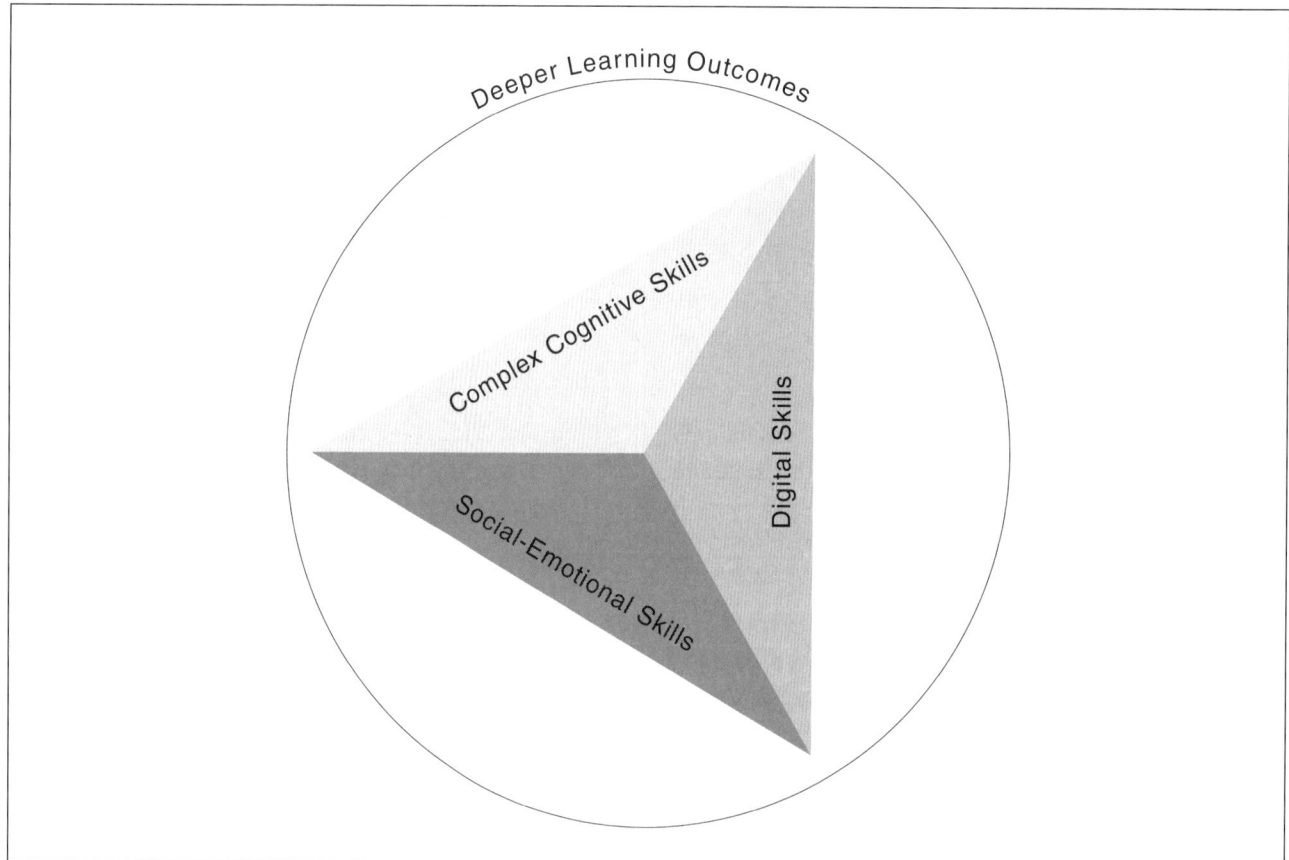

Figure I.2: Pyramid of deeper learning outcomes.

I asked somewhat rhetorically, "Does that mean we could make this a starter tool for introducing deeper learning and leave project-based learning (PBL) as an option?"

The art teacher flashed a grin. "Yep, and because I like visual things, I can see a template that anybody could follow—even young kids. It would be one simple tool that would start any student thinking critically, being creative, using technology, and getting through the curriculum. One flexible tool—a simple template for personalizing learning in any content with any student. Any teacher can adapt it to his or her style."

"If you pardon the expression, I get the picture you're painting. That said, this can't be a one time, quick-fix solution."

"I understand," she answered, "but think of this: one teacher could select a chapter and make a plan wherein kids sharpen their critical thinking as they analyze a story and then make a short video about it with some friends. Digital skills, creativity, and a better understanding of the story could be measured through one project that involves multiple interconnected skills—more than four Cs!" Figure I.2 is a visual example that blends the skill sets.

Richard jumped in with, "I get it. We could focus on any skills we think our kids need to know. I could focus on basic reading. Tom could stress digital skills right in math class."

"My vision," the instructional coach said, "would be different plans for each student. The plans could include skills from all three sets even as each plan focuses on just one. And if I take what I know about portfolios, I could see kids learning how to organize their completed work into folders."

After this conversation with the friends and colleagues of my coffee klatch, I reflected on what we had discussed and on the excitement of the idea of personalized learning plans mediated by teachers but individualized by students. The ideas could indeed become blueprints for personalized learning. I recalled how my mentor Reuven Feuerstein saw the teacher as a mediator of learning whose primary responsibility is the removal of self- and other-imposed limits on a student's potential to think and feel. He asked over and over:

> Who can presume to know what a child is capable of understanding? It is no more a

mystery than what depths of feeling a child can experience. Our job is to do all possible to change those perceptions and help the child become the best possible learner.
(R. Feuerstein, personal communication, 1995)

What grew from that night's conversation is the personalized learning agenda in this book. The personalized learning process as envisioned in this book speaks to the teacher's role as a heartfelt mediator of the mind. In the school environment, the teacher as mediator of the mind gives priority to learning processes over content. Preparing learners for their future world means helping them learn to self-regulate how their minds think and their hearts feel, so they are more effective learners. It means seeing how the parts are connected to the whole so that each student enjoys discovering new depths of learning.

How the Idea Works in This Book

After that first conversation others followed, including those with teacher teams, other colleagues, several students, and individuals I met through my consulting work. We discussed how to transform the seeds of that first conversation's ideas to create a practical tool that would carry students readily into deeper learning and indeed produce deeper learning outcomes for a lifetime. As a result, the personalized learning plan as a tool became a reality, one that any teacher—regardless of grade, teaching style, existing curriculum, assessment requirement, or student load—could adapt, scale, and sustain as a primary driver to deeper learning outcomes.

A blueprint for personalized learning plans and a blueprint for personalized teaching plans allow either to select which deeper learning skill set to highlight, and create a unique plan enabling each student with varied amounts of intervention to construct his or her own deeper learning outcomes. It also allows both teachers and students to assess whether the work produces the desired outcomes. To help teachers adopt and adapt an idea they are considering, this book furnishes elementary, middle, and secondary examples, including sample grade-level appropriate activities with corresponding playbooks. Playbooks come in two variations.

1. A *teacher playbook* is a task analysis of steps for guiding students through a personalized learning plan, an activity, or a lesson you have created and stored for future use.

2. A *student playbook* is a sequenced list of directions informing students how to complete an activity or task in a lesson, project, or personalized learning plan. In most lessons, you will see cooperative learning implemented as a basic tool for organizing communication in concert with other high-effect strategies. The activities are categorized by elementary, middle, and high school options, but with modifications you can use many across their designations.

This book asserts that professional learning communities (PLCs)—a continuous collaborative process of working together via "collective inquiry and action research"—are ideal for implementing personalized learning plans (DuFour, DuFour, Eaker, Many, & Mattos, 2016, p. 10). By working on a common personalized learning plan and its assessment, PLCs can pick a shared professional teaching goal and measure its effects more widely in the context of personalized learning plans for students. The personalized teaching plan structures team conversations and avoids loss of precious meeting time with meandering discussions. Mutual feedback during the planning and assessment phases (preferably without assigned grades), as well as after mutual observations in classrooms, ensures collaboration to produce a meaningful outcome from the planning, completing, and assessing of student personalized learning plans.

I have structured this book to highlight practical how-to tools to guide how and what students master as they develop to learn deeply. The book is neither mandate nor recipe. The fundamental tool, a personalized learning plan, is like a multi-use Swiss Army knife. That little red knife allows users many options for solving small and big problems. You are encouraged, but not required, to read the entire book before your first try making a personalized learning plan blueprint. The first chapter shows how to select an outcome and backward plan with a basic template to personalize one or many student learning experiences. You can apply the blueprint to skills of your choice from any skill set, and you can pick the content.

Following is a list of the four features I highlight in the book.

1. An emphasis on *how-to practices* first and *theory to explain* second adapted for grades preK–12 across the curriculum

2. An evolution, not a revolution, by refining practices that teachers have requested

3. A student-centered focus leading to deeper learning outcomes bolstered by student agency
4. A preference for adaptable evidence-based instructional practices

Focusing on How-To

This book's most distinguishing feature is its emphasis on how-to. No matter which hat I wear as an educator, I regularly hear my colleagues call for practical help that they can adopt or adapt on Monday. I've also heard that they are so eager for something that is easy to use quickly that they will accept quick fixes, Band-Aids, or busywork. The blueprint template is a response aimed to address the calls for an easy-to-use *how-to*, but it is not a bandage or quick fix.

The personalized learning plan may introduce a manual skill such as turning on a computer, or it may help develop a set of problem-solving skills or organizing a year of deeper learning skill planning across a curriculum. Even the most teacher-directed personalized plans with basic skill–teacher playbook goals advance student agency and improve learning of curriculum content and aligned deeper learning skills. By asking students to think about goals, strategies, and other implementation decisions, and by inviting them to self-assess and peer assess the outcome, goal-setting process, or both, you are advancing their social-emotional skill set.

As you and your students develop confidence and competence with the personalized learning plan template, you will begin to coach them in the investigation and solution of ever more complex real-world problems. Eventually, you can show them how to increase their ability to transfer what they have learned about learning and its partner mindset, grit, across the curriculum. When you are able to move students from personalized learning plans that help them master a standards-aligned deeper learning skill (for example, analyzing informational text) to its transfer into a real-world or authentic problem (such as applying for college, helping a grandparent vote, or investigating smog reduction in the neighborhood), you recognize how valuable your promotion of transfer and agency is to their personal academic growth and how much more worthwhile it is when compared to wasting time on test prep reviews.

With the blueprint template, you have a manageable method for moving students from being information consumers to being engaged idea makers and technology shapers who can explain, write, and take responsibility.

In the Middle Ages, a teacher's role was information giver; students gathered ideas from the sole source, pre-Guttenberg transmitter of knowledge, the learned university lecturer. In an information-saturated world, it has become necessary for learners to learn how to find information, sort it, and make sense of it so they can apply it. This makes knowing *how to learn*—how to gather information one needs to know, make sense out of the information, filter, and apply it—essential and what employees and citizens most need (Woodill, 2018). A personalized learning plan provides you with a rich opportunity to change yourself from information dumper to question asker. Figure I.3 shows how the blueprint templates, tools, learning, and teacher connect to one another.

In this figure, the result of personalized learning experiences appears in the outermost ring. The outcome of each personalized learning experience is a deeper learning outcome. Now, look at the center of the illustration. In the center sits the student *Personalized Learning Plan*—one of the blueprints. That is the outcome you want as the result of student planning. Moving out from the center, you see *Personalized Learning Plan Helping Tools*. These tools are things like prompts, activities, guiding rubrics, playbooks, playlists, and so on. In the next ring you see *Personalized Teaching Plan and Other Tools*. These are transfer, two-way feedback, digital tools, and agency, which connect to the desired 21st century skill sets. Lastly, you are back to the outcome: *Deeper Learning*.

Sometimes a personalized learning plan focuses on one small skill in one content area for one student—sort of a tiny home for a single novice scientist, reader, or mathematician. At other times, the template is a multi-week project-based learning unit for a whole class—a giant skyscraper. In every case, learners exit more educated than when they entered.

Digging Deeper Into Theories

Many authors have written about the need to personalize learning. Ideas abound. Some have presented ways to personalize with computer-assisted instruction (CAI). Others have suggested that it would be a good idea to personalize learning for students without relying on technology. This book rejects that notion. Because schools can no longer relegate the digital world to the closet, you will look at personalized learning through a digital lens that blends and extends prior online

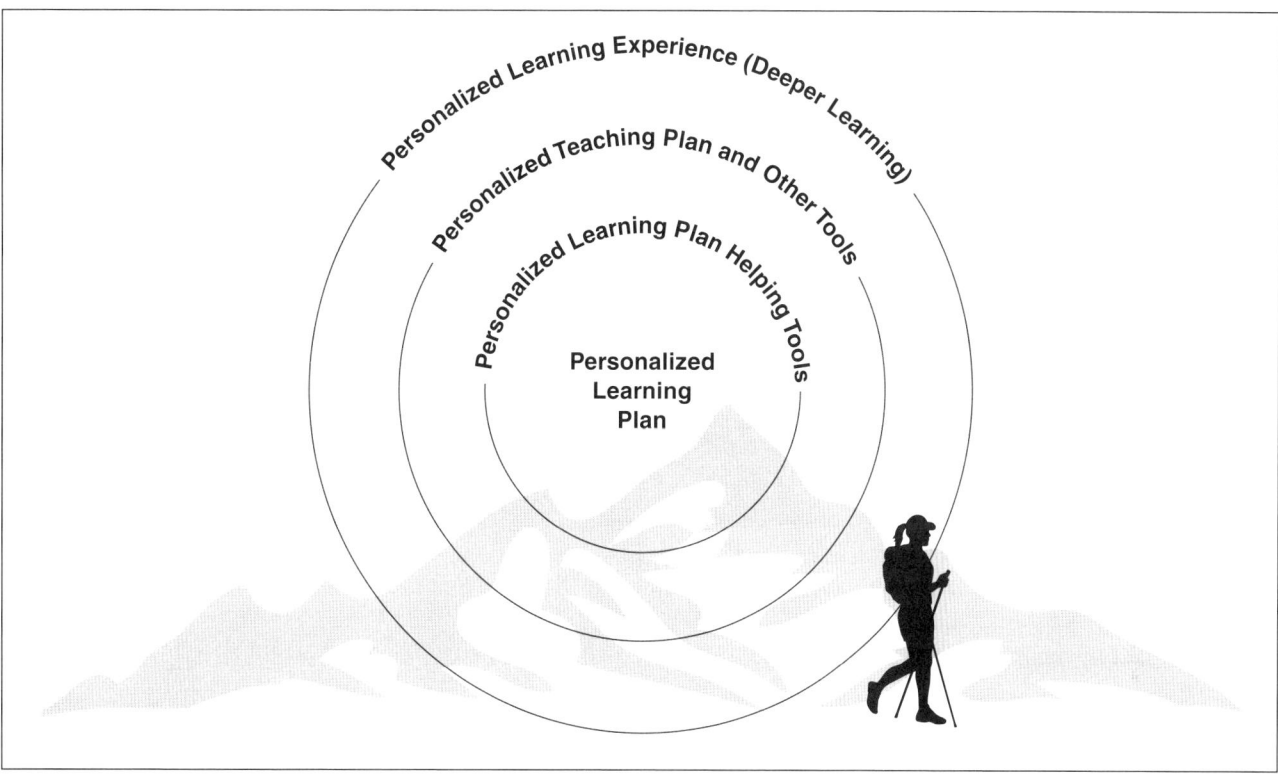

Figure I.3: Personalized learning's tools, results, and guide on the side.

practices in the novel personalized learning plan format by addressing the following.

- **Digital devices:** Digital devices can help personalize any type of learning experience with teacher and students as active digital makers, not passive key clickers. It targets digital management tools, digital templates, and internet sites which help you transform your classroom into a digital center where students make deeper learning. Whether calling on the internet to email or to learn coding, digital devices including smartphones and smartboards are helpful, necessary tools for all students. Pen and paper belong to an obsolete age.

- **Outcomes:** The inclusion of backward planning for every personalized learning plan allows you to teach *students* how to plan with the end in mind.

- **SMART goals:** Shifting goals from content coverage to the assessment of measurable skill development via outcomes applied to content with SMART goals lets you measure soft as well as hard skills with hard data. The measurement of SMART goals enables teachers, parents, administrators, and other third parties to see the effects of SMART-guided personalized learning plans. The SMART acronym in this book is adapted from Anne E. Conzemius and Jan O'Neill (2014) and stands for *specific, measurable, achievable, relevant* (formerly *results oriented*), and *timely*, and it announces criteria for a personalized learning plan's deeper learning outcomes.

- **Student-centered deeper learning outcomes:** Deeper learning outcomes are given preference in every personalized learning plan. The format itself facilitates goal planning, a crucial 21st century skill, and student agency, which requires that all students have a basic experience with deeper learning production.

- **Novel triarchic 21st century skills framework:** For the first time, 21st century skills are framed as three sets of skills different from the outdated four Cs originally set by P21 (2019). This book reframes the four Cs as complex cognitive (including creative- and critical-thinking skills), social-emotional (including collaboration and communication), and digital skill sets. Sets are the categories which include those specific, measurable skills which enable deeper learning outcomes. These skills are the prerequisites that students learn to improve so that deeper learning results.

- **Multiple tools:** For each skill set discussed in this book, you can open a chapter to discover multiple examples of specialty tools for engaging students with the targeted skills. These include playbooks, guiding rubrics, playlists, and activity samplers which show the how-to for the targeted skill templates. Tools are for teachers to share online or in print with students and are accompanied by playbooks to copy and share.

- **Guiding rubrics:** Four familiar *grading* rubric models are repositioned as four guiding rubric models for enhancing student agency via self-assessment in the context of two-way feedback. Playbooks detail how to prepare and incorporate guiding rubrics for deeper learning outcomes. So you can devote more time to feedback, the book offers the following ways to add grades after summative assessments if you must.

    1. Rated checklist (see the reproducible "Rated Checklist—PreK–3" on page 222 and "Improvement Rating Scale—Grades 3–12" on page 224)
    2. Single-point guiding rubric (see the reproducible "Single-Point Guiding Rubric—Grades 3–12" on page 226)
    3. Multi-point guiding rubric (see the reproducible "Multi-Point Guiding Rubric—Grades 3–12" on page 228)
    4. Open-ended guided self-assessment rubric (see the reproducible "Open-Ended Self-Assessment Rubric—Grades 3–12" on page 231)

- **Evidence-based practice:** Starting with goal setting, two-way feedback, cooperative learning, and graphic organizers, this book's treatment highlights how to prioritize evidence-based practices within inquiry lessons and projects. These lessons or products are the incubation chamber for the 21st century skills most likely to advance deeper learning.

- **Guide on the side:** You see how to *mediate minds* as a guide on the side (versus a sage on the stage), where you help students expand their agency through choices about what and how they learn. The term *guide on the side* takes on deeper meaning as you select multiple strategies, activities, and methods that let you wear this hat with aplomb. Watch for examples of what students, engaged by personalized learning plans and their teachers acting as guides, do and say to facilitate various skills.

If you recognize any of these ideas and say, "I do this already," such a reaction is welcome. It means you are not just a reader or a listener at the latest conference. It means you are an evaluator of possible new practices and one who acts from ideas that will help your students learn more and better. You pilot new ideas, assess the results, and decide on modifications (or you say, "Let's forget that"). When a new or even an old idea presents itself with the claim that it's a good idea for helping students, you consider it with prior knowledge in mind by examining how you might adapt and try it on for size.

How the Idea Works in Your Classroom

How do these four ideas play out in your classroom?

1. Remind yourself that this is a refinement, not an addition to your teaching load. As you challenge students to take on the responsibility to learn how to learn and how to bounce back with grit after setbacks, you will remove some of the weight of responsibility from your shoulders and transfer it to the shoulders of your students.

2. Know that a personalized learning plan can turn students on to the personal power of self-directed learning. Just show your administrator that a personalized learning plan is more extensive, innovative, and outcome driven, more than worth the time it will take you to make it. (For transparency, I must add, time saving only kicks in after you kick off the program and enable students to become efficient personalized learning plan users.)

3. Keep it simple and small. Pick an easy, manageable, crucial-to-implement SMART outcome for you or your students. Consider the following very basic outcomes.

    - *Elementary school*—Students increase the time spent on home reading by three minutes each day of the week.

- *Middle school*—Students record the average decreased time it takes for their group to clean up its maker space by two minutes a day.
- *High school*—Over three weeks, students increase by two the number of examples given for each point made in a weekly essay.
- *Teacher example*—Set up a secure portfolio site for storing each student's personalized learning plan by Friday.

4. Plan how you will find time each week for personalized learning plans to make teaching and learning more productive and fun for you and your students. All told, planning a personalized learning plan should require fewer than thirty minutes every two or four weeks. You must judge if time taken is worth it by measuring the SMART outcome.

These four actions will make you more efficient as a planner (one of the domains recommended for evaluating teacher performance). One complaint I have heard time and again, as with other sound practices such as SMART goals, cooperative learning, and evidence-based instruction, is that typical lesson plans are a meaningless and timewasting exercise spoken in terms like this: "I open the lesson plan form every Wednesday. I fill in the blanks for each hour as required. Hour one: reading groups. Hour two: mathematics circle. I just have to enter new dates. They are really fake plans" (C. Trenser, personal communication, March 15, 2018). Such lesson plans bear no resemblance to personalized learning plans and their supportive cousin, personalized teaching plans.

In my work helping teachers adopt the templates, some have preferred to jump right into the deep waters; others have carefully tiptoed to test the temperature. The former, with high risk tolerance, think through their personalized teaching plans with no hesitation, ready to offer plans to every class. The latter, more cautious, start with low-risk plans. Low riskers first try a SMART goal (Conzemius & O'Neill, 2014) with a specific, achievable student outcome. Both of these methods are acceptable.

How the Chapters Are Organized

Each chapter begins with a title and a synopsis of its contents, a driving question, and a sequence of guiding questions. Each provides information from which you may form your answer to that chapter-driving question. In each chapter, you will find a series of questions asking for the definition of the topic, what the concept looks and sounds like in classrooms, examples of piloted strategies, and helpful tool examples with playbooks, playlists, and sample rubrics. At each chapter's end, look for the Takeaways section to summarize your response to the driving questions and other prompts.

The book contains the following chapters and appendix.

1. The first five chapters introduce the blueprints—templates—and key skills for implementing and assessing the plan through the following chapters.
   - **Chapter 1** examines what a personalized learning plan template is and how to make your first plan.
   - **Chapter 2** shows how to boost engagement and create and maintain a reciprocal social-emotional culture of trust and mutual respect.
   - **Chapter 3** articulates how to prepare outcome-driven instruction and assessment.
   - **Chapter 4** shows how to expand student agency through personalized learning plans.
   - **Chapter 5** examines how personalized learning plans promote learning transfer necessary for deeper learning.

2. The next three chapters examine the three 21st century skill sets most responsible for deeper learning outcomes.
   - **Chapter 6** explores specific complex cognitive skills and how to develop students' complex cognition with personalized learning plans.
   - **Chapter 7** examines how personalized learning plans develop social-emotional skills, which enable deeper learning outcomes.
   - **Chapter 8** focuses on digital skills, explaining how and why they drive instructional practice, and what they do to ensure this inclusion.
   - The **conclusion** synthesizes what's been said about the personalized learning pathway to deeper learning outcomes.

3. **Appendix**
   - The **appendix** provides the personalized learning plan blueprints and other templates for you to replicate.

Visit **go.SolutionTree.com/instruction** for a list of state, national, and international standards that align with the work in this book, as well as online instructional resources, a glossary, and the free reproducible versions of the blueprints.

Takeaways

I hope you enjoy this book and find your way to adapt the concepts, strategies, and tools it offers to personalize deeper learning for your students. Here, you can enter ideas you want to take from this introduction and pose any *I wonders* to pursue as you read. In each subsequent chapter, the chapter ends with a similar invite as either an open-ended stem or an open-ended question. To prepare for Takeaway invites, you might find it helpful to keep notes. Identify the chapter name and number and then the driving question. As you read, highlight those sentences or paragraphs which build on your prior knowledge or introduce a new concept. At the end of the chapter, prioritize the points (as many as you want). Fill in your top three or more. At the end of the book, review your highlights, make a master list, and then identify those ideas you most want to act on.

The Takeaway lead-ins are purposefully open-ended. It's my experience that this format best allows each reader the agency to gather information most important to him or her. You make sense of the information you choose, and then move to applying what is most important for your students to become deeper learners.

TAKEAWAYS

Here are some examples of notes you might make on the introduction.

In this introduction, what I learned about personalizing learning for deeper learning outcomes is . . .
- The work world has changed and expanded the 21st century skills list.
- The lowest priority is recall skills. The fewest jobs will be there. More complex thinking needs to be the focus.
- Technology makes it possible to personalize learning so that students, not computers, do the deciding on what, how, why, and when to learn. It opens up ways to develop agency.
- I need to know how to include digital skills every day. Students need the skills to know how to learn with all the gadgets, and not more gadgets.

My *I wonder* is what I will learn in this book to answer these questions.

CHAPTER 1
PERSONALIZED LEARNING PLANS

> My sense is that we're ready for another industrial revolution in this country. The great minds and innovators of Silicon Valley would come through China and say, "The pipeline is full of ideas"—there's personalized medicine, biotechnology, new forms to power ourselves, clean energy, etc., etc.
>
> —*Jon Huntsman Jr.*

What company isn't offering something personalized? The word represents a boondoggle and a boon. Search online for *personalized*; watch an online video or the TV; read a magazine. See what you find. You're likely to find more examples than either of us can count of things that can, their proponents claim, be personalized. Some examples are as follows.

- Car interior
- Wedding list
- Health plan
- Baby shower
- Travel itinerary
- Insurance plan
- Solar energy for your home
- Dinner menu
- News feed
- Medical health portal
- Musical playlist
- Bank services
- Workout
- Financial plan

Technology provides the capability to make instantaneous, multiple variations of a standard product, service, or practice with the label *personalized*. We can buy personalized smartphones, SUVs, travel plans, or youth sports awards, all aligned with our individual lifestyle, age, beliefs, biases, and whatever interests we may each have.

- A roof repair appraiser can examine hurricane-damaged houses in one block and print out a personalized repair estimate while standing on a buyer's doorstep. The appraiser can adjust any owner's estimate on the spot so that the customer can see individual choices on color, size, and quality of all parts and price.
- A baseball coach can gather data from each pitcher's games and determine what ways the player can adjust her fingers to improve velocity, spin, and curve.
- Each family member, pressing a smart hub, can personalize a playlist of favorite programs available on Netflix, Hulu, Amazon Prime, Disney+, and multiple emerging digital networks.

- Hospitals have patient portals that contain all health records for that hospital and its affiliated doctors plus other hospital or health records the patient allows. The patient's health care providers and the patient have immediate access to a person's complete medical records, after-care summaries and instructions, future appointments, diet plans, accounts, links to share, and a prescription refill link.

Even students have taken up the personalized clamor with pleas like this one from a fifteen-year-old:

> Why are we pitted into a system of learning that doesn't take into account how we learn best and how we intend to apply our interests? When each night the mounds of homework I get prevent me from practicing my passions or furthering me to my goals, how can you expect me to be happy or fulfilled? (A. Roberts, personal communication, March 13, 2016)

This chapter answers its driving question by describing the ingredients for initiating personalized learning plans. It presents a blueprint for you to guide one student or your entire class toward deeper learning outcomes. Immediately after reading the chapter, you will be ready to adopt the replicable personalized learning plan template and its playbook, implement your professional teaching plan, and assess its results. Start-up suggestions, a chart detailing what sounds and sights personalized learning plans produce, and responses to frequently asked questions will further your trial implementation and assessment of the results.

Driving question: How do I personalize learning in my classroom?

What Is Personalized Learning?

Personalized learning within the context I describe is the result of an individual's self-directed learning. The learning is guided by a caring teacher's mediation with evidence-based instructional practices and selected technology tools for designing, implementing, and assessing deeper learning plans to attain individual goals. The goals aim to develop students' skills, talents, and interests by meeting personal learning needs.

Although learning can occur anywhere, anytime, with whatever a student chooses to learn, a student's formal classroom personalized learning materializes most strongly in a teacher-facilitated, collaborative climate. This learning depends on a skillful teacher guiding students to attain deeper learning outcomes relevant to their personal interests and unique needs.

You can examine my definition through its following four components.

1. **Outcome:** Personalized learning is the *result* gained from a student's planned, managed, and assessed learning *outcomes*. Sometimes, the words *outcome* and *goal* become confused. Outcomes are the specifics that determine you have reached your goal. The best, most valued outcomes are measurable and observable. Thus, when you declare your goal is to improve my ability to analyze a text, you begin by thinking about the specific aspects of that complex cognitive skill by asking "What does that skill look or sound like?" The same holds true when you or students have a big idea SEL goal such as *show respect* or a digital skill goal like *program an app*. In both cases, you want to know what each looks or sounds like. What does respect look and sound like in your classroom? What do the programming procedures for the app look like?

    Personalized learning plan outcomes may include mastery of a year's course content, a technology tool, deeper learning skills, or social-emotional competencies. With a personalized learning plan, you enable students to identify specific needs, to determine individual learning goals, to select strategies, materials, and digital tools, and to assess results so that the student's talents, interests, and learning needs are enhanced. Outcomes drive the plan because a student starts planning with the result in mind (otherwise known as *backward design*; Wiggins & McTighe, 2005).

2. **Process:** Personalized learning is the *process* by which students make choices to self-direct the planning, doing, and assessing of what, when, where, and how they learn so they can achieve their self-selected individual learning goals.

3. **Instructional and assessment practice:** Personalized learning is an *instructional approach* by which caring teachers enable

students to self-direct their learning and transfer what they have learned beyond classroom walls. Through guiding rubrics, teachers make assessment a key student-centered instructional tool.

4. **Technology:** Teachers engage students with *technology tools*. For instruction, these may include interactive whiteboards, PCs, notebooks, or laptops, internet access, 3-D printers, computer-aided instruction programs, and others. You can enable personalized learning with these tools as a means for students to make personal plans and for you to manage the process in a systematic way.

What Evidence Supports Personalized Learning?

Research identifies several important student benefits of personalized learning.

- Planning and goal setting are crucial cognitive functions. Many students arrive at school with undeveloped cognitive functions, including planning and goal setting. They may be impulsive and random, imprecise, and inaccurate collectors of information. These behaviors, many ingrained as bad habits, inhibit successful learning. Thus, the process of goal setting itself becomes a prerequisite for helping students overcome these habits and introduce effective learning, critical thinking, and problem-solving skills (Feuerstein, Rand, Hoffman, & Miller, 1980; Zelazo, Blair, & Willoughby, 2016).

- The planning process is most useful to promote collaboration, an essential *social-emotional* skill. Working in teams helps students develop their interpersonal and intrapersonal skills (Ryan & Deci, 2000) as called for in SEL standards.

- By providing students with the autonomy to set their own goals and determine what they are doing and then doing what they selected, teachers empower students' feelings of competent confidence and intrinsic motivation (Ryan & Deci, 2000). This leads to feelings of self-efficacy and the willingness to manage and direct their own learning (Guglielmino, 1977; Ryan & Deci, 2000).

- The interactive elements of the planning process, grounded in giving and getting two-way feedback from peers, teachers, and significant others, help students become more effective learners. When teachers call on two-way forward and backward guiding feedback reviews and recommend future improvements, they initiate the increased likelihood of positive action and higher achievement results (Hattie, 2012).

What Does a Personalized Learning Plan Look Like?

Like an architect's blueprint, the master template for a personalized learning plan is a document that will guide your students as they plan, implement, and assess their own self-made plans. After you familiarize students with the tool, you will change your teaching hat. Your new hat identifies you as a coach, a guide on the side. Just as a tennis coach follows a playbook to introduce her players to the game's key tool, the racquet, you will introduce your students to the template. As each student masters the template's basic uses, you will move the individual player's game forward on an individualized, personal track.

For you, this blueprint is an organization and management tool. For students, it is an immediate immersion into all three skill sets—(1) digital (for various technology competencies), (2) complex cognitive (for higher-order-thinking competencies), and (3) social-emotional (for executive functioning competencies). The process enables you to empower students as you individualize how they take increased responsibility for self-directed learning choices. Each blueprint will target a specific outcome, which encourages and enables students to develop measurable knowledge or skills specific to that blueprint. As students walk the planning path guided by their blueprints and your feedback, each will use evidence to take steps closer to competency. The evidence will show you that each is becoming more proficient in planning, completing, and assessing a personal learning plan with specific competencies measured.

Figure 1.1 (page 14) shows an example completed template. Refer to the appendix for the reproducible "Personalized Learning Plan" (page 212). As you review this template, note the key elements. You are encouraged to adjust vocabulary and number of parts to make it age appropriate.

- For grades K–2 students and students with specific special needs, you may think of this as an interview document. Instead of these students writing their answers, you can ask and record their answers in the template. You may also wish to reduce the number of elements in the plan. As these students gain writing skills, you can put a simplified template, such as the reproducible "Starter Personalized Learning Plan" (page 215), into their hands.

- For students in grades 3–12, think about how many elements will initiate their engagement. You can reduce any part. The template's adaption must include the outcome, at least one strategy and one rubric, and due dates. Expand from this basic template until students internalize the process.

- For English learners, you may wish to translate the template with Google Translate. Form a

Name: Jamie Rodrigues	**Grade:** 8	**Teacher:** Mrs. O'Shay
Start date: 4/10	**End date:** 4/22	**Check-up dates:** 4/14, 4/19

Content Focus

☒ English language arts
   Strand:
     ☐ Reading
     ☐ Writing
     ☐ Speaking and Listening
     ☐ Language
☐ Mathematics
☐ Performing or visual art
☐ Science
☒ Social studies
☐ World language
☐ Other: _____

Skill Set			
Basic Cognitive	**Complex Cognitive**	**Social-Emotional**	**Digital**
☐ Decoding	☒ Critical thinking	☐ Collaboration	☐ Basic
☐ Fluency	☐ Creative thinking	☐ Communication	☒ Applied
☐ Numbers	☐ Problem solving	☒ Self-direction	☐ Other: _____
☐ Operations	☐ Design thinking		
☐ Phonics	☒ Cognitive function		
☒ Vocabulary			
☐ Other: _____			

Feedback

Feedback is by:
   ☐ Self
   ☒ Teacher
   ☒ Peers: <u>Regina, Sophia</u>
   ☒ Other: <u>My mom, Alejandra</u>

Plans *Enter your response in the blank space after each request.*
My improvement goal:
To compare and contrast two sides of a protest debate.
What do I need to know for this learning plan?
What were reasons each side gave?
What people or resources will I call on?   • Newspaper stories   • Interviews from three people on each side for point of view   • YouTube videos of march and police reaction
What materials and equipment will I use?   • My laptop   • YouTube   • SurveyMonkey   • Google Slides
What strategies will I use to reach my goal?   • Make a contract to listen to others' ideas and do my fair share of work.   • Gather information from several sources on a Venn diagram.   • Present both sides of the conflict with data.   • Make our selection and conclusion.   • Make a slideshow that shows both sides of the argument.   • Include a conclusion and its reasons.   • Present to the class.   • Invite parents to the presentation.
What skills and talents will I apply?   • Comparing   • Being a teammate   • Making a decision based on facts   • Making a creative slideshow with figures   • Presenting to others
What are my criteria for measurable success?   • A slideshow with seven slides that earns our team four points out of five   • Our ratings from the audience will give us four points out of five.   • I work well with my teammates and resolve disagreements and find win-win resolutions. Regina and Sophia confirm this.
What evidence will I show?   • My two sides on slideshows   • My survey responses   • My feedback
How much time will I need?
We will need the whole schedule.
Notes:
I need help to learn how to make a slideshow.

Figure 1.1: Personalized learning plan—Example.

need-to-know tutoring group for each language. This small group will allow you to teach a minilesson in which you walk through the document in the needed language. As an alternative, you may wish to pair an EL student with a fluent English-speaking student as peer coach. When each student is ready for the document in English, make the change.

When you are starting the process with students who are in grades K–3, are learning English, or have special needs, try the barer-bones template shown in figure 1.2. It is limited to fewer questions. You can access the reproducible "Starter Personalized Learning Plan" (page 215) in the appendix. After a student demonstrates the ability to complete the starter template without you entering the basic demographic responses, add to the template.

For non-readers and non-writers, you complete this template after explaining each question and giving an example. Show the template on your interactive whiteboard or similar display, and brainstorm answers. Record the list so each student can select and copy an answer. Coach as needed. When students are able, let them ask and answer the questions on their own. Start with very specific goal inquiries, such as lessons for learning the alphabet's sounds and symbols. That would look like, *I want to learn how to pronounce the letter Q*, for example. Before introducing them to the template, check their prior knowledge of the words *goal* and *plan*. Your intent is to help them internalize these words even as they accomplish their stated goal.

The second tool, the teacher playbook, is a guiding sequence of instructions. The playbook, an example of which is shown in figure 1.3 (page 18), allows you to

Name:	Grade:	Teacher:
Start date:	**End date:**	**Check-up dates:**
Content Focus		
☐ English language arts **Strand:** ☐ Reading ☐ Writing ☐ Speaking and Listening ☐ Language ☐ Mathematics ☐ Performing or visual art ☐ Science ☐ Social studies ☐ World language ☒ Other: _____		
Skill Set		
☐ Basic cognitive ☐ Digital ☐ Complex cognitive ☐ Social-emotional		
Specific skill:		

Plans
Enter your response in the blank space after each request.
What do I want to do better?
Who can help?
What materials do I need?
How much time do I need?
How will I know I have made progress?
Other thoughts or ideas:

Figure 1.2: Starter personalized learning plan.

quickly fill in demographic information and check off plan-specific items such as a skill set, content area, and so on.

A teacher playbook for a personalized learning plan template will guide you as you introduce the template to students. Make notes and refer to them as often as you need. As you will discover, when digital notebooks are one-to-one in your classroom, you have the same opportunity to put your playbooks online. With an online copy sent to each student's electronic portfolio, you know you don't have to send a new blank for each new plan. When a student forgets the play, he or she goes to the playbook.

If colleagues join you in using personalized learning plans, you can start a permanent digital portfolio to follow each student through the grades. Each year, the personalized learning plan playbook will add questions and make student personalized learning plans more complex. These questions will give the next grade's teacher insights into each student's personal talents, digital skills, other 21st century skills, citizenship skills, and college and career readiness. Figure 1.4 (page 19) is an example of a starter playbook for students learning the alphabet. The example models a simplified template. Adapt the example as needed.

1. **Make necessary variations.** For prewriters, students with special needs, students learning English, or students who struggle, modify items in the plan. You may also wish to simplify the language by using more conversational words (for instance, "I want to learn how to…").

2. **Show or share the template.** Use the whiteboard or share to students' digital devices. If multiple students are working with one device, each should upload an electronic portfolio online or to your available equivalent. Remember to explain the words *goal* and *plan*.

3. **Ask students to complete, or help them complete, the master or starter personalized learning plan.** Fill in the information for students who aren't yet writing. As they need to practice writing, give them pieces of information to copy into the blanks. If needed, make paper copies with larger space for young writers to print in. Indicate all start dates, interim dates for formative assessments for check-ups, and end dates.

4. **Determine a focus skill.** Check one. You can adapt the form for students. If a student is working in one skill set, such as analyzing (complex cognitive) or listening to others on my team (social-emotional), you may encourage one targeted skill. If your students are ready to take on more, you can include two or maybe three skills. However, avoid overload.

5. **Fill in the names of those who provide feedback.** Leave blanks where appropriate. You will designate who gives feedback. Sometimes only you will give feedback, sometimes peers, and sometimes both. Peer feedback is especially important when teams are working with a common plan.

6. **Students fill in the blanks in the Plans section.** Each student completes this section, even if an answer is the same as that of others in a team or the class. Each keeps a copy in the portfolio.

7. **Share, demonstrate, and guide practice.** In addition to modeling and monitoring first personalized learning plans, guide practice for sharing the template to an electronic portfolio. Coach and give feedback. Modeling happens when you walk the class through the steps for completing a template for a skill, preferably with an example from your personal experience. After checking for understanding of what you modeled, watch students as they make their own and help as needed. Continue monitoring during this guided time by checking their template entries, asking clarifying questions, and giving warm feedback. Later, you will continue coaching to see how each student is following the completed plan.

8. **Guide two-way feedback.** You can give and get written or verbal feedback by digital exchange, by face-to-face conferences, or a combination. Conduct one four-to-five-minute conference per month with each student. Depend on the template to frame your conference discussions by directing your probes and warm feedback from the plan. In addition, if all are following the same blueprint, you can share feedback to all with specific but nameless feedback directed at all or some.

9. **Measure progress.** If you save the plans and rubrics, you can assess progress made over several plans. You might measure data on a single criterion by rubric ratings, number of students who accomplished a goal, and more.

10. **Reflect.** At least once per month, do a whole-class reflection on the pluses and minuses of the planning process. Start with a short rubric so students can think of ideas for improving the process. The elements of a guiding rubric do not change based on the number of students included. Whether you are targeting a whole class, one or more groups, or an individual, the format doesn't change. What will change are methods and procedures you use for the reflection.

Figure 1.3: Teacher playbook for personalized learning plan templates.

*Visit **go.SolutionTree.com/instruction** for a free reproducible version of this figure.*

What Are the Personalized Learning Plan Processes?

The approach to making personalized learning plans has three major processes: (1) planning, (2) guiding the implementation, and (3) assessing the outcomes. Each plan starts with the blank personalized learning plan template. In students' first personalized learning plans, you do lots of guiding with your feedback. As students get used to the process and gain practice, you let students do more of the guidance themselves.

1. Planning

    a. Copy the template. With the data from your needs assessment, select the target digital skill or skills.

    b. Determine the students' SMART outcome.

    c. Complete the guiding rubric.

1. Determine which students to involve, such as one student, a small group, or the whole class. Complete the template's demographic section. When students are starting to read and write, you can enlarge the form and let them copy the information you share on the whiteboard. As their basic skills improve, use the template for practicing oral reading (singly or in chorus) and writing their responses.

   If you have digital notebooks available, plan to start students sketching pictures and words. The following abbreviated steps, from the Illinois Early Learning Project (n.d.; https://illinoisearlylearning.org/pa/project-planning/children-sketch), can get you started. That website has directions for later sketch work.

   a. Set various items on different tables and group students at each.

   b. Explain to the students that they will be sketching an object, including its shape and texture, "sizes of its parts, how many parts it has, [and] its location relative to nearby objects" (Illinois Early Learning Project, n.d.). Say that sketching is done quickly.

   c. Provide a clipboard, a piece of paper, and a pencil to each student and allow all students to stand where they need to as they sketch.

   d. Discuss the sketches when they are done.

2. After a sketch, ask questions such as the following.
   - "What feelings are in this picture?"
   - "Can you tell me a story about this picture?"
   - "What other objects can you draw that make this sound?"

3. Collect sketches, one per letter of the alphabet, in student portfolios until you reach the end of the alphabet. Help students bind their sketches into an ABC book to share with parents.

4. End the unit with practice choral reading or a reading circle with the sketchbooks. Invite students to share positive feedback with statements such as, *What I like about (student's name) book is . . . .*

5. When students are making their sketches and presenting books, intervene at least once a day to ask, "Why are you making these sketches?" Ensure their *whys* are in response to the words *goal* or *plan*.

Figure 1.4: Teacher starter playbook for personalized learning plan templates—Example.

*Visit **go.SolutionTree.com/instruction** for a free reproducible version of this figure.*

   d. Select the activities you believe will help your students achieve the outcome. Select activities to guide their learning.

   e. Set the pacing.

   f. Share your plan with a colleague.

2. Guiding

   a. Introduce students to the plan with an advanced organizer of your design that engages and excites their interest.

   b. Review norms for peer interactions.

   c. Introduce the guiding rubric.

   d. If included in the plan, set partners.

   e. Initiate the first activity with a student playbook.

   f. Check for task understanding.

   g. Walk about the classroom, observing with the guiding rubric and giving helpful feedback.

   h. Assess the first activity with the guiding rubric and continue to the next activity or assessment.

   i. If products are included, conduct show and tell.

   j. Guide reflection with questions starting from the rubric.

   k. Shut down devices and transition to the next lesson.

3. Assessing

   a. Review your observations, student products, and, if possible, feedback from colleagues and your supervisor. You may also wish to solicit parent feedback.

   b. Complete the open-ended rubric (which asks open-ended questions or gives stems such as *What did you do well with this personalized learning plan?*).

c. Use data for the next personalized learning plan. File the plan, student samples, notes, and rubric in your electronic or paper files.

The following six steps are another way of looking at the process, and you can follow them if your school lacks a curriculum for teaching a skill you want to teach.

1. **Decide on the skill outcomes for your students:** You can define which skills will benefit your instruction tied to your content and to any skill sets you include.

    - *Select skills*—You may have skills presented in a curriculum or standards. For digital skills, you might not (and you will learn how to address that in chapter 8, page 175).
    - *Assess needs*—This applies to any skill set. Make a needs assessment. With selections from the list, you can use SurveyMonkey or a similar tool to gather data from a random selection of students. Distribute the survey either a few days before starting a content lesson that involves internet research or as a need-to-know check. With the results, add need-to-know strategies to ensure students learn how to perform the skills.

2. **Develop a guiding rubric:** With the identified skills, analyze the task and make SMART criteria for assessing the process and results from your instruction.

3. **Design your personalized teaching plan:** Complete the template for the lesson. Focus your lesson either on the digital skill outcome or its application in a content lesson. For instance, in standards announced by the National Council for the Social Studies (2010), students are asked to explore the complex influence of scientific findings and technology on human values, the growth of knowledge, and behavior. Middle school students examine new technologies such as the wheel, printing press, and the automobile so they can compare these with other technologies they may be more familiar with, such as the internet, WiFi, and smartphones. For a lesson aligned with this standard, students will learn to compare one technology invented several hundred years earlier with one invented more recently, perhaps even in their lifetime. In a personalized learning plan with a guiding rubric for *analyzing* for cost, positive and negative effects, social impact, and connection to their lives, students will show that they can examine each by multiple factors and compare each factor. In this case, they must show they can apply the skill in course content.

4. **Add a personalized learning plan:** Add a template emphasizing the digital skill selected. Decide the level of student participation in planning and assessing the template. Share the template and playbook to student devices.

5. **Coach:** As students work alone or in teams, circulate with the guiding rubric in hand and encourage students' management as you coach with two-way feedback.

6. **Assess results:** Gather and analyze data from personalized learning plans and other assessments in this lesson. Determine next steps.

The rest of the book, led by questions, takes you through these steps.

How Do I Launch Personalized Learning Plans, and What Should I Include?

Assuming that your classroom is an environment in which all students feel psychologically secure sharing ideas and feelings in small groups or with the whole class, you can launch the process. If not, you will need to address any issues that block the two-way communication inherent in the process. In that case, chapter 2 (page 35) might contain helpful ideas.

You can launch in at least four ways.

1. Invite one or two students at the start and then expand the number as you become more comfortable, confident, and competent with this tool. Although your desired ideal outcome is personalized learning plans produced by every student at least once per quarter, you may elect to start with one student or a small, select group before including all. You may also elect to require personalized learning plans as often as once per lesson or project.

2. Hold off and spend the first quarter of the school year establishing a healthy culture in which feelings of mutual trust and respect are

dominant and no one feels concerned about peer ridicule. Again, chapter 2 can help.

3. Select social-emotional skill development as the outcomes for the first round. Communication and collaboration, two of P21's (2019) original 21st century skills, allow multiple opportunities for introducing plans while simultaneously establishing a culture of respect and trust. For specific SEL models, search frameworks such as the following.

   - Your state's department of education
   - The Organisation for Economic Co-operation and Development's framework for social and emotional skills (n.d.b) organizes SEL skills around what is called the five-factor model, or the big five personality indicators, including (1) collaboration, (2) emotion regulation, (3) engagement with others, (4) open-mindedness, and (5) task performance. These indicators break down further in definition of certain characteristics including empathy, critical thinking, and many more.
   - The New York State Department of Education's (NYSDOE; 2018) social-emotional learning benchmarks spotlight self-awareness, self-management, social awareness, interpersonal skills, ethical decision making, and responsibility in personal life, school, and beyond. The NYSDOE (2018) guidelines offer proficiency levels broken into (mostly two-year) grade bands.

4. Consider any combination of the first three.

When you search, browse the site you have selected with a topic if necessary. For instance, browse *NYSDOE* and then *SEL*. If possible, go to the next level on the site and search a topic such as *social awareness*.

You can begin the process even as you act to ensure your classroom climate is capable of sustaining it. The easiest way to start is to adapt the personalized learning plan template. It is a simple, concrete tool to replicate in a digital or printable template for each student you want to engage. If you prefer, try the template with just one or two students, assess how well it works, and call on this knowledge to include more students.

The six steps in the playbook in figure 1.5 guide your start. Adjust these steps to fit your class.

You will determine which outcome will most benefit the students you elect to include. Later, you can increase their agency to decide not only outcomes, but also ways to attain the outcomes. See starter ideas in table 1.1 (page 22).

It is preferable, but not required in initial plans, to prioritize deeper learning skill sets that experts have identified will be most valuable for students' understanding of core ideas in your curriculum. As you bring a skill into play, remember that knowledge is necessary but not sufficient. The aim of personalized learning plans is to have students transfer knowledge to action. Yes, they must know about a skill, but the transfer that leads to deeper understanding and increased competence

1. Go through the personalized teaching plan, determining the outcomes and elements you seek—strategies, resources, digital tools, and so on.
2. Introduce the personalized learning plan template to students. Check for understanding.
3. Walk students through the plan you have made. Explain that the first personalized learning plans you are sharing will become theirs. Later, they will be expected to make their own. With early elementary students, start with the goal or the finished product. As students mature in their ability to take responsibility and write their own plans, expand how much is contained in the personalized learning plan.
4. As students work on and through their plans, coach from the side. Clarify and encourage.
5. Guide reflection and add feedback.
6. Advance to the next skill (for example, primary collaboration: [1] I do my role, [2] I take turns, [3] I let others speak, and so on). Increase student agency as appropriate for each element. Add other 21st century skills in later plans.

Figure 1.5: Teacher playbook for getting started.

Table 1.1: Outcome Ideas

Grades or Needs	Outcomes
Elementary school	A basic, standards-driven skill such as "ask and answer questions about key details in a text" (RL.1.1; National Governors Association [NGA] & Council of Chief State School Officers [CCSSO], 2010a)
Middle school	Engineering design skills such as "Define the criteria and constraints of a design problem with sufficient precision" (Next Generation Science Standards [NGSS], 2013)
High school	Taking notes during a lecture, analyzing informational text as they read their resources, brainstorming project design ideas, or preparing a college application (Commonwealth of Pennsylvania, n.d.)
Behavioral challenges requiring individualized education plan to improve communication with peers	Identifying "words and actions that may support or hurt the feelings of others" (Ohio Department of Education, 2019)
High school English learners	Responding "to critical commentaries on a range of issues from illustrated models or outlines" (World-Class Instructional Design and Assessment Consortium, 2007)

comes from showing that they can do it. A second level of transfer follows with students' showing how well they can apply a skill in different situations or in different subjects. Chapter 5 (page 105) will take you on a deeper dive into transfer.

Whenever possible, incorporate technology in the planning process. By incorporating digital tools as you build personalized learning plans, you replicate the current digital workplace in which technology provides the predominant work tools. The personalized learning plan template is made so you can scan, adapt, and share a copy with digital devices or present a copy for all to see on an interactive whiteboard anytime you need to coach a team or the whole class. For example, with a full-blown inquiry, model how to fill in the blanks, show exemplary responses, show playbooks, and make all-class playlists by asking "How do you think you would . . . ?" as you distribute the opportunity to respond around the classroom (Rosenthal & Jacobson, 1968).

A student's personal portfolio includes the following items.

- Skills to develop into competencies
- Preferred strategies, such as a fishbone graphic organizer
- A list of guiding questions to use in a team collaboration
- Notes on team roles and responsibilities
- Summaries of key ideas
- Names of favorite resources, including websites
- Playlists
- Guiding rubrics
- Reflection journals
- Important templates
- Past work
- Feedback from the teacher and peers
- Grading rubric (optional)

Middle and high school students may also add a self-management rubric if you want them to call on the playbook as a strategy promoting their self-organizing skill or their categorizing skill.

It will help to set up a system you and students will need for storing documents and giving two-way feedback. If you don't already have a digital system, Google Docs and Google Drive provide a simple, interactive document-storage system. You may find one or two tech-savvy students who can maintain and coach you on the mechanics. If you create an electronic folder for storing all documents, upload the master template and the interview master into a document folder on your desktop. As you proceed, you can include other downloadable documents to share with students and show them how to share documents and create their own secure folders. After you have finished introducing students to the personalized learning plan, email or text a letter home to parents inviting participation in a parent night demonstration of your system.

If you have a limited number of digital devices for individual use, you can assign teams to a device and send each student a template for inclusion in a personal digital portfolio. If your classroom is a digital wasteland, you can print out copies that students can store in hard-copy portfolios.

What Does Personalized Learning Look and Sound Like in a K–12 Classroom?

In a K–12 classroom, where personalized learning takes place, you—the teacher as coach and guide—are at students' sides, allocating set amounts of time and support to allow, encourage, enable, develop, and enrich student choices about what, how, when, where, and why they each will pursue their self-determined goals. The predominant sounds students hear from you are interrogatory and congratulatory.

Personalized learning also looks and sounds like students engaged in rigorous tasks matched to their talents and interests. They are stopping to think and answer probing how and why questions followed with requests for examples and proof. Working alone, but more often with peers, they answer your complex thinking questions about complex ideas and ask thoughtful questions themselves, they call on technology, and they make informed judgments about the products they make. The aim of personalized learning plans, shared by teacher and students, is to advance each student's know-how as an empowered, self-directed learner adept at knowing how to design, problem solve, and make decisions as an ever more effective high-agency learner seeking deeper learning outcomes.

What are the specific looks and sounds of teachers and students that indicate personalized learning is alive and well in a classroom? Overall, you will observe students engaged in making, doing their plans, and assessing the results. Visitors can look and listen to how you talk and act on the side to guide students' engagement in rigorous inquiries. Visitors can do the same by observing students' mindful engagement, hearing the language they are using. Table 1.2 (page 24) provides samples of what teachers and students may do or say while engaged in planning, accomplishing, and assessing personalized learning plans.

What Is the Potential for Personalized Learning in My Classroom?

Your personalized learning plan template adoption will create opportunities to customize each student's learning. The most beneficial outcomes result when you set this up as an ongoing process. You can tie each lesson to a personalized learning plan. When you are new to the process, aim for one personalized learning plan per unit. Use this same guideline when students are novices to personalized learning plans. Any fewer and your students are unlikely to take the process seriously enough.

Whether you are an elementary, middle, or high school teacher, you can accomplish the following.

- Individualize instruction in any number of subjects.
- Customize when, how, what, and where your entire class learns in a week or semester.
- Shape how a team interacts with peers or how each student targets outcomes that range from vocabulary recall to transfer of design thinking in a capstone project.
- Ask question after question with higher-order-thinking prompts and cue those who struggle to respond.

If you teach single content in the upper grades, you can engage students in the following.

- Selecting outcomes in understanding your content
- Choosing ways to improve how students learn your content
- Developing deeper learning skills to transfer

You do not need to restrict personalized learning to what happens inside your classroom. The anchor is the student's contact with you, face-to-face or online to plan for personal skill development anywhere, anytime, anyplace, but first with you, either in your classroom or remotely.

- You can help students be more complete with homework or turn it in on time. How? Make one of these topics (such as handing in assignments on time) the personalized learning plan goal and continue working for the goal overtime until you both see a SMART result.
- If students are engaged in internships, you can collaborate with their mentors to set goals and

Table 1.2: The Looks and Sounds of Personalized Learning

Looks Like: What Teachers Do	Sounds Like: What Teachers Say	Looks Like: What Students Do	Sounds Like: What Students Say
• Share personalized learning plan templates with students. • Allocate fifteen minutes weekly for students to plan, do, and assess personal learning decisions. • Ask how and why guiding questions. • Walk among students to observe and guide personalized learning activities from the side. • Ask clarifying questions. • Share exemplars. • Review a student plan in a one-to-one or small-group conference. • Lean toward a student to give warm one-to-one feedback. • Review warm feedback with groups or all on digital devices. • Share feedback about progress, challenges, and more on a SMART Board for all to see. • Share rubric samples.	• "Let's walk through this planning template." • "This is what I like about your plan . . . ." • "I am not clear about your goal to . . . ." • "My suggestions for improving your plan (this part of) are . . . ." • "Can you give me an example of . . . ?" • "Tell me why you chose to . . . ." • "How will this strategy help you . . . ?" • "How are you helping your team?" • "What if you considered . . . ?" • "What might be a different way to . . . ?" • "Tell me how doing . . . will challenge . . . ." • "Why?" • "May I suggest that . . . ?" • "It's your choice to . . . ." • "How do you think you will use . . . ? • "If you were to change any part of your plan, what would it be?"	• Make entries onto the template. • Complete talent and interest surveys. • Answer complex questions. • Ask questions and respond to peers. • Explain individual responses about planning and assessing their ideas. • Collaborate in pairs or threes to reflect on common outcomes. • Give and get feedback in a gallery walk or other structured strategy. • Enter completed work in a digital folder. • Organize folders with plans, rubrics, and artifacts.	• "What I want to understand is . . . ." • "The skill I need to improve is . . . because . . . ." • "In this plan, I intend to . . . ." • "Here is how I . . . ." • "My reason is . . . ." • "What I do best working with a team is . . . ." • "Can you give me an example of . . . ?" • "You helped me most when . . . ." • "I found it hard to . . . ." • "I helped the team when I . . . ." • "I am proud that I . . . ." • "I appreciated how you . . . ." • "I need your help to . . . ." • "The pluses of working with you were . . . ."

plan what's most important to learn during this time outside school.

- If you are taking students on a field trip, you can prepare them with plans that identify what they learned from the excursion.
- If you teach in a virtual school, you can add personalized learning plans to guide each student's unit of study.

How Will Personalized Learning Plans Help My Remote Learning Instruction?

The coronavirus pandemic (World Health Organization, 2020) turned classroom instruction inside out and upside down. The pandemic disrupts not only how, what, where, and when students are taught, but is also causing major disruptions in students' and teachers' home lives. Some teachers are still designing and redesigning their interactions with students—flying solo by the seat of their pants. No matter what one's teaching style, personalized learning plans offer solid direction for planning, doing, and assessing remote learning.

When using personalized learning plans, follow these guidelines regardless whether instruction is face-to-face or virtual.

- Stay with your standards-aligned scope and sequence.
- Think about adjusting lessons so students focus on deeper learning outcomes (chapter 3, page 53). Pay special attention to chapters 6–8, on

crucial complex cognitive thinking and social-emotional and digital skills. They are highly desirable skill sets for enhancing remote learning.

- Review how personalized learning plans—with playbooks, guiding questions, and guiding rubrics—will help students acquire the self-direction necessary when learning at home.

If you're teaching remotely, be sure that any of your selected ideas will work well with your remote learners. The following tools can help with this instruction as well.

- **Classkick** (https://classkick.com) is an app and web-based instructional tool that lets elementary teachers take their classrooms paperless, see students working on assignments in real time, and give and get feedback during remote tasks. The app helps monitor student engagement, alone and when working in teams.
- **Nearpod** (https://nearpod.com) is an elementary digital dashboard that looks like a music producer's panel. It allows students to log in to whole lessons. Teachers can *fold* video, shareware, and PDFs so students can interact online.

How Do I Ready My Class for Personalized Learning?

Personalized learning won't just happen. You will make it happen by giving students a tool to use, the template, and the skills to succeed with that tool's capability to guide their own learning for a lifetime.

- The bad news is that if you don't make personalized learning a key course outcome, chances are that some students might get it, but most won't. The majority will just float along hoping to get a grade but not really understanding your course. You ready your class by making personalized learning a key outcome.
- The good news is fivefold.
    1. Infusing personalized deeper learning outcomes into what and how you teach enriches the learning *results* your students take out the door at year's end (Evans & King, 1994).
    2. The blueprint helps you with assessments that leave a measurable trail of student accomplishments.
    3. The blueprint advances students' goal planning as quintessential lifelong learning—anytime, anyplace, any teacher, any skill set.
    4. By taking charge of the technology available for classroom learning, you can more easily manage personalized learning plans as tools to advance students' digital skill development.
    5. With personalized learning plans, you establish your role as the engine driving what and how students learn. No matter how quickly students take full charge, you are still the chief driver. When you first introduce personalized learning plans, students may have the least agency. First comes knowing the process; then comes their increased responsibility for planning and assessing the results. Like novice Junior Maine Guides, in the personalized learning environment, your students first explore how to find their paths through the woods and then go on their solo survival trips.

The start of formal personalized learning requires a few hours to create the personalized learning plan template and if possible, ask a PLC group or other peers to assess your first take. Next, you may want to piecemeal instructions to your students, assessing each part along the way. You can do this in fifteen minutes per day over one or two weeks. Once students fully understand the template and take full responsibility for entering its content, the process may use as little as ten minutes per week. With the template, you and your students have a blueprint from which you can set both small and big goals. To gain a sense of the variation in scale that's possible, imagine designing a tiny prefab house and building a giant skyscraper!

When getting yourself ready to introduce personalized learning plans, it helps to anticipate frequently asked questions by students. The following are some predictable questions you might get from middle and high school students.

- Do we have to? (This one is sometimes a whine.)
- Will we be graded?
- How long will this take?

- How do we make a personalized learning plan? An outcome? A goal?
- What's a SMART goal?
- Do we have to? (More whines)
- Do I have to do it by myself?
- What goals do you want us to pick?
- Can we do it in class?
- Can I work with somebody?
- Can I pick my partner?
- Why doesn't anybody else have to do this?
- How much time will we have?

You have already read the short answers to these questions. As you continue reading, you will gather information about ways to respond. For instance, regarding grades, personalized learning plans rely on guiding rubrics for assessing goal-driven student performance. Assessing is not grading. In chapter 3, you will read that the primary purpose of guiding rubrics is to motivate students' self-management of their personal learning goals. Criteria in a guiding rubric are assessed on a performance range, most often from 0 points, which means *not yet*, all the way up to 4 points, which is *wow*, and describes exemplary performance. The teaching aspect of the statements makes clear what a wow performance requires. If your school requires grades, you can add up the points, create a scale, and record a grade for each personalized learning plan. Add that score to test and quiz scores, and you have a multidimensional grade to give. However, before you go this way, review the research about how extrinsic rewards like grades can undermine intrinsic motivation advanced by feedback centered on goals (Murayama, 2018).

You may distribute templates weekly, biweekly, or by lesson, project, or unit according to the pace you set. You will ask students to store their drafts, plans, selective artifacts, and assessments in Google Docs or an equivalent learning management system (LMS) provided by your district, private school, or charter group.

What if students resist? Any change that takes students out of their comfort zone can bring a fight or flight response. Keep your cool. Offer encouragement and support to solo passive resistors, even going so far as to coach one-to-one while other students are preparing their plans. A buddy is another option. For the active resistor, offer some choices, including the chance to opt out and work alone in an individual personalized learning plan. For group resistance, divide and conquer. Separate a group so all work alone, or redistribute individuals. At all ages, working alone is generally not a desired choice. If a student or a team chooses to work alone, it is important that you hold all to the same standard, regardless of working alone or collaborating. Also remember that active fighters are like one dog barking at other dogs. They are frightened. Find the fright and address each student's concern.

What does it look or sound like when addressing such fears? Table 1.3 charts options for teachers, counselors, or administrators. The *looks* and *sounds like* options respond to refusal statements. As you respond, mix and match your responses to fit students' reactions.

Table 1.3: Addressing Students' Fears

Student Reaction	Response Looks Like	Response Sounds Like
• "I'm not working with her!" • "I want to do it myself. He won't do his share." • "He's too slow. I can do it myself." • "They never help. I do it all." • "I get better grades. She'll pull me down."	• Eye contact, head nodding • Leaning toward but not invading space • Silence • Reassuring smiles with nods • Making a list (with permission) • Checking the list with student • Staying present • Ignoring interruptions	• "I see you are (*emotion such as anger*). I would be too if (*event*)." • "If you had to work with (*other student*), how might you make sure he (*helps*)?" • "Can you tell me why?" • "Why do you think they . . . (*don't help*, for example)?" • "How do you think your response will make (*the other student*) feel?" • "What would you say back if someone told you . . . ?" • "What options would be OK with you to . . . ?"

How Can I Address What Students Need to Know With Personalized Learning Plans?

Throw out rigid adherence to a curriculum or textbook. Maintaining inflexibility in a curriculum's scope and sequence can hinder personalized learning. Instead, you can adopt the personalized learning plan's functions so you can initiate personalized learning pathways in your classroom on Monday. You may introduce a personalized learning plan at any time, but doing so is often helpful at the start of a new lesson. Surprise your class with the personalized learning plan. Your first step might be selecting a single complex cognitive skill embedded in instruction and in a personalized learning plan. If your students lack prior knowledge of how to compare and contrast ideas or how to infer, you don't need to follow scope and sequence to teach prior-knowledge or thinking skills. Instead, you find a different way to deeper learning results.

The following are examples of teachers who, when encountering lack of prior knowledge or foundational skills in their students, respond on an as-needed basis by taking alternate routes to deeper learning.

- When reading *Alexander and the Terrible, Horrible, No Good, Very Bad Day* (Viorst, 2014), a first-year third-grade teacher found her students could not recognize common, proper, and possessive nouns, a grade-one standard. She decided to drop the prescribed third-grade standard of finding relevant clues to draw conclusions and substitute a review plan for the nouns. Her supervisor said, "They do have to recognize the types, but not by finding single answers. Don't confuse means and ends. You can stick with Alexander. He will show your children how to find common and proper nouns in a story they love. Forget the workbook. Ask Alexander" (S. Stroud, personal communication, May 22, 2019).

- When fifth-grade English learners were asked to reason abstractly in a science unit, the teacher's needs assessment led her to adapt her standards-aligned project intended to show her students how to represent data in graphical displays to reveal patterns of daily changes in length and direction of shadows, day and night, and the seasonal appearance of some stars in the night sky. She said, "Before they can reason, Bloom says they have to recognize key facts. My students can't remember the names of the planets, and they kill the pronunciation. I turned my textbook reading lesson into a project for posting a hall mural on newsprint. I got them into teams. Each team had a planet or star to name, day and night movement to graph, and summaries of key facts to write. We did a round-robin where every team explained their section. My method was different from colleagues', but I got there just as well" (A. Paul, personal communication, April 12, 2015).

- When a seventh-grade standard dictated that students *recognize when meaning breaks down and use self-monitoring strategies including making predictions, recalling purpose of reading, and activating prior knowledge to confirm understanding*, the teacher planned a unit for comparing King's (1963) "Letter From Birmingham Jail" with Henley's (1888) "Invictus." When she found three in thirty students had no prior understanding about how to make predictions, she scheduled a needs-to-know minilab to introduce the three and two others who asked for a prediction skill. She introduced a graphic organizer in a team structure. Her department chair lauded this evidence-based strategy (M. McGuire, personal communication, January 2012).

- When a tenth-grade geometry teacher discovered that a sophomore who arrived in the middle of the semester didn't understand the difference between rational and irrational numbers, she thought about transferring the student to basic mathematics. "My first thought was she has to learn in the proper order. I don't have the time. My collaborative teammate showed me how she uses personalized plans to differentiate. That worked" (R. Radoco, personal communication, October 10, 2018).

How Do I Ensure I Cover My Standards During Personalized Learning?

As you know, a hallmark that sets student-centered personalized planning apart from traditional scope and sequence approaches is its reliance on deeper learning outcomes driven by 21st century skills. *Scope and sequence* describe the ideas and concepts that are covered in a course or curriculum. All topics (scope) are listed in the order (sequence) that they appear.

This book's mindful emphasis says no to covering the textbook from first page to last, each chapter in order, and testing to see what students can remember. It says yes to understanding core ideas, not by recalling the content, but by applying the key thinking skills to the content.

Most K–12 content standards call for students to think critically or creatively about content (Anderson & Krathwohl, 2001; Bellanca, Fogarty, & Pete, 2020). Advanced content standards often call for problem solving, either tightly structured (as in mathematics) or loosely structured (as in science and social studies, such as those by the NGSS Lead States [2013]). A *tightly structured problem* requires a precise set of procedures to secure a precise, predictable, accurate solution. Figure 1.6 is a tightly structured geometry problem.

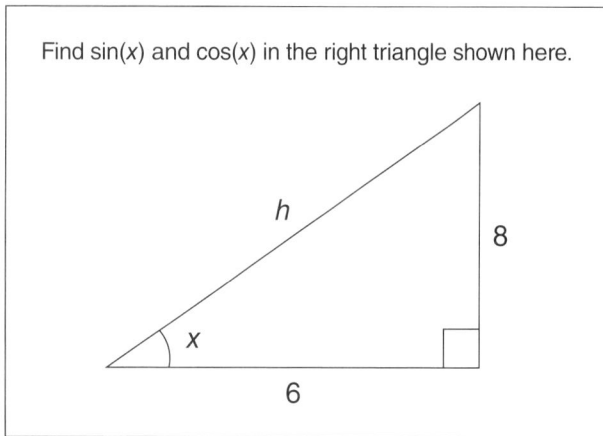

Figure 1.6: Tightly structured geometry problem.

Loosely structured problems ask students to generate multiple possible solutions to a complex, ill-defined problem with unclear goals and missing information. An example of such a problem: How can we end the COVID-19 pandemic? Students might seek ways to solve annual flooding from a river that flows through their town. There is no pre-set solution in a loosely structured problem, and the problem itself may be multifaceted. Place emphasis on gathering information, evaluating possible solutions, and designing a solution the student thinks has the best chance to work.

Few standards ask students to recall (Bellanca et al., 2020). Yet recall verbs (such as *is, name, define, describe, identify, label, list, match, outline, give, recognize, reproduce, select, state*) dominate tests and quizzes in every discipline and grade and are chief drivers of daily instruction in a high percentage of classrooms. Where test and quiz items push for recall, often with single-answer questions, essays also tend to favor the obsolete focus on regurgitation rather than thinking. Following are some examples of single-answer questions and prompts.

- What are the names of three musicals?
- Name the three characters in this story.
- True or false: Uranus is a moon.
- Fill in the blank.
- List three reasons . . .
- Select the correct answer.

The fact that state and national standards mostly call for complex thinking to develop students' intellect tells us that the most significant fourth R is *reasoning*, not *regurgitating*. In addition, the most recent predictions of which skills future employees will need make no mention of recall. Instead, the cognitive abilities set reigns first, and content skills sit fourth, below complex problem solving (Desjardins, 2018). The skills students must learn shift dramatically in favor of reasoning.

Note the call for complex problem solving, creating, comparing, describing patterns, and so forth in the following standard examples; the verbs are italicized. These examples show how the shift has already begun at the standards level. What must follow is administrators who stop pushing test preparation, both formal (when time is stolen from the curriculum to rehash what students have already forgotten), or informal (when teachers continue handing out fact quizzes and tests to drive their instruction). In place of recalling facts from the three Rs must come assessments that drive a standards-aligned reasoning curriculum.

- **Mathematics:** "*Use* addition and subtraction within 20 to *solve* word problems involving situations of *adding to, taking from, putting together, taking apart,* and *comparing,* with unknowns in all positions, for example, by *using* objects, drawings, and equations with a symbol for the unknown number to *represent* the problem" (Florida Department of Education, 2014).
- **Art:** "With limited guidance, *create* musical ideas (such as answering a musical question) for a specific purpose" (Department of Defense Education Activity, n.d.).

- **English:** "*Compare and contrast* the adventures and experiences of characters in stories" (NGA & CCSSO, 2010a).
- **Science:** "*Use* observations of the sun, moon, and stars to *describe patterns* that can be *predicted*" (NGSS Lead States, 2013).

Complex cognitive skills embedded in a standard tell *how* students are expected to succeed at each grade with higher-level thinking skills. For example, *plan* and *investigate* to *describe* and *classify* . . . or *analyze* character. When you match the future jobs lists not only with the Common Core State Standards, but also with standards promulgated by individual states and national organizations such the International Society for Technology in Education (ISTE), the Collaborative for Academic, Social, and Emotional Learning (CASEL; SEL), NGSS (science), and the National Art Education Association (arts), you can easily see the emphases on the complex thinking, problem solving, and other 21st century skills that promote deeper learning. Calling on these standards will enable you to hit the target for any personalized learning plan. Even if the testing in your school drives recall-focused instruction, your students can reap the benefits after you take the time in each lesson to address the 21st century skills shown in the standards.

- The **Common Core State Standards** (CCSS; NGA & CCSSO, 2010a, 2010b) and their state siblings highlight complex thinking verbs and initiate 90 percent of the standards (Achieve, 2017), and the majority of the reviewed states' standards includes "college and career readiness in their ELA and mathematics curricula, and the majority of states displayed a 'strong' rating—the highest available—for clearly and fully addressing each [college and career readiness] element within their amended state standards" (Bellanca et al., 2020, p. 2).
- In the **Next Generation Science Standards** (2013), you find a plethora of complex cognitive verbs such as *plan*, *conduct* an investigation, and *classify*, not as commands to recall information, but as information to think and act. For some people, critical thinking is seemingly intuitive, but like any skill set, critical thinking needs to be taught and cultivated. Unfortunately, educators are unable to deposit the skill directly into their students' heads. While the theory of critical thinking can be taught, critical thinking itself needs to be experienced firsthand.
- In **CASEL** (n.d.b) social-emotional learning (SEL), cognitive skills such as *metacognition* (thinking about one's thinking) and self-management are central to executive skills and personal decision making. The OECD (n.d.b) says that "though social and emotional skills are often called 'non-cognitive skills,' the term is an obvious misnomer since every aspect of mental functioning is based on some form of information processing and cognition" (p. 24).

In various state standards, complex thinking skills stay with the higher-order complex thinking verbs that should drive instruction. Note the following state samples.

- **Wisconsin social studies standards:** "Wisconsin students will *construct* meaningful questions that initiate an inquiry," "gather and evaluate sources," and "develop claims using evidence to support reasoning" (Wisconsin Department of Public Instruction, 2018).
- **Texas technology standards:**

    The student uses creative thinking and innovative processes to construct knowledge, generate new ideas, and create products. The student is expected to:

    (A) *identify*, *create*, and *use* files in various formats, including text, raster and vector graphics, video, and audio files;

    (B) *create*, *present*, and *publish original* works as a means of personal or group expression;

    (C) *explore* complex systems or issues *using* models, simulations, and new technologies to *develop* hypotheses, *modify* input, and *analyze* results; and

    (D) *analyze* trends and *forecast* possibilities. (Texas Education Agency, 2012, p. 6)

The Department for Children, Schools and Families (2008) reinforces this perspective:

Pupils who are critical and creative thinkers will be prepared for a rapidly changing world where they may have to adapt to several careers in a lifetime. Many employers want people who can see connections, have bright ideas, are innovative and are able to solve problems. Good critical and creative thinking abilities provide pupils with the tools needed for independent and life-long learning.

> Helping pupils improve the skills of critical and creative thinking cannot be a 'bolt-on' activity but should permeate each lesson. Teachers should structure activities that build on pupils' abilities, interests and experiences. This creates opportunities for pupils to develop these skills in a 'safe' environment where they feel able to take risks. (p. 3)

You can add a standard that requires higher-order thinking as a goal in the personalized learning process in an effort to attain proficiency in those areas.

What New Skill Sets Will I Need to Teach?

Please note the word *sets* in skill sets. Authors advocating the inclusion of critical thinking and creativity in 21st century classrooms, myself included, have not always considered how teachers might measure thinking skills. We also may have highlighted the now modified sets to be included or simply called for generic critical thinking or more creativity without identifying the specific measurable skills that make up the sets of mental cognitive processes, and ignored the rising importance of the digital and social-emotional sets.

After being immersed in cognitive instruction since 1970, new data have driven my thinking about 21st century skills several steps forward. After editing *Deeper Learning: Beyond 21st Century Skills* (Bellanca, 2015), while examining articles contributed by researchers and practitioners, I concluded that 21st century skills without an endgame shortchange classroom implementation of deeper learning outcomes. As new studies emerged, I recognized that the P21's (2019) generic four Cs give short shrift to emerging skills identified outside school walls—skills considered critical for future employment and 21st century citizenship.

My discussions with colleagues and a review of other educators' data from the World Economic Forum (2020) helped me relabel and regroup the skills most desirable for future citizens and workers into three new skill sets based on the most recent research. By recognizing the need expressed in these documents and reinforced by colleagues and educators with whom I was working, I revised my thinking to add two previously excluded sets, social-emotional and digital, to the mix. Based on multiple sources of data from the World Economic Forum, futurists, and those on the front lines of the classroom, I added these two to the established third set, now relabeled *complex cognitive*.

By separating complex cognitive skill sets from manual and basic cognition (recall) and categorizing the complex cognitive skill sets within two subsets—(1) critical thinking and (2) creative thinking—by regrouping the four Cs' communication and collaboration in the social-emotional skill set, and by acknowledging the real-world need to recognize the digital skill set as the most important, we see how 21st century skills are evolving as a pyramidal taxonomy with an emphasis on head (complex thinking) and heart (social-emotional skills). Hands (manual) includes memory skills with an emphasis on information recall and means eliminating recall as a higher-order-thinking skill. Although they may contribute to higher-order thinking, short- and long-term memory work in different parts of the brain. This taxonomy includes the totality of future citizen and job skills in the deeper learning discussion.

The Complex Cognitive Skill Set

Consider the word *complex* when you are reading about the complex cognitive skill set. *Complex* and *cognitive* are joined together in a recent marriage fostered by constructive learning theorists—who assert that "people actively construct or make their own knowledge and that reality is determined by the experiences of the learner" (Kratochwill, Cook, Travers, & Elliot, 2000, p. 256)—and employment researchers (De Fruyt, Wille, & John, 2015). By separating *basic* cognition or *recall* from what we know as *higher-order-thinking skills* (such as analysis, idea generation, and evaluation), cognitive scientists advance our understanding of what the brain contributes to learning. Simultaneously, they show us how recalling from memory has been misconstrued as a necessary function to be mastered before the introduction of constructive, complex thinking skills can start. With the almost infinite information available via the internet, we no longer have to squeeze facts into the limited storage of our brains. To avoid being overwhelmed with tsunamis of facts and figures flooding our brains from an ever-increasing number of technology-driven sources, it seems more important that we and our students become thinkers, mindfully in charge of picking and choosing the data we need and thinking critically about data sources. Increasingly, brain research and cognitive psychologists have shown us how creative- and critical-thinking skills power our learning (Utami, Probosari, Saputro, Ashadi, & Masykuri, 2018).

By removing the recall skills from the complex set, teachers can specify measurable, higher-order-thinking skills for inclusion in the daily curricula, first and foremost, as the skills of choice that most enable students to deepen their content understanding (Hewlett, 2013) and enable skill transference.

The removal of fuzzy generic labels such as *critical thinking* or *creative thinking* in favor of a taxonomy of specific, standards-delineated higher-order skills aids teachers in writing SMART outcomes and goals, which are specific and measurable. Just as the generic term *breakfast cereal* includes many cereals, while specific names delineate types such as bran flakes, muesli, and oatmeal, allowing parents to decide which specific cereal is healthiest, the specifying of measurable standards-aligned skills in subsets such as critical and creative thinking allows teachers to select the specific, measurable skills that are realistic for students to perfect as they pursue deeper learning outcomes (Bellanca et al., 2020).

Picking a specific complex cognitive skill can be as easy as picking a state or national standard to head a lesson. As you will see in chapter 6 (page 119), you need only refer to a lesson's content standard, look for a key verb, and include it in your student's personalized learning plans. The following example illustrates the steps.

1. Select the standard.
2. Highlight an outcome-producing verb (for example, *edit*).
3. Determine what students will show they can do when they edit a file.
4. List these factors as criteria for a guiding rubric and playbook.
5. Outline a personalized learning plan with the outcome stated to show the edited product.

Bloom's (1956) top levels and the two upper floors of Robin Fogarty's (1999) three-story intellect will provide ample options that pair with your learners' complex cognitive needs. Note in figure 1.7 that for the first time, the 21st century skill building, the three-story intellect, has a date matching the style and content fit to this century's evolving taxonomy of complex cognitive skills.

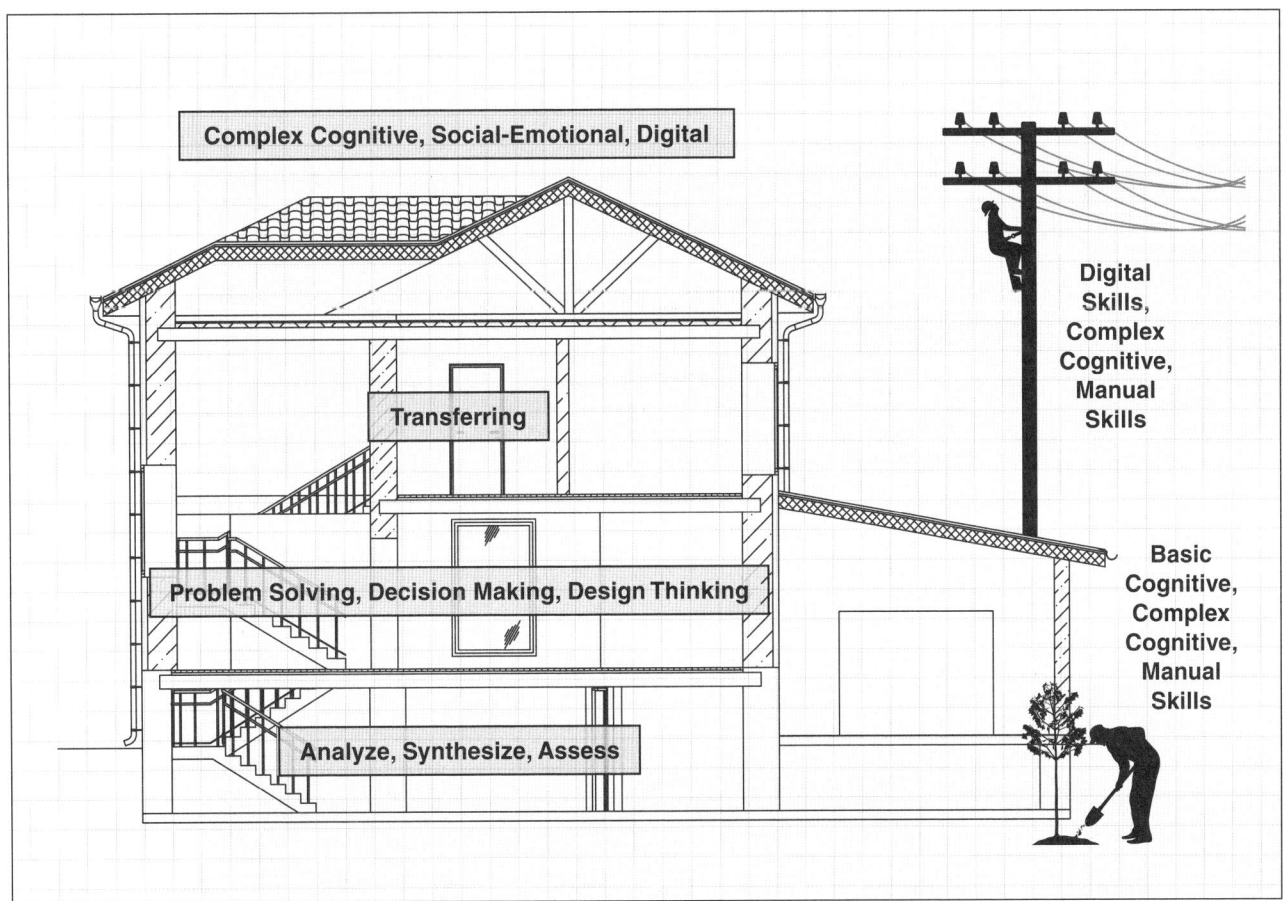

Source: Adapted from Anderson & Krathwohl, 2001; Fogarty, 1999.

Figure 1.7: The 21st century three-story intellect.

The Social-Emotional Skill Set

The *social-emotional* skill set is identified by future employers as important to unlocking future learning doors by 21st century graduates. This set connects skills involved in communicating and collaborating as well as in managing one's own behavior for the present and the future. SEL, as defined most succinctly by CASEL (n.d.a) is:

> the process through which children and adults acquire and effectively apply the knowledge, attitudes, and skills necessary to understand and manage emotions, set and achieve positive goals, feel and show empathy for others, establish and maintain positive relationships, and make responsible decisions.

I recall how often SEL skills were once derided as *soft* and not worth classroom time. SEL theory, research, and best practice, mostly ignored for decades, contradicts those who would mock attention to how students feel and interact in the classroom.

- As early as 1962, David W. Johnson, Roger T. Johnson, and Edythe Johnson Holubec (2008), one of the earliest research teams, focused on cooperative learning and introduced research showing the power of this method to produce academic results superior to individualized learning. They also made clear the importance of positive, face-to-face interaction and social skills as necessary components of classroom life.

- When Reuven Feuerstein, Ya'acov Rand, Mildred B. Hoffman, and Ronald Miller (1980) introduced mediated learning experiences as crucial for cognitive development, they included goal setting, decision making, knowledge application, and self-regulation of behavior as essential cognitive functions.

- Malcolm Knowles (1975), an early voice calling for self-directed learning with its emphasis on goal setting, planning, and self-assessment, introduced his humanistic theory in the 1950s. He called for learner-constructed contracts or plans to guide learning experiences.

- John Hattie (2012) identified self-grading as the instructional strategy producing the highest achievement results. His research made a strong connection between self-grading and SEL's call for motivating students' self-awareness and self-management.

The Digital Skill Set

Initially, digital skills were not counted among 21st century skills. Business and education leaders have called for digital skills to head those lists. Employment futurists, such the World Economic Forum's Adam Jezard (2018), speak to the economic benefits, saying that technology "embraces everything from basic to advanced IT skills, data analysis, engineering and research. These are the skills that are likely to be the most highly rewarded as companies seek more software developers, engineers, robotics and scientific experts."

The College Board's chief of global policy Stefanie Stanford (2019) offers an additional reason to promote teaching digital skills when she advocates for transforming "digital natives" into "civic leaders." Under the headline "More Coding Instruction Would Be Helpful," Mader (2020) says:

> There's a crucial reason to broaden access to computer science. It isn't just a huge part of our economy, it's an inescapable part of our civic life. From campaigning to media coverage to voting, technology is deeply intertwined with democracy. If we're going to keep a government of the people and by the people, we need a lot more tech savvy among the people. Our students may be digital natives, but we have to educate them to be digital citizens. We need a generation ready to shape technology—and reckon with all the ways it's shaping us.

Indeed, the need for graduates with competency in digital skills is twofold. Facility with these skills enhances the lives of individuals while also allowing them to contribute more fully to their communities and world. However, the relevance of digital skills burgeoned suddenly. Since technology first exploded like lava from an undiscovered volcano, its spread has wreaked havoc in the education community. Unlike in the European Union and Australia, many in the education community in the United States struggle to acknowledge the eruption's impact.

In the United Kingdom and United States, where some districts have embraced the ISTE (n.d.) student standards, a growing number of school leaders are moving from an emphasis on technological tools to a realization that digital learning requires more than ever an emphasis on skills for students to manage the proliferation of new gadgets, apps, and computer-assisted instruction programs, to buy and often play with. Just as every day brings a sunrise, the tech industry pumps out a new app, a new update of digital devices, or a new AI innovation. The next step is for districts to recognize the need for formal, standards-aligned digital skills curricula with time allotted to differentiated instruction equal to that scheduled for English language arts and mathematics and not just for technologically gifted and talented students who get to take a coding class. According to Mader (2020):

> I would argue that we all must be tech aware—even strive for fluency. There are many ways to be a productive member of the tech community—as salespeople, designers, trainers, consultants and success managers—that don't require one to be a coder. The tech community requires diverse talent to serve an increasingly diverse customer base.

Yet another imperative exists for developing digital skills. The development of these skills works to erase the wrongheaded emphasis on digital hardware, the toys of technology. Playing with toys keeps people in a state of perpetual childhood. There, they remain suspended, dependent on others to fill desires, pushing to sell goods and services to those who can't think for themselves. The inability to use and think about technology in a sophisticated way promotes a culture of consumption rather than one of creativity and humanistic principle. By developing student expertise with the skills to manage technology, toys become tools to self-manage choice-filled lives, so those living these lives become, as Mader (2020) writes, shapers of technology. I call these shapers of technology *digital thinkers*.

Since digital thinkers are made, not born, teachers are the essential go-to source for developing the complex cognitive and social-emotional skills that enrich our future citizens', employees', and leaders' learning and lives. It is not sufficient to simply buy and use a digital tool. It's essential that users not only learn how to use the new device, but how to use the device to identify and solve problems, think creatively, and communicate.

Unlike computers, teachers can coach the nuances of feeling and problem solving, nuances that computer programs cannot. For instance, a computer program can determine whether a letter written on Word meets technical criteria: no spelling errors, correct punctuation, specified format, specified length, number of words, and so on. A teacher is needed to assess tone, meaning, problem solving, and evidence of thinking. When coaching with a guiding rubric in hand, the teacher can ask open-ended questions like the following that initiate student complex thinking and problem solving.

- *Clarifying questions* may ask for brief examples—for example, "Can you show me an example of how making a decision about what app to use increases your voice and choice?"

- *Skill-specific questions*, followed by feedback to the response, show how well the student is using a complex thinking skill—for example, "How did you analyze Dumbledore's motives? I liked your first idea but I am not sure about the second. Can you tell me more?"

- *Feeling tone questions* invite students to tell how they felt about their work and hear confirming feedback—for example, "Please tell me how you feel about your finished work. What do you like or dislike? Thanks for sharing."

In the absence of district or school leadership or funds for equitable time and resources for digital skills, you as an individual teacher are not powerless to integrate digital skills as full-blown outcomes in your daily planning—and you don't have to introduce separate digital skill units, purchase special materials with your own dollars, or invent new curriculum during your planning period to do it. By assessing which digital skills your students will need, you can turn to free online digital curricula (chapter 8, page 175) from Europe, Australia, and a few North American districts. You and your peers may have to take initiative and choose the digital skills which will most help your students become 21st century deeper learners via personalized learning plans and not wait for Godot.

TAKEAWAYS

As in the introduction, I invite you to compose your own list of key ideas from this chapter to save for constructing your own blueprint for a professional teaching plan.

CHAPTER 2
ENGAGEMENT AND TRUST

The personalization of learning is not just for pretending kids will have choices in what they are going to learn. Rather, it is building environments in which teachers have the time and skills to know their students and can adjust the pace, the materials and surroundings so they can meet the needs of all learners.

—George Wood

Consider sophomore Mona, who says she hates her classes. "My teachers are nice enough . . . I guess," she tells her mother, "but I feel so dumb. When I say anything, I'm afraid all the kids will laugh at my accent."

"Did you talk to your teachers about this?" her mom asks.

"No. I'm afraid they'll holler at me for not speaking up. It's safer in the back row. I never have to say anything, and my teachers don't know I'm there."

Mona is struggling because there are important elements missing from her classroom experience: these are communication, collaboration, and the resulting mutual respect and trust with her teacher and classmates. What helps create and sustain these elements in a classroom? With a definition of engagement at the start, this chapter answers its driving question. It identifies the conditions that will maximize the production of deeper learning outcomes resulting from the introduction of personalized learning plans. With added templates and playbooks, the chapter gives multiple grade-level how-to examples for building a climate of mutual trust and respect and for developing social-emotional skills that enable students to engage in meaningful ways with peers.

Driving question: How do I engage students in deeper learning via personalized learning plans?

What Is Engagement?

Engagement can be surface level, but it needs to be deep. Surface engagement asks students to use their hands to make (*make a poster*) or legs to perform (*run a one-hundred-yard dash*). In the classroom, surface learning engages students with manual and basic cognitive tasks (*write a sentence, fill in the blank,* or *take notes*). In surface engagement, minimum criteria direct the functional task. "Today, class, you are each copying a diorama of Fort Ticonderoga," a teacher in a surface-level classroom might say. Little emphasis is on thought or feeling.

Deep engagement involves students' minds in solving authentic problems, reflecting, making real-world decisions, and assessing what and how they learn. In deeper learning, engagement is the result of challenges that require a student to use her or his mind and feelings to complete an activity or project while simultaneously developing complex cognitive, social-emotional, and digital skills to achieve an outcome. In classrooms that engage in deeper learning, one might hear the following. "Work together to figure out why this fight happened and agree how you will avoid fighting in the future." Or, "Our outcome this week is to show how we can use our geometry knowledge to design a quilt," or even, "Our outcome is to design a robot that can pitch a ball four feet." Note that each of the preceding statements asks students to think and feel, collaborate, or create.

What Conditions Promote Deeper Engagement?

Assuming your classroom environment already furnishes physical security and safety for all students and staff, the preeminent condition for deeper engagement is a healthy learning climate. This is an environment in which you and each student proactively build reciprocal trust and respect for all so that the maximum productive teaching and learning can occur each day.

In this environment, not only is everyone physically safe, but everyone also feels safe and secure from verbal-emotional abuse or ridicule from any person in the classroom at any time. All can express honest opinions and feelings during the many engagements when giving and getting feedback through the process and task collaborations. This classroom would look like what educator and psychologist Thomas Armstrong (2012) describes as a "place where students with all sorts of labels come together as equals to form a new type of learning environment" (p. 159).

Except in small schools that have only one class of students who stay together until graduation, it is most likely that your class contains at least one student who is a newcomer, or, as some wont to be exclusive might put it, a stranger, when the semester starts. You must insist that what follows is behavior by all to build the trust of all while respecting each and welcoming the newcomer. Your leadership role asks you to initiate, model, coach, and assess social-emotional growth in what Armstrong (2012) calls a "new type of learning environment" (p. 159).

Your leadership is revealed by the words you speak and the deep engagements you initiate (Stenger, 2014). Later sections in this chapter tell you how to build this trust and respect, and what evidence to look for to ensure it exists at healthy levels.

Where Do Communication and Collaboration Come In?

Two words, highlighted by P21 (2019) and captured in many SEL standards, express what, why, and how to extend the reach of a warm, healthy climate into every nook and cranny of your classroom, making it an emotionally safe place for you and your diverse students. What are these words? *Communication* and *collaboration*.

When teachers lecture or assign students to finish worksheets, climate is about keeping students on task. The *I talk, you listen* teachers' worry arrives when one student bullies another, one jokes on Instagram, another falls asleep, two whisper on the side, one sneaks out of her digital worksheet by going online to craft a fortress, two text a secret note, three don't hand in homework, two don't take notes, and so on. These noncompliant students fail to cooperate with the teacher and misuse communication. This places students and teacher at odds, and it plants seeds of disrespect when the teacher disciplines the offenders and expands distrust on both sides.

A collaborative climate encourages different behavior. For instance, when students make agreements and sign contracts with specific cooperative norms, mutual respect and trust grow (Henschke, 2012). Personalized learning plans, another form of cooperative contract, provide transparency. If nothing else, personalized learning plans help you get to know students and build their trust. When a teacher challenges students to inquire and solve authentic problems they care about, students bend heads together and figure ways to help each other. In my experience, the more challenging the collaboration, the more interpersonal communication follows. It is likely you will see evidence of social-emotional skills such as empathy and perseverance as bonding students talk together.

Although past generations of school evaluators have denigrated inclusion of these so-called *soft* SEL skills, they must rank as high as basic skills. Analysis of a nine-country longitudinal study by the OECD (2015) asserts that, "Children's capacity to achieve goals, work effectively with others and manage emotions will be essential to meet the challenges of the 21st century" (p. 1).

Nowhere is it more ludicrous to say students need only the *content* of science or mathematics to succeed than in hard-skill science, technology, engineering, and mathematics (STEM) curricula. The job description in figure 2.1, representative of more than one-hundred twenty-five jobs in the careers section of a major metropolitan newspaper, accentuates the preference for candidates with strong communication and collaboration skills. Note in the job criteria how many employers expect communication and collaboration skills.

With employers understanding the high degree of difficulty required for people to work together to solve difficult problems such as writing a program for a specific audience, identifying customer needs, and contributing to team efforts, job descriptions are calling for applicants prepared as much with soft skills as with technical expertise and problem-solving abilities.

As personalized learning plan outcomes, collaboration and communication provide multiple social-emotional skills. Whether readying students to work together or write essays, teachers can insert skills from any set into these plans. Like other SMART outcomes, students will assess with measurable criteria. Students who feel a need to develop any of these skills can choose to include them as outcomes. Even when communication or collaboration skills are *not* explicitly targeted, teachers developing agency can structure teams to develop personalized learning plans.

How Can I Gauge the Level of Mutual Respect and Trust in My Classroom?

You can gauge respect and trust—the social-emotional health—of a classroom climate in two ways.

1. There is an absence of toxic talk and action. No mean girls or boys. No bullies allowed. No sarcastic remarks or show-off interruptions (Willis, 2009).

2. You can see and hear students' self-managed behaviors. This visible evidence provides data that show students and the teacher believe that mutual respect and care are important. Self-managed behavior looks and sounds like a student planning, carrying out, and assessing a personalized learning plan without direction from a teacher or other adult. It also looks and sounds like the student carrying those behaviors into family life, other classes, and a part-time job. Table 2.1 (page 38) lists those self-management behaviors.

---

new

IT Support Specialist
Business Inc.   4.2 ★
Springfield, USA

$20 an hour

➤ Easily apply

Our IT technician performs maintenance, sets up company networks, and troubleshoots for computer users on location. Some IT technicians also design websites, write content, and offer their services on live chat lines for user support. It isn't unusual for an IT technician to run a help desk, assisting customers and employees with computer and network issues. IT technicians can either work specifically for a company's staff or its customers, but some may be responsible for supporting both.

5 days ago   ·   Save job   ·   More

Source: Adapted from Indeed, n.d.

Figure 2.1: IT support specialist job description.

Table 2.1: What Self-Management Looks and Sounds Like

Looks Like	Sounds Like
• To a high degree, planning, doing, and assessing a personalized learning plan contract • Including emotional control as a personalized learning plan outcome • Using self-control to manage impulsive responses • Carrying out an agreed-on responsibility in a team (such as when one is recorder) • Carrying out agreed-on classroom responsibilities (such as taking attendance) • Taking on service responsibility • Keeping a schedule of school and home responsibilities • Putting forth best effort on homework • Using self-control to manage self-recognized foibles	• "I am pleased that . . . ." • "This is a time for me to say *no*." • "It would be better if I did . . . at . . . ." • "No, I don't think it's responsible to . . . ." • "Yes, I could help by . . . ." • "This is what I accomplished in my schedule . . . ." • "I can change my priorities so that . . . ." • "I am sorry that . . . ." • "As your friend, I would like to help by . . . ." • "I can't accept bullying. I won't participate." • "Let's work this out together." • "Let's see how I can help solve this problem."

Assuming that your classroom is already a place in which mutual respect, trust, and collaboration are norms, you can introduce personalized learning plans as early as the first week of school. There is no better approach than to designate the collaboration set as the core skills for raising the level of trust and respect as you further develop students' team skills for more productive problem solving, decision making, and design thinking. Focusing on these skills, however, does not mean you put aside what you have always done, such as establishing rules that don't allow bullying behavior, creating guidelines about smartphones, and modeling respectful behaviors.

If you did not do so in your first week with a new class, you can take time during the week prior to introducing the template to ensure that your climate is sufficiently healthy for encouraging students to ease into the process. The behaviors in table 2.2 are signs of a healthy classroom.

The experience of faculty at the Jen School, a last-chance school in Des Plaines, Illinois, for severely disruptive adolescents, and at similar schools that rely on restorative justice practices to help struggling students become engaged learners, shows that teachers can create healthy climates even with the toughest of the tough. When it comes time to set up and maintain a healthy climate, Craig Maki (2019), Jen School's founder and first principal, notes the important responsibilities of the principal and each teacher:

> There is no doubt in my mind that the school's adults make or break the climate. When it is toxic, we spend our days as firemen and policemen. We are not here to put out fires. It is our responsibility to provide the climate and expect the kids to do their part. (C. Maki, personal communication, March 12, 2018)

If you must adapt this blueprint to ensure all necessary safety for engaged learning, so be it. If the chance should throw you a class mix of toxic students, an all-class personalized learning plan can be your go-to advanced organizer for establishing a culture of respect. If your class contains one or two who make it difficult for others to engage, you can focus the disrupters' personalized learning plans on basic behavior goals. Once you feel confident that your class is able to walk a path of mutual respect, you are ready to dive into the process with a test of the deeper learning waters.

The reproducible "Interview Questions" (page 217) can generate important background information which will help you with the personalization process. It will also help defensive students meet you more as a person. This does not mean you want or need to befriend the student. It does invite the student to dialogue safely with you and break down barriers initially erected to fend off adults. Repeat as often as necessary that *every answer is confidential* and *students have the right to answer any item or to pass*. This right is paramount to true learning.

You may share the interview document in confidence with each student on a digital device. If your classroom lacks sufficient digital devices, scan and print it for each student to keep in a private portfolio in a locked cabinet near your desk.

Table 2.2: What a Healthy Classroom Looks and Sounds Like

Looks Like	Sounds Like
• Heterogeneous groups between two and five students work together. • Special needs students are included in heterogenous groups. • All roles are shared equitably. • All listen to each other without interruptions or talking over. • All make encouraging statements to each other. • Students resolve conflicts with respect for others' feelings. • All come to meet with required materials. • All avoid put-downs and gossip. • All give each other warm feedback and positive suggestions. • Each volunteers to help others. • All take responsibility for physical care of the classroom. • All celebrate each other's success with high fives and other hurrahs. • Brainstorming of ideas without judgment	• "Will you join our group?" • "That's a good idea because . . ." • "Can I help you . . . ?" • "Let's figure a way to solve this." • "Can you give us an example for . . . ?" • "I appreciate it when you . . ." • "It's time to clean up. Let's each do a fair share by . . ." • "Bravo!" • "Let's make a list and vote." • "How would you feel if . . . ?" • "Three cheers for . . . !" • "Give me a high five!" • "That sounds like propaganda to me." • "That sounds like gossip to me." • "Let's divide this task so we each do a fair share." • "Would you like to hear my feedback?"

Developing each student's sharing skills helps maintain the mutual respect and trust which supports the process. When you set up a digital network and include portfolios, team activities, peer feedback, team plans, and, most notably, teamwork co-assessments, you reinforce the expectation that collaboration and communication are a top priority. By initiating the SHARE acronym, you enable students to develop specific social-emotional skills. Post and review SHARE with the class before incorporating one or more into personalized learning plans. Visit **go.SolutionTree.com/instruction** for a free reproducible version of this acronym.

S = Seek best ideas

H = Help each other

A = Attend to others' feelings

R = Respect others' ideas

E = Expand, expand

How Do I Engage Students in Peer Interviews?

You and your students must collaborate to build and maintain the classroom culture of mutual trust and respect each day of the year so that students can work together in a productive way. Trust building is not a one-and-done activity. Nor does it happen without your leadership. A helpful trust-building strategy is the peer interview with a common set of questions and guiding norms. A perfect time to introduce peer interviews is when you launch personalized learning plans. You can extend these interviews with added questions one or more times each semester.

A trust-respect culture must be reciprocal. As noted, this culture must ensure that students will respect each other and you. This is crucial for success of the personalized learning plan interview and for its impact on the class culture, where all students hopefully feel they can interact safely and be assured that what they say to each other will be helpful and supportive. The more you help students form positive bonds, a process that can begin with peer interviews, the less likely it will be that you see off-task behavior, negative comments, and mean behavior.

The interview playbook in figure 2.2 (page 40), which corresponds with the reproducible "Interview Questions" (page 217), provides a task analysis for interviewing students with the interview template. After your first trial, you may wish to adjust the interview steps.

How Do I Promote Reflection?

It's easy to skip reflection activities in a time-pressed classroom. Because reflecting comes at the end of a lesson

1. Review the reproducible "Interview Questions." Decide what to add, remove, or otherwise change. Set a flexible schedule that allows time for complete interviews. Elementary students may need more time over several days.
2. Review SHARE with students.
3. Upload and store your final document into a desktop folder.
4. Share the "Interview Questions" reproducible with the whole class. For students who may have their own laptops or notebooks, share the template to their devices. If you don't have digital devices for your students, print a copy for each student.
5. Check students' prior experiences with personalized learning plans. Discuss the purpose, benefits, expectations, and procedure for your approach.
6. Play both roles in a demonstration interview. Fill in your personal answers on the template shown on the interactive whiteboard. In middle or highschool classrooms, invite a student to be your partner to ask the questions and record.
7. Invite students to contribute to a whole-class list in response to the question "In a personal interview, how do you want your partner to show respect for you and your ideas?" Write one or two examples to start the list. If you don't see an important pro-respect word after students have no more ideas to give, add to the list.
8. Share the document so each student can upload a copy to a personal folder. (See playbooks for creating a digital portfolio accessible by each student, and for creating a manila folder portfolio for each student, figures 8.5 and 8.6, page 199.)
9. Pair students for the interviews. Check for understanding on how to fill out the answers. Each takes a turn as the interviewer. Invite interviewers to follow the ideas generated on the shared respect list.
10. Keep time, noting when most pairs are near completion before giving a final time's up notice. Walk among students and give encouragement, but don't be drawn into conversations.
11. Post the following guiding questions.
    - What does the word *share* mean to you?
    - Why is it important to share in a team?
    - Who is involved in sharing?
    - How do you share?
    - How would you seek best ideas from a group?
    - When can sharing happen?
    - Where can sharing happen?
    - How specific is your statement?
    - How will you measure the outcome?
    - What is authentic about your plan?
    - What is the time schedule?
    - What is easy about sharing?
    - What is hard about sharing?
    - What have you learned today about sharing?
12. Pairs who finish the interviews first can begin discussing their responses. When all pairs are done with interviews, prompt a whole-class discussion of each question. Seek multiple responses to each question from between three and five random students for each letter of SHARE. Record all responses. If the list is incomplete, add your own ideas before checking that all ideas are worthwhile or removing those that the students don't think fit the classroom's trust norm.
13. Optional: Schedule one-to-one conferences to review each student's responses. For grades 8 and up, allow between ten and fifteen minutes per interview. For grades 7 and earlier, reduce the number of questions and the time. You may delay conferences to later in the semester, after you have ensured that students will engage in teamwork, so you do not have to monitor on-task behavior and can conduct short conferences without distraction.

Figure 2.2: Playbook example.

Visit ***go.SolutionTree.com/instruction*** *for a free reproducible version of this figure.*

or project, time can run out when students are highly engaged and miss the end time. However, when you skip reflection, you miss the most teachable moments.

Reflection asks students to stop and think about what they have learned and how. When you ask them to think about their learning, you not only slow impulsive thinking, you move into the uncharted and difficult waters of metacognition. Figure 2.3 has reflection question examples.

Social-emotional skills, in turn, get a boost because those who monitor their thinking can, in turn, be conscious of their emotions and restrain themselves from being impulsive (Krishna & Strack, 2017). As such, it follows that lack of impulse control can block academic achievement. If you refer to teacher evaluation models such as Charlotte Danielson's (2019) Framework for Teaching Evaluation Instrument, you will see that proficient use of the skills that promote metacognitive reflection will place you in rare company: "The teacher uses a variety or series of questions or prompts to challenge students cognitively, advance high-level thinking and discourse, and promote metacognition" (p. 67).

As with other instructional proficiencies, you benefit from knowing how to facilitate metacognitive practices that include even the most hesitant. When prepped with guiding questions, shy students are more likely to share. Round-robin responses rely on evidence-based practices such as wait time (allowing time to go by before offering an answer to questions students are struggling with), equal distribution with each student called on to speak in a round-robin, and open-ended prompts so that all students are encouraged to reflect. Round-robin responses also help you avoid calling on the same quick volunteers over and over (Los Angeles County Department of Education, 2019). You launch round-robins with the six steps in figure 2.4 (page 42) showing a playbook sequence for an equal distribution strategy with the round-robin response.

Insist that all listen and honor each response. Put-downs or wisecracks are not allowed! Move, in order, through the class until all have responded. What do you do when a student breaks the social contract and makes silent or verbal fun of another's response? As with other unacceptable behavior, first try the nonverbal approach: stare and head shake. A second offense merits an in-class time-out sitting next to you and a private one-to-one discussion in which you identify a consequence for repeat offenses. You may write a personalized learning plan just for this student. It should focus on a social-emotional skill that constitutes a desired behavior.

After students have learned to reflect with SHARE, you can add guided peer-to-peer interviews through the year, designate these partners as peer-support teams, and keep the teams together through a quarter or more. Figure 2.5 (page 42) is a playbook to help teams work together over time. Select those items important to you and your students.

What Activities Are Best for Building and Maintaining Trust?

Building trust into a personalized learning plan blueprint takes time and hard work by you and by the students. Maintaining trust is equally challenging. By modeling the trust behaviors that you seek, you make

---

- What frustrated you? How did you handle it?
- How was teamwork important for this activity?
- What was hard about your teamwork? What was easy?
- What was hard for you in the problem solving? What was easy?
- What are some skills you needed to be good at teamwork?
- What are some skills needed to be a good problem solver?
- What is another situation where you had to use teamwork to solve a problem?
- How can you use what you learned in this experience in situations outside the game? Why do you think so?

Source: Adapted from Sepp, 2012.

Figure 2.3: Reflection questions—Examples.

*Visit **go.SolutionTree.com/instruction** for a free reproducible version of this figure.*

1. Ask an open-ended prompt and then ask each student to reflect on it in silence for a moment.
2. Ask each to stop and think, draw a picture, or write a response on a note card before you designate who will start the round-robin.
3. After the wait, ask for a volunteer to start.
4. After the first response, with a nod of your head, ask each in turn to the first student's right-hand side to answer or to say, "I pass." Always honor a pass as well as give individual wait time.
5. You may record unduplicated answers on the interactive whiteboard or just listen and thank students for sharing. If a student says, "My answer is like number four," invite that student to share in his or her own words. With a multiple-question response such as SHARE, you can switch to a different item after you have several responses for each item, for example, moving from asking how students seek best ideas to how they help each other.
6. End a session with a review of SHARE, asking "Which of these skills did you do best today?" or "How is your progress with . . . ?"

Figure 2.4: Teacher playbook—Round-robin responses.

*Visit **go.SolutionTree.com/instruction** for a free reproducible version of this figure.*

1. Match paired partners. Start dialogue with each student completing his or her own personalized learning plan template and then meeting with partners. Keep the interview teams together at least eight weeks. Change only those teams you see not working well.
2. For a novice personalized learning plan class, walk through the interview and provide examples for each question or prompt. For individual novices, pair with experienced student partners who can coach the novice. Do this if you have a new language learner or a student who is a challenged communicator.
3. After peers review and give positive feedback on each other's personalized learning plans, take advantage of the chance for students to complete prompts for building trust ("I like how you…," "I think it's a good idea that you are…," "I wonder why…," or "I am concerned . . . .").
4. Post the completed plans around the room. Host a gallery walk in which students use sticky notes to complete the prompt "I like . . ." and attach it to the wall or a bulletin board.
5. Students may take a copy of the personalized learning plan home and secure parent or guardian feedback. Keep the original copy in the student's portfolio. Students will each need access to their secure electronic folders.
6. Students return their plans to you after getting feedback from parents or guardians, storing interview results in a portfolio (this is preferably online but can be in a manila folder). You may review and conference with students to coach each with the interview results in mind.

Figure 2.5: Teamwork playbook.

*Visit **go.SolutionTree.com/instruction** for a free reproducible version of this figure.*

what you value transparent. You put the cap on the well when you provide honest support to those who struggle to show the respect that leads to trust, but you also ensure that there is accountability for those who violate the norms.

Lectures and films about mutual trust and respect are nice, but are generally much less effective than a menu of engaging activities that teach students how to respect and build trust with each other. With the reproducible "Interview Questions" (page 217) as an engaging starter activity, respect will follow as students discover positive characteristics about each other and their cultures. In a personalized learning plan–friendly environment, scheduling one engaging trust-building or collaboration activity per month—more often if needed—with the opportunity afterward for students to reflect on the activity's value produces not only more fruitful conversations among students but advances competence with the 21st century deeper learning skills of cooperation and communication.

The following classroom-tested activities build your classroom culture.

- Prompt Circle
- Shapes Made Perfect

- Science Scavenger Search
- Engineering Feats
- Collaborative Class Puzzle
- By Any Other Name

Try one of these activities, selected or modified for your students' maturity, twenty or thirty minutes before embarking on a new unit. In many cases, you can tie the fun into a review of the prior unit's content. Remind students why you are taking this time before starting an activity. After the activity is over, guide a five- or ten-minute reflection so students can connect the fun learning with the serious rationale of building trust and respect. The activities work for any grade level with some modification if necessary.

Prompt Circle

Follow these three steps for the Prompt Circle activity for older students or Magic Circle for elementary students (Davenport, 2018).

1. Seat students in chairs in a circle.
2. Decorate a canoe oar, table tennis paddle, or some other object.
3. Hand the paddle to one student, who responds by answering the prompt while other participants listen to him or her and then pass the paddle to the right once finished. Give an open-ended prompt. The prompt might look or sound like the following.
   - "Today, I learned . . ."
   - "This morning I want to learn more about . . ."
   - "I am pleased that I . . ."
   - "I am worried that . . ."
   - "In this lesson, I discovered . . ."
   - "I am proud that I . . ."
   - "I do my best when . . ."
   - "I wish . . ."

All students except the student with the paddle are active listeners looking at the paddle holder in silence and waiting. When students feel psychologically safe, you can invite paddle holders to amplify their responses with examples or a story. Adapt this strategy with similar Magic Circle activities with early learners (Perry, 2017).

Shapes Made Perfect

You can make this a review of various shapes. Follow these four steps for the Shapes Made Perfect activity with all ages.

1. Invite pairs to blindfold each other and then give them a rope to hold.
2. Ask them to drop the rope at your signal and to take three steps to the right from where they were standing.
3. Wait a moment and invite the pairs to return to the rope, pick it up, and try to work together to lay it out in a perfect geometric figure which you have assigned.
4. When finished, everyone can remove their blindfolds and sit in a circle. To begin a discussion, provide prompts such as "What I learned about trusting my partner is . . ." or "I was glad when . . ."

Science Scavenger Search

Follow these four steps for the middle school Science Scavenger Search activity. To adapt this for high school science students, make the list from objects in your curriculum: for example, in chemistry, use an object to measure a gas, a tool to hold a beaker, and the like.

1. Match students in teams of three; one should serve as a recorder.
2. Have teams search for junk equipment needed to complete an experiment based on a list of functions like the following. Some of these functions are open to interpretation. You can vary this with a list of lab equipment and materials for floating a paper boat or other object which they can make and include in a team competition game.
   - Can start a fire
   - Holds water
   - Measures ounces
   - Binds together
   - Covers
   - Tastes good
   - Flavors
   - Spins
   - Cuts
   - Screens

3. When a team has an object to match each function, it must make a set of instructions for producing a solid or liquid that is edible and market it to sell with a brochure. (You can find brochure templates in Word, Google Docs Templates, or Canva.) First finished wins.

4. Provide closing prompts for the class such as "What we discovered about our creative teamwork is . . ."

Engineering Feats

Follow these two steps for the Engineering Feats activity. As an alternative, have students build the tallest towers. This would work for grades 5–up.

1. Split students into teams of five each. Provide each team with forty straws and twenty marshmallows and explain that they must work to build the longest bridge that withstands your handmade earthquake. Set a time limit that requires fast thinking and collaboration.

2. After a winner is announced, start a whole-class conversation with prompts such as the following.
   - "By working together, we learned to . . ."
   - "We worked best as a team when we . . ."

Collaborative Class Puzzle

Follow these three steps for a Collaborative Class Puzzle activity for grades 2–12.

1. After a lesson in which students study famous people (scientists, mathematicians, world leaders), invite trios to create sketches from the lives of these famous people. Encourage older students to include background images taken from the person's life.

2. Cut the sketches into puzzle pieces, put the pieces in a sandwich bag, and give the pieces to another team. New teams will assemble the puzzles on a classroom bulletin board.

3. Afterward, provide concluding prompts such as the following.
   - "To re-create the puzzles, it was best when we . . ."
   - "We learned how to trust each other when . . ."

By Any Other Name

Follow these five steps for the By Any Other Name activity, which works for grades K–12. Prewriters can draw on large pieces of paper.

1. Give each student five or ten small sticky notes.

2. Invite each student to write one word per sticky note that describes the qualities they like friends to have.

3. At a signal, each student posts the notes on a wall or bulletin board. Silently, students are free to move any note into a group that is its synonym.

4. When everyone is done, invite one student to label one group with a larger sticky note.

5. End by brainstorming a list of feelings students experienced during this activity by starting with the prompt, "When someone . . . I felt . . . because . . ." Discuss the completed list.

How Do Cooperative Learning and Team Problem Solving Maintain Trust?

Teams are a constant, and not just in sports or for software engineer careers. McDonald's has a team development program required for every franchisee (McDonald's Corporation, n.d.). The Army, Navy, and Marines rely on teamwork, especially in programs such as the SEALS (Gleeson, 2019), where teamwork is considered a matter of life and death. Emergency-room medical teams connected by digital notebooks, Amazon.com management teams meeting with FaceTime, and rapid-response forest-fire teams are other examples of teams working together often with sophisticated technology to solve problems and build trust. Likewise, PLCs are becoming more common in schools (Taylor, Hallam, Charlton, & Wall, 2013). What do these groups all have in common? They are an accepted way of increasing productivity via the core social-emotional skill of trust.

You may already include cooperative learning as a key instructional strategy. If you are familiar with the effects research (Marzano Research, 2020) and cooperative learning's benefits for your students, the only new information provided here will be suggestions for adapting what you already do well within the process. If you are a light user of the process, or if cooperative learning is not something you have adopted, the material that follows here will suggest easy steps forward for you to take via the personalized learning plan process.

What Does Research Say About Cooperative Learning?

Cooperative learning is supported by one of the strongest research traditions in education, with thousands of studies conducted across a wide range of subject areas, age groups, ability levels, and cultures. The results, in general, suggest that cooperative learning develops higher-order-thinking skills, enhances motivation, and improves interpersonal relations and peer relations (Johnson, & Johnson, 2018; Slavin, 1995).

In the mid-1960s, when brothers David and Roger Johnson (1999) first researched the impact of cooperative groups on achievement, they ended up showing the superiority of cooperation over other "learning alone" methods. The cooperative group proved to be the highest-producing achievement-promoting model when compared with the all-class lecture-test model and the individualized worksheet model. The research from Johnson and Johnson (2018), Slavin (1995), and others stirred a fire that still smolders. In spite of cooperative learning's effectiveness being corroborated by researchers and meta-analyses (Hattie & Clarke, 2019; Marzano, Pickering, & Pollock, 2019) naming cooperative learning one of the most effective methods for raising student achievement, many advocates of 21st century skills have ignored the studies or derided the practice as old hat—even as they call for increased collaboration in today's classrooms.

Although many how-to books such as *Blueprints for Achievement in the Cooperative Classroom* (Bellanca & Fogarty, 2003) facilitate cooperative learning theory in practice, Father Time has pointed his finger at a few cooperative tactics that more specifically pass his test for creating a reciprocal culture of trust and respect. Whether informal or formal, these selected tactics raise achievement. When well facilitated, these tactics bond students as they build the climate of trust and respect fundamental for producing deeper learning outcomes. Additionally, in remote learning, digital skills will enhance student team learning when they work *asynchronously* (at different times).

Informal Cooperative Learning

Informal cooperative learning tactics rely on variations of think-pair-share. Variations include write-pair-share, draw-pair-share, paired partners, and 2-4-8. In think-pair-share, two students think or work alone to complete a single task (think), they agree on one answer (pair), and they describe (share) it with the class or match with another pair to form four and then a group of eight. When working on personalized learning plans, pair students. *Two heads are better than one* is a favorite motto reiterated by veteran teachers using cooperative learning strategies. Structured pairs work even with reflection as students in pairs think, draw, or write alone, talk with a partner to synthesize what they learned, and then share the result with the class.

This quick engagement tactic lets you structure wait time and other achievement-producing tactics validated in Teacher Expectations and Student Achievement (TESA) studies (Kerman, 1979). By linking think-pair-share to an open-ended question about a recently completed task, you increase the chances that even a shy student, or those needing time to stop and think, can prepare a response. You also can ask for multiple responses. Think-pair-share slows down dominating, impulsive responders, and increases the number of students who raise their hands. As an informal cooperative learning tactic, you can easily embed think-pair-share into a lecture to check for understanding, to maintain attention, or to increase engagement. It is equally helpful when students are engaged in group work and you want to check their thinking and problem solving by asking them to stop and think.

An open-ended question is crucial to think-pair-share success. When aiming to promote thinking, closed questions asking for single facts are a dead end. They are grounded in memory, not cognition: "What tree did George Washington cut down?" "Who shot President Lincoln?" So too is asking for students to recall a list of items: "What were three causes of World War I?" "Name the three largest states." Fact questions advance short-term memory located in the hippocampus, and long-term memory in the neocortex. Critical and creative thinking spring from the two-sided prefrontal cortex, the home of complex cognition (Moawad, 2020). Table 2.3 (page 46) provides examples of open-ended think-pair-share questions to stimulate complex thinking as students plan or assess a personalized learning plan.

Table 2.3: Think-Pair-Share Questions

Elementary School	Middle School	High School
• "What do you want to accomplish with this personalized learning plan?" • "What would you like to do better in (*subject*) this year?" • "Who can help you complete this personalized learning plan?"	• "How can working in a team help you learn better?" • "What are two ways you prefer to study (*subject*)?" • "How did this personalized learning plan help you?"	• "What ideas are most important for you to put in this personalized learning plan?" • "How did working together help you achieve your outcome?" • "What would you like to share that will help (me, your peers) help you in this class?"

Formal Cooperative Learning

Formal cooperative learning is an ideal tactic to initiate personalized learning plans. By identifying a single outcome for teams, you remove the primary responsibility of facilitating plans from your shoulders as you help students develop teaming skills in search of their common outcome. In this way, you increase student agency as members follow the personalized learning plan template to plan, implement, and assess their plans together. By structuring the teamwork, you make your implementation monitoring easier, and you harness the power of many minds and hearts to think and problem solve together.

When you want to develop students' team skills, you can structure teams of between three and five students to complete a content study guided with a shared personalized learning plan (such as why bullies exist, learning the differences between wealthy and impoverished neighborhoods in your city, or the common characteristics of John Steinbeck's novels). You form the teams; students provide a driving question to answer or single goal for the team to reach. Each member is accountable for a specific role, expected to call on interpersonal communication skills to help the team bond in pursuit of the shared outcome, and asked to assess not only the content outcome but the thinking and cooperating that produce the outcome.

If you organize *base teams* which stay together for a semester, you will stand a better chance of facilitating mutual trust and respect in each team and developing each member's team skills. Eventually, teams arrive at the point where members can agree among themselves on establishing roles and responsibilities, team norms, the personalized learning plan outcome and, as you increase their agency, the cognitive strategies and all aspects of the personalized learning plan assessment. Base teams do not prevent you from setting up other formal teams for specific learning tasks across your curriculum.

The playbook examples in figures 2.6–2.8 (pages 47–48) show variations of formal cooperative learning activities made grade-level appropriate and aligned with class norms for trust and mutual respect (which are not required but do help). Prior to starting, outline timelines, task, strategy, and team sizes. If you are experienced with cooperative learning, you will recognize how role and outcome identification are always included in a formal cooperative learning activity. You may also see how graphic organizers and jigsaw structures are included as strategies to increase team collaboration.

Before you start a personalized learning plan–enriched lesson that relies on teams, you review class norms, time, strategies, and technology tools, team contracts, and roles and responsibilities. You will provide a collaborative rubric. Note this playbook is a much shortened version. It is appropriate for students being introduced to their first personalized learning plan. Those more experienced with personalized learning plans can add personalized learning plan elements to increase their planning behavior or allow experienced teams to create their own criteria for collaborative success.

What Activities Are Best for Transferring Team Skills to Decision-Making Scenarios?

Cooperative learning works best when students rely on team skills to solve both tightly structured problems and loosely unstructured problems (Wismath & Orr, 2015).

Tight Problem Solving

As discussed in chapter 1 (page 11), tight or well-structured problems are solved by recalling a set of

Engagement and Trust

Team size: Two or three students
Roles: Recorder to mark our choices, timer to keep us on time, coach to make sure we agree
Norms: 1. Listen to each other. 2. Speak with inside voices. 3. Be positive with each other. 4. Agree on our choice.
Time: Ten minutes for ten days
Assessment: A checklist rubric to assess collaborative skills
Task: Decide which of these tasks or activities your team will select. ☐ Increase our info-text reading rate _____% in the next month. ☐ Decrease the number of spelling errors in our chapter summaries by _____% in the next month. **Outcome:** A chart showing the increase or decrease selected. Complete a two-sentence summary after reading one story per week.

Figure 2.6: Formal cooperative learning playbook—Elementary school example.

Team size: Five students
Roles: Guide keeps time and engagement of all, facilitates discussions; recorder completes one online template with team-gathered info; checker asks clarifying questions about individual summaries; encourager identifies strong points in each summary; reporter presents group's final summaries of five articles jigsawed among the five members. In the jigsaw, each member watches one online video or reads one article about presidential powers, collects key points per guiding questions, and adds to the matrix.
Norms: 1. Listen. 2. Don't get loud. 3. Be supportive. 4. Come to an agreement.
Time: Eight class periods over eight days
Assessment: Individual quizzes: content of articles read, understanding of presidential powers. Rubric is two single-point rubrics based on collaborative norms and presentation content.
Driving Question: To what degree have the last two presidents and the current president changed the office's constitutional powers? Or you can talk about presidential powers.)
Outcome: A matrix chart presented, as a team, to the class. The chart will show up to three changes in power with each president, the legislatures, and the Supreme Court.

Figure 2.7: Formal cooperative learning playbook—Middle school example.

Team size: Five students
Roles: Guide keeps time and engagement of all, facilitates discussions; recorder completes one online template with team-gathered info; checker asks clarifying questions about individual summaries; encourager identifies strong points in each summary; reporter presents group's final summary of five articles.
Norms: 1. Listen and be respectful. 2. Agree to listen to all sides. 3. Search for a win with any conflicts.
Time: Ten class periods and self-directed time out of class
Assessment: Four-point guiding rubric for each norm
Task: Do jigsaw research with fair-share distribution of ten articles related to lesson topic. Display class-made bubble map showing articles' key ideas with connections to final summary of all research. Each team jigsaws reading of ten online articles about one of five social media sites for teens to answer the driving question, How are social media changing to meet concerns of parents? Individuals from each team with same social medium agree on common response. List five concerns backed by data from articles read. Present with charts in a shareware display.

Figure 2.8: Formal cooperative learning playbook—High school example.

procedures and performing each exactly as learned. When you log into your computer, you solve that problem by going through rotely recalled steps. In the same manner, students assigned to solve a mathematical problem follow a given set of procedures and arrive at a predictable result. Structured problems that people solve daily at work include using a coffee machine, turning on and logging into their computer, and accessing email. Likewise, tightly structured problems are the norm in mathematics, directed by standards which call for students to "make sense of problems and persevere in solving them" (NGA & CCSSO, 2010b). The CCSS and many state and provincial standards of mathematical practice ask students to be precise and accurate with procedures as well as reason logically to arrive at understanding (NGA & CCSSO, 2010b).

In the field, experts disagree about the roles of rote recall and reasoning. Many teachers hinge procedures on memory, especially in the early grades. Some who teach algebra and geometry do the same. Mary Jo Dulin, a physicist who teaches mathematics to incoming STEM students at the University of Sydney contends that even in a statistics course, memorized procedures have their place if for no other reason than to conserve time when reasoning (M. J. Dulin, personal communication, 2017). Dulin points to problems that rely on what students can do with linear algebra formulas for solving statistics problems: "Recalling the deviation formula is one example I invite my students to memorize" (M. J. Dulin, personal communication, 2017).

The following are examples of tight word problems. These numeracy problems show how recall of the numerical functions is required to solve the problem.

- **Elementary school:** Marisa read her book for twenty-five minutes on Monday and thirty minutes on Tuesday. How many minutes in all did she read? (Procedure for two-column addition)

- **Middle school:** Marisa received three detentions in the fourth quarter. She received three other detentions for the first and second quarters combined. She received twelve for the whole school year, so how many detentions did she receive in the third quarter? (Procedures for addition and subtraction)

- **High school:** You take a 1,300 mile round trip to New York to see the Yankees play your favorite baseball team. How much time will you save on the 1,300-mile trip if you average 70 miles per hour (mph) compared to averaging 60 mph? If your car gets 25 miles per gallon (mpg) at 70 mph but increases to 30 mpg at 50 mph, how many gallons of gas would you save on the 1,300-mile trip at the lower speed? If gas costs $2.30 a gallon, how much money do you save? Is the saving in time at the slower speed worth the extra cost? (Recall procedures for addition, multiplication, division, and subtraction.)

Elementary School Activity: Problem-Solving Procedures

Follow these steps to try problem-solving procedures for grades 3–6.

1. Pair students and invite them to select between the role of recorder and the role of reporter. Review norms for teamwork.
2. Make clear the outcome of this personalized learning plan. It is for students to recall without prompting the procedures for solving Marisa's reading problem (in the first bullet on page 48).
3. Identify the procedures, present the first problem, and ask the pairs to follow the procedures to find the solution for two trains speeding to each other on one track. One is going 90 mph and the other is going 60 mph. They are 1.5 miles apart. How long before they crash?
4. Repeat this approach with additional train problems until your check of recalling the procedures hits a 90 percent success mark. If you prefer, you can start the pairs with a problem and then arrive at a class consensus about the procedures. Repeat with more difficult two-train problems until your class hits the 90 percent recall expectation set as the personalized learning plan outcome.
5. After each round, debrief students on how well they followed the best procedures.

Middle School Activity: Precision and Accuracy

Follow these five steps to try a precision and accuracy activity.

1. Put students in a trio with roles, norms, and other guidelines you set.
2. Make clear the outcome of this activity: It is improving precise calculations for a geometry problem. Provide a guiding rubric to assess precise and accurate measurements as well as their answers.
3. Share the driving question. In this case, it might be something like "How can we find a general expression for the area of a triangle on a grid if its vertices have coordinates $(5,5)$, $(x,0)$, and $(0,y)$?"
4. Provide the grid and invite teams to show their work with a list of recommended problem-solving procedures and their reasoning on a large, posted sheet of paper. Before teams start, share this guiding rubric.
5. Debrief with the rubric three to five times with various measurement problems. Measure each student's improvement in making precise and accurate measurements.

High School Activity: Perseverance

The upper-grade Pennsylvania Standards for Mathematical Practice (Commonwealth of Pennsylvania, n.d.) stress application of procedures and reasoning in problem solving. For example, "Apply geometric concepts to model and solve real-world problems" (Commonwealth of Pennsylvania, n.d.) is an example that asks students to create a model for solving a problem not listed in their textbook. This standard directs a problem-based lesson that will enable teams to transfer tight problem-solving procedures (mathematical problem-solving skills as called for in the standard) into a scenario that requires loose problem-solving skills and mindsets (Duckworth, 2016).

Follow these five steps for a problem-solving process that combines geometry procedures with student perseverance—a social-emotional skill.

1. **Present a real-world problem like this one:** The local river overflows with each spring rain. The overflow damages many homes in the community. Several students' families have been flooded out.
2. **Make clear the outcomes for this activity:** Produce a workable solution to this problem, and show evidence of perseverance in finding a workable solution.
3. **Provide a guiding rubric for showing evidence:** To what degree did I stay with the task when (1) a teammate disagreed with my idea, (2) my idea was not achievable (like a SMART goal), (3) my teacher gave me negative feedback, or (4) my geometry was off?
4. **Ask the driving question:** "Using what we know about geometry, how can we modify the riverbanks to prevent home damage?"
5. **Debrief:** Use an open-ended rubric after each activity and post a chart showing class progress.

Loose Problem Solving

For *loose problem solving*, you can ready your teams to solve unstructured or ill-structured problems. These problems are the type that they may see in real-world social, political, or scientific situations (Simon, 1973). To resemble situations in the real world, ill-structured problems have unclear goals and incomplete information and in real life, these problems often are solved through collaborative effort. When problems are taken from students' concerns about their daily life situations, they are labeled *authentic*. Authentic problems are more likely to arouse student interest and willingness to solve them (Alioon & Delialioğlu, 2019; Ryan & Deci, 2000).

For these authentic scenarios, set up formal cooperative thinking teams with roles, responsibilities, norms, rubrics, and a common goal. The first problem-solving tasks will expose students to the challenges of problem solving in teams. However, to help students learn from this first experience and advance collaborative problem-solving proficiency, you need to add team self-assessment with reflection questions. These questions will ask what students learned from problem solving and teamwork and challenge them to improve the skills. Based on their self-assessments, you can encourage students to select one problem-solving skill or team skill to include as the outcome in their next personalized learning plan.

Think how you might use the following examples.

- Elementary school example: Team Cup Pyramid
- Middle school example: Survive
- High school example: All Hands on Deck

Elementary School Example: Team Cup Pyramid

Follow these four steps for the Team Cup Pyramid activity.

1. Invite teams of five to tie one piece of string for each member to a rubber band.
2. Review the time, roles, norms, and outcome.
3. Instruct each team member to hold one piece of string. Each team will attempt to lift a paper cup by expanding and contracting the rubber band and stacking a total of six cups in a freestanding pyramid. You can share a video like that at https://bit.ly/327LcWS for an example as well.
4. After all teams finish the building task, ask students questions like those in figure 2.3 (page 41). Guide a reflection with open-ended prompts on what the task taught about team problem solving.

Middle School Example: Survive

Follow these seven steps for the problem-solving activity Survive.

1. Set up teams of three and have students decide roles.
2. Review norms for teamwork and provide five diverse pieces of equipment (or simply a paper list) to each team. For example, you might hand out thirty feet of clothesline, a small pot, a can filled with coffee, a one-inch nail, and a pencil. The team has washed up on an unknown rock island, totally barren of plant and animal life and will have to find a way to survive with only these materials until rescued.
3. Provide outcomes.
4. Ask the driving question: "How do we survive until help comes for us?" You may want to review the steps for solving a loose problem, but you don't have to.
5. Give the teams ten minutes to answer the questions using at least three of the objects. They will have an added four minutes to prepare their presentation of the answer, how they used the tools, and their reasoning.
6. After each presentation, other class members may ask clarifying questions.
7. Supply guiding questions to prompt discussion of what was learned from this experience and what skills or ideas about problem solving and working together could carry forward in other situations or a future plan. You can share a four-column chart like the one in figure 2.9 on the whiteboard for classifying responses.

High School Example: All Hands on Deck

Follow these ten steps for the tight problem-solving activity All Hands on Deck.

1. Because students will complete this hands-on scenario to find radius and circumference,

Guiding Questions for Reflection

1. What did your team do well to solve the problem?
2. What specific teamwork skill does each person on the team most need to improve?
3. What specific problem-solving skill does each person need to most improve?
4. What help does your team need to improve?

Did well	Team skill to improve	Problem-solving skill to improve	Help needed

Figure 2.9: Sample reflection questions with chart.

*Visit **go.SolutionTree.com/instruction** for a free reproducible version of this figure.*

check prior knowledge about key vocabulary words: *circle*, *radius*, *area*, and *circumference*. To fill in any gaps, invite one student to the whiteboard and ask him or her to pick one glass from several you have ready, use a marker, and outline the circle.

2. Invite students with prior knowledge to come up and mark with different colors each of the terms as they explain the meaning.

3. Have another student pick a different size glass and do the same tracing, and then ask other volunteers to repeat the term identification.

4. Ask a volunteer to hold up each of the remaining glasses and ask for identification of the terms in relation to each sample.

5. Split students into heterogenous teams of five and review roles and norms.

6. Detail your guiding questions. Then distribute figure 2.10 (page 52) to each team and preview the questions. Let the teams know these cues and clues will help solve the problem.

7. Outline the outcome and provide each team with the following supplies.

    - One foot of string
    - One paper clip
    - One 12-inch ruler
    - One sheet of 8.5 × 11-inch paper
    - One pencil

8. Explain the task: create a circle on the paper using only the tools provided. For their circle, they must provide the measurements for area, radius, and circumference. Every person on the team must contribute to the measurement and the solution.

9. After all teams complete the task (about twenty minutes), guide a class discussion with the guiding questions this way: Pose a question, give each team several minutes to prepare an answer, and then survey answers from several teams before asking the class to agree on a single, final response.

10. Conclude the discussion by asking for the similarities and differences between the tight problem solving for the mathematical measurements and the loose problem solving for determining how to get all hands on deck to make the measurements.

- What jobs did your group come up with? What were the responsibilities for each job?
- What agreements did you make so that all made a fair-share, all-hands-on-deck contribution to the solution?
- What were the measurements you made for each key term: radius, circumference, and area? What formula did you develop for the measurements?
- What answers did you find for the measurements?
- What skills did you call on for your collaborative problem solving?
- What steps did you take to make sure you solved the measurement problem with the tools provided?
- What was the most difficult part of this challenge?
- What was your most significant learning about collaborative problem solving?

Figure 2.10: Guiding questions.

*Visit **go.SolutionTree.com/instruction** for a free reproducible version of this figure.*

TAKEAWAYS

Add the ideas you want to take away about creating a trusting, respectful climate supportive of personalized learning plans.

CHAPTER 3
OUTCOME-DRIVEN INSTRUCTION AND ASSESSMENT

When we are no longer able to change a situation, we are challenged to change ourselves.

—Viktor E. Frankl

Outcome-driven instruction is familiar to well-prepared educators. They plan lessons backward, with an end in mind (Wiggins & McTighe, 2005). This chapter shows another picture of backward planning's outcome-driven planning process. This snapshot of outcome-driven personalized learning plans shows how to engage students in a deeper understanding of course content driven by personalized learning plan skill outcomes.

How-to examples start with basic skill outcomes and expand to outcomes fostering the complex cognition that is the hallmark of deeper learning. Grade-level templates and playbooks show how to prepare guiding rubrics. A list of research reports provides evidence to support this approach. Then this chapter goes to the heart of the book—putting personalized learning plans and personalized teaching plans into action. If you are a school leader with professional development responsibilities, this chapter guides you in helping your faculty adopt personalized teaching plans, a master personalized teaching plan template with its playbook, and rubrics.

Driving question: How do students assess outcomes in a personalized learning plan?

What Is Outcome-Driven Instruction?

Outcome-driven instruction starts with a plan for teaching a simple one-week lesson and progresses to facilitating a multiweek project-based unit. As a teacher, you will replace traditional sequential plans that start with a goal statement. By starting your plan at the back end with a SMART goal (Conzemius & O'Neill, 2014), you will be better able to see your result and determine your success. To prepare a goal as an outcome, you identify the result or what learning you want to come out of your plan.

When planning to engage students with the blueprint, you create a personalized teaching plan. You can see the reproducible "Personalized Teaching Plan" (page 219) in the appendix and read more about it in chapter 3 (page 53). This ready-to-use template helps you construct, use, and assess personalized learning plans for students. That is your outcome to keep in mind as you extract information from this book.

When you start your personalized teaching plan by stating your instructional goals as one or more SMART accomplishments or outcomes, you make your goal more specific so that you can measure the result and see that you are not just covering material. Thus, your end in mind will be a document you can hold in hand. It will detail a plan that contains your selected strategies, tools, and tactics. You will make your selections based on your desire to help your students enter the starting gate of personalized learning. Like a jockey in the Kentucky Derby, you will have a chart, a playbook, which plans how your students will hold high the victory roses at the end of the race.

Figure 3.1 provides you with a step-by-step roadmap for planning, coaching, and assessing your personalized teaching plan with a personalized plan outcome. Like *going over the river and through the woods*, it shows how a well-planned trip begins with the end in mind, *grandma's house*—the most important element, the end we want to keep in mind from the moment we leave home.

Keep in mind that there may be modifications along the way, but everyone involved in the process will know the anticipated outcome in detail before beginning.

Your own personalized teaching plan, a modification of the personalized learning plan template, will assist you when creating your students' personalized learning plans. A personalized teaching plan best begins with the

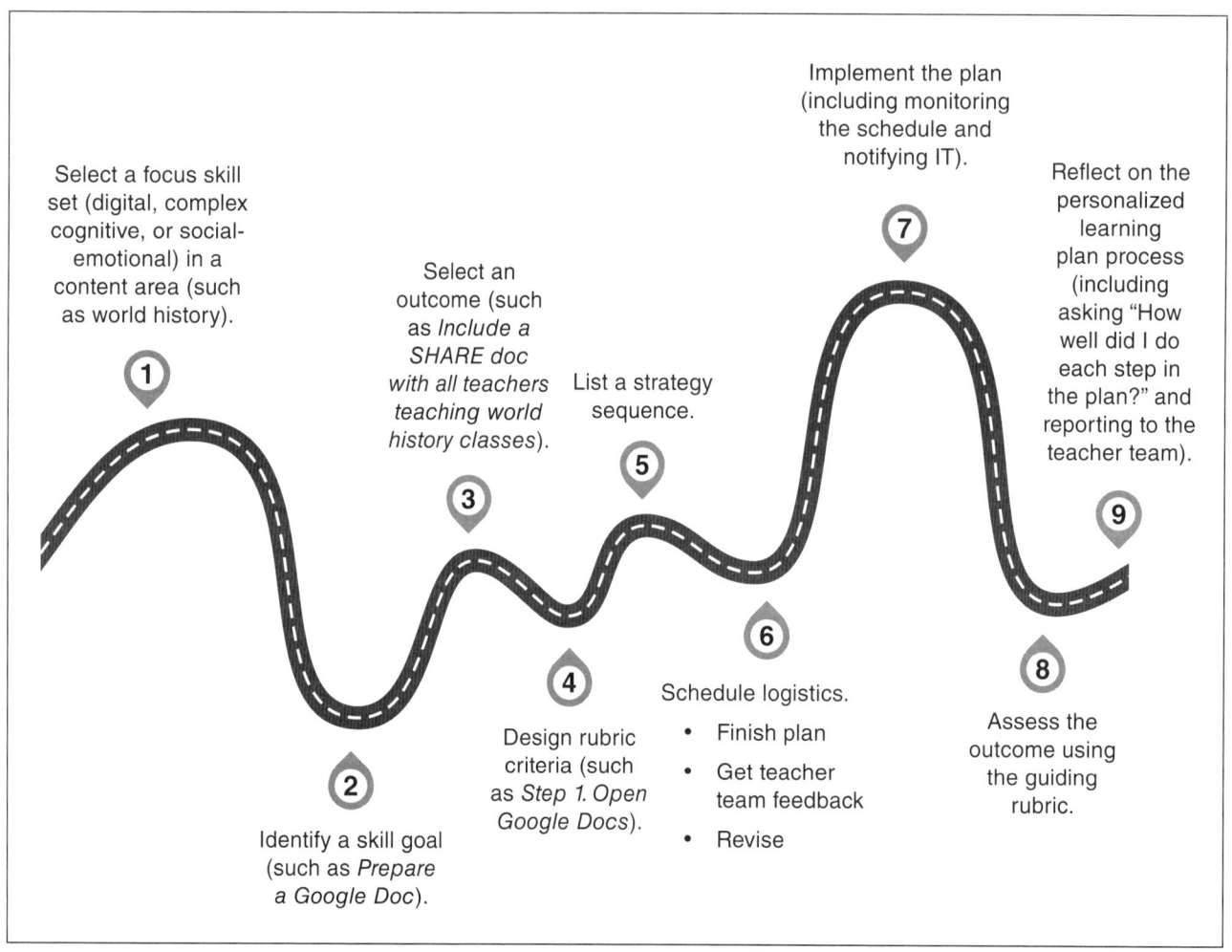

Figure 3.1: Creating personalized teaching plan outcomes—A roadmap.

*Visit **go.SolutionTree.com/instruction** for a free reproducible version of this figure.*

resulting outcomes students will achieve. Short-term outcomes to drive a weekly lesson or project are likely to improve overall outcome gains.

Outcomes that feature skills from the skill sets will advance students into deeper learning. Figure 3.2 shows examples of student goals and outcomes to measure from the pyramid of deeper learning outcomes in figure I.2 (page 4).

Consider Mary Ellen, a fifth grader, who loves animals. At home, she cares for two gerbils, a cat, three goldfish, and the family poodle. When her cat caught a chipmunk in the yard and deposited it at the back door, she knew it was a gift, but cried anyway. When her teacher asks for volunteers to feed the classroom pets, her hand is the first up. Mary Ellen tells her teacher that she wants to do her class project on horses; she wants to know all about them.

"That's wonderful, but that may take you several years," says the teacher, Mrs. Johnson, smiling. "For this project we only have this month's science days. When you study horses, what is most important for you to know?" Mary Ellen says she first wants to know how to feed a horse.

"I think you have time to learn that. You can research the information and maybe interview a horse owner on Skype," says Mrs. Johnson.

"Oh, yes," Mary Ellen exclaims. "Could I also try to feed a horse myself?"

"It may be tough to find a place, but it is worth a try," responds Mrs. Johnson. "We can put that in your research. Now, I think you have a start on making a goal about what you want to know and do when you finish the project. That will be your outcome."

The following five steps are the playlist Mary Ellen's teacher followed.

1. Like an architect, the teacher prepped the student to start filling in her personalized learning plan. What was the teacher's end? As with the personalized teaching plan, it was outcome driven: the student's completed plan.

2. The teacher would coach Mary Ellen to start at the end of her plan by asking her to delineate the details of her selected goal as a specific, desired outcome. Mary Ellen would demonstrate how to feed a horse.

3. To measure what Mary Ellen knew and could do, the teacher posed a driving question to focus on her ability to apply the new knowledge: "What are three important points to remember when I feed a horse?"

4. Next came the guiding rubric to assess how well Mary Ellen could perform three points and show her proficiency in a measurable way. The teacher coached the student as she created the rubric.

5. Finally, Mary Ellen and her teacher planned the actual tasks.

The guiding rubric, prepared before the final task in the personalized learning plan, would allow Mary Ellen and her teacher to progress from the already determined result stated in the outcome to the outcome's final assessment at the end. While learning about the horse and then applying the information, the rubric steered the student until she achieved her outcome and the teacher's. Figure 3.3 (page 56) shows the guiding rubric Mary Ellen developed with coaching from her teacher.

	Digital	Complex Cognitive	Social-Emotional
Goal	Share an open-ended assessment doc.	Improve my predictions when reading a story.	Manage my portfolio.
Outcome	Peer assessment with rubric showing SHARE tasks 100 percent completed for three tasks	A teacher assessment showing five correct predictions	A list of criteria for organizing my portfolio

Figure 3.2: Pyramid goals with outcome and goal examples.

56 PERSONALIZED DEEPER LEARNING

Name: Mary Ellen	**Teacher:** Mrs. Johnson	**Period:** 3
My project: How to feed a horse	**Date:** 4/15	**Check-up dates:** 4/19, 4/26

Feedback is by:
- ☐ Self
- ☒ Teacher
- ☐ Peers: _____
- ☐ Other: _____

My goal: I want to be able to feed a horse.

My outcome: A certificate from my riding coach saying I showed, in one week's time, that I can feed my horse according to stable guidelines

Rate each item.
0 = Not yet
1 = A little bit
2 = Yes, I did
3 = More than asked

_____ I looked for information in one print source.
_____ I looked for information in one online resource.
_____ I recorded notes from each source in my portfolio.
_____ I identified at least two things to remember from each source for when I feed my horse.
_____ I found a horse owner who liked my ideas.
_____ I used what I had learned by reading when I fed a horse.
_____ I studied the stable's feeding guidelines.
_____ I showed the horse owner I know how to feed a horse by following stable guidelines.

Total score:

Add your points and your teacher's points as one total:

What did I do well when I fed a horse?

What was my evidence?

Figure 3.3: Guiding rubric—Example.

How Do I Apply Design Thinking to Personalized Learning Plans?

As with other skills in this set, you increase the value of activities by adding personalized learning plans. You may build the plans around an empathy activity for the entire class or select some single element for meeting a small group's need.

The design thinking process is a problem-solving model developed at the Hasso Plattner Institute of Design at Stanford (2018). Rather than make the end result or outcome a solution to a problem (such as a shortage of rental housing for urban poor), design thinking focuses on a need (Why do the poor need housing?) and the empathy to ensure the *need* is met, not just the *problem solved*. Figure 3.4 shows the design thinking process. As you think of students who may need empathy so they can function more successfully in your classroom, adapt your problem solving to the design thinking cycle.

Early in our conversations, my mentor Stan said the word *relevant*. He used the term as a criterion for my lesson goals which he hoped would become SMART outcomes. He repeatedly quoted actor Richard Cushing (as cited in Forbes, n.d.): "Plan ahead: It wasn't raining when Noah built the ark." I made a list of similar quotes from voices across the ages.

- Malcolm X (BlackPast, 2007): "Tomorrow belongs only to the people who prepare for it today."
- Eleanor Roosevelt (BrainyQuote, n.d.): "It takes as much energy to wish as it does to plan."
- Confucius (n.d., as cited in Hughes, 2018): "A man who does not plan long ahead will find trouble at his door."
- H. K. Williams (1919, as cited in Doyle, Mieder, & Shapiro, 2012): "Remember, if you fail to prepare, you are preparing to fail."

How Do I Plan for Deeper Learning Outcomes?

Planning for outcomes, starting with the end in mind, has long been common in business and industry. Author and business guru Stephen R. Covey (2004) is credited with introducing the phrasing "Start with the end in mind." Writers Grant Wiggins and Jay McTighe (2005) pioneered outcome-driven learning in education.

By designing lesson and project plans with SMART goals (AchieveIt, n.d.; Conzemius & O'Neill, 2014) and measuring deeper learning results at the end, you are more likely to collect assessment data that mark

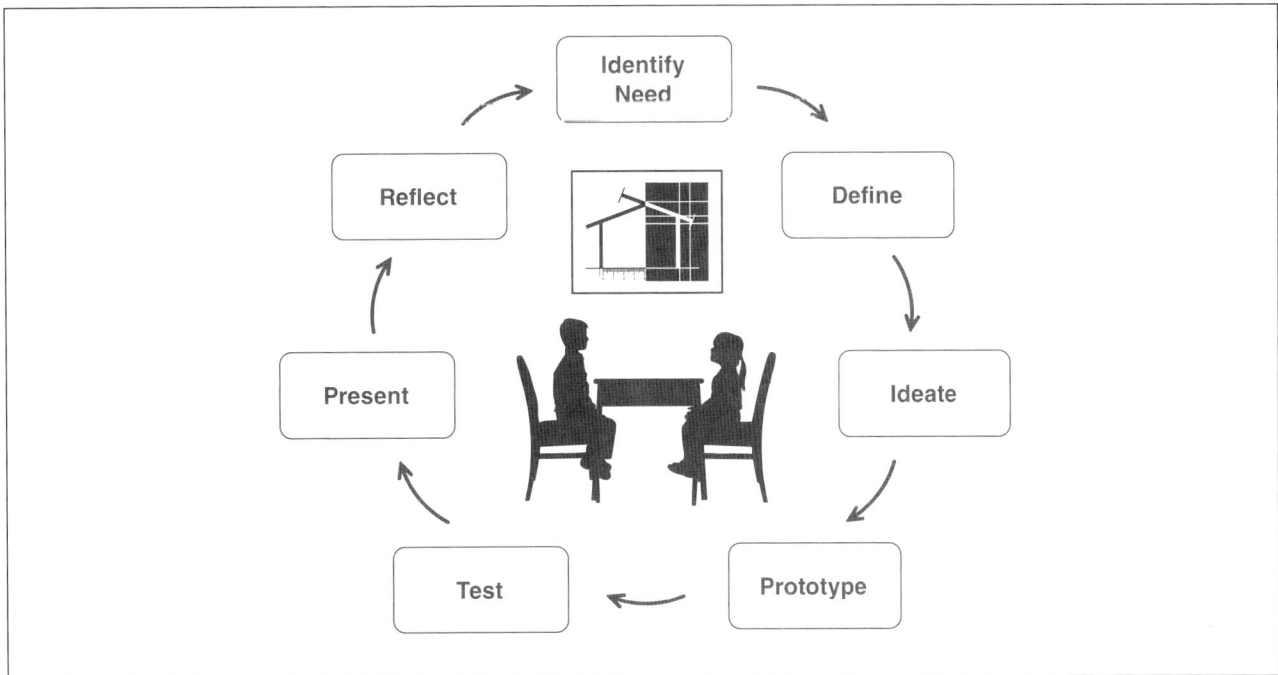

Source: Adapted from Hasso Plattner Institute of Design at Stanford, 2018.

Figure 3.4: Design thinking cycle.

students' arrival at the desired finish line. It also provides you with data about the effectiveness of the process.

S = Specific

M = Measurable

A = Achievable

R = Relevant

T = Timely

Although some districts provide professional development to advance backward lesson planning, the approach is not a run-of-the-mill practice when it comes to making deeper learning skill outcomes. Instead, backward plans tend to target standardized test scores for outcomes.

Outcome statements aimed at raising standardized test scores are inadequate in schools bent on readying tomorrow's citizens to learn, labor, and live in the work world. As with traditional lesson plans and IEPs written to cover material and comply with policy or law, such outcomes waste teachers' time and talent. Current attempts to limit outcomes to content are not very SMART in the meaningful sense. They fail to meet the criteria for an effective teaching and learning outcome that will ready students for their futures. Because most standardized tests are driven by dated outcomes, the recall of basic skills and facts via standardized test-driven outcomes ignores, above all else, the *R* for *relevant*. To be relevant and fully SMART, they should more closely reflect researcher and education writer Linda Darling-Hammond's (1997) thought: "A democratic education means that we educate people in a way that ensures they can think independently, that they can use information, knowledge, and technology, among other things, to draw their own conclusions."

As leading voices and critics of this century's continued reliance on the obsolete, irrelevant curriculum, instruction, and assessment practices of past centuries say (Bellanca & Brandt, 2010), it is too easy for teachers to confuse students answering questions at the end of textbook chapters, listening to lectures, giving one-word answers, completing digital worksheets, and finishing workbook pages—all common ways to cover the curriculum—with learning in ways that are relevant and engaging for today's students. Tests, quizzes, class participation, homework, and essay scores may be easily graded and show what curriculum goals were covered, standards touched on, or facts and procedures recalled, but do little to tell what all students have accomplished in reaching relevant, deeper learning outcomes meaningful in their present and future lives.

How Do I Make Deeper Learning Competency My First Priority?

Deeper learning competencies call for instruction and assessment methods which differ from those that lead to recall competencies. Start by determining, preferably with your school's instructional leader, which deeper learning competencies are the preferred outcomes in your school. Next, work with your collaborative team members or a grade-level team to plan a trial personalized learning plan. As you implement, call on these colleagues to observe and give feedback. Added eyes and ears will help you refine your personalized learning plan. Peer coaching for teachers has five impacts (Annenberg Foundation for Education Reform, 2004, as cited in Aguilar, 2013).

1. Coaching allows teachers to apply their learning more deeply, frequently, and consistently than teachers working alone.

2. Coaching supports teachers to improve their capacity to reflect and apply their learning to their work with students and also in their work with each other.

3. The conditions, behaviors, and practices required by an effective coaching program can affect the culture of a school.

4. Coaching increases in teachers' use of data to inform practice by evidence, rather than by individual and sometimes conflicting opinions.

5. Coaching promotes the implementation of learning and reciprocal responsibility when colleagues work together and hold each other accountable for improved teaching and learning.

For teachers intending to implement personalized learning plans, their proficiency as facilitators of their students' academic success should inform their competencies. With feedback from their instructional leader or peer coaches, personalized learning plan novices can select competencies to improve from frameworks for planning instruction. With Charlotte Danielson's (2019) Framework for Teaching Evaluation Instrument in hand, the novice teacher might select planning ("Setting instructional outcomes" as something to improve) and pay special attention to incorporating differentiated activities that lead diverse students to the selected personalized learning plan outcome.

With this selection, the teacher can begin walking the pathway from a raw skill to a competency and a proficiency. A skill is what a teacher or student does to perform an act. For instance, making an outcome SMART or assessing how well a student applies and extends knowledge are skills. When teachers or students show mastery of the skill so they can make near transfer in a lesson, they have competence. For instance, if a sixth-grade mathematics teacher who is a personalized learning plan novice wants to implement three strategies to help students achieve an outcome such as "Apply and extend previous understandings of numbers to the system of rational numbers" (NGA & CCSSO, 2010b), the teacher must first teach two skills: (1) apply and (2) extend. Students will show competence when they make the first applications without her help to the system of rational numbers; they will show proficiency when they can do so independently in a variety of real-world scenarios.

A teacher shows his or her *skill* by writing the first guiding rubric with appropriate criteria in a format and language for students. After piloting the first personalized learning plan rubric with students, this teacher *shows competence* by designing rubrics for other personalized learning plans without coaching. Proficiency is clear when the teacher transfers what he or she has done in rubric design to full lesson assessments.

In the absence of a schoolwide approach, start with a grade-level team or subject-specific collaboration. If you're a singleton or your school doesn't function as a PLC, team up with a colleague or a peer who works in another school. No luck? The last choice is to go it alone.

With a decision about which competencies are first, make your plan and call on research-backed methods and tools that prove engaging as you develop your choice of the skill set–based competencies in table 3.1.

The table shows the specific skills that fit into the sets discussed in more depth in the skills' specific chapters.

The most practical way to start students on the deeper learning path is by having them follow a plan with its guiding rubric for one skill from your preferred set. If your classroom culture needs attention, start with the SEL set. If the culture is sufficiently positive, go to complex cognition. In either case, you can infuse the digital skills with others you select from SEL or complex cognition.

To best measure the cognitive and social-emotional engagement you design, call on effective learning strategies based on 21st century constructivist theories (including cooperative learning, hypothesis testing, nonlinguistic representations, two-way feedback, and others highlighted through this book). Frame these activities with an outcome-based plan not only for planning, but also for *assessing* any complex skill outcomes or final product. To the degree that you facilitate students' cognitive and emotional engagement, you will see and hear evidence of what and how students are thinking, problem solving, collaborating, and communicating so that they understand the complexities of your content. In this way, you can examine their thinking as it happens and the results of that thinking—the deeper learning outcomes—when the lesson, unit, or project is finished.

Whenever you set up the learning situations, the cognitive and social-emotional activities which engage students' minds and hearts, you complete the essential first step that enables you to observe and assess their deeper learning outcomes. What you observe becomes fodder for measuring the following.

- The type of thinking and feeling
- How much thinking and feeling are occurring
- The quality of those engagements

Table 3.1: Skill Set–Based Competencies

Complex Cognitive Competencies	Social-Emotional Competencies	Digital Competencies
• Critical and creative thinking • Problem solving • Decision making • Planning • Metacognitive thinking	• Managing emotions • Being self-aware and socially aware • Having collaborative, caring relationships • Displaying social responsibility	• Finding, managing, and storing information • Communicating and collaborating online • Finding and managing online services • Managing social media and other digital tools

Source: P21, 2019.

Figure 3.5 is a backward design playbook that spotlights how to choose a cognitive, social-emotional, or digital skill as an outcome. This example walks you through a sequence of tasks for helping students take a complex skill and develop it over time into a competency you can observe and measure as a desired outcome.

Any of the three major skill sets are open for you or students to pick as a personalized learning plan outcome. Just as you would do with other skills such as hitting a forehand shot in tennis, painting a mural, or growing orchids, you aim for a competence with the targeted skill; demonstrated competence with the specific skill is the outcome the student is pursuing. Competence seldom results from a single try. It develops over time as a student's confidence builds from previous gains. From a teaching perspective, it is wisest to plan any competence as an outcome, not a journey. It is also wise to create multiple plans with one specific skill over time so that your students have time to practice and become proficient. When all are not progressing at the same rate, you also can differentiate each plan most fitting the pace of each student. Figure 3.6 is an example of a playbook for students.

When you share a playbook in students' online storage depots, you do not have to repeat instructions each time you ask students to apply a specific protocol. When differentiating, you do not have to change the protocol in the playbook. Likewise, in other classes, students can access this playbook's protocols to enrich their reading of text in print or online. If you lack access to a storage file, print it for inclusion in their portfolios.

How Do I Create My Personalized Teaching Plan?

Some teachers are already implementing advanced deeper learning, including project- and problem-based learning. These teachers are familiar with evidence-based strategies such as cooperative learning and graphic organizers, SMART goals, and higher-order-thinking questions. They seize the advantage to wrap what tasty

1. Determine the major skill set (complex cognitive, social-emotional, or digital).
2. Decide what specific competency you want to assess (analyzing, generating ideas, self-managing, opening the program Word).
3. Visualize what this competency looks like and sounds like in your specific content area (language arts, social studies, calculus) and with this skill (analyzing informational science text, analyzing fictional characters, writing a three-page essay with Word).
4. Construct a guiding rubric to track improved competence with the targeted cognitive skill. Criteria should detail what questions to ask and actions when reading to analyze.
5. Lead students through a looks-like brainstorm or other activity to experience the skill. (For example, model the skill by brainstorming all the ways they use social media.) Remember, brainstorming aims to produce multiple unjudged responses. It can appear as a playlist or a mind map.
6. Invite students to complete the task (generating ideas) and to self-assess with a targeted skill rubric that you show on your interactive whiteboard or share to digital devices.
7. After the first round, discuss what students learned about using the skill ("What are the key questions you ask and answer so you are analyzing the text?").
8. After assessing the first personalized learning plan targeting this select skill, invite students to increase the challenge by naming the same skill and assessing its use with other material. For instance, after using brainstorming to generate ideas about analyzing a book's main character, brainstorm how to generate ideas about analyzing a historical figure (informational text). Next, transfer the skill by analyzing best uses for a new app or ways to confront a bully.
9. Conduct a summative assessment.
10. Guide a reflection of the process (through brainstorming, for instance) with a review of what worked well, what could be done better, and what help they needed with the process.

Figure 3.5: Teacher playbook targeting a deeper learning competency.

*Visit **go.SolutionTree.com/instruction** for a free reproducible version of this figure.*

1. Underline each major point with a highlighter.
2. Highlight repeated major points with parentheses.
3. Circle or color code key words with markers.
4. Write questions and attach sticky notes to the page.
5. Index ideas with headers for major ideas and sub-headers for contributing ideas on a sticky note (different color).
6. Star top five ideas made.
7. Sequence major ideas in order of importance with a back-page sticky note.

Figure 3.6: Student text analysis playbook—"How do I analyze text?" example.

*Visit **go.SolutionTree.com/instruction** for a free reproducible version of this figure.*

figs they have long eaten within the leaves of a new personalized teaching plan. Those who are deeper learning novices tend to be the most cautious. At first, some object with strong *yes, buts*: "I've already read about these practices" or "I don't have time." However, I point to the notion of *plan, do, assess* and ask, "Have you tested the waters and tried these ideas?" With empathy, I show how a personalized teaching plan is a replacement for, not an addition to, their lesson plans. My intent is to awaken them to the distinction between knowing about deeper learning practices and acting on what they know.

In retrospect, I find that personalized teaching plans have been my most successful tool for encouraging the hesitant to act. I encourage teachers to ask themselves what from the chapters they read could be most important for helping them introduce personalized learning plans. Often, they respond with something like "Unlike lengthy planning for project- and problem-based learning, the personalized learning plan is a wide doorway to deeper learning." Together we gather ideas they already prefer from the chapter takeaways, prioritize them, and walk through the template together. I immerse them in learning to make personal plans for students by doing a SMART personal plan for themselves.

Figure 3.7 (page 62) is an example of a completed personalized teaching plan template for a third-grade literature reading lesson. (Review it with SMART criteria.) Although the selected standard expects students to learn how to determine the main idea or theme and then the key details ("Recount stories, including fables, folktales, and myths from diverse cultures; determine the central message, lesson, or moral and explain how it is conveyed through key details in the text" (NGA & CCSSO, 2010a), other standards from English language arts, such as "Describe characters in a story (e.g., their traits, motivations, or feelings) and explain how

their actions contribute to the plot" (NGA & CCSSO, 2010a) and "Explain how specific aspects of a text's illustrations contribute to what is conveyed by the words in a story (e.g., create mood, emphasize aspects of a character or setting)" (NGA & CCSSO, 2010a) contribute to this plan's outcome (which promotes students' selection of relevant clues). To make your own personalized teaching plan, go to the reproducible "Personalized Teaching Plan" (page 219) in the appendix and adapt it to fit your needs and ideas.

Although this example targets a single elementary student, adjustments for older students, your whole class, or a small group are manageable. In all combinations, start with a preferred skill set with an age-appropriate skill that students need. Change your activities so they too are age appropriate and comfortable for you and your students to perform and ensure the instructions in any student playbook are likewise modified. With all other modifications, you make these decisions on your experience.

Figure 3.8 (page 64) details the playbook for the personalized teaching plan in figure 3.7. In the example, it is for a reading coach. If you are a teacher, you can follow this playbook.

When you arrive at your personalized teaching plan assessment, you will do well to have a guiding rubric to call on. As with all guiding rubrics, it is best to have it ready so you can review your plan before you start the template. Your guiding rubric can be a checklist to make sure you have included all elements. If you have one or more colleagues to coach give you feedback, try the single-point rubric. Use that template and select five to seven criteria related to a planning skill you want to improve or to the composition of your entire plan. Follow the playbook for the format you choose.

Name: Elias Dulin	Grade: 3	
Start date: 11/1	End date: 11/5	Check-up dates: 11/3 and 11/4

Content Focus

- ☒ English language arts
  - **Strand:**
    - ☒ Reading
    - ☐ Writing
    - ☐ Speaking and listening
    - ☐ Language
- ☐ Mathematics
- ☐ Performing or visual arts
- ☐ Science
- ☐ Social studies
- ☐ World language
- ☐ Other: _____

Skill Set

Basic Cognitive	**Digital**	**Complex Cognitive**	**Social-Emotional**
☐ Decoding	☐ Basic	☐ Critical thinking	☒ Collaboration
☐ Fluency	☐ Applied	☐ Creative thinking	☒ Communication
☐ Measurement	☐ Other: _____	☐ Problem solving	☐ Self-direction
☐ Numbers		☐ Design thinking	☐ Specific skill: _____
☐ Operations		☒ Cognitive function	
☐ Phonics		☐ Specific skill: _____	
☐ Vocabulary			
☐ Other: _____			

What is my improvement goal?
I want to know how students remember how to pick relevant clues.

Whom will I teach with this plan?
- ☐ One student: _____
- ☒ Small group: James, Alex, Nita
- ☐ Whole class

What SMART goals do I want my students or student to achieve?
- Three rhyming patterns identified
- Recall with 90 percent accuracy two questions to ask when finding relevant clues in literature there
- Two examples of three clues per idea from new story
- Ten projects connected to the reading

Feedback

Feedback is by:
- ☐ Self
- ☐ Teacher
- ☒ Peers: Erica LaSalle
- ☐ Other: _____

Teaching Plan *Enter your response in the blanks.*	
What is my improvement goal? I want to know how students remember how to pick relevant clues.	
Whom will I teach with this plan? ☒ One student ☐ Small group ☐ Whole class	
What SMART goals do I want my students or student to achieve? I want to achieve for my student (no more than three): • Identify three rhyming patterns. • Student recall with 90 percent accuracy; two questions to ask when finding relevant clues in literature there • Show two examples of three clues per idea from new story. • Conduct ten projects connected to the reading this academic year.	
What people or resources will I call on? Parent volunteers in projects and my team	
What strategies will I use to reach my goal? Use this playlist. 1. Engage all with lion-tiger movie and brainstorm with Venn on whiteboard 2. Read aloud lion story excerpt and model big idea and clue ID 3. Model picking same-sound words 4. Increase responsibility with whole class 5. Cooperative groups of three with roles and new stories and gallery walks 6. All-class Venn diagram on bulletin board 7. Team projects for museum from list of ideas 8. Formative check-ups with guiding rubric for two questions or rhyming words 9. Provide tutorials as needed 10. Presentation of museum to invited guests 11. Summative assessment 12. Final reflection	
What materials and equipment will I need? SMART Board, chart paper and markers, six or eight of each for each student: • Stories or excerpts • Folders or portfolios • Materials for each team project	
How much time will we need? Two weeks	
What are my criteria for success? See outcomes above. I also want to see 95 percent engagement with no more than one behavior correction per session.	
What measurable evidence of learning will I show? Individual summative scores on grading rubric; two formative assessments per student and one summative	
What other things do I want to note here? I hope to see five volunteer parents helping with projects.	
☐ I have attached my pacing chart. ☐ I have attached the rubric.	

Figure 3.7: Personalized teaching plan—Example.

1. Help teacher identify a specific skill (reading to find relevant clues) as her SMART outcome.
2. Follow the personalized teaching plan. The first questions are demographics that help you keep a record. File it for your next coaching session, and have the teacher keep a copy.
3. Coach the teacher through the planning questions in the Teaching Plan portion of the template.
4. When it comes to strategies, provide the following plan.

    Step 1. Select three to five short examples of age-appropriate stories or excerpts.

    Step 2. Review with teacher the two basic prompts for finding relevant clues.
    - What's the big idea?
    - What clues told you so?
5. Practice with the teacher on the first story. Do as much practice as the teacher needs.
6. Plan the introduction. (Play a detective game, hunt for clues or scavenger hunt with clues to identify a specific object; this is also a good time to post guiding rubrics for the reading outcomes and the final project.)
7. Bridge the idea of hunting to the idea of finding right (relevant) clues to understand the big idea in a story.
8. Read the first story aloud and model answering the prompts that you show (poster, whiteboard) for all to see. Highlight the prompts as the first of two student outcomes.
    a. You will recall the two prompts for finding clues to a story's (excerpt's) big ideas.
    b. You will read two stories and identify correct answers to each prompt each time.
9. Choral read the second story with guiding prompts reviewed before the start. Ask the class to brainstorm responses to each prompt. Post answers for all to see; discuss which are best ideas and why.
    a. You will recall the two prompts for finding clues to a story's (excerpt's) big ideas.
    b. You will read two stories and identify correct answers to each guiding prompt each time.
10. Form cooperative groups of three with the best reader (give each student a copy of the third story or excerpt), plus a recorder who will write answers on large chart paper, and the question answerer. Monitor and coach as needed. Teams must agree on first answer (big idea), and all five must add at least one idea to the second. Post signed charts around the room and do a gallery walk asking students to find answers that are like theirs and different from theirs. After students sit, ask for examples of similar and different responses. End by asking students to tell how the prompts help them understand the story or excerpt.
11. Add student team practices (keep same teams) as time allows. This is the most important activity in the day. Extend time as needed for sufficient practice through Thursday as well as differentiated coaching sessions.
12. Send final story home for independent reading with the two prompts. Encourage students to share reading and answers with someone else in the home.
13. Follow up. As soon as Wednesday afternoon, begin preparation for team projects.
    a. Excite the students with the project idea. Projects will extend what they are learning about relevant clues and big ideas. If you want, add social-emotional, art, social studies, or digital outcomes.
    b. Share a list of artifacts students might produce and encourage them to add their ideas.
    c. After each team selects a product related to the lesson's two main outcomes and the theme content (lions and tigers), instruct parent volunteers to help teams gather materials and equipment needed. Advise parents to be guides on the side. Let students make products their way.
    d. Each afternoon while parents are helping, differentiate instruction for individuals or small groups who need more guided practice with the reading outcomes.
14. Friday: test day. Showing a new story, choral read the questions to test major outcomes. Allow time for each student to write or speak responses.
    a. Question 1: What's the big idea?
    b. Optional questions 2–5: true-false, multiple choice, fill-in-the-blank, short essay; all to check knowledge.
15. Tabulate scores and celebrate by opening the classroom museum to invited guests. Each team will stand by its display and answer visitor questions.
16. Save the last hour for students to reflect on what they learned about big ideas and relevant clues.
17. With the SMART criteria, create a SMART rubric to assess your degree of success with the students' personalized learning plans.

Figure 3.8: A personalized teaching plan playbook—Coaching for main idea and relevant details example.

Do I Help Students Construct *Authentic* Outcomes in a Personalized Learning Plan?

The adjective *authentic* describes objects that are not false or copied, such as an authentic antique that has an origin supported by unquestionable evidence. Used to describe an outcome, authentic says you have written an outcome that you can verify, with unquestionable evidence, that has great importance to your students. The evidence comes from their past or present spoken words or actions as a quintessential need to understand or accomplish.

You might ask, "How do I learn from my students what has great importance to them?" The answer is to stop, look, and listen. Think about the following middle school examples.

My students say the following kinds of things.

- "I don't know how."
- "Why do I have to?"
- "I need to know . . . ."
- "I don't understand."
- "I can't."

My students won't do the following.

- Remember mathematical facts.
- Think.
- Write a sentence.
- Solve a tough mathematics problem.
- Take a stand independent of their friends.
- Respect others.
- Challenge a bully.

My students are interested in the following.

- How they look and dress
- What friends say
- Social media
- Music fads

These examples may or may not fit your students. You can find out more from middle and secondary students by just asking. If the question is confidential, it is likely you will stir more honest responses. For instance, pick a medium that you know students love, such as a smartphone, and share an open-ended survey tool (such as SurveyMonkey) with them. Challenge them alone or in teams to come up with a confidential survey of their peers to ascertain authentic interests, defining the word in this context, for what they want to learn about. Do not restrict interests to your course's subject matter. Go for what most interests them in their daily lives. Have the class collect team responses and vote on the top five most meaningful or relevant to them. Now you can design authentic lessons to plan around their *I want to learn* needs. If topics fit your subject directly (say you teach social studies, and students are interested in protests following George Floyd's death or the Black Lives Matter organization, or you teach science and they are interested in the eclipse coming next week) or indirectly (say you are an art teacher, and students are interested in women leaders or their heritage, or you teach mathematics and they're interested in wildfires, immigrant parents, or how fast a virus spreads), it's up to you how to include the issue in your lesson or personalized learning plans.

To help students write authentic outcome statements with their interests in mind in their personalized learning plans, ask them to assess the first outcome statements you wrote when you introduced the practice. Share the SMART acronym (visit **go.SolutionTree.com/instruction** for a free reproducible version) for all to see. These five criteria will guide students' self-assessment and your feedback as you show them how to construct personalized learning plan outcome statements. Defining an outcome at the outset allows students to create their plans backward. SMART lets each student declare where he or she is going with a plan yet to be made. Like taking a trip to grandmother's house, they determine that her house is a goal to reach before they start mapping out how they will get there.

This sample rubric in figure 3.9 (page 66) shows how to help middle and high school students make it a common practice.

What Is Outcome-Driven Assessment?

Outcome-driven instruction consists of lessons, projects, and personalized learning plans that start with the end in mind, an outcome with sequenced activities to ensure that a student's performance shows skill mastery. You start your plan by conceiving what you want students

Name:	Class:	Period:
Teacher:	Date:	

Outcome statement:

To what degree does your goal meet each criterion?
0 = Not at all.
1 = I have lots of work to do.
2 = Change some parts.
3 = Add a tweak.
4 = Bravo!

See feedback for scores equal to 1–3.

Criterion To what degree is this outcome SMART?	Feedback
____ Specific: It is a simple sentence that describes a significant result I want.	
____ Measurable: I can count items that show how many or how much.	
____ Achievable: I can get this done with the resources I know are available.	
____ Relevant: This is my choice and I can explain how it will help me.	
____ Timely: It states an end time I can manage.	

Figure 3.9: Guiding rubric—Assessing SMART outcomes example.

*Visit **go.SolutionTree.com/instruction** for a free reproducible version of this figure.*

to take away or the results you want to see coming from their work. You then provide the strategies most likely to produce that result.

It means that you set up your rubric as an assessment tool that also is an instructional tool. For the outcome in your plan, the rubric specifies the criteria for knowing the student has demonstrated competence with the outcome. Does the rubric show the knowledge to be gained? Does it specify the desired skill accomplishment? By understanding the importance of the criteria and checking or getting feedback throughout the project, lesson, or plan, you help students understand by doing what they will accomplish.

Note how guiding rubrics are incorporated into all personalized learning plans: at the start, in the middle, and at the end. Unlike the traditional grading approach, guiding rubrics are transparent. There is no secret reason for a grade that appears only when a student or parent wants to know "Why did you earn this grade?" From the beginning, the criteria make clear what's expected of students and align study with the end in mind. Along the way, the student becomes the first person evaluating his or her performance with feedback from the teacher and peers. From every direction, the student hears "Keep your eye on the ball—the final outcome."

What Outcomes Can I Assess With a Personalized Learning Plan?

If you prefer a directive teaching approach and rely on lecture or programmed learning as your dominant teaching method, there is no need to worry that personalized learning plans will devalue your style or subvert your preferred model of instruction. The same is true for any teaching style. By allotting five to ten minutes every two weeks to insert personalized plans in your schedule, you can continue to lecture, offer direct instruction, use cooperative teams for science labs, enable project-based learning, or take extensive learning expeditions. No matter how you are teaching your students, adopting personalized learning plans allows you to develop through assessment-rich instruction any skill you determine will help students become more effective learners.

- If *lectures* are your main teaching tool, students can set goals for improving their notetaking or studying from their notes. If you ask questions, students might set a goal to improve how well they answer with evidence.

- If *direct instruction* is your teaching model, personal goals may include listening to and following instructions, staying on task during guided practice, and improving the quality of homework or handing all assignments in on time. With these goals, align outcomes that require your students to start moving toward deeper learning as they plan, take responsibility for, and assess a personalized learning plan.

- If you focus on manual or basic cognitive skills, the template will ask students to add goal setting to their skill toolbox. You will be empowering students to assume increased self-direction in improving these skills. Through a school year, create a sequence of personalized learning plans aimed to improve perseverance as a goal with specific outcome statements geared to assist students in developing resilience. This experience can point them toward the more challenging complex cognitive skills included in the SEL set shown in figure 3.10.

Consider the following outcomes and how you can assess them in a personalized learning plan.

- If you are striving to improve student **mindsets** (Dweck, 2006), you can help students develop their intrapersonal skills, other intelligences

Manual	Basic Cognitive	Complex Cognitive	Social-Emotional	Digital
• Lift a rock. • Plug in a lamp. • Dig a hole with a trowel. • Hammer a nail. • Start an engine. • Hang a coat. • Plant a seed.	• Write a sentence. • Spell a word. • Enter a question mark. • Pronounce a word. • Compute a number set. • Recall a mathematics procedure. • Recall an answer to a fact.	• Analyze an historic event. • Generate ideas to solve a problem. • Compare animals in a family. • Sequence activities in a personalized learning plan. • Assess outcomes. • Differentiate. • Set priorities.	• Be aware of oneself. • Be aware of others. • Collaborate with others. • Care. • Respect others. • Encourage someone. • Give support.	• Find information online. • Store a personalized learning plan in an online portfolio. • Select and manage online tools. • Communicate via Microsoft Word. • Share a personalized learning plan in a network. • Compose with an online tool. • Collaborate in an online network.

Figure 3.10: Deeper learning skills—Examples.

(Gardner, 1983), or cognitive functions (Feuerstein et al., 1980). The functions persistence and patience are the prerequisites for grit and resilience or the ability to hang in there when the going gets tough. Being precise, being accurate, controlling impulsivity, focusing, and adapting are also cognitive functions you can develop as student mindsets.

- If promoting social-emotional skills, you can align with Gardner's (1983) interpersonal skills. In this skill set, students may make goals for developing such skills as self-control, expressing feelings with appropriate words and actions, listening to peers, taking pride in successes, asking for needed help, offering help, showing appropriate affection, showing awareness of others' feelings, respecting others' differences, and celebrating others' successes.

- If your students need to target digital skills, having students follow safety and security internet guidelines as a precursor to opening the computer, Word, Google Docs and other Google tools, researching online, making citations, opening and using apps, sharing documents, and evaluating or creating websites will make for lifelong learning outcomes.

- When completing a project or inquiry lesson, students may assess how well they are completing the entire lesson or unit. They may also assess their engagement or quality of work with any personalized learning plan element such as how well I ask my driving question, do research, work with my team to design a product, make my presentation, and engage in reflection. Of course, they can also assess the outcome of the project or lesson.

- **Setting goals and assessing** the personalized learning plan will help those students who are random or episodic thinkers. They may have lots of facts in their heads but need help to organize their ideas. They may be episodic thinkers who can't connect facts or ideas together. The blueprint's sequential format will guide them in organizing the flow of ideas.

- *Skills transfer*, **or transfer of learning,** is the most important and most challenging outcome that a student can include in a deeper learning personalized learning plan. What is being transferred? In addition to knowledge or information gathered in the research phase of a project, students can transfer the essential 21st century skills into macro-thinking processes such as *design thinking*, *problem solving*, and *decision making*. Here they are *setting goals for deeper learning outcomes* (Bellanca et al., 2020).

For more information, see the How Do I Assess How My Feedback Impacts Student Agency? (page 98) section.

What Do Outcome-Driven Assessments Look or Sound Like?

Both formal and informal outcome-driven assessments are productive road signs. After students develop their outcome statements, an informal assessment of class dialogue might look (written on the whiteboard) and sound like (spoken words) the following.

Teacher: "*Here is an example of a personalized learning plan from last year's world history class. I will show you how we can decide if your personalized learning plan rubrics are strong.*"

[Written on the whiteboard] From the historic biography I picked, I want to give three reasons why this person was a hero with three examples for each reason in my essay. If I get this done by April 1, this is the number I need for an A grade.

Teacher: "*Now let's look at the rubric for assessing this outcome. Here are the criteria that guide this assessment. We will call on each other to help decide to what degree the statement does what's described. Look at this.*"

[Written on the whiteboard]

_____ *Specific: It is a simple sentence to describe a significant result I want.*

_____ *Measurable: I can count items that show how many or how much.*

_____ *Achievable: I can get this done with the resources I know are available.*

_____ *Relevant: This is my choice and I can explain how it will help me.*

_____ *Timely: It states an end time I can get to.*

Teacher: "Let's check the vocabulary. What words don't make sense in this context? [Waits] OK. I see no hands, so I am going to give a score to each criterion. I will explain each score; 4 is the highest.

First, specific. A 4. It tells me exactly what my wanted outcome is with very few sentences. [Pause] Questions? [Pause]

Second, measurable. I give it a 4. Can you see the two sets of 3? I can count those. [Points and counts seconds]

Third, achievable: A 2. The statement doesn't say anything about resources. The author needs to tell about the format she will use for notetaking and reporting. [Pause]

Fourth, relevant: A 3. She wants an A grade. That needs to tell *why*. [Pause]

Last, timely: A 4. She gives the due date." [Pause]

Ricardo: [Pauses to count] "1."

Teacher: "Thumbs up and down? [Pauses to count] Bravo! Now let's see what to change to make a perfect score. What would you do? Tell us the criterion and then your idea. I want as many ideas as we can think of . . . "

An analysis of this dialogue shows three examples of informal outcome-driven assessments.

1. Explaining the SMART criteria
2. Asking students to explain or give criteria examples
3. Providing positive feedback on their responses

In addition to starting a lesson with these three, you can coach students with criteria, questions, and feedback with any element you select at any time. Consider the following examples.

- "I'd like to cut in a moment. I'm reading your outcome, and I don't see how you would measure it. Am I wrong?"
- "I hear you telling me that you will finish this project in ten days. That seems fast to me."
- "I notice the second criterion on your problem-solving rubric says 'We described the problem.'" Can you give me a few specifics about how that would look or sound?"
- "I appreciate the full scope of your SMART criteria. I especially like how you have *relevant*, the R in SMART. You picked a problem that you obviously care a lot about."

Whether you designate an all-class outcome or transfer the selection agency to your students, the driving force is *their* needs as learners. Do they need individual attention to basic mathematics or reading skills? Notetaking? Collaborating? Digital research? After that comes your professional assessment, including intuition, of the students' readiness to facilitate the learning-to-learn skills that lead to deeper learning outcomes (critical thinking, creative problem solving, and transfer).

Table 3.2 (page 70) provides a selection of age-appropriate personalized learning plan outcome statements developed with the SMART criteria in mind. You can also imagine how assessments would pair with these outcomes.

After students (or you) assess and fine-tune outcome statements, the assessment process moves from outcomes to the rubric the students will use. The rubric will guide students to reveal the degree to which they achieved the criteria that promote the desired result via strategies they selected.

What Tools Work Best When Assessing Personalized Learning Plan Outcomes?

In place of grading quizzes and tests to check information recall, rubrics are the common tools for assessing skill development and personalized learning plan products. For both, the preference is the *guiding* rubric. You can replace a traditional grading rubric with a guiding rubric to add information to your normal tests and quiz format about a student's overall performance.

When an outcome calls for knowledge and understanding, tests and quizzes are adequate checks sometimes helped by guiding rubrics. When an outcome calls for skill development, skill transfer, or applying a tool to make a product, guiding rubrics provide the most agency-rich assessments. If you must grade performance outcomes, use a format that awards points that recognize the degree of accomplishment or amount of development over time. This will enable you to have your guiding rubric do double duty as a grading rubric.

Table 3.2: Leveled Outcome Statements Developed With SMART Criteria

Elementary School

English Language Arts: Today, I want to retell a story I read by naming six events in order from start to end.

Science: By Friday, I will make a rain gauge and keep a three-week daily record on a chart that shows daily volume.

Mathematics: This week, I will complete ten word problems with no errors and explain my thinking on solving problems on a single sheet placed in my Google folder.

Music: This month, I will practice thirty minutes daily with a smartphone recording of each session assessed on a rubric shared with my French horn teacher before our session on May 30.

Maker Project: This week I will use scrap materials from our classroom bin and mount and seal a Wordle chart about my no-bullies-here campaign.

Middle School

English Language Arts: My aim this week is to complete a five-paragraph analysis of character in my selected story with no grammar, spelling, or sentence errors. My analysis will show one example of what the character said or did and one example of what others said about the character.

Science: Today, I will make a bar graph to display on a share-slide and show the relationships between kinetic energy, the mass of two bottle cars I make, and the speed I generate with two different sized rubber bands.

Mathematics: On Thursday, our team will submit three correct measurements of a circle and explain in a three-minute podcast how we did each one using only a piece of string and the formula.

Social Studies: By February 20, we will present the results of our community survey recommending safe passage school routes to the principal in her office.

Performing Arts: This quarter, I will compose and perform a two-minute dance in the Alley mode in our school's dance festival.

High School

English Language Arts: Our team will make a six-minute oral presentation. My part will be to explain the four conclusions we came to about our book's author's purpose with one example per conclusion with proper citation.

Mathematics: I intend to design a wooden floor with an inlaid geometric pattern of rectangles and squares in proper proportion. I will show my design on chart paper with the correct measurements for one unit applied within a 20 × 40-foot room. It will be ready by January 12.

Science: I want to complete my lab record sheet by the Friday deadline with all seven questions answered correctly and with two examples for each. I will share my sheet with my teacher via Google.

World Language: We want to interview two Latinx DACA students about their experiences with Immigration and Customs Enforcement. We'll do it in their language before the end of this month and create a collage with at least seven images labeled in that language.

Career and Technical Education: My partner and I will build a plastic car to show our solar-powered model of the future. We will submit plans that meet the criteria for a contest and enter the model in the contest before the April 7 deadline.

Capstone Project: Our team will complete a wall mural showing the contributions of Native American physicists to laser science developments. We will unveil our work on the science hall wall on May 20.

What Is a Guiding Rubric?

A *guiding rubric* is an instructional tool and an assessment tool in one. It highlights the most recognizable characteristics of a skill, practice, or action, and the understanding of a concept targeted by a personalized learning plan. By providing students with guiding rubrics *prior* to teaching a skill or topic introduction in a personalized learning plan, you initiate a deeper learning dive. As students check on the rubric while completing the personalized learning plan, they reinforce what is most important to *know*. With the final summative review, best aided by your feedback, they demonstrate what they can *do*.

Align the guiding rubric with the outcomes. Add other guiding rubrics to assess important contributing outcomes. By presenting criteria for determining an outcome's most desired results at the start of the lesson, the guiding rubric allows students to do three things: (1) plan backward for how to attain an outcome important to them, (2) assess themselves formatively as they implement the plan with a teacher and perhaps peer feedback, and (3) conclude the lesson or project with a summative assessment bolstered by final feedback from others.

How Is a *Guiding* Rubric Different From a *Grading* Rubric?

First, consider the similarities.

- Both allow you to assess standards-aligned skill development such as how to punctuate, how to analyze informational text, how to solve a two-step problem, how to open a Word document, or how to inquire.
- Both allow you to identify benchmarks to score a student's depth of understanding of a concept such as *All living things are made of cells*, the Pythagorean theorem, causes of the civil rights movement, or following copywrite ethics, as well as a student's use of a learning tool such as a potter's wheel, a 3-D printer, a compass, or a graphic organizer. You or students may make a guiding rubric for a final product such as a cardboard boat that floats, a slideware presentation highlighting Ludwig Mies van der Rohe's influence on modern architecture, or a budget for a dream vacation.
- Both allow you to assess a student's mindset or skills for team collaboration. In short, the possible content is always the same, as is the potential final from the transformation of the rubric's score into a grade.

Now, consider the differences list in table 3.3.

Table 3.4 (page 72) lets you compare and contrast the different *characteristics* of grading rubrics versus guiding rubrics.

Rather than talk to students about what they are expected to learn in a unit, show a completed *guiding* rubric. You introduce students to a guiding rubric as a reciprocal learning strategy. A *reciprocal* strategy allows for dialogue between the student and the teacher. Ideally, the student shows her work, the teacher or peers give feedback, and then the student self-assesses before returning the final rubric to the teacher for inclusion in the student's portfolio. If you must grade the product, select a format such as the multipoint rubric, which allows scoring.

The walk starts with steps through an initial self-assessment on a sample rubric. This engages students in learning how to fill in the rubric. This walk-through ends with each student having assessed a sample concept or skill you have provided. Some need coaching to fully grasp this. In the course of a school year, you can make it your own teaching outcome to coach all students on the skills and dispositions so they can self-direct how they create and self-manage their personalized learning plan guiding rubrics.

Table 3.3: Grading Rubrics Versus Guiding Rubrics

Grading Rubric	Guiding Rubric
- This is a tool for teacher evaluation of student performance. - It is 100 percent teacher-made and controlled. The format is usually multi-point with teacher vocabulary. - It is intended to end with a number or letter grade.	- This is a tool to enrich and refine what or how a student is learning; two-way feedback is the most important ingredient. Instruction is provided as students match rubrics to outcome criteria, receive teacher and peer feedback, self-assess progress, and attain outcomes. Teachers and peers share feedback, and a dialogue ensues among all parties (Hattie & Clarke, 2019). - A teacher or the students may make this rubric as an instructional strategy so that assessment informs learning. - A guiding rubric may be followed by a grade, but the primary purpose is to inform or instruct. Its secondary purpose is to promote student reflection and self-management. Both purposes are achieved by helping the student look back at prior knowledge and skills or forward to improvement.

Table 3.4: Where Grading and Guiding Rubrics Overlap

Grading Rubric	Both	Guiding Rubric
Extrinsic Motivation		**Intrinsic Motivation**
Teacher made and directed	Assessment of content	Teacher models and moves to student self-assessment and self-directed learning.
Multi-point	Criteria or benchmarks	Three formats with emphasis of warm feedback forward and backward
Teacher vocabulary		Student reading level
Grading scale oriented	Range of performance	Optional grading (no grading preferred in personalized learning plan formative assessments)
Purpose is to assess student performance		Purpose is to instruct through criteria guiding feedback
Optional feedback from teacher	Formative and summative assessments	Feedback as guide from teacher and peers
Ends a lesson, project, or unit		Developmental criteria over a semester or year
Teacher may retain in portfolio		Teacher retains rubrics and artifacts for comparison over time

What Does a Guiding Rubric Look Like?

You can spot guiding rubrics in four common rubric formats: these include the rated checklist, the single-point rubric, the multi-point rubric, and the rubric with guiding questions. With whichever format you select, you will assess degrees of development over time as well as reinforce the students' understanding of the key content or skill to be mastered. You use the same format for introductory, formative, and summative assessments, taking as much advantage of two way-feedback as possible. Prior to the summative assessment of the skill or content understanding you want to develop, give and get feedback without grades. If you are guiding performance of the same rubric target over a longer time through multiple personalized learning plans, it is best to delay any grade. You may want to avoid grades totally.

With each guiding rubric, you create alternative teachable moments. You can add options for student self-assessment informed by your feedback as well as feedback from peers, parents, and other involved adults. By sharing these rubrics online with students, you enable reciprocal dialogue about each student's personal improvement over time. With storage of all copies in each student's portfolio, you and the student can look back to see progress made. Lacking digital resources, you can set up a paper-based portfolio with folders stored at your desk.

When calling on rubrics to guide learning, each of the formats has different pluses and minuses. There are four options for guiding rubrics.

1. Scorable checklist
2. Single-point guiding rubric
3. Multi-point guiding rubric
4. Open-ended self-assessment guiding rubric

Refer to the appendix (page 211) for the following reproducible templates to share with your students.

- "Rated Checklist—PreK–3"
- "Improvement Rating Scale—Grades 3–12"
- "Single-Point Guiding Rubric—Grades 3–12"
- "Multi-Point Guiding Rubric—Grades 3–12"
- "Open-Ended Self-Assessment Rubric—Grades 3–12"

Scorable Checklist

You may call on this simple checklist multiple times during a personalized learning plan to assess its outcome. This rubric relies on easy-to-score criteria with levels of quality named. You and students can score the degree to which the student has shown progress in attaining the outcome. You have options to add a feedback column or open-ended response guides at the end of the rubric for summative comments, questions, or next-step advice. This format is a starter guiding rubric and is easiest to incorporate into a grading scale if you elect to grade plans.

In figure 3.11, the teacher's chosen creative-thinking outcome shows four criteria. In this example, students only write their names. In later versions, when students are able to read, the teacher will add *I* to each criterion so the student can self-assess.

In figure 3.12, the teacher has set the norms. All students are expected to follow these norms, but the teacher extends the rubric so that each student may pick a *power goal*, the number-one outcome to be included in the final grade. Note that feedback from the teacher and classmates will be included. The teacher also expects students to reflect on their progress with the three open-ended questions.

Single-Point Guiding Rubric

This guiding rubric is the best for promoting two-way feedback. You list criteria in a middle column and open space for comments noting what is positive about a performance of each criterion and suggestions for improvement. Because this rubric is meant to promote written feedback and dialogue, there are no quality scales for the criteria. In the assessment process, you, a

Name:		
I saw or heard that		
____ You added many ideas.		
____ Your ideas were different.		
____ Your ideas added to others' ideas.		
____ You helped make the final idea special.		
Project title:	**Date:**	**Class:**

Figure 3.11: Rated checklist for guiding creative thinking—Elementary example.

*Visit **go.SolutionTree.com/instruction** for a free reproducible version of this figure.*

Name:	Date:	Teacher:
Class:	Period:	Grade:
Check-up dates:		
Team names:		
Feedback is by:		
☐ Self		
☐ Teacher		
☐ Peers: _____		
☐ Other: _____		

Figure 3.12: Rated guiding checklist for classroom norms—Secondary example.

continued →

Score each response.
0 = Not yet started
1 = Most of the time this is hard to do.
2 = With help I can do this in the classroom.
3 = I can do this most of the time by myself in this classroom.
4 = I do this all of the time by myself in this classroom.

Final score: You will have the chance to assess your personal goal for your norms at least three times in this unit. Your teacher will OK your goal.

____	I will respect each person in our art studio and the work by making positive comments.
____	I will build trust with the teacher and my classmates by providing helpful feedback.
____	I will care for all materials and equipment.
____	I will complete my fair share of work on all collaborative tasks.
____	I will work on my art tasks to build my art understanding, appreciation, and skills.

Other:

My personal outcome for this unit (select one from the previous section or agree with teacher on another):

My outcome:

What am I doing, or did I do, well with this outcome? (Earn up to three points per time.)

What do I need to improve? (Earn up to three points per time.)

What help do I need to improve? (Earn up to three points per time.)

Place your completed assessment in your portfolio.

Visit go.SolutionTree.com/instruction for a free reproducible version of this figure.

designated student, or both write feedback to the student identifying how expectations were exceeded or suggestions for improvement. The student or the team considers the feedback and incorporates it into the assessment.

In a personalized learning plan, the single-point format provides the richest opportunity for you to promote student agency, allow for two-way feedback, and encourage student self-reflection. It also allows a solo response or a team response. You may make either section (stated criteria or open-ended responses) optional.

The single-point guiding rubric in figure 3.13 focuses on assessing collaborative research skills. Notice the spaces for feedback before and after each criterion.

Multi-Point Guiding Rubric

This rubric most closely resembles the standard grading rubric. This format may have between two and five points. However, as a guiding rubric, this format is written in age-appropriate language, not in teacher language. By using age-appropriate vocabulary, you avoid

Teacher:	Period:	Class:
Date:	Check-up dates:	
Name:	Date:	Topic:
Names:		
Roles:	Recorder:	Timer:
	Reporter:	Other:
☐ Online ☐ Print		☐ Team ☐ Individual
Feedback is by: ☐ Self ☐ Teacher ☐ Peers: _____ ☐ Other: _____		
	Enter your responses in the appropriate column. Add pages as needed.	

Better than expected because . . .	Criteria	Suggestions
	We (I) conducted a systematic search for our topic.	
	We (I) can explain our search procedures.	
	We (I) agreed on article selection decisions.	
	We (I) summarized five articles with who, what, why, where, when, and how included as appropriate.	
	We (I) made complete citations.	
	We (I) rated helpfulness of articles from 0–5.	
	We (I) each performed our jobs.	
Respond to each with a list: • What we (I) did well • What we (I) need to improve • What questions or help are needed		

Figure 3.13: Single-point guiding rubric for collaborative research—Secondary school example.

*Visit **go.SolutionTree.com/instruction** for a free reproducible version of this figure.*

possible off-target assessments caused by students' insufficient reading readiness. (See Appendix A: New Research on Text Complexity, at https://bit.ly/3lLQaj4, for more on this topic.) When the multi-point guiding rubric follows SMART guidelines, it allows for numbers to distinguish degrees of quality for each criterion.

For feedback purposes, it is important to allow open-ended elaboration about the quality of any item. At the end of this format, you have the option of adding open-assessment prompts such as "What did you do best, what will you improve, and what help do you need?" or "Plus, minus, and questions to ask" about a designated single element or the whole experience. For a personalized learning plan, the most agency-friendly plus-minus charts prompt students to pick whatever they want to rate about their total experience: What were the pluses and minuses about your experience with this personalized learning plan? A narrower prompt asks a student to respond about a specific element of a lesson or project: What were the pluses and minuses you noted about your goal setting with this personalized learning plan?

As with the other formats, two-way feedback options are more important than any grades given. If you must grade, emphasize to students and parents the value of two-way feedback in formative assessments for achieving a personalized learning plan outcome. At the end of a plan, you can give solo grades based on how much improvement the student has made.

Figure 3.14 is a guiding rubric resembling the classic grading format but aimed at teaching the student the criteria for the measurement task. The criteria here highlight *learning to learn* how to find area and perimeter by engaging students in that task and reflecting on the process, not the answer.

Name:	**Grade:**			
Teacher:	**Period:**		**Date:**	
I found the area of the basketball key that shows my thinking with a labeled equation. My calculation was error free, including the units.	I used an OK area strategy and showed my thinking with the correct equation, but with two or three errors in calculation or units.	My strategy was partially OK, but I didn't find the area or, if I found it, I had more than four errors in calculation or units.	I had no strategy.	I had no strategy and I didn't find the area.
I found the perimeter of the basketball key that shows my thinking with a labeled equation. My calculation was error free, including the units.	I used an OK perimeter strategy and showed my thinking with the correct equation and two or three errors in calculation or units.	My strategy was partially OK, but I did not find perimeter, or I had more than four errors in calculation or units.	I had no strategy.	I had no strategy and I didn't find the perimeter.
I double-checked all calculations to see exact numbers and letters in correct spots (100 percent accuracy).				
My score: _____ **Give reasons:**				

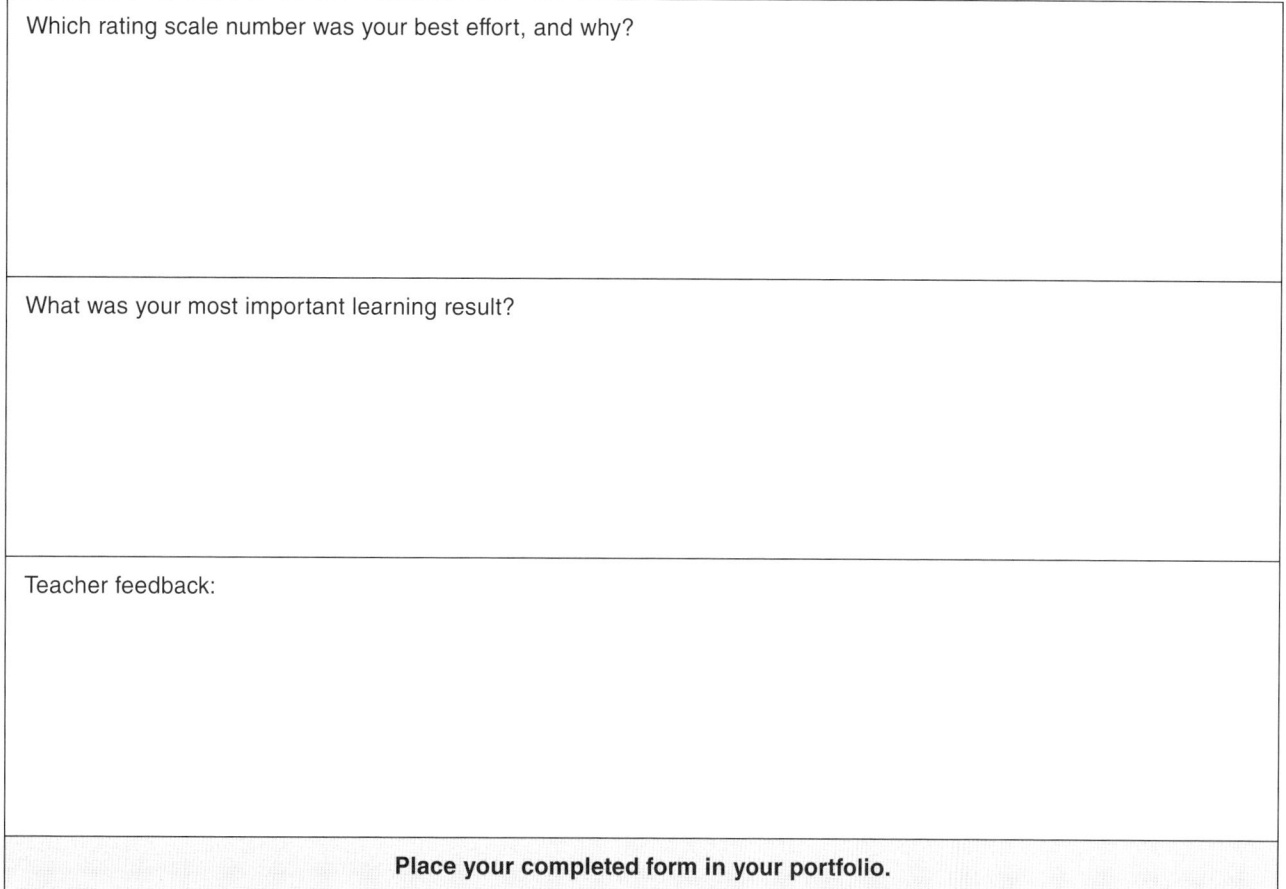

Figure 3.14: Multi-point guiding rubric for area and perimeter measurement—Secondary example.

Open-Ended Guiding Rubric

This open-ended guiding rubric encourages fluent, flexible thinking. You can also call on its three guiding questions when you are coaching students working on their targeted personalized learning plan skills. If it is a confidential chat with one student, the questions are informal assessments. Couple think-pair-share with the questions for formative assessments that are asked and answered but not recorded. With groups, structure a round-robin with these three prompts.

You will find this model helpful when you want to stretch students to think about options more flexibly or with students able to set their own criteria and be fluent with their examples and reasons. Because this rubric prompts thinking with three open-ended questions, it facilitates the most agency. If you are required to give grades, Pass or Fail should satisfy for this open model, especially if you keep the artifacts and plans with the written summative rubrics in portfolios. Figure 3.15 (page 78) presents a sample completed open-ended guiding rubric.

How Do I Assess My Personalized Teaching Plan?

When you have completed your teaching plan, review its rubric and enter your change ideas on the template. Share the plan and then return to the rubric to assess how well it worked for you. Remember that the "best laid schemes o' Mice an' Men/Gang aft agley" (Burns, 1786). Prepare to modify your plan.

After a first try you may need to make adjustments for your second go. If more than 15 percent of your class is still struggling, modify the elements in your personalized teaching plan. For the 15 percent, it is best to increase differentiation of strategy with tutoring and small-group practices. Try not to reduce expectations inherent in student outcomes. Once satisfied with your students' performances with your first personalized teaching plan, move to the next skill they need. For instance, with the reading example, move to a new skill or increase the level of difficulty. You can retain the same

Student name: Zita Bogdanovich	**Date:** 12/1		**Teacher:** Ms. Kahlstonovitch
Grade: 9	**Period:** 4		**Topic:** Weather effects

Skill: Making predictions from data

Feedback is by:
- ☐ Self
- ☒ Teacher
- ☐ Peers: Tom, Roger, and Inez
- ☒ Other: WXYZ weather person

What we (I) did well:

I arranged for our guest weather person to visit and gave her our team's questions before our meetup.

I chaired the questions so everyone got to ask at least one and do a follow-up.

I emailed her a thank-you card signed by all.

I read and summarized my two articles on predicting Dallas weather in spring.

I found and summarized my data on Texas Tornados and gave that to the team.

I applied what I knew about making predictions to our data.

What we (I) need to improve:

I need to stop arguments in our team.

My article summaries needed more specific reasons to back up my main idea.

In my presentation, I confused Roger, who wanted more facts.

I didn't always arrive at our online meetings on time.

I got discouraged over all the reading.

I had fun making and gathering data from my backyard windmill.

What questions or help are needed?

I need help from Ms. K with writing summaries.

I need more encouragement than I thought to stick with tough reading.

Figure 3.15: Open-ended guiding rubric.

approach—modeling and then increasing the challenge and responsibility for reaching the new outcome with cooperative groups—before you end with a stimulating high engagement mini-project.

Although your students may seem to be covering less material with your plan, remember that less is more. By engaging students' minds in a few stimulating activities replete with collaboration and communication, you enable them to move Xunzi's (2014) admonition "Tell me and I forget. Teach me and I remember. Involve me and I learn" more quickly into action. You only need to remind yourself, "Remain firm about your goals, but flexible about your methods" (Donahue, 1992, p. 127), as you compose your first plan.

Figure 3.16 presents a guiding rubric to self-assess teaching performance for the reading plan in figure 3.8 (page 66). Modify it, and invite your grade-level team and supervisor to observe and give feedback.

What Are My Responsibilities in a Personalized Learning Plan Assessment?

You have ten responsibilities. The more you increase student agency with any one responsibility, the less you are responsible to do yourself.

1. Identify outcomes.

Name: Elias Dulin	Grade: 3	Date: 11/7

Scores:

0 = I haven't started yet.
1 = A first step: you need to do better.
2 = This is a good start.
3 = This looks good.
4 = Wow, I got it!

To what degree I did the following:

- _3.5_ Engage my students as active thinkers about literature they read
- _3_ Highlight the prompts they need when they read for relevance
- _4_ See evidence that they internalized these prompts
- _2.5_ Promote teams working together
- _3_ Encourage their decision making

I got feedback from my:

- _X_ Peer
- ___ Supervisor

The feedback told me:

That my kids were really engaged. "All I saw were bottoms up when they buried their heads together." "They seemed to enjoy reading each other's pages on the gallery walk." "I want to see if this works. I want their scores."

My Summary Assessment

What I did best in this lesson was:

Plan. It took a lot more time, but the end saved me time wasted with bad instructions and kids goofing off. Being specific about the group jobs really helped. I had only one student whine, "I don't know what I am supposed to do." I moved away from my giving directions and allowed kid decisions.

What I will improve next lesson is:

I need more stories. I want to make the lesson longer. Some of the students needed more practice, and I have to figure how to allow that to happen.

Help I need is:

Getting more stories and more variety

Figure 3.16: Engagement rubric for assessing a personalized teaching plan—Example.

Visit go.SolutionTree.com/instruction for a free reproducible version of this figure.

2. Select, create, or co-create guiding rubrics.
3. Set up a record storage system.
4. Schedule personal feedback time.
5. Dialogue with students.
6. Ask for and listen to students' feedback.
7. Capture need-to-know teachable moments.
8. Communicate with parents.
9. Prepare playbooks.
10. Prepare playlists.

Identify Outcomes

To start, determine student goals. These goals are akin to students' personal learning destinations. Before students start a lesson or project, you help them find personal and specific learning performance goals. You help transform these into SMART outcomes. You can provide outcome examples as models and support for reaching the goals. At the start, with students as novice planners, you lead with your questions and then help to turn goals to SMART outcomes. As they become experienced, you gradually turn students loose to frame their own outcomes in their plans. This is not just a gradual release of responsibility; it is an increased cognitive challenge. Use your coaching skills to stretch students outside their comfort zones as they learn to plan with the end in mind.

Select, Create, or Co-Create Guiding Rubrics

There are more than enough rubrics and checklists available online for teachers to adapt as *grading* rubrics. Online sites provide easily adapted examples for basic skills, the four Cs, and any content. For personalized learning plans, you must adapt traditional grading rubrics so they contain performance outcomes and the criteria to guide students through their planned performances. Guiding rubrics add insurance that students will advance in their content knowledge and in their process skills development, which results from implementing their plans. As with personalized learning plan outcome statements, you provide initial guiding rubrics. But in the name of agency, you will move students from their dependence on you and your models to learning how to create their own and become the self-managers that are asked for in social-emotional standards.

Set Up a Record Storage System

Strong, personalized feedback benefits from a systematic record-keeping system. Guiding rubrics contain the protocols and formats that provide opportunities for rich, two-way feedback. The easiest system to set up is in Google Docs. Blogs and wikis provide added storehouses so you and students can file the artifacts, rubrics, comments, and records in private electronic mailboxes. Each box is one student's official portfolio. Only you and the student can access the box as you converse about that student's progress.

Schedule Personal Feedback Time

To ensure you get to every student, and especially those with extra need for personal feedback, prepare a weekly schedule. This schedule can be your major communication link with the students most in need of attention. The schedule will remind you when to target half of your guiding feedback time to those who are struggling most to achieve their personal goals.

Dialogue With Students

The more often you can hold a personal tête-à-tête with each student, the more you will activate metacognition—number one in strengthening recall and advancing deeper learning outcomes (Hattie, 2009). In my professional experience, individual at-desk conferences that help students learn-*from*-doing should take up to 75 percent of the time you devote to personalized learning. As you give feedback to individual students on preset personal goals, review data in the student's portfolio, and discuss responses to questions from the student (intertwined with the student's additional feedback to you), you will soon recognize why two-way feedback is such a major influence on achievement and motivation (Hattie & Timperley, 2007).

Ask for and Listen to Students' Feedback

You can rely on the research data that point out that student feedback to teachers is too seldom given or received and that powerful benefits may be gained when it is given and received (State of Victoria, 2020).-Using this feedback builds a climate of trust and respect like no other method. When you act on student feedback, especially feedback you invited, students gain the highest achievement advantage and make the strongest gains (Hattie & Timperley, 2007).

Capture Need-to-Know Teachable Moments

You can predict some teachable moments when students first arrive in your classroom at the beginning of the school year. However, you are not all-seeing. Prepare for the first unforeseen scenarios by embedding activities into your lessons and projects that you are *sure* students need to know. However, it is also important, especially in deeper learning projects, to stop and structure personalized learning plan minilabs for one or more students who have skill and knowledge gaps you uncover. These will work best when you can trust the rest of the class to stay engaged while you take time out at a side table. You can also encourage individuals to self-identify need-to-know background knowledge for how to perform a task. In those cases, take the time to ask any others if they want to join the minilab. With high trust, students who do need to know will come forward without fear of negative comments.

Communicate With Parents and Guardians

Two-way communication encourages parents and guardians to give feedback on how they see their children performing and accept specifics of a student's performance. Personalized learning plans increase the chance this two-way talk will happen. When communicating with parents and guardians, make the student's personalized learning plan the center of attention, preferably with the student present and leading the personalized learning plan walkthrough. Explain the personalized learning plan's purpose and let the student explain the chosen skill, why it was chosen, and progress being made. This is a good time for the student to show artifacts related to the personalized learning plan. After the chat, tell the parent or guardian what you like about the student's progress. Again, your best role is guide on the side. Encourage everyone to ask questions and give helpful feedback with lots of *I likes*. Next, invite parents or guardians to discuss any concerns and end with giving you feedback.

When discussing parent or guardian concerns, call on your active best listening skills. Avoid becoming defensive. Ask for clarification, paraphrase, summarize, and listen some more. After discussing each concern, acknowledge its legitimacy and collaborate with the parent or guardian to find a mutually agreeable plan to resolve the issue. Be sure to engage the student when making any agreements. Don't forget outcomes and a schedule for the next conversation about the student's progress.

When a face-to-face conference is not possible or parents or guardians don't want the student in the conference, the next option is a virtual conference, preferably with a video connection. Whatever configuration works, be sure to end the conference with parent feedback *to you*. Although parents may push for what they know—grades—you can overcome this entrenched preference by providing copies of plans, a grade tabulated from rubric summaries, and samples of student work generated via plans.

Prepare Playbooks

A playbook is a sequenced checklist of steps or procedures needed (sometimes required) to prep for or complete a complex task. Surgeons use playbooks. Airplane pilots use playbooks. Online customer service agents use playbooks. So do auto mechanics who are checking your car engine. If you watch team sports on TV, you will notice coaches carrying clipboards or digital notebooks. These contain all the plays and plans for that game. Players receive their first playbooks at the beginning of tryouts, study them, and get ready for practice. Each week, coaches modify the playbooks to fit the next game. Playbooks help all stay on the same page.

In figure 3.17 (page 82), a teacher playbook in checklist form, you see a *Don't forget to do* sequence of SHARE procedures. Start with this sample and add or subtract items. Reuse your final SHARE playlist in its entirety once you have established what works for you and your students. For higher agency, encourage students to modify the playlist or to start from scratch and make their own.

Figure 3.18 (page 82) is the playbook for the outcome of a playlist of research sites that middle school students will find. Each team keeps a copy of its digital notebook and stores the playlist and rubric in its online portfolio, ready to share it with the teacher when asked.

Prepare Playlists

In the digital world, playlists organize music, podcast topics, workout regimens, and recipes. Online notebooks allow space for multiple personal to-do playlists. Siri and Alexa share music playlists as well as grocery lists, and your phone can list favorite apps and prescribed medicines. Note that playlists differ from playbooks. *Playlists* enumerate ideas; *playbooks* sequence instructions.

Playlists work well in high-engagement classrooms—especially if students have access to digital devices. If students have access to digital devices, you can share idea lists or invite them to brainstorm their own playlists. Playlists allow you to identify the following.

- Favorite items to cover in a personalized learning plan
- Books or articles for student reading
- Best practices to include in a personalized learning plan
- Ideas for outcomes
- Banked rubrics

Name:	Date:	Grade:
Teacher:	Check-up dates:	Item:
Notes:		

☐ Topic shared with students
☐ Personalized learning plan format and protocols reviewed
☐ Outcomes identified by: ☐ me ☐ students
☐ Guiding rubrics completed and SMART approved
☐ SHARE system clarified with students
☐ Assessment schedule set
☐ Feedback schedule set with: ☐ teams ☐ individuals

Figure 3.17: Teacher SHARE playbook—Example.

*Visit **go.SolutionTree.com/instruction** for a free reproducible version of this figure.*

Please follow these instructions.
☐ Set up your team's roles and review the collaboration rubric in your portfolio.
☐ Review your personalized learning plan outcome statement for researching internet sites about global warming.
☐ Search the internet for materials. Follow the research rubric from last month. (It's in your portfolio.) Check it every day.
☐ Make a playlist of possible sites and copy the URLs to your personalized learning plan.
☐ Choose sites for a final playlist of recommended sites for others to read.
☐ Include full citations and share.
☐ Assess your work and your teamwork with the rubrics. Be sure to schedule a feedback session with me. Share your final document with me.
☐ Upload all rubrics and products into your online portfolio.

Figure 3.18: Student playbook for global warming research—Secondary example.

*Visit **go.SolutionTree.com/instruction** for a free reproducible version of this figure.*

The following grade-level-appropriate playlist examples show a teacher-made list for elementary students (figure 3.19) and a list generated by high school students (figure 3.20).

How Do I Keep Personalized Learning Plan Playbooks, Playlists, Rubrics, and Artifacts Organized?

The most helpful way to organize these tools and artifacts is to set up a storage system for student portfolios on free cloud storage such as Dropbox and Google Docs. The system can include important plans, rubrics, playlists, playbooks, and artifacts. If possible, each team member should retain a copy of the team's artifacts in a subsection of the team portfolio. Teams can scan, photograph with their phones, or share documents. If you lack adequate digital devices for solo or team storage, you can use a manila folder with paper copies of student work securely stored in your desk. If you have sufficient digital devices with at least one per team, you can set up online portfolios in a free learning management system (LMS) such as Google Docs. When keeping online portfolios, assign a confidential code to each student. Each student and you should know this secure, protective code.

After you show students how to use the system, it will be each student's responsibility to store artifacts you designate in their portfolios and keep the portfolio organized. You may devote a class period to a lesson on the critical-thinking skill of categorizing, with the

Outcome-Driven Instruction and Assessment 83

Playbook
☐ In your team, look at the playlist. Read all the topics.
☐ Pick one or more project topics that interest all members.
☐ If you choose more than one, discuss and vote for one.
☐ If you can think of a like project, add it to your list.
☐ Copy the project you pick onto an index card.
☐ Everyone signs the index card to say that they agree on this topic.

Playlist: Project Topics			
Pets	Our friends	Favorite TV shows	Tabletop games
Flowers	Airplanes	Favorite _____	Books we like
Our neighbors	Friends	Vacations	Heroines and heroes
Our neighborhood	Sports	Outside games to play	Favorite foods
Our families	Famous people	Video games	Problem to solve

Figure 3.19: Playbook and playlist ideas—Elementary example.

*Visit **go.SolutionTree.com/instruction** for a free reproducible version of this figure.*

Playbook
☐ Select your personalized learning plan outcome.
☐ Review the list of possible projects and select your project and medium.
☐ Review playlist for approved sites and contact instructions.
☐ Rank desired sites from the site list. Preview the site photo.
☐ Avoid site duplication and submit your site requests to the class committee before the deadline.
☐ Check off all completed tasks on this list and store the final in your portfolio.

Playlist: Possible Projects		
Wall mural	Freestanding sculpture	Image painting
Sidewalk mural	Video projection	Photo collage
Freestanding mural	Slide projection	Single blown-up photo
Wall sculpture	Large painted portrait or image	

Figure 3.20: Playbook and playlist ideas for community art projects—Secondary example.

*Visit **go.SolutionTree.com/instruction** for a free reproducible version of this figure.*

portfolio as the medium. Of course, it will not surprise you that all can't keep their portfolios organized. This will give you the teachable opportunities to turn the need into a personalized learning plan for *categorizing* and then ample opportunities to assess formative *organizing* performances.

Figure 3.21 (page 84) shows an example portfolio playbook in checklist format. To reinforce what students should include and avoid students saying, "What am I supposed to put in my portfolio?" make sure that students store and refer to this playbook.

What Logistics Are Necessary for a Personalized Learning Plan Assessment?

After students are familiar with the process of self-assessing a plan before, during, and at the end of the planned time, you may need to allocate less time for this task. For instance, in the first quarter of the year, you direct the rubric completion, step by step. In the second quarter, you can set up pairs or trios for each personalized learning plan. Ultimately, you increase the challenge for managing the self-assessment by encouraging each student to gather feedback and then solo self-assess.

The options give preference to technology tools as the go-to assessment means. If your classroom lacks sufficient technology, you can rely on chart paper to display samples and make paper copies of templates to store in folders. If using paper templates, team volunteers can carry out functions such as materials distribution, collection, and portfolio storage. Figure 3.22 presents a general teacher playbook. Instead of a sequence of instructions, this example shows tasks categorized by elements. You can adapt this playbook as a guide showing you what to include in a playbook.

Name:	Date:	Grade:
Teacher:	Subject:	Period:
Check-up dates:		

Playbook

Check off items as you finish each task.
- ☐ Identify myself by first and last name, class, and period on my portfolio's front page.
- ☐ Identify classmates who will give feedback.
- ☐ Provide a table of contents with dates and a personalized learning plan topic.
- ☐ Place items for each personalized learning plan in a dated sequence.
    - ☐ My plan
    - ☐ My guiding rubric
- ☐ Products to show work
- ☐ Feedback labeled from teammates by date
- ☐ Teacher feedback by date
- ☐ Other feedback by date, labeled with who gave feedback
- ☐ My feedback responses
- ☐ Playlists made
- ☐ Artifacts made
- ☐ Other artifacts labeled

Figure 3.21: Portfolio playbook—Example.

Visit go.SolutionTree.com/instruction for a free reproducible version of this figure.

Time:	Fifteen minutes to initiate or review each new rubric prior to start of lesson or project; ten-minute formal interim assessments; fifteen-minute summative assessment (Add five minutes per round of feedback. All times approximate to grade levels and student familiarity with the process.)
Place:	Desks or carrels for solo work; computer stations for teamwork (Students with phones, notebooks, or laptops may give feedback and complete self-assessment outside of class.)
Materials:	Rubric template copies to display or share; chart paper option to display plus paper copies; playlists and playbooks
Technology:	Interactive whiteboard; computers or mobile devices per each student or per each group; internet access; LMS share capability with journal and portfolio options
Teams:	If the personalized learning plan allows for teams, continue the same pairs or trios with roles, responsibilities, and collaboration guidelines (It is your decision when to switch teams after their first personalized learning plan assessment. From an agency point of view, encourage teams to make this choice after you are comfortable with your directed process.)

Figure 3.22: Category-style playbook.

Visit go.SolutionTree.com/instruction for a free reproducible version of this figure.

TAKEAWAYS

This organizer encourages you to reflect on what you read in this chapter about connections among outcomes, rubrics, and personalized learning plans. Enter your takeaways here.

CHAPTER 4
STUDENT AGENCY

All that is valuable in human society depends upon the opportunity for development accorded the individual.

—Albert Einstein

During his long, unjust imprisonment by South Africa's apartheid government, Nelson Mandela shared his version of William Ernest Henley's (1888) poem "Invictus" with fellow inmates. The poem addresses the essence of human agency, the feeling of confidence in one's own freedom to take charge of his or her own life. As this personal sense intensifies, so does the individual's readiness to voice ideas and feelings in spite of restrictions imposed by others. After reading the poem many times, the isolated Mandela asserted his agency and chose to voice his own version.

In the original poem, Henley (1888) talks about how, despite being injured and contending with looming horrors, he feels in charge of his own decision making: "I am the master of my fate / I am the captain of my soul."

This chapter looks at why and how teachers are making the shift from providers of information to facilitators of deeper learning with increased amounts of student agency. It poses many questions: What is student agency, really? How much power and authority are teachers willing to give over to students so they can feel like masters of their own ships? What are the advantages to teachers and learners with agency? What methods work best to develop and enable agency? Where do personalized learning plans fit into student agency?

Driving question: How do I empower student agency with personalized learning plans?

What Is Student Agency?

Student agency is both a driving force and a result. *Agency* is one's deeply felt right to make free choices and to share those choices in one's *authentic* voice. In this context, *authentic* describes the expression of one's personal beliefs and ideas strongly felt. For instance, although disenfranchised from voting by the framers of the Constitution, American women and the descendants of black slaves raised their voices in protest and won the right to choose those who made law. More importantly, empowered by increased agency, both groups continue forward to expand their right to choose.

In the school context, students push for the right to choose what, when, how, and where they will learn (or not learn) and to express their choices in whatever legal ways they elect. In middle schools, many students for the first time experience voting choice for representative school leaders. By sixth or seventh grade, students have a first chance to choose elective courses. When a teacher selects PBL, students may find themselves making choices about the content of a project, who is on which team, and how to make a product of their choice. The more complex and meaningful the choices offered, the more able the students are to develop their sense of agency, feeling they are the captains of their ship and masters of their own souls. As students develop this young sense of agency, they plant the seeds for becoming self-directed learners. In high schools given to promoting agency, students not only have expanded choice opportunities in student governance and uncensored school newspapers, they are asked more and more to make choices that enable them to grow and develop their personalized sense of agency (Bradley, 2014).

In a classroom context, agency is stimulated by students' right to make choices free from the limits of socioeconomic class, religion, gender, ethnicity, ability, customs, or instructional policy or practice. Not all secondary schools are ready to offer such meaningful choices, as shown by challenges of LGBTQ+ students who want to participate in sports traditionally restricted to a specific gender and schools restricting what courses students may elect as their school administrators insist on ability grouping.

The promotion of agency in and out of classrooms becomes more vitally necessary as each Century 21 day passes. The unpredicted COVID-19 pandemic lay bare the inability of so many students thrust out of their safe nests, their walled classrooms, and away from the security of highly structured school days into ill-structured, unsupervised remote learning time where they were unsure what to do. Many may have asked, "What am I supposed to do? How do I accept the overnight charge to learn without a teacher over my shoulder, holding my hand, telling me what to do?" Such reactions were not the responses of students with strong integrity, efficacy, and agency who are more focused and engaged, choose tougher challenges, and concentrate better during those challenges (Johnston, 2004). Nor were they ones likely to show their agency and "exert influence on their educational trajectories, their future lives, and their immediate and larger social surroundings" (Klemenčič, 2015).

What Does Research Say About Promoting Student Agency?

Researchers Richard M. Ryan and Edward L. Deci (2000) answer *why* when introducing what became seminal research:

> The fullest representations of humanity show people to be curious, vital, and self-motivated. At their best, they are agentic and inspired, striving to learn; extend themselves; master new skills; and apply their talents responsibly. That most people show considerable effort, agency, and commitment in their lives appears, in fact, to be more normative than exceptional, suggesting some very positive and persistent features of human nature.
>
> Yet, it is also clear that the human spirit can be diminished or crushed and that individuals sometimes reject growth and responsibility. Regardless of social strata or cultural origin, examples of both children and adults who are apathetic, alienated, and irresponsible are abundant. Such non-optimal human functioning can be observed not only in our psychological clinics but also among the millions who, for hours a day, sit passively before their televisions, stare blankly from the back of their classrooms, or wait listlessly for the weekend as they go about their jobs. (p. 68)

If you are a teacher who sees too many students frozen when taken outside the comfort zone of their classrooms or who are lethargic, or who hears too many parents and teachers bemoan low motivation and outright refuse to carry the torch of self-directed learning and students saying "These projects are too hard. Why don't you just tell me what to do?" or repeatedly ask "Do I have to?", you have your answer to this question. In short, the answer is actively promoting agency so it is easy to find "the curious, vital, and self-motivated," the students who will "extend themselves; master new skills; and apply their talents responsibly" (Ryan & Deci, 2000, p. 68).

What Does Agency Look and Sound Like in a Classroom?

When students make important choices about their own learning, they develop the feeling of agency. That feeling leads to increased confidence in making their own choices. In turn, the feeling grows. By imagining a stop-action video of students engaged in self-directed learning, you can visualize discrete instances of what they say and do as agents of their own learning. Each frame indicates the degree and quality of their agency. For example, in a remote classroom, a middle school science teacher asks student teams to apply what they have learned about group inquiry to a flotation problem. They will have to figure out how to set up the experiment amongst themselves even though they are physically separated. She gives each team a template and a rubric to guide decisions—nothing else. One group is excited about the chance to think like scientists. Several others have doubting members. One group shrugs but disappears. What this teacher knows about agency is that responses to open-ended assignments tell much about students' feelings of agency. Do they welcome choosing how they will carry out the task, which team member will do what, how they will help each other, and how they will know the quality of their work? Or do they moan and groan about the task, showing little or no interest in making choices?

It is important to remember that agency is a feeling. One student's feeling may seem superficial, but feels important to her. She is willing to select a book to report all by herself. She does this. Her self-confidence now says to her, "If I can do this, why can't I pick what I report?" Another feels more agentic: "I know I am a good writer. I don't just want to report about the main character. I want to compare her to other women in history and how they made their voices heard." A third, the most agentic in her class, says, "I want to make a stronger statement that more people will hear. I want to make a podcast with an interview of the author and talk about women's voices in our history. I know I can do it well."

Lucy M. Guglielmino's (1977) Self-Directed Learning Readiness Scale (SDLRS; www.lpasdlrs.com), or Learning Preference Assessment, was a groundbreaking device that offers a concrete playlist to researchers. The scale tells what self-directed learning sounds like. Guglielmino's (1977) full scale, which requires a fee, identifies the most important characteristics of self-directed learners as individuals who are feeling a high degree of agency with their freedom to choose as they pursue their learning goals. By adapting the scale, you can identify specific and measurable outcomes for personalized learning plans. For instance, you might select the all-important and measurable skill of goal setting and turn it into a SMART outcome that reads *In the next thirty days, my goal is to intern at the Chicago Architecture Center. I will receive an evaluation of my internship with at least a 4.25 out of 5 rating and three specific examples of my creative, on-the-job problem solving to include in my college application.*

Scan the full scale to find other elements of self-directed learning needed by your students and fit them as criteria into a guiding rubric. A sample may look like this guiding rubric in figure 4.1 (page 90) based on SDLRS results that indicate a self-directed learner is one who is "persistent in learning" (Guglielmino, 1977). Remember that you are using the criteria to deepen the student's understanding as well as to assess persistence.

Your challenge when learning how to promote agency is to pinpoint the most salient characteristics, attitudes, and skills that are hallmarks of agency. For students who are not yet goal setters, you know that increased facility at goal setting will signify one step forward toward self-direction. You might say the same of other indicators from the SDLRS.

With a clear sense about other characteristics, attitudes, and skills necessary to promote agency, you can call on the scale to assess students' self-direction and what you must do to advance their ability to self-regulate specific behaviors that are stepping stones to higher agency. For instance, from the SDLRS, you might transform the statement "I work very well on my own" (Guglielmino, 1977) into a personalized learning plan outcome such as *In the next ten days, I will give my teacher a time chart and ten fifty-word summaries that show how I stayed on task each day as I completed my reading tasks working alone without any reminders or breaks.* Note the emphasis on *I* and the student's self-regulation. With a corresponding rubric as a guide, the student gets to take charge of her home study, make daily choices about staying on task, and reflect on her choices. To the degree that she succeeds, she can take pride in her agency.

Table 4.1 (page 90) gives additional examples of agency from two perspectives: (1) teachers (and what they say and do to promote the feeling of agency via self-directed learning) and (2) students (and what those who are working to improve self-direction say and do as they own their agency by expressing their choices with confident voices). As you review these options, decide which you already do and which you could add to your toolkit.

Student name:			
To what degree do I (you):		1 = Not at all 2 = Once or twice a task 3 = Consistently during every task	
Tell myself "I can finish this."		Keep the finger of blame pointed to myself	
Start working without hesitating		Ignore interruptions while getting the job done	
Stay with the job until it is finished		Tune out self-doubt	
Find ways to climb over an obstacle		Ignore mean words	
Stick to my plan		Act on constructive feedback	
Ask for what I need to go forward		Check daydreaming during the task	

Source: Adapted from Guglielmino, 1977.

Figure 4.1: Rubric—Persistence in learning.

Visit **go.SolutionTree.com/instruction** *for a free reproducible version of this figure.*

Table 4.1: Agency From Two Perspectives

What Teachers Can Do to Develop Self-Direction in Students	What Teachers Can Say to Coach Agency
• Add personalized learning plans for students. • Schedule project- and problem-based learning units with student decisions about the elemental parts (what the driving question is, what strategies they will use, how they will self-assess). • Organize inquiry-based lessons with students asking the questions. • Schedule personalized learning plans with student-determined, student-managed, and student-assessed outcomes. • Develop self-sufficient learning teams. • Ignite critical and creative thinking with students calling on prior knowledge of how and what they have learned. • Plan for deeper learning outcomes for all students. • Encourage student choice in all lessons and projects. • Engage students with two-way feedback. • Coach for grit and transfer. • Provide media options for students to select. • Include student self-assessment and reflection in lessons and projects. • Help students learn to learn skills so they can self-assess transfer ideas and higher-order-thinking skills.	• "This is a challenging problem. How do you propose to solve it?" • "What is your goal? What outcome are you looking for?" • "Why do you want to learn this? Why this way?" • "What is the driving question for your plan?" • "How are you going to make sure you achieve your outcome?" • "What are you choosing to do here?" • "How will you know you reached your goal or achieved the outcome you want?" • "What have you done well today? How could you improve in the future? What help do you need?" • "What have you learned about this skill that will help in this lesson? In future lessons or projects?" • "How can I help you be more successful?" • "What can I do to help you stick with your plan?" • "What barriers are in your way?" • "What are the challenges? How will you overcome them?" • "What will give you the most trouble when you do this?" • "How are you going to organize your time?" • "What is your team responsibility in this plan?"
What Self-Directed Students Do	**What Self-Directed Students Say**
• Identify their own outcomes and driving questions. • Self-select learning strategies and media.	• "My goal is to . . ." • "I want to . . . because . . ."

- Define and complete products.
- Invite help and feedback.
- Schedule tasks.
- Give warm feedback (page 101).
- Self-assess team roles.
- Self-assess outcomes.
- Transfer new learning.
- Ask and answer questions.
- Co-create and assess roles and responsibilities in a team.
- Engage in inquiry-based lessons from start to finish.
- Structure project- or problem-based learning plans by doing the following.
    - Selecting topics or issues to investigate
    - Identifying outcomes and ways to measure
    - Framing the driving question
    - Determining the strategies, resources, media, and tasks
    - Deciding on team roles
    - Scheduling formal feedback
    - Self-assessing content, teamwork, thinking, and problem solving during and after the project
    - Reflecting on transfer
- Engage in or lead team activities.
- Volunteer for room-management roles.
- Volunteer for class jobs (attendance, library).
- Mentor new students.
- Guide guests.
- Be the teacher's technology genius.
- Use an LMS with their own portfolios.
- Share ideas via classroom technology.
- Participate in classroom justice management team making and adjudicating classroom guidelines and responsibilities.

- "I plan to . . . so I get this result . . ."
- "Roadblocks I encountered were . . ."
- "I overcame these barriers when I . . ."
- "The most challenging part of this was . . ."
- "What I did well was . . ."
- "What I could do differently next time is . . ."
- "Help I need from . . . is . . ."
- "It helps (doesn't help) me when . . ."
- "I am proud that I . . ."
- "The way I will do (or did) this was . . ."
- "I would like you to tell me how I . . ."
- "I will (did) use this skill or idea . . . to . . ."
- "Uses I see for solving problems like this are . . ."
- "It is important for me to stick with . . . because . . ."
- "It was my responsibility to . . ."
- "I wonder why . . ."
- "I am curious to understand . . ."
- "I think I can do better because . . ."
- "I want to do better because . . ."
- "I would like to try a different way to . . ."
- "My options are . . ."
- "I am interested in trying to . . ."
- "Here is my (our) plan for . . ."
- "This is my schedule for . . ."
- "My preference is . . ."
- "In the future, I . . ."
- "I will help with . . ."
- "My future learning plan is . . ."
- "My college (trade school) goal is . . ."
- "I want to become a . . . I will do this by . . ."

How Do I Determine the Degree of Agency Appropriate for My Students?

Student agency is best visualized on a high to low continuum, as shown in figure 4.2 (page 92). Though it exists on a spectrum, the three major points on that spectrum follow.

- **Low:** You *allow* students limited voice and choice, letting them, for example, choose what team they will join, where they will sit in a classroom, who will be a partner, what materials to research, what novel to read, what practice questions to answer, or what requires asking permission for. (Can I hand in this assignment later? Can I go to the bathroom? Do I have to . . . ?)

```
┌─────────────────────────────────────────────────────────────────────────────┐
│        ●─────────────────────────────────────────────────●                  │
│                                                                             │
│         High agency              Middle agency              Low agency      │
│   You actively promote and plan   You encourage agency by planning   You allow procedural choices. │
│   for authentic choices that      inquiry lessons with strategies that                              │
│   stimulate intrinsic motivation  require students to make choices                                  │
│   and include multiple opportunities  and give feedback to you.                                     │
│         for self-assessment.                                                                        │
└─────────────────────────────────────────────────────────────────────────────┘
```

Figure 4.2: Student agency continuum.

- **Middle:** You *encourage* student voice and choice by, for example, setting up an inquiry lesson such as how simple machines work, why Abraham Lincoln changed his mind about slavery, or how to make a financial plan. In these lessons, you may allow students to brainstorm, choose digital tools, work in teams, select roles, volunteer for class-management roles, and make class rules. In addition, you coach them to plan, complete, and assess personalized learning plans.

- **High:** You *intentionally develop and amplify* student voice and choice. For example, after reviewing an exemplary personalized learning plan, you approve student-planned personalized learning plans and highlight self-assessment for skills chosen by students. PBL is the instructional model for all content, and your role is limited to feedback coach and content expert. Students make all choices regarding procedures. Self-selected teams change for each PBL, with students choosing what to investigate.

Ideally, all classrooms enable agency at the middle to high level. Teachers commonly desire student agency but also worry that they do not know how to provide that agency (Dignath-van Ewijk & van der Werf, 2012; Vaughn, 2018). The *how* rests among the practices identified in tables 4.1 (page 90) and 4.2. Additionally, by inviting students to target the characteristics outlined in Guglielmino's (1977) SDLRS in one or more personalized learning plans, you determine the quality and quantity of agency appropriate for expanding the specific skills. Because these characteristics are crucial to how teachers decide how much agency to provide, review figure 4.1 (page 90) from the SDLRS as your starter guide for self-directed learning behaviors to target in personalized learning plans. For agency's sake, you may want to share the list with students and allow each to select one target behavior.

For elementary students, schedule one two-week personalized learning plan with guided formative self-assessments fifteen minutes every day. Plan think-pair-share pairs, magic circles, or other formats so students can share with open-ended stems to guide them: "I am pleased that . . . ", "I'm proud that . . . ", or "I'm making good progress because . . . ." For middle and high school students, save fifteen minutes of class time each week for students to self-assess, perhaps with open-ended guides such as Mrs. Potter's questions, or share with stems as paired partners or trios. Individuals can choose whether they need to carry on a personalized learning plan skill for added weeks or start a new skill. It is helpful when working alone to set up pairs and trios for two-way feedback.

To the degree you already have, or will, adopt one or more of these methods is the degree to which you will observe agency in your students. If you hold on to low-agency practices that dictate orders to students, you bypass opportunities to expand their intrinsic motivation and instead require rewards and punishments to keep them on *your* track. These tables help you listen and look for concrete examples to measure the agency in your classroom. The tables are specific to developmental levels, as elementary students and middle and high school students use different words when talking about the choices they are free to make, the actions they choose to take, and the skills that help them control their learning. Table 4.2 provides middle and high school examples.

If you are comfortable with low-level support, commonly allow procedural decisions, and are ready to move out of your—and students'—comfort zones, you can advance to the second level by empowering all or even just a few students with the skills for self-regulation and self-directed learning. You can call on table 4.2 to help guide from the side, monitoring progress and ensuring all stay engaged.

You see the most significant student agency gains when you decide to go for the biggest impact at the highest agency level. At this level, you make plans for projects saturated with opportunities for self-directed learning. You target specific deeper learning skills and talents which promote students' decision making as they plan, complete, and assess their own learning experiences. In his seminal definition, Malcolm Knowles (1975) describes this as "a process in which individuals take the initiative with or without the help of others in

Table 4.2: Levels of Agency

What Teachers Design	What Students Do	What Students Say
Low-level agency *The teacher allows opportunities for student voice and choice.*		
<ul><li>Thinking strategies such as graphic organizers, open-ended prompts for discussion (*explain why*, *compare*), volunteers requested to answer question or do task</li><li>Formal cooperative groups with prompts to understand, analyze, or evaluate ideas</li><li>Peer pairs, think-pair-share with open-ended prompts</li><li>Book and article reading choice; learning method choice (online or print), personal topic essay choice, digital story choice</li><li>Individual projects, games, journals, portfolios, or personal playlists</li><li>Flipped lessons</li></ul>	<ul><li>Select practice problems on a worksheet.</li><li>Select topics for essays.</li><li>Select research topics or resources.</li><li>Complete written prompts to teacher questions.</li><li>Select materials for journals and portfolios.</li><li>Volunteer answers in class discussion led by the teacher.</li><li>Engage in think-pair-share and paired partner tasks and respond to prompts.</li><li>Engage in partner lab work.</li><li>Observe and comment on others' work during gallery walks.</li><li>Create exit tickets.</li></ul>	<ul><li>"I am doing the odd numbers on this worksheet."</li><li>"I have selected option four on the computer screen."</li><li>"I want to write about my sister's struggle with cancer."</li><li>"I want to ask how atoms are formed."</li><li>"I would like to be the one who . . ."</li><li>"I want to read about blue whales."</li><li>"I am going to read this book."</li><li>"I used the page checker from Class Tools."</li><li>"Our answer is . . ."</li><li>"We learned that a square is . . ."</li><li>"We think that Paul Martin was a good prime minister because . . ."</li><li>"I liked how our team shared . . ."</li><li>"Our team discovered how to research . . . ."</li><li>"Your example helped me because . . ."</li><li>"I was pleased our team agreed on a definition of . . ."</li><li>"What we did well in this experiment was . . ."</li><li>"The help we need to improve is . . ."</li></ul>
Middle-level agency *The teacher encourages student voice and choice.*		
<ul><li>Increased opportunities for self-direction in teamwork, hands-on activities, labs, problem- and project-based-learning, inquiries, and personalized learning plans</li><li>Initial processes based on students' prior experiences with each element</li><li>Increased opportunities at each strategy element or model by encouraging students to accept increased challenges and by coaching improvement with guiding rubrics as needed</li><li>Guiding rubrics to encourage skills transfer to more difficult content models</li><li>Volunteer opportunities or different answers to open-ended questions</li><li>Constructive feedback for work in progress as well as lesson, unit, or project end</li></ul>	<ul><li>Engage in cooperative inquiry with the teacher deciding who will determine roles, rules, responsibilities, and assessments during the task and encourage increasing agency as students learn how to work in teams.</li><li>Engage in differentiated amounts and degrees of agency based on prior personal performances.</li><li>Engage in maker labs, science labs, or other hands-on activities with teacher-determined amount of student voice and choice (set goals and outcomes, select activity, select materials, select assessment format).</li><li>Students respond to teacher or peer provided.</li></ul>	<ul><li>"I agree to the role of . . ."</li><li>"I am responsible for . . ."</li><li>"I am not sure of how I will . . ."</li><li>"As recorder in this team, it is my job to . . ."</li><li>"I wonder . . ."</li><li>"What I know about being the team leader is . . ."</li><li>"From this list of goals you gave me, I want to . . ."</li><li>"I can improve most if my next outcome is number . . . on the list."</li><li>"Our team has voted to do the . . . experiment on the list."</li><li>"Team, let's review our norms for brainstorming and voting."</li><li>"Your feedback tells me I can add . . . to our plan."</li><li>"Our team would like to use the following approved sites . . ."</li><li>"The big idea we want to investigate is . . ."</li><li>"You have told me that I could improve . . . by adding (removing, modifying) . . ."</li><li>"We agree that our solution needs more . . ."</li></ul>

continued →

• Constructive peer feedback throughout student work and at its end • Design elements required and how much choice is allowed per element (picking strategies)	• Engage in PBL inquiry via teacher-prescribed learning strategies (cooperative learning plus graphic organizers, guiding questions, hands-on activities) to make a whole-class presentation; assess performance with set rubrics. • Solve ill-structured authentic problems. • Work with teacher-made all-class personalized learning plans with teacher-designed and assessed outcomes and guiding rubrics. • Review teacher feedback on a guiding rubric and give feedback.	• "Our team will use what we know about brainstorming and then vote on an idea for this project." • "Let's review the roles and responsibilities for this task and decide who does what." • "Our plan is to use a matrix to distinguish characteristics of . . . " • "Here are the strategies we plan: . . . " • "We intend to jigsaw the topic . . . " • "What if we use the . . . strategy here?" • "For our presentation, we plan to do the following: . . . " • "I have selected these criteria for the guiding rubric for . . . " • "We understand that during this project, our team will agree on the strategies (guiding rubrics, products) to use after you have approved the plan." • "Here is what I have done well for this outcome." • "What suggestions do you have for us?" • "What I could improve in the next round is . . . " • "Help I could use is . . . " • "I appreciate the feedback. What I will do differently is . . . " • "When making choices about . . . in this personalized learning plan, I will try to . . . " • "I want to choose how . . . " • "I appreciate how you . . . "

High-level agency
The teacher intentionally develops and amplifies student voice and choice.

• With students, personalized learning plans focused on attributes, attitudes, and skills that are the hallmarks of student agency
• Digital skills in all plans
• Personalized learning plans, with students choosing and assessing all elements aligned to lessons, units, and projects
• Team collaboration in high-engagement, project-based inquiry, problem-based learning, and personalized learning plans
• Learning stations, science, and maker labs to stimulate hands-on work
• Opportunities for students to seek different answers or solutions in all tasks
• Opportunities for all to give and get feedback to partners in a round-robin
• Celebrations for attempts to answer questions without disparaging wrong or inadequate responses
• Opportunities for near and far transfer (page 96) of personalized learning plan skills in the context of lessons and projects
• Opportunities for students to plan, do, and assess complex cognition needed to increase agency
	• Brainstorm and select deeper learning outcomes for class, teams, or individuals plus a strategy and options for student-made personalized learning plans and rubrics to include teacher and peer feedback.
	• Plan, do, and assess deeper learning experiences based on interests and standards.
	• Determine changes in learning plans.
	• Brainstorm and select best ideas for increasing student agency.
	• Select online research sites and articles.
	• Engage in two-way feedback with peers and teacher.
	• Value increasing their deeper learning skills for near and far transfer.
	• Think about what and how they are learning as related to college and career futures.
	• Express pride and pleasure in learning.
	• Reflect on their goals.
	• Adopt goal setting for learning outside of class.
		• "For my personalized learning plan, I wonder if . . . "
		• "I would like your feedback for this plan (strategy, rubric)."
		• "We have followed the template. Could you give us your feedback about . . . ?"
		• "This is what I am (or we are) interested in for this project. I (we) would like your feedback on . . . "
		• "We have voted on this way of including your suggestions to . . . "
		• "I am changing my personalized learning plan. Do these meet the criteria for . . . ?"
		• "We have changed our plan with your feedback about . . . "
		• "Assessing our choices in this project, we are pleased that . . . "
		• "Assessing my (or our) choices in this personalized learning plan, I am (or we are) proud I (or we) . . . "
		• "I did my best work in this group when I . . . "
		• "We could have made a better choice by . . . "
		• "We voted to ask . . . to help us . . . "
		• "We appreciate your help to . . . "
		• To peer team:
		  • "We have to choose . . . "
		  • "It is our responsibility to . . . "
		  • "Let's vote on . . . "
		  • "All who agree, give a thumbs-up for . . . "
		  • "There is (is not) a consensus on . . . "
		  • ". . . has suggested we . . . What do we want to do?"
		  • ". . . has told us this is our decision. How should we proceed?"
		  • "Let's vote on our response to . . . 's feedbac."
		  • "How do we think our freedom to make learning choices will play out when we are in college (trade) classes?"
		  • "How do we want to assess this project?"

diagnosing their learning needs, formulating goals, identifying human and material resources, and evaluating learning outcomes" (p. 18).

The degree to which you see the behaviors, hear students' choice-making words, and see their actions indicates how ready they are to take their freedom and responsibility seriously when deciding what and how they learn. From low-agency lectures or programmed learning tasks during which students' only agency may be to take notes or select a different computer key, to high-agency models of teaching such as problem-based or project-based learning in which students face choices in every element, your eyes and ears gather data on how much student agency is in practice. If you observe students not making good choices or hear agency, you may have to engage in a heart-to-heart talk in which you address the issue. A private conference is appropriate for one student. When it is a larger problem, address those involved and call on your problem-solving skills to come up with agency.

The personalized learning plan is a strong force for boosting student agency, because it not only allows multiple opportunities for student voice and choice, such as choosing outcomes, choosing projects, potentially co-creating guiding rubrics, offering peer feedback, incorporating feedback, and offering student-to-teacher feedback, it structures the chance for reflection on their feelings of accomplishment and the chance for helpful feedback from an important other—you. As agency develops, any apathy about self-direction gives way to interest not just in choosing how one learns, but also in selecting issues that adults may not wish to discuss as the subject matter of learning in classrooms or remote stations.

When completing the personalized learning plan, students may show increased amounts of higher agency in one or more of the following ways.

- By selecting and developing skill outcomes to create, implement, complete, and assess as personal goals
- By increasing choice making when planning with the personalized learning plan template
- By giving and taking warm peer feedback when asked
- By organizing and maintaining a folder or portfolio with completed playbooks for each plan, and by creating and editing those playbooks

- By reviewing personal progress over time with an increasingly sharper eye
- By communicating about progress and folder or portfolio contents to parents, peers, and teachers

How Do I Encourage and Develop Student Agency?

My experience helping teachers adopt strategies for promoting agency tells me to bypass low agency. Teachers with classrooms mired in low-level choices should at least go to mid-level. All can go to high by adopting personalized learning plans as the starting point. By jumping to other high-level strategies and turning *do* statements into *I need to learn how to promote agency by* statements, teachers have not only collected a database of information that tells them where to start, but also created student need-to-knows, which they can turn into student personalized learning plan outcomes.

If students are coming from a class with little experience making mid-level choices, it's important that teachers assume responsibility for making each element through Lev S. Vygotsky's (1978) lens of increased responsibility by scaffolding the choices they make using the gradual release of responsibility. This translates into your modeling the steps for completing a personalized learning plan. Students complete the plan, and then you assess the result. You also guide a reflection so students can directly identify their increased feelings of competence and confidence. With a second personalized learning plan, preferably with a playbook, you and students construct the plan together. The students with the playbook carry out the plan. You give feedback and guide students' self-assessment and reflection. You can repeat this step as often as is helpful. Next, students help each other in pairs with you offering feedback on all elements including self-assessment feedback and reflection. Figure 4.3 (page 96) shows sample need-to-know statements adapted from the high-level agency in table 4.2 (page 93).

With the information you collect, you can prepare need-to-know minilessons that fill in missing background skills from levels 1 and 2. The following examples are grade-level-appropriate minilessons for identified need-to-know labs. A different skill is targeted in each scenario.

High-Level Agency Statements	Need-to-Know Adaptions
Please rate how well you can do each item by using the scale. Share any ideas or questions about any item. For those items that you give yourself a 0 or 1 for, rewrite it as a need-to-know statement. Rating scale: 0 = I don't know how to do this. 1 = I can do this with help. 2 = I am doing OK. 3 = I can show others how.	
Students brainstorm and select deeper learning outcomes for class, teams, or individuals.	____ Brainstorming for deeper learning outcomes
Students select online research sites and articles.	____ Picking online sites and specific articles to read so I can reach the outcome
Students engage in two-way feedback with peers and teacher.	____ I am comfortable giving positive feedback to my teammates.
Students listen to positive feedback from peers without discomfort.	____ I am comfortable getting positive feedback from my teammates.
Students give positive feedback to the teacher.	____ I am comfortable giving positive feedback to my teacher.
Students are comfortable hearing positive feedback from the teacher.	____ I am comfortable getting positive feedback from you.

Figure 4.3: Need-to-know statements.

Visit **go.SolutionTree.com/instruction** *for a free reproducible version of this figure.*

Key statements regarding the following scenario include "Even if I have a great idea, I can't seem to develop a plan for making it work" and "It takes me a while to get started on new projects" (Guglielmino, 1977).

Jackie, a fourth-grade teacher, noticed that several of her students were not starting to write their ABC books. One told her, "I don't care about books" while others chatted excitedly as they sketched the letters; another just stared into space. With most of the class busy, Jackie slipped a note to the five she was inviting to meet at the language arts learning center. She announced that anyone interested in joining the familiar need-to-know group should "Hop on over!"

Later, Jackie started the group by saying, "I see that some of you are having a tough time getting started with your ABC book." After a series of "how many" probes, she offered, "It sounds to me you all know what to make and that you all can recite the letters from A to Z. Am I correct?" When she got blank looks, she added, "How about just a thumbs-up or down?" Confirming all thumbs-up, she started a round-robin alphabet count until confirming each response with a "Yes!", "Hurrah!", or "Way to go!"

More prompting questions led her to understand that the group's common denominator was not knowing how to get started. She decided to show how to stop, think, and make a plan before starting the assignment. She started with A. "A for me is an alligator!" She clapped her extended arms and flashed wide eyes. "Who knows what an alligator is?" Many hands waved. "Me." "Me" "Me". "OK," she said. "I see Alison with an A's hand up."

Knowing the benefits of a good plan to start a project like the ABC book, she led them through planning by making steps to follow. She started by showing the group how the finished book with all the letters and pictures they drew was their goal. If they could, they were able to add the animals' names. At this point she walked the five students through the steps of gathering materials they would need. With their attention falling off at this point, she invited everyone to make a first sketch of their favorite letter. She knew she could regather them on the next day for feedback, more letters, animals, and the rest of the plan. After everyone returned to their desks, she watched each student start.

Here is a secondary-level need-to-know minilesson related to nanotechnology, a science elective. The skill is making a plan that I manage. A key statement regarding the following scenario includes "In a classroom situation, I expect my instructor to tell all class members exactly what to do at all times" (Guglielmino, 1977).

Gina had complained to her parents that her teacher was disorganized: "He never gives good instructions. He just asks questions when I don't know what he wants us to do." After an earful from Gina's mom, Mr. Reardon, the nanotechnology teacher, invited Gina to talk with him during her free period. He listened as she explained how she struggled in classes where the teacher didn't tell the class exactly what to do: "It's really hard in your class because we have these big projects. I need to know what to do—all the steps like in a recipe."

After Gina specified several instances where lack of precise instructions confused her, Mr. Reardon proposed a possible solution so Gina would know how to handle open-ended instructions. "I like to think I am helping you to think like a scientist. That requires two types of thinking. Sometimes you have to be open to exploring ideas and making your own decisions, and sometimes you need to follow precise instructions. I sense that the former, the open-ended questions, makes you uncomfortable. I would like to propose that you make your next personalized learning plan focus on learning ways to deal with open-ended instructions. I will help with that if you want, and I will be more attentive to helping you learn that open way of thinking. I already know you are a really good student who works hard on every assignment. You attend to details as well as any student I've taught. I do want to help make it easier so you can lower your anxiety with open-ended problems. How does that sound?"

Taking the risk to acknowledge student needs has proven to be a valuable teaching strategy for increasing student motivation. From the time Donna M. Ogle introduced the KWL organizer in 1986, teachers have developed a variety of prior-knowledge checks to identify missing knowledge or experience (Bransford, Brown, & Cocking, 1999; Knight, 2018). Steve Zipkes and his colleagues at Cedars International Next Gen High School, where every lesson every day is PBL, have made the need-to-know lab a common strategy (S. Zipkes, personal communication, September 2020). Even when teachers can predict with accuracy what background knowledge students will need to know, the first day of a new PBL starts with a whole-class need-to-know brainstorm. Through the PBL activities, teachers keep an eye out for emergent needs. Either the teacher or student can ask for a workshop (S. Zipkes, personal communication, September 2020).

When teachers introduce a new way of teaching or a new topic to study, few students are in the habit of automatically checking their prior knowledge. Teachers cannot possibly predict everything students need to know before they start a unit. Often, the need to know does not spring up until the middle of a lesson. Combining a KWL strategy in a need-to-know assessment at the start or in the middle of a lesson gives increased assurance that students don't confuse themselves. As you note their needs, it's important to have a way to respond as you put information into practice.

How Do I Promote Agency With Two-Way Feedback?

When employing personalized learning plans, two-way feedback is what you want to take place between you and your students, and among your students. Sometimes it flows back and forth between two students who invite others' ideas on a personalized learning plan or lesson's product; sometimes a teacher invites feedback about his or her methods; at other times, students give and get feedback from the teacher on a mutual concern. There is no single way the flow must occur. What is important is a teacher being willing to hear student voices and students feeling comfortable enough to respond. By its nature, two-way feedback—another of the highest-effect methods Hattie (2009) identifies—announces to students that their voices are important. Opportunities for two-way feedback appear throughout the process directed to a single student, teams, or the whole class. Specific instances include before, during, and after.

- Defining the outcome
- Selecting materials
- Completing learning tasks or strategies
- Attending need-to-know labs
- Developing the guiding rubric
- Making products
- Presenting products

- Assessing
- Reflecting
- Conferencing, including with parents

Begin two-way feedback as early in the school year as possible, with an explanation of what your feedback method is, its goals, and how it will work with personalized learning plans. Rely on the interactive whiteboard to share a guiding rubric. Without singling out any individual or small group, select a completed class activity and share the key points about what was done well and how improvements could be made without violating any individual's confidentiality. You can share this information as a presentation as your lead into the process.

Even if you design every element and hand a personalized learning plan to students, you have allowed them low-level agency. You can enrich those opportunities as soon as you introduce two-way feedback with open-ended prompting questions like those in table 4.3. Unlike one-word closed questions, which require a single right answer, an open-ended question leaves it up to the respondent to *choose* what and how much to say. This allows a teacher to acknowledge the quality of thinking with feedback like, "I appreciate how many ideas . . . (the uniqueness of your ideas, the depth of your ideas)."

At this level, the more open-ended prompts you can provide, the more agency you are promoting. If a student struggles with these, drop back to forced-choice prompts such as "Do you feel you need more time to reach this goal, or do you want a smaller goal?", "Do you want to know more about . . . or about . . . ?", "Do you need more help doing . . . or . . . ?" When you hear a student say things from the middle-level agency row in table 4.2 (page 93), such as "I agree to the role of . . . " or "I am responsible to . . . ", slowly move forward to those agency strategies.

At the high level, where students make far more decisions about their personalized learning plans, two-way feedback will look more like a conversation. At this level, students may say "I need you to help me with X" and after providing the help or guidance, you might ask, "How did the help I gave you benefit your work with creative thinking? Learning transfer?"

How Do I Assess How My Feedback Impacts Student Agency?

The personalized learning plan allows you and students to personalize student goals as SMART outcomes and tightly align any guiding rubric you and students aligned with the SMART outcome with the following three standards for effective goals.

1. A = Achievable (Do you feel you can produce this outcome in the time and with resources you have chosen?)
2. B = Believable (Given this is a new goal for you, how convinced are you that you have the talent or skills to accomplish the results you want?)

Table 4.3: Open-Ended Prompts

Prompt Type	Example Prompts
Goal prompt	• "What can you tell me about how you think you can achieve this goal?" • "What help will you need from me?" • "What are the difficulties you feel in this goal?" • "What do you need to know that will help you do well?"
Strategy prompt	• "What do you feel . . . will help you reach the goal? If not, what might?" • "How do you want me to change?"
Self-assessment prompt	• "How well did you reach this goal?" • "What score would you give each benchmark? Can you tell me why?"
Feedback prompt	• "What do you like about this plan?" • "What would you change?" • "What help do you want from me?"

3. C = Conceivable (How SMART is the outcome for this plan?)

When students' positive feedback aligns with the ABC standards, you know you are close to making goals manageable and measurable chunks that students will judge possible to do. When verbal and nonverbal clues tell you a student's agency is low, you know you must increase the stakes and numbers of choices the student can handle. Table 4.4 shows the ABC prompts that clarify to what degree feedback will empower students. Teachers ask themselves these questions before and while they work with students to clarify and decide their personalized learning plan outcomes.

How Do I Provide Agency-Enhancing Feedback?

With your ABC feedback, a student is more likely to accept what you say and transform your words into actions and ideas into performances that lead to personalized learning plan outcomes. Add in strong opportunities for students to reciprocate with two-way feedback, and the odds increase. The following guidelines help you provide feedback that enhances student agency.

- Set feedback criteria.
- Establish norms for respectful two-way feedback.
- Encourage peer feedback.
- Build teamwork skills.
- Guide the feedback process.
- Develop feedback skills.
- Save all feedback.

Set Feedback Criteria

With SMART criteria in a guiding rubric, you benchmark specific behaviors to which students can respond. Specific, measurable, achievable, relevent, and timely criteria allow you to target those behaviors that will make the most difference in a student's accomplishments. Refer to the section What Tools Work Best When Assessing Personalized Learning Plan Outcomes? (page 69) in chapter 3 for more information about rubrics.

Establish Norms for Respectful Two-Way Feedback

In a reciprocal climate with strong student-teacher relationships, a personalized learning plan gives you and students increased opportunities to talk with each other. With the template, you collaborate in construction of a mutual agreement. When you attach guiding rubrics to a personalized learning plan's outcomes, you make it easy on yourself and students to share specific feedback, guided by specific criteria.

These conversations are practical means to influence what researchers note as strong influencers of academic achievement. A comprehensive review of school climate research (Maxwell, Reynolds, Lee, Subasic, & Bromhead, 2017) supports the understanding that a positive school climate promotes students' abilities to achieve more highly, exerting "a powerful impact on academic achievement." For example, academic emphasis (Goddard, Hoy, & Hoy, 2000; Hoy & Sabo, 1998), academic optimism (Smith & Hoy, 2007), and strong teacher-student relationships (Cook et al., 2018; Martin & Collie, 2019) are particularly influential. Specifically, student-teacher relationships effectively work as a protective factor for school adjustment including academic achievement as well as

Table 4.4: Reveal Agency Level With ABC

Feedback Standard	Questions That Reveal Agency Level
Achievable: I think I can.	• Do students feel they can achieve or accomplish the outcomes in the personalized learning plan with my feedback? • Is that feeling based on evidence from prior helpful feedback from me?
Believable: I believe I will.	• Do students believe or have the confidence in themselves to achieve the personalized learning plan outcome with my feedback? • Do they believe that my feedback is helpful enough to achieve the outcome?
Conceivable: I know what I want done.	• Have students conceived or thought through the plan with my feedback so they can make the progress required? • Do they see my feedback as helpful and hopeful?

conduct and behavioral problems, especially for adolescents transitioning from middle school to high school (Longobardi, Prino, Marengo, & Settanni, 2016).

With a guiding rubric, a teacher keeps feedback focused on criteria. The prompts give precedence to those the rubric guides him or her to emphasize. For instance, with a rubric for *getting started on a project*, a stop-and-think criterion on the rubric signals the kind of feedback the teacher might give a student who impulsively starts a task willy-nilly. The teacher can block out other observations and say, "Alexander, I see you have jumped right in. What is it that you are hoping to accomplish? What is your plan?"

At key points while completing the personalized learning plan, the criteria promote voice and choice by encouraging self-assessment fueled, when asked, by your feedback. The first feedback is teacher strong. As the student begins to internalize the feedback and the teacher takes one, then two, and then three steps back to increase student agency, and when she observes his increased self-management—stopping to think before he starts a plan—then the teacher shifts to warm feedback to encourage more agency. Ultimately, she can ask the student to self-assess how competently he stops to think before acting.

Encourage Peer Feedback

Whenever possible, promote two-way feedback between students. Peer feedback offers various benefits, not the least of which is that "reviewing peers' work is also likely to help students become better reviewers of their own work and to revise and improve their own work" (Rollinson, 2005, as cited in Double, McGrane, & Hopfenbeck, 2019). Peer two-way feedback can occur by setting up peer teams with two or three students per team. These teams stay together so they can grow comfortable getting and giving SMART two-way feedback. In this way, you add to the sharing culture in your classroom as students develop friendships, continue to build trust and mutual respect, and expand their interpersonal relationship skills.

Build Teamwork Skills

In the cooperative learning literature, Johnson and Johnson (n.d.) designate groups like critical-friend teams, which stay together over extended time, as *base groups*. By staying together through a semester, students are more ready to develop their teamwork trusting each other sufficiently as friends who can critique each other's work without damaging their team relationship. These teams are ideal for working together on personalized learning plans, especially when students share a personalized learning plan or the base group members are sticking with a personalized learning plan beyond a single lesson.

In addition to long-term base groups in which students can become friends, you may move students in and out of short-term groups. In this way, students have many more opportunities to build positive relationships and build a cohesive whole-class climate with multiple opportunities for you to structure peer-to-peer feedback.

When students are giving and getting feedback in a peer group, you engender agency by first guiding and then letting each team decide its logistics: time, exchange method, norms, roles, and so forth. If you schedule personalized learning plan base group meetings for twenty to thirty minutes per week, you will provide sufficient time to advance skills for two-way feedback. The more you encourage this practice, the more you will see evidence of improved interpersonal relationships (page 37) that foster mutual trust and respect and end with better achievement results. This evidence will include students giving and getting the honest, warm feedback that is a hallmark of effective critical-friend teams. It is also likely that you will see students relying on these skills as they interact with others (including you) outside their time, in other situations.

Of course, you are more likely to gain observable results if you prepare students to give and get ABC feedback. In the setup for critical-friend base groups, model for your class what appropriate feedback looks like and sounds like. For guided practice, peer conferences advance knowledge and skills for getting and giving warm feedback. You can encourage students to use sticky notes or index cards to share feedback. The cards and notes are a recording medium. When feedback is in writing, especially when multiples are involved, it makes it easier for students to step back, read each note, and save the feedback with other products from the lesson or project. If you present guiding rubrics on single-point templates, you can coach more easily.

Guide the Feedback Process

Guiding rubrics allow you to structure and build skills for two-way peer feedback. The single-point rubric in figure 4.3 (page 96) shows criteria identifying helpful behaviors by someone giving warm feedback. The reproducible "Single-Point Guiding Rubric—Grades 3–12" (page 226) is a template you can use. With its emphasis on feedback, a student can distribute copies and request feedback from several peers, and collect and consider all copies. When multiple students are involved, you heighten agency by letting each team set the logistics and follow norms for feedback that you and the class have agreed on.

After peer reviews, the teacher may add feedback as well. The touchy issue that may arise involves trust. Does the teacher trust everyone has followed norms and not read peer feedback, or does the teacher read what the peers said? My experience says *trust until a norm violation occurs*. Then handle the misbehavior as you would other trust breakers.

When considering other management issues for feedback such as how often to review personalized learning plans and rubrics, what data to keep, and what follow-up support to give, keep it simple. Do it once per grading period unless your eyes and ears tell you otherwise. Don't let the rubrics take over. Remember the *process* to enable self-directed learning is primary. The paper merely facilitates that process. Figure 4.4 (page 102) shows a single-point guiding rubric for elementary peer feedback.

Develop Feedback Skills

As found in the sayings of Buddha (as cited in Kyōkai, 2008), "Whatever words we utter should be chosen with care for people will hear them and be influenced by them for good or ill" (p. 83). These words may have special resonance for a teacher, especially one guiding students in effective and empathic ways of delivering feedback. You help students share feedback so that their peers will be influenced for good, not ill. The following options exist for how students may share feedback.

- **Warm feedback:** New team peers react best to warm, or encouraging, feedback. When you encourage students to give warm feedback by focusing on what a peer did well, predictable defensive resistance is lowered. Warm feedback accentuates the positive by highlighting a specific accomplishment. The following sentence stems suggest ways to deliver feedback that highlights the positive.
    - "I am pleased that you . . . "
    - "I see your description of specific examples of what you did well, such as . . . "
    - "I like the way you . . . "
    - "Here's a bravo for how you . . . "

- **Cool feedback:** After a student's openness to warm feedback signals she is ready to accept a challenge to think more deeply, it's vital to check for receptivity to cool feedback. While maintaining a warm tone, feedback givers build on sharing what their peer has done well by asking permission to give constructive critique: "Would you mind if I give you constructive criticism about your responses in this rubric?" When the feedback receiver indicates that it's OK, peers are set to probe each other with such questions as the following. However, a *no* is a *no*. Observe it and let it go. If a student falls into a *no* pattern, have a private conference to determine the reason (usually a fear) and come up with a plan to move ahead with OKs. When selecting a stem, react to the students' words or work. Mostly you will ask for clarifications. These examples show various ways to probe so that students clarify or expand their thinking in a personalized learning plan. Similar stems could probe any other subject's artifacts.
    - "I wonder how this statement . . . fits your goals?"
    - "I can't tell if you want to do . . . or . . . . Which do you prefer?"
    - "How does this idea fit with your plan's outcome?"
    - "I need a clearer picture here. Can you give me an example?"
    - "I'm confused by this statement. Will you explain it in a different way?"

- **Hard feedback:** If a student agrees, peers can provide the most difficult feedback to give and to act on: hard feedback. By trusting a peer's words suggesting significant changes in personalized learning outcomes or approach, a student receiving hard feedback signals readiness for change. It is important that all suggestions for change communicate empathy couched in an encouraging tone. With hard feedback added to peer two-way dialogue, peers might prompt dialogue through questions, such as those that follow.

Name: Roderick	Date: 9/23
Feedback is by: ☐ Self ☐ Teacher ☐ Peers: Johnna ☐ Other: _____	

Example	Criteria	Suggestions for Improvement
You looked at me and didn't talk when I talked.	You listened.	I don't have any.
You wondered why I chose that quote for my project, because you didn't know what it meant.	You didn't make fun.	Give an example.
You said I could try this one website you used before.	You gave positive suggestions.	I could always use more suggestions, so maybe offer more?
You weren't mean when you weren't sure about what the quote meant.	You respected my ideas.	I felt relieved that you weren't mean, so I don't have suggestions.
Your website idea can give me more ideas for making my project better.	You helped me reflect or look forward.	Maybe if you ask questions like Mr. B does, I can think about what I've done in the past to reflect.

Figure 4.4: Single-point guiding rubric for peer feedback–Elementary example.

Visit go.SolutionTree.com/instruction for a free reproducible version of this figure.

- *Analysis*—"How does your selected strategy help you achieve your stated outcome? Let's explore alternatives."
- *Evaluative*—"What are the pluses and minuses to your strategy?" and then discuss a different tack.
- *Hypothetical*—"What will happen if . . . ? And what will happen if . . . ?"

Save All Feedback

Feedback that helps students improve a personal performance requires time to reflect on the given ideas. After reflection, time is needed to revise a plan and take new actions. As a guide on the side, working in tandem with students instead of determining their entire paths, you want each student to adopt a way to observe progress over time. It helps if you establish a record system that the student manages. The system will offer a place to store feedback along with plans and artifacts. Through the school year, students can retain their feedback and other important documents and assess their progress.

You can set up your classroom storage system either with manila folders or preferably, with digital folders in Google Docs or an equivalent LMS. If needed, provide a playlist and protocols to show students how to make and access their personal folders (page 199). Each student will manage her folder with each rubric and its artifacts organized by date and subject. When students repeat a personalized learning plan because they needed more development, they should bundle the materials so that you and others with access can review progress over time. When it comes time for parent-teacher conferences, students present a table of contents along with selected documents.

Figure 4.5 is a sample playlist for a table of contents. This playlist is workable in manila folders stored at your classroom desk or in each student's digital folder. If online, students can set up a portfolio master folder with labeled subfolders. Only you and the student should have access (via codes) to the confidential portfolio. Figure 4.6 is a student playbook for creating a table of contents.

> Dear student,
>
> Please make and store this folder as instructed by me. You will receive an A (Acceptable) or a U (unacceptable) each quarter. The criteria for an A is having all items organized as per the following table of contents and all items being present. If you are unsure where to place an item, first check with your learning team. If they can't help, email me at teacher@teacher.edu with your question.
>
> Please don't wait to enter your items in the folder. My exact collection day will be unannounced. Different teams will have different dates. You will have opportunities each month to update your folders. If you are absent on those dates, see me to discuss your options.
>
> The table of contents is as follows. File items in the folder by the date you complete them.
>
> 1. Folder title (the lesson or project title) with your first and last name and the date completed on the tab
>   a. Personalized learning plan template
>   b. Guiding rubrics
>   i. Teacher feedback
>   ii. Peer feedback, including the giver's first and last name
>   iii. Other feedback, including the giver's first and last name
>   iv. Self-assessment
>   v. Final (summative) assessment
>   c. Artifacts
>   d. Final product evidence (photographs and explanatory notes)
>   e. Additional unmentioned items

Figure 4.5: Student table of contents playlist.

*Visit **go.SolutionTree.com/instruction** for a free reproducible version of this figure.*

> 1. Follow the playlist order.
> 2. Make dividers for each set of project, lesson, or unit items.
> 3. Sequence items by date completed.
> 4. When entering rubrics, make sure you date and file them accordingly.
> 5. Take photographs of final products with dates and write notes about them that anyone can understand.
> 6. Add each item to the portfolio on the day you finish the project, lesson, or unit.
> 7. Get help from your learning team as needed.
> 8. Keep the contents secure. Do not share your access code.

Figure 4.6: Student table of contents playbook—Example.

*Visit **go.SolutionTree.com/instruction** for a free reproducible version of this figure.*

How Do I Find the Time and Place to Give and Get Two-Way Feedback?

An important part of promoting two-way feedback is making thoughtful decisions about time and place for the process. Your desk, a private corner, or outside the classroom are locations that allow for the privacy you will want for intentional one-to-one or small-group conferences. Otherwise, you may confer informally at students' desks or workstations. When you want to give feedback to small groups, schedule one group at a time. If you need to give feedback specific to one student, schedule a conference in a space that is as private as possible.

When you are scheduling private or small-group conferences in elementary school classrooms, pick a time each day and bunch the conferences. With thirty students in your class, scheduling fifteen minutes twice a day will enable you to give personalized learning plan feedback to each student each week. In middle and high school classrooms, schedule twenty minutes one day per week over a month; for more intense conferencing, you might schedule formal feedback conferences at the rate of four per day. If you are teaching grade 6 or higher, consider scheduling conferences during a planning period that aligns with students' free periods or study halls. You also have the option of conferring before and after school hours or during lunch. With rubrics to focus the feedback, you will need fewer than five minutes for most group or individual conferences.

Each student should see the rubric, and the dialogue should focus on benchmarks. If students have questions about what to do next, either allow a few minutes extra or visit those who need more understanding at their desks or workstations for a tutorial, or schedule time outside school hours.

For conferences to succeed *during* class, it is essential that your climate supports differentiation. You must be able to trust other students to stick with the work scheduled for them. For instance, if your style is lecturing, you would talk for the first half of a period and confer during the second half, one student at a time, when other students are starting homework, working together on peer feedback, checking notes, reading, or completing some other assignment. If you employ active learning strategies such as cooperative learning, you will find it easier to differentiate assignments that allow you to schedule conferences.

TAKEAWAYS

This organizer gives you the chance to ready yourself for adopting methods to increase student agency.

CHAPTER 5
SKILL TRANSFER

I have been impressed with the urgency of doing. Knowing is not enough; we must apply. Being willing is not enough; we must do.

—Leonardo da Vinci

When Apollo 13's crew radioed, "OK, Houston, we've had a problem here," the problem was an unexplained explosion (as cited in Woods, Kemppanen, Turhanov, & Waugh, 2015). What followed was mission control's collaboration with the Apollo crew to return them safely to earth. Together, they transferred book knowledge into problem-solving action. They did as Johann Wolfgang von Goethe (as cited in Faust, n.d.) advised, "Knowing is not enough; we must apply."

Knowing how to apply and transfer information to solve real-world problems, make pivotal decisions, or design innovative solutions may be more important than recalling facts and procedures. Although teachers at levels as early as preschool (Eastern Connecticut State University, n.d.) encourage students to apply critical- and creative-thinking skills in a variety of ways, they often lack the know-how to promote intentional *transfer* of complex thinking skills into more complex patterns of thinking such as problem solving, decision making, and design thinking (Harding, de Barba, & Goh, 2016).

You will find answers to this chapter's question as you investigate how to integrate skill transfer into lessons and projects that promote deeper learning outcomes. You will compare different purposes, types, and tools for bridging the three complex thinking skill sets into tight and loose problem solving, design thinking, and social-emotional rich decision-making scenarios across the curriculum. By using grade-level examples, you will discover how to integrate these skill-rich deeper learning patterns across the curriculum.

Driving question: How do I activate learning transfer to produce deeper outcomes?

What Is Learning Transfer?

Learning transfer is the effective application of current knowledge, skills, and mindsets into a new situation or context. In the K–12 classroom, the simplest transfer occurs when a student uses prior knowledge (how to use end punctuation, for example) or experience (how to score in basketball practice with a layup, for example) to apply what she knows in a new context (such as punctuating a paragraph or scoring with a layup in a game) or to produce a new outcome (such as a paragraph without end punctuation errors or a rebound to score a two-point basket).

When aiming for deeper learning outcomes, students transfer a complex thinking skill (such as analysis) to understand more difficult material (analysis of a character to analysis of an entire short story) or one complex skill (such as drawing conclusions) into a new, more complex skill (such as drawing conclusions into problem solving). Transferring deeper learning outcomes requires achieving outcomes more complex than applying or using. Transferring across contexts or in novel situations is a tough thing to master as well.

Researchers have provided insights into the value of learning transfer (Baldwin, Ford, & Blume, 2017; Perkins & Salomon, 1988). Their studies note that the most productive transfer occurs when students are asked to apply deeper learning skill sets to understand more fully what they are learning—the content of each course's curriculum. Others note this:

> The knowledge gained needs emotional support to be made useful and applicable in the real world. This insight may play a key role in helping mitigate a longstanding educational problem—the lack of knowledge transfer from one course to another (within and across disciplines) and from school to the real world. (Immordino-Yang, 2016, as cited in Schmidt, 2019)

However, because most classroom practices are geared to prep students for recall test scores rather than deeper learning outcomes, in classrooms, transfer becomes the most important goal to ready students for their futures (Foley & Kaiser, 2013; Furman & Sibthorp, 2013; Hung, 2013; McKeough, Lupart, & Marini, 1995). Those teachers who have yet to leave behind the call for recall can rest comfortably knowing that their students too will benefit from purposeful transfer. Author and school superintendent Michael McDowell (2021) claims that "students need a rigorous and relevant program of study that enables them to develop expertise *within* disciplines and experience *across* disciplines" (p. 21).

Students can transfer their knowledge and skills by proximity (near and far), direction, or depth. They may transfer an idea or skill gained in one course to new material in the same course or another course, perhaps the following week. For example, a student might transfer the know-how of asking and answering questions from work in language arts to a science project about penguins. Students deepen their understanding of a class's material and transfer that to other courses. Imagine the impact on students' performances if they summarized what they learn from notes they have taken before they took the final test. Using personalized learning plans to push that transfer shouldn't be ignored.

Proximity Transfer—Near and Far

Proximity is the label for the most common transfer types. There are two types of proximity transfer: (1) near and (2) far (Matthews, 2018). Young children, including elementary students, start with *near* transfer. For instance, when pre-readers learn to take sounds, connect sounds to letters, and sound out letters into words, their transfer is near. They apply the knowledge they already have to something in close proximity to that knowledge. The context is familiar (Matthews, 2018). To ensure that students apply what they learn about using letters to making words, and then to gaining comprehension or meaning, teachers promote near transfer by design—teaching specific letters to form words; words then form meaning.

Near transfer to contexts similar to those in daily lessons can often happen with little teacher effort. By teaching a lesson designed to lead to an observable near transfer, teachers raise the odds that students will advance a skill's development or a concept's understanding. If teachers merely cover the material and students memorize the letters and the words, the chance for transfer is nil. If a teacher highlights how letters become words and words become sentences by pushing each next step, students can apply near transfer.

Near transfer extends when teachers ask students to take one of the following two actions.

1. Connect ideas or apply skills learned in one lesson (rhyming in a sonnet, for example) to another lesson (reading iambic pentameter in Shakespeare's [1595/1997] *Macbeth*).

2. Connect ideas or apply skills learned in one content area (rhyming in a sonnet) to another (meter in music class).

Eventually, students develop near transfer competence by connecting a complex skill (analyzing a poem) into a thinking pattern such as problem solving (analyzing a geometric problem).

Although near transfer is common in K–12 classrooms, the more important *far transfer* is not. In fact, "there is no focus on the future utilization of learning" (Thalheimer, 2020). Near transfer becomes far when a student, teacher, or new coursework asks students to apply knowledge or skills to real-world problems outside the classroom. For instance, in elementary grades, this means students calling on what they have studied about natural animal habitats in a classroom lab as they search for habitat examples on a field trip to a local forest preserve. In middle school science, this may look like a field trip to a local fun park to examine force and motion principles applied to roller coasters. In high school sociology, a teacher may promote far transfer by facilitating projects transferring Thomas Paine's social justice concepts to students' examination of court systems or into an investigation into law as a career. For any of these attempts, students must activate transfer of multiple complex skills in the inquiries. Teachers can enable this activation by increasing the amount of quality instruction.

Depth Transfer—Shallow and Deep

When prompting near and far transfer, you distinguish shallow from deep transfer. *Shallow* transfer is what happens when students recall a learned procedure and use it to complete a near task. For instance, in mathematics, the student remembers the procedures for solving a two-step speed problem and follows it from memory on practice equations in a digital program or paper workbook. In language arts, the student recalls end punctuation rules as she completes sentences in a paragraph with a period.

In contrast, *deep* transfer happens when students call on a familiar complex critical-thinking skill such as *construct* or *determine why* to solve a new problem. Deeper transfer is necessary to produce deeper learning outcomes. Examples follow.

- In fifth-grade science, a teacher prepares students *to support an argument* that plants get the materials they need from air and water. In the next month, she prepares a deeper transfer language arts lesson for students *to support an argument* that a narrator's point of view in a short story influences how events are described in the story. Personalized learning plans for the lessons highlight transfer of skills *to support an argument*.

- In sixth-grade social studies, a teacher invites students to analyze historic events for cause and effect. With a personalized learning plan, the student calls on understandings of how to *analyze* and *find cause and effect* learned in English class last year. The student then combines the two to complete this complex thinking task in science.

- In eleventh-grade physics, the teacher presents students with a real-world problem scenario about light sources. From a need-to-know lesson that provides students with a model to solve ill-structured problems, the students apply the model to solve the light scenario and gain deeper understanding of light sources. The teacher includes a personalized learning plan to help students focus on deeper learning skills.

Directional Transfer—Backward and Forward

Students also can transfer backward and forward, and into and out from. With *backward transfer*, students reflect on past learning experiences (Archer, Eyster, Kelly, Kowalski, & Shanahan, 2014). They recall past understandings about content and about utilizing skills they are being asked to address in a current lesson or project. This ability to access prior knowledge is crucial to constructing new knowledge. It also destroys the myth that memory has no value. As students learn to check prior knowledge, they are activating their transfer back skills. The most common look-back strategies and tools are those such as graphic organizers like the *what we know how, about, and to do* in figure 5.1 (page 108). Another common approach is *who, what, when, where, why*, and *how* guiding questions that prompt backward transfer at the introduction of a lesson or project.

When teaching students how to call on backward transfer, the combination of collaboration, graphic organizers, and prompts enables students' reflection. Examine figure 5.2 (page 108), a look-back example of analyzing a character in a novel, short story, or drama. There, you can see examples of backward transfer prompts easily added to lessons or spoken as passing words.

What We Know How to Do	What We Want to Know	What We Have Learned to Do
Look at what character says, actions, and what other characters say about . . . Look at how other characters treat . . . Look at what narrator says about . . .	Is character telling the truth? Obvious signs Hidden clues Others' behavior If the narrator doesn't like the character What the narrator or other characters don't say about the character How can we use this exercise with a movie or TV story?	Look at hidden clues in character descriptions. Use what other characters say and do to judge truth telling. Use clues to decide how others feel about the character. Ask "How are characters linked?"

Figure 5.1: Analyzing a character in a short story.

*Visit **go.SolutionTree.com/instruction** for a free reproducible version of this figure.*

A way I learned to identify what I needed to know to analyze a main character:
An example that helped me read a story last year:
Last year, I learned how to _____. How will that help me _____ today?
Last week, we worked on writing summaries. Complete the following sentence: I will share all ideas with the class. When I write a summary, it is a good idea to:

Figure 5.2: Prompts to elicit backward transfer—Example.

*Visit **go.SolutionTree.com/instruction** for a free reproducible version of this figure.*

Forward transfer is when you can see how knowledge or a skill might be applied (Archer et al., 2014). It occurs each time a student imagines future coursework or life scenarios in which the skill or knowledge might be beneficial. Teachers can facilitate forward transfer in many ways, including asking students to do the following.

- Design an application of key understandings about a topic just studied (such as the periodic table), an experience just completed (field trip to study dinosaurs at a local museum), or skills utilized (precise evaluation in mathematics problem solving).
- Look ahead in time and use creative thinking to estimate or predict possible applications that are either near or far. The teacher can use guiding prompts such as "How might you use your skill of predicting in your next science class?"

Common forward transfer methods include prompts for a think-pair-share or write-pair-share, a graphic organizer (such as that in figure 5.3), or a crystal ball four-corner brainstorm activity. After identifying the forward target, prompts you might include follow.

- How might you use what you learned about . . . ?
- Imagine that you are . . . (taking a test next week, in a college class, applying for a job, starting a new class). Tell me the steps you would follow.
- In this lesson, how would you call on what you know about writing in the program Word to help in the new situation?
- How will knowing how to . . . help you in your first job?
- How do you think a recruiter will react if you describe your problem-solving skills in your application?

Figure 5.4 (page 110) shows a teacher's playbook for a forward transfer activity. Students can use the brainstorm playlist (chapter 6, page 119) if they need help getting started with it.

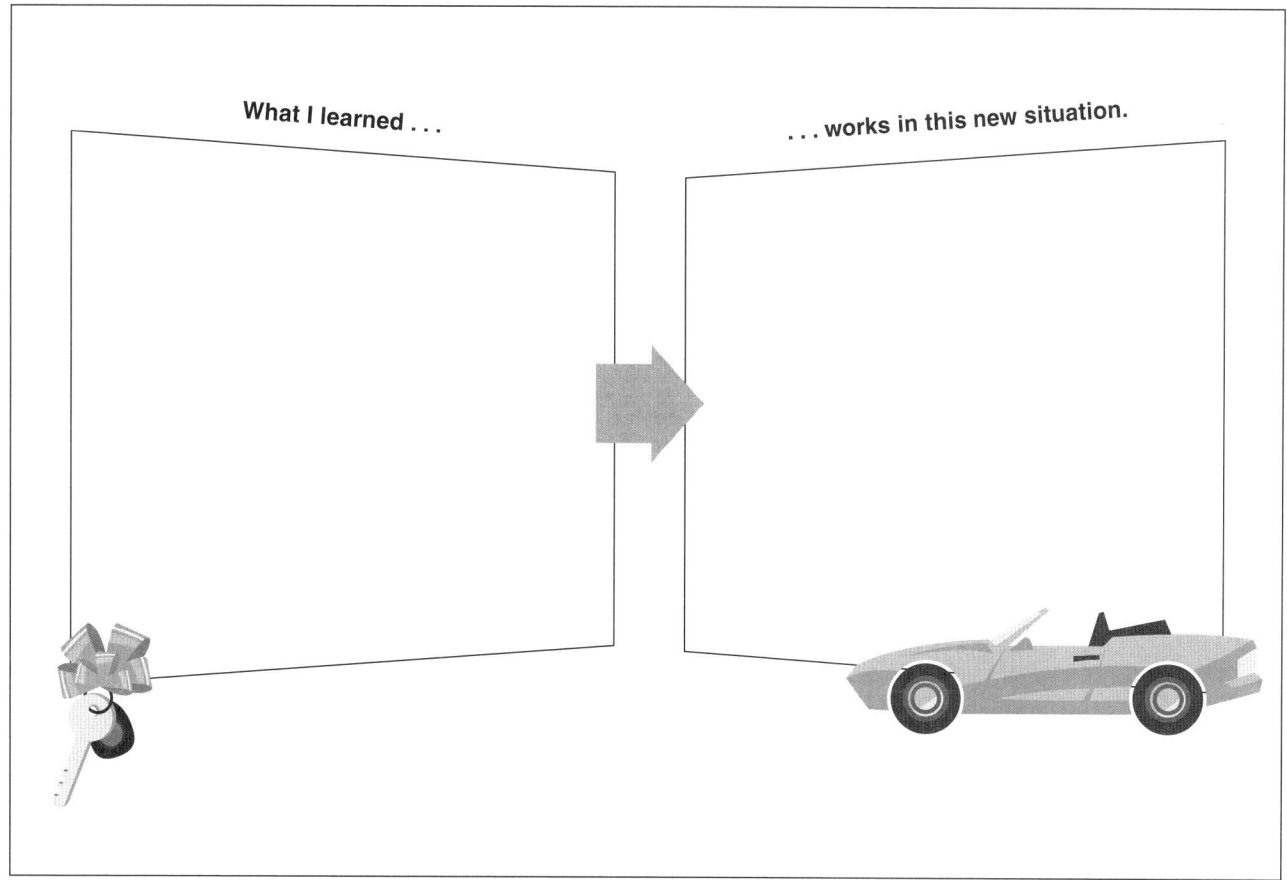

Figure 5.3: Forward transfer graphic organizer.

Visit **go.SolutionTree.com/instruction** *for a free reproducible version of this figure.*

1. Set up five member teams.
2. Share the playbook in figure 1.3 (page 18) with each team.
3. Ask the driving question: "How do we use what we can do with Word in an essay to write a blog?"
4. Decide on outcomes like the following.
   a. A list of five or more ideas that shows ways to use Word in a blog
   b. A finished blog created with Word
5. Provide a rubric to guide transfer of what students know about and can apply when writing a blog. Each student will have her or his own rubric to guide assessment.
6. Each team determines roles and responsibilities (such as leader, timekeeper, digital recorder, presenter, and coach) and reviews the team contract based on class norms.
7. Participate in brainstorming a list of ideas to transfer from Word to writing a blog.
8. Each member completes a personalized learning plan with a transfer skill as the outcome.
9. In your team, make a second list of what members know about the format, content, and so forth for a blog. If you're unsure, search online. Brainstorm a list of what the team knows about how to use Word for a blog. See the brainstorm playlist if you need help getting started.
10. Teams use Word to write a blog on a topic of the team's choice.
11. Check your blog with the transfer rubric your teacher provides.
12. Plan follow-up blog-making with rubric-based feedback to show the student's improvement in near skill transfer.

Figure 5.4: Forward transfer (digital task playbook)—Team brainstorm, middle school example.

*Visit **go.SolutionTree.com/instruction** for a free reproducible version of this figure.*

Why Should I Focus on Learning Transfer?

A major meta-analysis (Thalheimer, 2020) captures twenty-four reasons why it is important for educators to teach for transfer. For K–12 educators, the following findings apply directly to their personalized learning plan adoption.

- Skill transfer occurs most potently to the extent that teachers' learning designs strengthen knowledge and skills.
- Learners who set goals are more likely to transfer their skills.
- Learners who use goals to trigger action planning will be even more likely to transfer, compared to those who only set goals and take no action.
- Learners with supervisors who encourage, support, and monitor learning transfer are more likely to successfully transfer their skills.
- The shorter the time between learning and transfer, the more likely that training-generated knowledge creates benefits for skill transfer.
- The more success learners have in their first attempts to transfer what they've learned, the more likely they are to persevere in more transfer-supporting behaviors.

How Do I Plan for Transfer?

Transfer does not happen for students just because they sit in your classroom. Students learn to transfer learning when your classroom functions as a healthy, supportive, and encouraging home for the mind (Costa & Kallick, 2004; Thalheimer, 2020).

1. In this context, ensure students can generalize and draw conclusions about persons, places, objects, ideas, values, skills, and beliefs. You can assess their ability by asking "How do you think . . . connects with . . . ?"
2. Help students look beyond immediate learning situations and hypothesize how their new understandings and skills are relevant to new situations. Ask them for a forward transfer with "What if . . . ?"
3. Help students connect what they already know and can do as creative and critical thinkers to the generation of new ideas. Ensuring that your students can proficiently transfer critical- and creative-thinking skills makes it more likely they will be ready to do so on their own. Ask them to transfer forward with "What do you want to try next?"

To ensure students become active and mentally and emotionally engaged in accepting the transfer challenge, if you have not already done so, take responsibility for creating a reciprocal learning climate where trust and mutual respect are the norms among you and the students. As you saw in chapter 2 (page 35) throughout, you make it psychologically safer for each learner to risk sharing novel thinking and problem solving. In addition, you create those healthy conditions that allow for warm two-way feedback.

At the beginning of a deeper learning lesson with a transfer outcome, you can anticipate which students might need your help. This will be especially true for those who have locked themselves into thinking there is always one right answer. These students are likely to be uncomfortable with thinking outside the box to find several diverse and nuanced answers. Others will lack the skills to think through the task, even if you have spent time explaining the *how*.

To help students who struggle to link skills they demonstrated in one dimension with a new context, you start by diagnosing the challenges.

- One student fears failure about giving a wrong answer or a half-right answer.
- A second student fears she doesn't know how to think divergently.
- A third fears "you'll be mad at me" for not giving the answer "you want."
- A fourth fears peer ridicule.
- A fifth fears being "dumb."
- Another is a literal thinker.
- A sixth student doesn't recall enough about the subject to transfer learning.

Your diagnosis followed by empathic words and reassuring tone helps students address fears and insecurities while trying to transfer. As you coach for transfer, you help students gain confidence by increasing feelings of competence. If you feel comfortable setting up future transfer role plays or asking students to write and share future scenarios after they have brainstormed their ideas for resolving these concerns, you can do so in a lesson and follow solutions generated with a personalized learning plan. This places you in a position for coaching for transfer.

Whether coaching one student or several struggling with transfer, your positive words delivered in a warm tone can help conquer fear and encourage students to make new connections. The acronym ARREST identifies six coaching responses, shown in figure 5.5. Beginning with the letters A and R, mix and match these as you read body language and words, remembering that your job is not to make students feel good, but to help them work through their fears. You help them use what they have learned about thinking, collaborating, problem solving, and the other deeper learning skills.

With these skills, you start coaching with a mini-brainstorm. You may ask multiple "What if we . . . ?" questions in an encouraging tone to coax responses. Celebrate each small advance until the student relaxes, shows confidence, and lets answers unfold.

A = Acknowledge the feeling or concern.	"Are you scared to . . . ?" "You sound concerned that . . ."
R = Recognize the reason.	"Is this hard because . . . ?" "Are you not sure how . . . ?"
R = Restore confidence and competence.	"Let me help you . . ." "Would it help if we tried together to . . . ?"
E = Encourage	"What if you tried to . . . ?" "That's a good first step. Now, . . ."
S = Step ahead.	"Let's stop and think about some added ways to . . ." "Let's make a list to . . ."
T = Toast the tiny triumphs.	"That's the way to do it!" "Hurrah! You did it!"

Figure 5.5: ARREST coaching responses.

*Visit **go.SolutionTree.com/instruction** for a free reproducible version of this figure.*

Consider the following elementary and high school examples. Note in each example how the teacher, as coach, guides the ARREST interactions.

Elementary School Example

A second-grader is struggling to identify information about Amelia Earhart in a social studies personalized learning plan with the standards-aligned outcome, "to gather information from one or two sources with guidance and support from adults and/or peers" (Illinois State Board of Education, 2017). The teacher crouches low beside the boy's desk. She empathizes with his frustration, acknowledging the emotions caused by his difficulty finding the information. In guided reading, he had followed a newspaper graphic to find the answers to questions posed in a matrix organizer, such as who, what, and when questions. With a story to read on his own, he shied away from the organizer. The teacher had directed the class to read the Earhart text by transferring forward.

The teacher smiles, and acknowledges that the task to find the information about the main character "is tough." Then she chunks the task. You can see the ARREST letter in parentheses pointing out coaching responses.

Teacher: "It looks like you aren't sure where to start." (A)

Juan, softly: "Uh-huh."

Teacher: "What if I helped you look for just one bit of information? . . . and then we see what else to add. Will that work for you?" (R)

Juan: "I guess."

Teacher: "OK, let's just try it. Do you remember that 'who?' is the best place to start? It will help you look. Let's go to the first question. Who were the people involved in preparing Amelia Earhart's plane? Can you find that?" (R)

Juan shakes his head back and forth without speaking.

Teacher: "That's OK. There is a lot to look for. Let's just try this: What's the pilot's name in the title?" (A, E)

Juan: "That's easy. Amelia Earhart."

Teacher: "Good job. That's one name, one *who*. Now read the first paragraph and see if you can find another name." (T, E)

Juan: "I think I see three. Wilmer Stultz, Louis Gordon, and George Putnam."

Teacher: "Bravo. You did it. That wasn't so bad, was it?" (T)

Juan: "No."

Teacher: "Great. Now I am going to ask some other questions with the organizer. I want you to read the next paragraph. Look for when *Amelia flew her last flight,* where *she left from,* what *her type of plane was,* and the reason *why she made that flight.* Now remind me what the key question words are." (T, S)

Juan: "When . . . where . . . what and why?"

Teacher: "Bravo. You got it. Just remember when you learned how to ask questions to gather information. You are looking for facts. I remember how well you did with your basal reader. You can answer on this newspaper organizer with who, when, where, what, and why. Take your time. When you see one answer, put it with the question. Stop and think. One step at a time. You can do this." (E, S, T)

High School Example

A twelfth-grade physics team starting a project-based engineering unit disagrees about the transfer requirement. For its product, the class had decided to build a miniature roller coaster. Teams will compete in a force measurement contest. Noticing the disagreement, the teacher stands behind the team's workstation and listens. Zeroing in on the disagreement, she interrupts the discussion.

Teacher: "You folks are really going at it, but it sounds like you are going around in circles. I'd like to offer some suggestions so you can move forward." (A)

Recorder Student: "That would surely help, I think. At least for me."

Teacher: "I see the rest nodding yes. Thumbs up? OK. It sounds like two of you want to evaluate the whole design process, and two others just want to do the creative-thinking skills. One wants to assess how you are applying the math." (A)

Chief Engineer Student: "I'm just afraid we'll get it wrong. And I don't know how to get all five of us to agree."

Timer Student Julie: "And we're wasting lots of time arguing."

Teacher: "I hear these concerns. Let's see how I can get you moving. What if we review what this project's playbook says about the outcome? Laura, would you read it for us?" (A, R)

Student Laura: "Each team member will decide what they want to assess as an outcome that measures transfer. Each will select the direction, content, and distance of the selected skill or idea."

Teacher: *"I would like you to reread that statement. I want two answers. First, who decides what is the transfer outcome? Second, what's being decided about transfer? Thumbs-up for that approach? Good. Please write while I wait." [time passes] "I see most are done. Laura, let's start with you. Question one—who decides?" (T, R)*

Student Laura: *"It says, 'Each team member.'"*

Teacher: *"Jaime?"*

Student Jaime: *"Sí. I agree."*

Teacher: *"I see you all shaking your heads yes. Is that what you were doing?" (R)*

Student Ivan: *"No. I thought we all had to agree. I guess we don't."*

Teacher: *"Great. Then that's settled. Now let's go to the second question. Anna-Maria?" (T, S)*

Student Anna-Maria: *"I think we all decide on our own. It just reminds us how many choices we have."*

Student Ivan: *"I say yes, too. That means I can see how well I use calculus in our roller coaster. That would be a deep forward transfer for me. Tomas could do his design thinking, and the others pick whatever skills."*

Student Laura: *"Does that mean I can keep working on precision? That's been my thing this quarter. I still need to work on it."*

Teacher: *"What do you think?" (S)*

Laura: *"Yes."*

Teacher: *"Bravo! Let's make one final check before you go back to your planning. Just let me see—thumbs-up? Thumbs-down? OK, you each will determine what you will transfer?" [waits] "Good. I look forward to seeing each idea. If any of you has a specific concern left, let me know how I can help." (T)*

What Do Far and Near Learning Transfer Look and Sound Like?

What students do and say when transfer is a *planned* outcome indicates how engaged and comfortable they are with accomplishing transfer's complex-thinking, designing, decision-making, and problem-solving requirements. Table 5.1 (page 114) has examples of behaviors that educators use to promote this transfer, and of what they can see or hear when promoting near and far transfer.

Observe and note where your students' actions and remarks lie in this table. If you see no far transfer occurring, review your inquiries and provide novel contexts in which to challenge students. Call on personalized learning plans as a medium to accomplish far transfer, especially when you are stressing more complex personalized learning outcomes. This requires your careful scope and sequence pre-planning to ensure including the skills you want transferred in multiple lessons or projects.

The CCSS and many alternative ELA standards early on identify ask-and-answer questions. The NGSS highlight inquiry. Because of time pressures, teachers can integrate the two sets with a series of informational text and science activities. The personalized learning plans will focus first on asking questions in science lessons, and then for near transfer in added science lessons and eventually in other content lessons. Here is the outline for that approach.

1. Plan a personalized learning plan with the focus skill: ask-and-answer questions in science.
    a. How to ask and answer questions
    b. Near transfer
    c. Far transfer

Consider this multigrade transfer scope-and-sequence example.

1. Plan parallel lessons.
    a. *Ask questions* introduced
        i. Elementary school: Living things
        ii. Middle school: Energy
        iii. High school: Introduction to plate tectonics
    b. Ask questions for near transfer
        i. Elementary school: Non-living things, plant needs
        ii. Middle school: Forms of energy
        iii. High school: Moving plates
    c. Ask questions for far transfer
        i. Elementary school: How people use plants
        ii. Middle school: Energy applications
        iii. High school: Plate boundaries

Teachers also may follow a scope and sequence of questions to ask which proceed from factual (*who*,

Table 5.1: Transfer Sights and Sounds

Teacher Promoting Near Transfer Looks Like	Teacher Promoting Near Transfer Sounds Like
• Scheduling time for students to look forward and predict how they might apply a new reading, mathematics, or other skill in a similar problem today • Scheduling time for students to look back and see how they used a new reading or mathematics skill in a similar problem • Providing students an opportunity to develop a new skill with different media in next project • Providing students with different examples of a new skill and asking to use in homework • Asking students to make a personal goal for using a new skill or idea in new problems or situations next week	• "Let's look at three examples. How are they alike? Different?" • "Where have you learned something like . . . in the past?" • "What connections do you see here among . . . and . . . ?" • "How are the characters in this story like characters you have read about in last week's story?" • "Using what I showed you about rules, what rule could you make for how to solve this problem?" • "Now that you can do this problem in different ways, what advice would you give about how to . . . ?" • "Where else in this classroom do you think you could use the information you have just learned about . . . ?"
Teacher Promoting Far Transfer Looks Like	**Teacher Promoting Far Transfer Sounds Like**
• Leading a brainstorm of a list of similar projects completed in past years • Asking students to reflect on importance of new ideas to future encounters • Sharing a Venn diagram on interactive whiteboard to show how problem-solving skills apply to different types of problems students will be doing next	• "In what other course you are now taking could you use this reading, math, or thinking skill . . . ?" • "How could this . . . skill help you to plan for . . . next year?" • "Wow! I love how you are seeing the future benefits of . . . so you can . . ." • "I want you to review what you learned in last year's coding course so you can program an app in this course."
Student Making Near Transfer Looks Like	**Student Making Near Transfer Sounds Like**
• Using different media to learn same material in a class • Practicing a skill with examples • Reflecting on how to use an idea or skill in a course • Bridging what is learned today to the next day's lesson • Writing an empathic outcome in a new plan for talking with sister • Writing an evaluation to self-grade a new plan in tonight's homework	• "Let me explain why and how I use . . ." • "I don't understand how to connect . . ." • "My goal for applying this skill next week is . . ." • "I can use . . . when I answer this question in my next assignment." • "These three examples show how I can . . . for this class." • "What I have learned about using this example is . . ."
Student Making Far Transfer Looks Like	**Student Making Far Transfer Sounds Like**
• Using number skills from elementary grades in algebra • Writing an art essay about an idea learned last year in ELA • Comparing two figures in American history with character analysis methods learned in freshman English class • Solving a statistics problem by applying skills learned to compare data sets in pre-algebra • Picking next year's courses based on what students need for a solid college application • Reviewing a critical-thinking skill (such as *distinguish*) learned last year to build a plan for a science experiment this year	• "When I get stuck in another class, I can use this skill to . . ." • "Next year when I study . . . this skill will help me . . ." • "My goal for next year is . . ." • "If I analyze this informational document today, I can add . . ." • "I predict this skill will help me make the varsity next year because . . ." • "What I have learned in this class will help me in other classes by . . ." • "What I learned last year about . . . will help me to . . ." • "I intend to apply this idea . . . in my next job when . . ." • "This skill will benefit me next year because . . ."

Visit **go.SolutionTree.com/instruction** *for a free reproducible version of this table.*

what, where, when) to reasoning (*why, how*) to complex thinking (*how to compare, how to justify*). The following bullets spotlight key ingredients for initiating far transfer of deep learning skills.

- Lesson design strengthens results for transfer.
- Students set SMART goals.
- Peer collaboration and feedback are part of the SMART goal creation.
- Teacher feedback is included.
- Coaching is planned to promote transfer of any targeted skill in a personalized learning plan.
- An immediate start-up is planned.
- Criteria for self-assessment are planned.

How Do I Assess Transfer?

As the two scenarios on pages 112 and 113 illustrate, format options for rubrics are similar to those for assessing the three skill sets. When you construct guiding rubric criteria for transfer outcomes, you decide among these options: (1) assess all with the same rubric, (2) give each team its choice, or (3) as in the physics-engineering discussion, give maximum agency to each individual.

Figures 5.6–5.8 (pages 115–117) show sample grade-appropriate transfer rubrics. By introducing these rubrics at the start of a lesson, you can guide students to focus on the transfer skills they are developing in a personalized learning plan. Before the lesson, present the rubric with the material and skills you want to review through the lesson before using the rubric for a summative assessment. Don't forget that *I (we)* identifies the author of each copy. *I* indicates the student's self-assessment, and *we* indicates team feedback with the same instrument. It is best to add the rating scale when you are changing the rubric from a formative guiding rubric, with its emphasis on feedback, to a summative grading rubric. There is little need to add the paperwork with rated formative assessments being scored and placed in the gradebook.

Name: Missy Gulogo	**Date:** 1/7
Story: *Alexander and the Terrible, Horrible, No Good, Very Bad Day* (Viorst, 2014)	
Topic: Using my ideas	
Circle One	
I (you) shared ideas with the team.	😊 😊
I (you) selected one idea as the best to help Alexander.	😊
I (you) explained why your idea was a good idea for helping Alexander.	😊 😐
☒ Teacher ☐ Student _____	
Teacher feedback: I was happy to see your four ideas. Please give another reason yours was a good idea. **Student:** Dina	
Optional rating scale: 0 = Not yet (straight face) 1 = Good thinking (one face) 2 = Great ideas (two faces)	

Figure 5.6: Single-response guiding rubric—Elementary school example.

*Visit **go.SolutionTree.com/instruction** for a free reproducible version of this figure.*

Name: Guadalupe	Date: September 27
Teacher: Mrs. Boeglin	Check-up dates: 9/12 and 9/19

Feedback

Feedback is by:
- ☐ Self
- ☒ Teacher
- ☐ Peers: _____
- ☐ Other: _____

Target idea or skill to apply: Transferring knowledge of the Constitution to my community

Specific idea to apply: How everyone, especially seniors, exercises the right to vote

Beyond Expectation	What Is Expected	How to Improve
I found out when women got to legally vote.	I checked back to see what I knew about an idea or skill I was going to learn to use.	I am OK.
I wanted to see if everyone knew how to vote, especially senior women.	I took what I learned about the Constitution and applied it in a situation in my community.	Fix the idea to match senior women.
I wrote my plan on the template you gave.	I described my idea and explained my reasons for the connection.	You asked me to survey more senior women.
I had eleven examples.	I was ready with examples for defending my application.	You said my list was good.

Draw a picture showing how you bridged your ideas into a community example.

(Me wheeling across the bridge to seniors)

Summary of feedback:

Teacher: Thumbs-up for your essay. Thanks for telling me how you will fix your main idea. All other paragraphs fit together well.

Student: I will fix the title and the introduction paragraph so it's about senior women.

Figure 5.7: Single-point guiding rubric for learning transfer—Middle school example.

*Visit **go.SolutionTree.com/instruction** for a free reproducible version of this figure.*

Name: Robin Sexton	Date: 10/15	Grade: 11	Period: 7
Class: American studies	Teacher: Mrs. Hapernathy and Mr. Thomas		
Team members: Jason Janos, Miranda Daniels			
Start date: 9/6	End date: 10/14	Check-up dates: 9/13	

Feedback is by:
- ☒ Self
- ☒ Teacher
- ☐ Peer: _____
- ☐ Other: _____

Transfer target:
- ☒ Skill: <u>Transfer of an idea</u>
- ☐ Idea
- ☐ Mindset

Below, pick the number that most represents performance for each item this week in your team. Place the score in column 1 under the criterion.

Criterion	3	2	1	0
Understanding a new idea or skill we learned for future use	Our (your) team summarized, in its own words, what we learned in this lesson, what and how we were transferring, the direction of the transfer, and the target, plus reasons for each.	We (your team) summarized the ideas and skill we learned and wanted to transfer. We noted what we would transfer and its direction as well as the target of the transfer and had one general reason.	Our summary focused on one idea or skill that we wanted to transfer and the target. No reasons given.	We (your team) could not summarize what we learned.
Projecting what we know about the new idea into the future	We (your team) brainstormed a list of between three and five ideas of how this might be useful in future classes and this class, plus reasons for each.	We (your team) brainstormed two ideas of how this might be useful in this class or in future classes, plus one general reason.	We (your team) brainstormed one idea of how this might be useful in this class or in future classes, but no reasons.	We (your team) have no idea what we could do with what we learned.
Using a new idea or skills	We (your team) brainstormed two or three specific ways this will help us (your team) in this and other classes and explained how.	We (your team) brainstormed two specific ways I might use this, one for this class and one in the future, and explained one reason.	We (your team) brainstormed one possible use for this but cannot explain how or why I think so.	We (your team) do not know what we (you) can transfer—not a clue.

Figure 5.8: Multi-point guiding rubric for learning transfer—High school example.

Visit **go.SolutionTree.com/instruction** *for a free reproducible version of this figure.*

TAKEAWAYS

What have you learned or had reinforced about transfer? What will you do with personalized learning plans to increase transfer in future lessons and projects?

CHAPTER 6
THE COMPLEX COGNITIVE SKILL SET

Education is not the learning of facts, but training the mind to think.

—Albert Einstein

The desire to be fast (when completing an assignment or assessment), or not knowing how to transfer knowledge, may thwart any attempt to think critically.

The student Eleanor asserted, "I'm done," as she handed her test to Mrs. Malcolm, her sixth-grade mathematics teacher.

Mrs. Malcolm looked over the page. "But you answered only two. The rest are blank."

"Yeah," Eleanor said, "but I'm the first one done."

"That's fine. But did you stop and think about the other questions?" the teacher asked.

Eleanor shook her head. "I thought you wanted us to go fast. You keep saying we have to work fast."

"Yes, I did. But you do have to stop to think first."

Eleanor has fallen into a speed trap. She has convinced herself that speed comes first, with her weekly tests, her daily quizzes—with everything. Once she starts a test, she dashes helter-skelter to the finish with characteristic impulsivity. She doesn't stop to think. Sometimes, she jumps in without listening to a single instruction. As much as her teacher encourages her to stop and think, Eleanor can't control herself. Impulse control, a prerequisite for critical thinking, seems beyond her reach.

Mrs. Malcolm has known many like Eleanor. It troubles her how many new middle-grade mathematics students are missing the mortar that holds the bricks of thinking in place. Without the ability to reason joined with the ability to self-regulate, students struggle with the complex thinking needed to do well in her mathematics classes. She once thought their difficulty was the inability to compute. After she learned more about basic cognitive functions, she looked at the basics in a different light. Her students' impulsivity was a headache, but their imprecise and inaccurate thinking (especially in mathematics) was a migraine. Not being able to infer, she thought, was like a bad case of the flu.

Complex cognition is crucial to academics, college, and careers, as well as with general life skills. As with other chapters focusing on the social-emotional and digital skill sets, this chapter describes best practices for integrating the complex cognitive set into personalized learning plans. This chapter features two subsets: (1) critical thinking and (2) creative thinking. After a definition and rationale for each subset, the chapter presents established, evidence-strong strategies as key ingredients in personalized learning plan templates. The selected tools promote critical thinking and creative competencies as well as their transfer into problem-solving and design-thinking projects. Grade-level examples with templates, charts, guiding rubrics, and other tools show how complex cognitive skills transferred into deeper learning content produce deeper learning outcomes.

> **Driving question**: How do I develop students' complex cognition with personalized learning plans?

What Is Complex Cognition?

Neuroscientists tell us that in the part of the brain called the *cerebrum*, the frontal lobe of the cortex is associated with reasoning, planning, problem solving, language, and higher emotions, such as empathy and altruism (Moawad, 2020). The temporal lobe is associated with hearing, speech, memory, and emotion (Moawad, 2020). From this description, we know that complex thinking and memorizing are distinct mental operations emerging from different parts of the brain, a distinction that allows for the separation of memory, a basic operation with its own skills, from higher-order thinking, with its unique skills (Moawad, 2020).

The expanding field of cognitive psychology reinforces brain research discoveries about how students learn by constructing new understandings from prior knowledge (Bransford et al., 1999). For the first time in history, teachers are learning how complex thinking is being extracted from the side-show of something nice for gifted children and featured in the center ring as learnable skills essential for all.

If you review state, national, and provincial standards, you can see the influence research on deeper learning has brought at all levels. If you call on a standard to frame your lessons, it is likely that you are looking through a lens that considers the implications of brain research.

You will note how standards rely on action verbs that help students learn how to think with complex cognition about the content in each standard statement (Bellanca et al., 2020). Most such standards make it possible to build a personalized learning plan around a critical- or creative-thinking skill and complex problem-solving skills. When you feature the critical-thinking skill in a standard (which doesn't mean vocabulary and names are not important), you move the focus from learning recall to learning to think in complex ways.

The following analyses of examples of critical-thinking skills emphasized within standards reveal the classic importance of such skills by showing how these two different examples are similar in their separate calls for students to compare.

- "Explain major differences between poems, plays, and prose, and refer to the structural elements of poems and drama" (4.RL.3.1; Indiana Department of Education, n.d.). This standard asks that fourth-grade teachers prepare students to explain differences so they can demonstrate how to categorize the list of literary forms. Both—explaining the differences and categorizing the forms—are complex cognitive acts.

- "Plan and conduct an investigation to compare the effects of different strengths or different directions of pushes and pulls on the motion of an object" (K-PS2-1; NGSS Lead States, 2013). This standard directs kindergarten teachers to plan an inquiry, a process that requires students to ask and answer questions as they compare different effects of their investigation.

With an emphasis on complex thinking skills, key verbs delineate which complex thinking skills students need in order to understand the content in a standard. Some refer to identifying these verbs as part of *unpacking* or *unwrapping standards*. For instance, ELA standards call for instruction applying a specific thinking skill such as *compare* to a specific *what*, such as characters in a story. The verbs in standards make a clear distinction between complex thinking and memorizing. Even if you search standards with a fine-toothed comb, you will struggle to find standards for recall. For instance, where you read *compare*, you will not find *recall a list of differences* or *recall the different steps when . . . .*

What Skills Make Up the Complex Cognitive Skill Set?

When you separate complex cognition from the basic cognitive or recall skill set and divide the complex thinking skill set into two subsets, you reorder Bloom's (1956) revised taxonomy (Anderson & Krathwohl, 2001) into critical and creative subsets. Each subset encompasses specific skills. These are the verbs you can view as mental acts. Contrast the columns in table 6.1 to see complex cognition's subsets.

It is likely you already do some activities and strategies that promote complex cognition. You may call it by another name, but each time you teach to a standard, it's highly likely that you are also teaching a complex thinking skill identified in your standard. If you ask higher-order-thinking questions, structure cooperative learning groups, or call on graphic organizers such as Venn diagrams, fishbones, or matrices, your odds increase. So too with brainstorming. These high-effect strategies not only engage students to a greater degree, they intensify critical and creative thinking.

When you foster these strategies with personalized learning plans, you promote complex thinking skills and ready students for attaining deeper learning outcomes.

As you pair the strategies with personalized learning plans, the playbook for developing complex cognitive skills in figure 6.1 will come in handy.

Table 6.1: Critical and Creative Thinking

Critical Thinking	Creative Thinking
Analysis or Convergent Thinking Skills	Synthesis or Divergent Thinking Skills
Categorize, compare, separate, discriminate, differentiate, choose, compute, modify, operate, schedule, judge, determine, critique, justify, appraise, argue pro and con, assess, conclude, defend, estimate value, explain why, grade, judge, rate, score, select, and *value*	*Create, design, fuse, hypothesize, invent, develop, arrange, assemble, collect, combine, compose, connect, construct, develop, devise, formulate, generate, join together, plan, integrate, prepare, produce, rearrange, reconstruct, relate, reorganize, set up,* and *synthesize*
Transfer to tight problem solving	Transfer to loose problem solving and design thinking

Source: Anderson & Krathwohl, 2001; Bloom, 1956.

1. Assess what your students can do with your curriculum as critical or creative thinkers.
2. Determine their readiness.
3. Go to the curriculum standards for your subject and grade level.
4. Go to the most frequently stated verbs as a whole.
5. Select the verbs or verbal equivalents that appear.
6. In order of priority, adopt your top choices as the thinking competency outcome you will plan, develop, and assess in a *personalized learning plan.*
7. Schedule thinking skills.
8. Select your rubric format and criteria.
9. Engage students in completing *personalized learning plan* strategies.
10. Invite teaching peers to give feedback during planning and implementation.
11. Revise, adjust, implement, and repeat as needed.
12. Identify other needed thinking skills or transfer to problem solving or a design-thinking scenario.

Figure 6.1: Teacher playbook—Developing complex cognitive skills.

Visit **go.SolutionTree.com/instruction** *for a free reproducible version of this figure.*

What Is Critical Thinking?

Critical thinking is thinking analytically, separating fact from opinion, assessing credibility, analyzing statements, comparing sources, differentiating by data, and much more. No more than two centuries back, news was spread by horseback riders galloping from town to town. Telegraph lines used to speed news across great plains. News sources now abound and technology pounds multiple perceptions, interpretations, and opinions into every hand, car, and home moments after an event.

Consider this scenario: Carlos turns the TV off and says, "I don't get it. One person promises one thing. The next, another. How am I supposed to decide who to vote for? And then there are the claims about *fake news*. One always says the media is fake news. And if the other guy *isn't* lying, they claim it's the media that is. Who knows what the truth is?" Comedian George Carlin (Carlin & Urbisci, 2005) told his audience something important in a serious moment: "I'll tell you what [politicians] don't want. They don't want a population of citizens capable of critical thinking." Why not?

Just as it became important for last century's schools to graduate citizens and employees able to read at the fourth-grade level because that's what the local newspaper required, learning institutions must heed an ancient proverb: "Do not confine your children to your own learning for they were born in another time" (Quotes.net, n.d.). Following that advice, some teachers, defying the recall-test norm, integrate critical thinking into lessons. Some go so far as to add cooperative learning or other high-effect practices such as graphic organizers or higher-order-thinking questions in their direct instruction or lecture. The first hope might be that their students will earn higher test scores. The second hope might be that students will become more engaged. The third might be that students will recognize the value of critical thinking and gain a lifetime skill.

What Is the Relationship Between Content and Thinking Skills?

Even as cognitive learning psychologists embrace emerging research theories and educators follow with new evidence-based practices aligned with theories about how the brain works (Bransford et al., 1999; Center for Educational Innovation, 2020), it is important that educators not misunderstand and throw the baby out with the bathwater. Some incidental change is occurring. Innovative high schools, for example, are adding courses such as nanotechnology and programming. Middle schools are adopting coding and media. They are forming what Harvard's curriculum guru Heidi Hayes Jacobs (2010) calls *Curriculum21*.

Whatever the content in a curriculum, primary classroom emphasis on the basic skills is not likely to disappear. However, in the fast-evolving 21st century, content (which has been considered most important) shares the throne more and more with process. The two together are like a petri dish holding a swirl of bacteria. How the scientist discovers what's in the dish depends on her problem-solving skills. Those skills become as important, if not more important, than what's in the dish. After the scientist solves this problem, there will be more to challenge her problem-solving skills. Those skills are no longer ignorable. As educators' understanding shifts from believing that learning is an empty dish to be filled until nothing more fits, to believing it is a dish that may have many different living things to be examined, the focus will continue to grow on what process skills are needed to identify each tiny new creature.

When it comes to understanding the necessary process skills' role in 21st century classrooms, corporate training and development practitioners are several steps ahead of school-based professional development specialists. When it comes to recognizing the connection between critical and creative thinking and problem solving, corporate trainers understand the need for employees to meet the challenge of complex problems with complex problem-solving skills:

> To become a problem-solver, you are on a mission to learn the art of thinking critically and creatively . . . a creative problem-solving process is an innovative one that allows you to move from your current undesired position to the desired position. (Training Express, 2020)

In the most frequently experienced loose problem-solving scenarios, learners—who may be students or adults at work—are expected to think both *divergently* with creative-thinking skills or *convergently* with critical-thinking skills. Effective problem solvers must know how to define a loose problem that has an unknown solution (critical thinking), gather information from all the available sources (critical and creative thinking), generate possible solutions (creative thinking), analyze the data (critical thinking), and implement a unique solution (critical and creative thinking). In short, loose problem solving engages minds in near transfer of critical and creative skills into a more complex problem-solving process and points to far problem solving.

Consider this scenario from the Westchester, Illinois, school district. After grade-level teams introduced students to grade-level and content-specific problem-centered PBLs, the middle school faculty elected to try an all-school problem-solving project (K. Looper, personal communication, July 2020). They asked the community to identify the problem to be solved. Votes tallied led to a project to find a solution to the annual spring floods which rushed water from the river flowing through the center of town into basements galore. First they took the skills they had developed in the prior grade level projects and applied these skills to the flooded basements. They followed the loose problem-solving process until they settled on a solution to share with the city council. After their presentation, the council voted to accept three of their ideas, and the students went on to prepare new solutions found through their complex thinking skills.

How Are Educators Responding to the Need for Students to Know How to Think?

The need for students to function as high-performing critical thinkers receives two main responses. First comes the response of those who believe in the rub-off effect: "If I teach rigorous content, the students will have to do more critical thinking." The rub-off effect is defended by teaching to the standards with some acknowledgement of how important the 4Cs may be. With it, teachers prioritize assessment-driven content outcomes, hoping that higher-level discussions, graphic organizers, and projects will cause higher-order thinking to rub off. This leaves hope that at least some students leave a class with these skills sharpened.

The second approach, adopted by a smaller number of schools, looks to instruct explicitly for deeper learning outcomes on a regular basis. This means that instruction is not aimed to produce proof of recalled information as happens in the rub-off approach. This second group looks like what is advocated by transfer researcher Will Thalheimer (2018): there is evidence of content understanding strong enough to transfer through many courses and beyond to the higher grades. The deeper learning outcomes from this mode of teaching will not produce accidental or haphazard transfer like the rub-off efforts do. In spite of outdated assessment practices, which drive shallow instruction, deeper learning outcome-driven instruction is happening to varying degrees in classrooms and whole schools (Hernandez et al., 2019).

How Do I Create a Guiding Rubric for a Critical-Thinking Skill?

When you want students to assess a critical-thinking skill in a personalized learning plan or a lesson, the complex cognitive skill set is most likely to help you target one of its specific and measurable skills. You can get some help from state, provincial, and national standards (Bellanca et al., 2020). Instead of reading a standard from the content priority point of view (the direct object), as is the most common way of responding to a standard, focus on the cognitive skill (the verb). Highlight the critical-thinking skill that should be featured as students learn about the information.

Standards' verbs are a gold mine for complex thinking outcomes. This makes personalized learning plans a practical tool for developing a wealth of critical-thinking skills. In personalized learning plans, they give you the chance to feature the standards-aligned critical-thinking skills most likely to appear in newer standardized tests, such as Smarter Balanced (www.smarterbalanced.org). Even if standards don't lead your instruction or you are not ready for organizing instruction with loose problem solving or design thinking, these activities provide ideas to start your students on the path to deeper thinking. For help unpacking standards and aligning instruction and assessment with the verbs in them, you might investigate *Common Formative Assessment: A Toolkit for Professional Learning Communities at Work* by Kim Bailey and Chris Jakicic (2012).

To include SMART outcomes and criteria in your rubric, avoid the general term *critical thinking*. That term is neither specific nor measurable, nor is its fuzziness likely to seem relevant to students. Start with the playbook in figure 6.2 (page 124).

The sample rubric in figure 6.3 (page 124) models the result of taking a state education department's (Georgia Department of Education, 2013) generic standard for critical thinking in a high school class—"Exhibit critical thinking and problem solving skills to locate,

1. Select the power standard for the upcoming personalized learning plan, lesson, or project.
2. State the SMART outcome.
3. Add the criteria.
4. Determine the format.
5. Add demographic information.
6. Determine times and persons for feedback.
7. Set a summative assessment date.
8. Review with students.

Figure 6.2: Teacher playbook—Critical thinking.

Name: Tomasina Tomas	Grade: 11	Date: 3/15
Period: 7	Teacher: Ms. Jones	Class: Fashion, merchandising, and retailing I
Check-up dates: 2/28 and 3/7	Critical-thinking skill: Analysis	
Outcome: This week I will search for and analyze five job websites and make a rating matrix based on five criteria.		
Feedback		
To what degree did you improve? 0 = I have not started to improve at all. 1 = I'm a novice. 2 = I'm working toward mastering this skill. 3 = I've mastered the skill. 4 = I've gone beyond mastery.		

Criteria	Rating and Reason	Feedback
Find relevant details about the job's skill requirements.	4—details all saved on a matrix I made	4—I agree.
Find relevant details about salary and benefits.	4—just like above	4—You organized the data and showed examples.
Determine my skill match.	2—not sure about my skills so can't really say	2—OK, let's make your next outcome focus on analyzing your skills.
Set categories to compare and contrast.	4—had good self-headers in my matrix and made it easier to compare	4—It was great and I liked the footnotes with details—nice touch. Shows your "go beyond."
Compare and contrast websites.	3—hard since each site used different words	4—It was hard, but you plowed through it, so I raise you a point. I love your grit.
Make a priority selection and explain.	3—ranked the sites and gave my three reasons for my 1 rating but was hard to do the middle ones because all similar	3—Good conclusion. Look closer at the middle one and come up with a way to pick out the fine differences. That's analysis at its best. Let's schedule a need-to-know conference.
Total	20	21

Figure 6.3: Guiding rubric for improvement—High school example.

*Visit **go.SolutionTree.com/instruction** for a free reproducible version of this figure.*

analyze and apply information in career planning and employment situations" (p. 2)—making it specific and measurable for a guiding rubric, and transforming the critical-thinking statement into an outcome. Teachers can adapt this model to write a similar guiding rubric for elementary and middle school students in any subject. With the teacher playbook in figure 6.2, examine this guiding rubric for a standards-aligned personalized learning plan.

The common critical-thinking skill *analysis* also appears frequently throughout federal, state, and provincial ELA standards such as this one: "Analyze how a particular sentence, paragraph, chapter, or section fits into the overall structure of a text and contributes to the development of the ideas" (NGA & CCSSO, 2010a). In figure 6.4, you can see the text allows the teacher to combine a reading unit with social studies. You can search online for the definition of *analysis* and find multiple definitions and descriptions to help you determine the criteria for your guiding rubrics.

In each chapter, Mrs. Dentley keeps focus on the standards-aligned task of analyzing paragraphs to show part-whole relationships. Her summative assessment does the same with no mention of Petry's (1955) book, Harriet Tubman, or the Underground Railroad. She has seen and heard sufficient evidence about the students' deepened understanding and appreciation of Tubman's accomplishments. The summative rubric assesses critical thinking. With this standard met, she feels ready to help them transfer analysis skills.

Consider having an introductory lesson instructing students about *analysis*, assessing what they learned with the rubric you create (like that in figure 6.4) and then, through several lessons, creating personalized learning plans focused on how they improve analysis.

Name: Sadie Deer	Date: 3/1
Grade: 5	Teacher: Mrs. Dentley

Text: Harriet Tubman: Conductor on the Underground Railroad by Ann Petry (1955)
Outcome: Tomorrow, you will analyze one paragraph from the first chapter's first page and show the class, on a slide, how you analyzed the connection to the story.
Check-up dates:
Feedback is by: ☐ Self ☐ Teacher ☒ Peers: Caitlyn Rossman ☐ Other: _____

Did Well	Criteria	How to Improve
You showed three examples of what Harriet Tubman said.	Find relevant details to show how the paragraph fits this book.	I thought they were good examples, but include exact wording and quotation marks when you quote something.
You made the three examples for your column titles.	Separate details into different columns.	n/a
I liked the titles.	Apply accurate labels.	n/a
	Determine connections to story.	I didn't see how you said the columns fit. Please tell me.

Figure 6.4: Guiding rubric—Analysis.

*Visit **go.SolutionTree.com/instruction** for a free reproducible version of this figure.*

What Strategies and Activities Promote Critical-Thinking Skills?

Along with guiding rubrics as the core instructional tool, you can select age-appropriate strategies (including graphic organizers such as Venn diagrams and compare and contrast) and engaging activities that advance specific critical-thinking skills. Consider the examples in the following sections.

Elementary School

The following activities promote critical-thinking skills in elementary school students but are adaptable for middle and high school.

Invent a Dinosaur

Follow these ten steps to invent a dinosaur.

1. Compose a personalized learning plan for a critical-thinking skill (such as *analysis*) inherent in this activity. Follow the template and walk students through the plan.

2. Invite trios to read about or watch videos about dinosaurs. Each team should pick a different dinosaur. (National Geographic Kids has slideshows showing specific kinds of dinosaurs, such as the iguanodon [https://bit.ly/2NmWVJC] and more. Visit https://kids.nationalgeographic.com/videos and search for *dinosaurs*.)

3. List selections in a matrix you show to the class, including species, what and how each dinosaur eats, and how each might have sounded.

4. After students read or watch the material, ask them to identify each part on the matrix.

5. Record responses. (If students missed the item, send the team back to their original source.)

6. When all functions are listed, each team selects numbers 1–6 from a die for each column. (You could change functions to body parts such as teeth, legs, and so on.)

7. Team recorders copy on index cards the name of the item and its specific type (such as *teeth—nine-inch incisors*).

8. Provide materials and let teams sketch or make a model of a new dinosaur with the parts they selected. They can name the new creature.

9. Display the completed creatures. In a circle discussion, discuss the physical attributes.

    - How is a body part connected to a function?
    - What do they think the attributes suggest about the creature's lifestyle?
    - How does looking at parts help us understand the whole creature?

10. Discuss *part* compared to *whole* and how finding each part of something helps us decide about the whole thing. Explore other animals, places, sculptures, and so on, where part-whole connections reveal something about the object and ask students for examples they could make. This is near transfer.

Tangrams

A tangram is a Chinese puzzle made from a square cut into seven pieces—five triangles, one square, and one rhomboid. Tangrams teach analysis of parts to whole. Students can use the following five steps to make figures from different pieces.

1. Share shape review models (triangle, square, and rhomboid, and include their names) with the class. Invite pairs to measure according to the sizes and cut a sheet of paper to make five triangles, one square, and one rhomboid.

2. Pairs arrange the shapes into a figure you or they choose and glue the pieces in place. (Visit www.education.com/tangrams for free examples to download.)

3. Ask the class the ways in which they helped each other think critically and list these ways.

4. Create a personalized learning plan and guiding rubric about making the pieces fit the whole picture. Use these prior to a next round of tangrams. See How Do I Create a Guiding Rubric for a Critical-Thinking Skill? (page 123) for help making that tool.

5. Optional: Bring in a new personalized learning plan so students can transfer their understanding of analysis to a new tangram. (If you need a model, go to the "Personalized Learning Plan," page 212.)

Middle School

The following activities promote critical-thinking skills in middle school students.

Word Clouds: Force and Motion

Try these five steps to link word clouds, force, motion, and critical thinking.

1. Conduct a science experiment about force and motion (such as a rocket launch competition) and include a personalized learning plan connected to the lesson. The outcome should be to define the key words *force* and *motion*.

2. Teams of three jigsaw articles or view a video about force and motion, collecting all words associated with force and motion.

3. With the words, they make two word clouds (www.wordle.net), one with the word *force* and the other with the word *motion*.

4. From the clouds, each team defines the two words on paper.

5. Host a gallery walk exhibiting each team's Wordle and descriptive definition.

Need-to-Know on the Go

With this analysis strategy, you wade into the planning process with the personalized learning plan template and rubrics. Follow these four steps.

1. When you observe that students need to know more about seeing how ideas connect (details to main ideas, details to details), announce a required need-to-know lab for those students and others who want to attend.

2. Create a figure with the blocks so students can see how parts relate to a whole.

3. Each student writes a part-whole personalized learning plan for part-whole analyses, creates a different figure, and explains the part-whole relationship.

4. In the next class period, continue the need-to-know lab with a task connected to the lesson. Coach application of the part-whole skill (analysis) and completing the plan.

High School

The following activities promote critical-thinking skills in high school students. You can adapt these for middle and elementary students as well.

Need-to-Know Survey

The outcome will show how well each student can analyze data on what the class needs to know prior to a lesson or project in your course. It refocuses the KWL (know, want to know, learned) advanced organizer strategy to read KNHWL (know, need to know, how we want to learn). Follow these four steps.

1. Prepare a whole-class personalized learning plan with analysis of gathered data from a KNHWL chart (like that shown in figure 6.5, page 128). A *do* outcome (as opposed to a *know* outcome) looks like these examples, whose verbs—italicized in the examples—identify the (do) action needed to produce the outcome.

   - *Elementary school*—Will *sketch* a picture of a favorite animal
   - *Middle school*—Will *produce and broadcast* one podcast discussing the upcoming school election
   - *High school*—Will *write* a summary of progress made to a critical-thinking goal

2. Determine specific analysis criteria in the context of the standard.

3. Write a SMART outcome, such as *At the end of this class period, you will enter a fifty-word spell-checked summary with a thesis statement and two evidence statements of what you accomplished with the current analysis goal.* Add criteria for analysis.

4. Construct a guiding rubric detailing the steps necessary for analyzing data and use it during the personalized learning plan. See figure 6.5 for help making that tool.

Build It Better

This activity looks at cause and effect through the following seven steps.

1. Create a personalized learning plan that has a cause-and-effect outcome and guiding rubric.

What We Know	What We Need to Know	How We Want to Learn
		Number your top five choices, with 1 being the one you want to learn most. ____ Read articles online. ____ Host an expert visitor. ____ Attend a lecture or demonstration. ____ Watch a YouTube video. ____ Do a hands-on activity. ____ Create a project. ____ Create a guiding rubric. ____ Do something else: _____.
Would you like to do this: ____ Alone ____ With a team		

Figure 6.5: Data-analysis KNHWL.

Visit **go.SolutionTree.com/instruction** *for a free reproducible version of this figure.*

2. Show the graphic organizer in figure 6.6 and identify the example topic: building a better car battery.

3. Set up teams of three, assign a process guide, recorder, and rubric checker, and share the guiding rubric.

4. Write *dead car battery* in the fish head (the outcome or the effect). Enter possible causes on the large bones. The possible contributing causes for a dead car battery might be, for example, *materials, methods, machines,* and *people*. Radiating from each contributing cause, brainstorm ideas that clarify these possible causes. For instance, for materials, it might be *crack on side of battery, no water, lost cap,* or *low acid*.

5. Share the driving question: "How do we make a better battery?" Invite teams to fill in each bone with brainstormed ideas.

6. Invite teams to agree on the most likely causes before creating a new plan for extending a more powerful battery's life.

7. Invite students to self-assess cause-and-effect thinking prior to a follow-up lesson on a subject in your content area with the same rubric. Create the rubric and contrast performances per the rubrics.

What Is Creative Thinking?

"What," Leonardo da Vinci may have asked his apprentices, "is creative thinking? Is it a talent which only some are born with like our duke was born with his divine right to rule? Or is creative thinking something any will learn from me?" After his apprentices finished their debate, da Vinci is said to have told them: "If you were not born with talent, you would not be here. That is why I give auditions. If you think you will learn from me, you are also correct. That is why you are paying a stipend to me" (as cited by S. Moore, personal communication, 1954).

The nature versus nurture debate continues (Domingue et al., 2018; Lakhani et al., 2019). Except perhaps in select schools devoted to the arts or other specialized fields, how you *nurture* the ranged talent thrust into your classroom is said to be more important than natural talent. Einstein (as cited in Root-Bernstein & Root-Bernstein, 2010) argued that creative thinking not only advances the arts and imagination but also impacts many other disciplines, including science. Perhaps that is why he advocated for teachers to cultivate creative imagination as a prerequisite to scientific advancement. Einstein saw the value in how you develop innate talent, and in valuing the process of development through learning, he was able

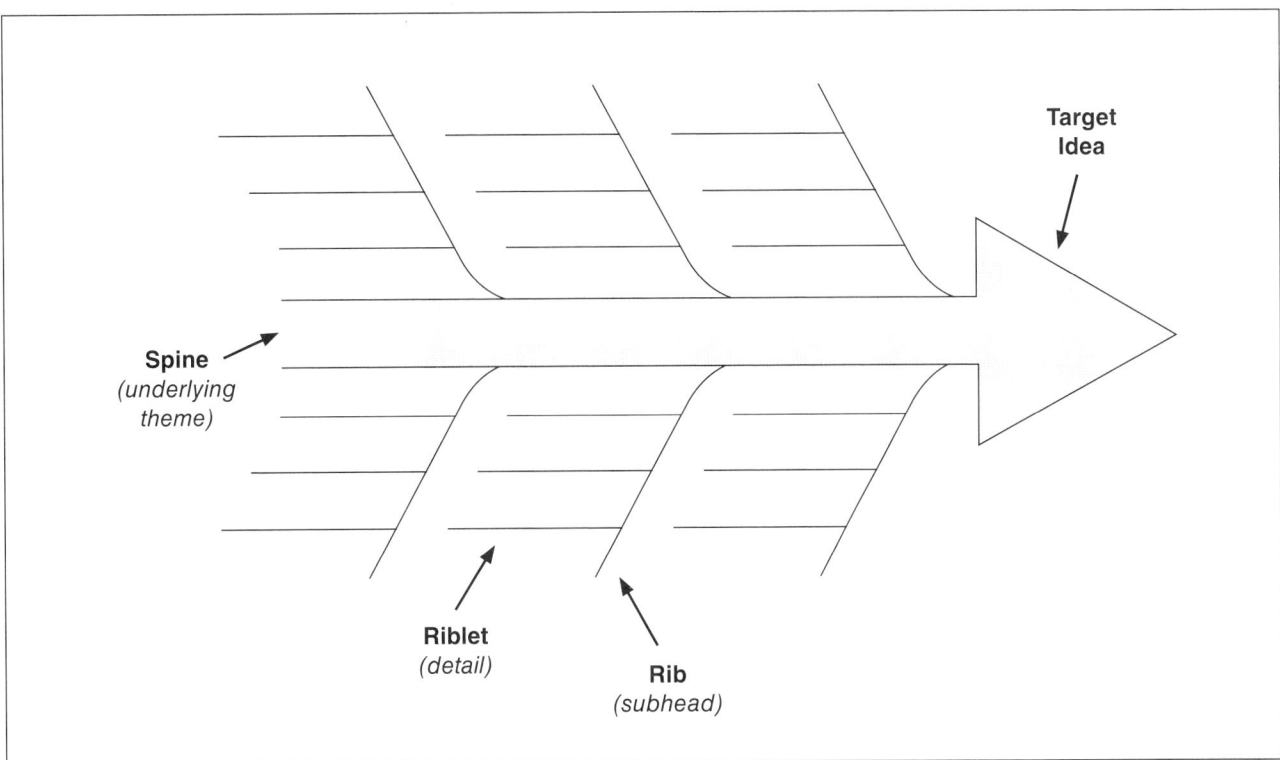

Source: Adapted from Bellanca et al., 2020.

Figure 6.6: Fishbone graphic organizer.

Visit **go.SolutionTree.com/instruction** for a free reproducible version of this figure.

to see surprising connections between disparate subjects and ways of thinking.

Dictionaries define creative thinking as the cognitive process of imagining or making original ideas while producing artistic work (Business Dictionary, n.d.). The creative process, or creativity, means making new connections between old ideas, discovering new relationships between concepts, or establishing new links that result in a novel outcome. Even billionaire investor Ray Dalio (as cited in Langlois, 2018) says, "I think it's also important for [students] to learn how to think creatively for themselves rather than just follow instructions."

You can highlight the following four skills when you foster creative thinking via a personalized learning plan: (1) visualizing, (2) ideating, (3) synthesizing, and (4) accessing the future. When you emphasize the skills in the VISA acronym, you will find it easier to blend creative-thinking skills instruction into your classroom.

V = Visualize (Imagine)

I = Ideate (Generate ideas)

S = Synthesize (Connect)

A = Access the future (Predict)

What Is Visualizing?

Visualizing is the cognitive skill of seeing in novel ways via the mind's eye. Some refer to this skill as *imagining*. Others might say *imaging*. It is a skill that helps students become more flexible and fluent in how they think as they view objects, people, processes, and events in different ways via their imaginations. Flexible thinking shows variations; fluency shows amounts in one or more variations, or quantities. Brainstorming is the skill that promotes both. As an output of creative thinking, a brainstormed list would include many (fluent) variations on a theme or idea. You can test your fluency by listing as many ideas as you can for increasingly complex thinking in your classroom. You can test your flexibility by seeing how many variations of each idea you can generate.

Although poets are expected to imagine, artists to dream, architects to envision, science fiction writers to fantasize, photographers to picture, school leaders to make a vision, astronomers to stargaze, and filmmakers to visualize, children are often stopped if they dare to daydream, stargaze, or imagine while on school grounds. In a 1934 study (Sackett, 1934), education research suggested that learning is improved when students are asked to rehearse in their minds, or visualize, completion of a motor task. Professors Tim Blankert and Melvin R. W. Hamstra's (2016) more recent study reinforces Sackett's (1934) findings by noting the significant gains when students imagine task steps.

What Strategies and Activities Promote Visualization?

This selection of activities delivers examples of age-appropriate strategies you can call on to promote visualizing. To integrate these into personalized learning plans for students of different ages, adjust the level of difficulty.

Elementary School

The following activities promote visualization skills in elementary school students.

My Goal

Try these three steps for a visualization exercise with an emphasis on goal setting.

1. Ask students to picture a goal for today in their minds. They can ask themselves, "What is important for me to do well? Accomplish? Get done?"
2. Guide them with questions to make a SMART goal.
3. Start a pair-share so each can share the goal with a partner. After repeating this for several days, move the pairs to share a weekly goal. At the end of each day they shared a goal, ask them to write exit tickets assessing a SMART quality that worked for them that day.

Picture Book: When I Grow Up

These three steps help students learn to visualize.

1. Ask pairs to do a pair-share about what they most want to be when they grow up. They should share what they would do in their dream job, where it would be, why they want the job, and what it would take to get it.
2. After sharing, the pairs help each other make a picture book with their answers. Provide materials so they can sketch images or magazines to cut plus other materials for binding the book.
3. Make personalized learning plans with getting the dream job as the outcome. Post the books before parent night. Ask each student to share the book and plan.

Building Block Toy

Ask your colleagues to donate interlocking blocks for this three-step project.

1. Invite students, alone or in pairs, to visualize a new robot toy they would like and could build. Show ideas to the class.
2. Students sketch their ideas and then each make a plan with a description of the toy as the outcome.
3. Display all and ask classmates to explain to one another "I like your toy because . . . " End with a reflection circle where each student explains how describing the image in detail helped him or her.

Middle School

The following activities promote visualization skills in middle school students.

Me Collage

This activity combines an act of creation with visualization in four steps.

1. Ask students to imagine how a talent they have will blossom in the next month or year. Allow time for reflection on what, when, how, where, and other details students can visualize as they see themselves accomplishing this goal.
2. Hand out materials so they can construct a collage or other art form that shows their new talent in action.
3. Introduce a SMART guiding rubric so they can write a plan with an outcome for the first steps to develop their talent.
4. In a team of four, invite each member to share a SMART talent goal and invite warm feedback from all teammates. For the feedback, students can use short *I like* stems. This should take about four minutes at most.

My Story

Follow these four steps.

1. Ask all students to think about a favorite story they have read at home or in school and then

imagine themselves as a character in that story. They could be a new character or replace a character.

2. Guide their images with reflective questions like, "What would you do? When? Where? How? Why?" and so on. Encourage specifics.

3. Afterward, students share the story with a partner who may ask clarifying questions and give warm feedback.

4. Students compose personalized learning plans with a guiding rubric for writing their own short stories. When stories are done, they use the guiding rubric for your feedback and peers'.

Analogy Central

The following two steps will help students improve their creative-thinking skills with unique and imaginative comparisons.

1. Through the year, teach a standards-suggested analogy form with your content in mind. If you are the language arts teacher on a grade-level team, plan how you can teach *analogy* per your standard.

2. Help students construct personalized learning plans for transferring analogous thinking into their content: analogies for numeric operations, for historic events, and so on.

Invent It My Way

Here are the steps for a visualizing activity.

1. Ask the class to imagine the steps involved in completing a task such as inventing a new way to study for a test.

2. Ask each student to visualize the steps with concrete images before they sketch images on paper or digitally.

3. Post each student's set of steps and host a gallery walk. Encourage combinations, enlargements, and reductions. Ask students to post sticky notes with added ideas, combined steps, or more steps.

4. Hold an all-class discussion about how this activity—seeing with the mind's eye—and the gallery walk improved students' ideas in number (fluency), differences (fluency), and quality. Discuss with them that intelligence experts consider fluency and flexibility signs of intelligence (Shi, Wang, Yang, Zhang, & Xu, 2017).

5. To further develop their flexibility and fluency, repeat the step-imagining activity with other topics that focus on improving learning skills. That might include steps for how to improve the homework process, be a better teammate, or write a better essay.

6. After each session, guide application of imagined ideas into personalized learning plans. When using this strategy multiple times, try brainstorming a list of ideas: What would they like to invent that would help them be a better friend, student, daughter, or son, for example? They can plan personalized learning plans with their selections.

7. Structure an activity for teams to make their own playbooks for how to invent. Integrate the best ideas into a single chart for the whole class.

High School

The following activities promote visualization skills in high school students.

Journey: A Storyboard

Visualize with high school students using this three-step process.

1. Invite students to take an imaginary journey to visit a cousin on another continent. Let them research this cousin's country and what daily life looks and sounds like.

2. They picture themselves interacting with the relative as they tour the country. After visualizing the journey, students create a list of skills (like those required in basic cognition, complex cognition, and social-emotional learning) needed to live and work there. They also create a storyboard with at least ten segments showing the cousin using one or more of these skills in daily life.

3. Extend this activity with a personalized learning plan for making SMART goals with the selected skills.

Public Sculpture

Students can use their imaginations with this two-step activity. You could combine this with the country research activity, so the sculpture would reflect where it exists and what matters in that culture or physical location.

1. Show the class a public sculpture and a public mural.

2. Each student writes an individual or team personalized learning plan to research public sculpture in your community, visualize and plan a public sculpture or mural connected to your content area, and make and display it. An example of connection to content is, if you teach world history, focusing on immigrants' contributions to our community. Allow time for peer feedback during and after the project.

Model Interview

Interviews are the vehicle for these visualizations in the following five-step project.

1. Assign cooperative groups of between three and five students to research a person who made important contributions in your content area. Jigsaw the selections by dividing responsibilities among teams or team members. For instance, if there are four people, each will interview one person and summarize the ideas for the others. Jigsaws also allow teams to gather and share information (for instance, one student reads about an animal's habitats, a second reads about diet, a third reads about predators, and a fourth reads about environmental benefits). They matrix the information to come up with a comprehensive study.

2. After researching this person, the team imagines what a day in this person's life looks and sounds like, creates a two-column chart of imagined actions and words, and constructs a plan for an imaginary interview.

3. Each team researches criteria for imagining and uses their findings to create a guiding rubric.

4. Teams present their rubrics to the class, asking for audience feedback.

5. You can extend this activity with a class discussion of what everyone learned from researching their chosen person and what might fit in a personalized learning plan.

How Do I Create a Guiding Rubric for Visualizing?

In the activities given in this section, note the choices you can make to integrate what you have learned about personalized learning plans to develop student skills. Look back over the activities and note the different ways available for developing these skills. Pick one of the ways and adapt the guiding rubric in figure 6.7 for a plan you think might work with your students.

What Is Ideating?

With the skill *ideating*, students generate different but related ideas. Their divergent ideas can range from

Name:	Date:	Class:
Period:	Content area:	Unit lesson:

Rating scale:

0 = All was dark.
1 = A glimmer of an idea
2 = Some light, some shadow
3 = Mostly sunny
4 = Basking in light

To what degree did I do the following?

____ Find a quiet place to relax.

____ Destress myself with even breathing.

____ Picture myself performing.

____ See myself near my goal.

____ See myself reaching my goal.

____ Try different methods to explore surroundings in my image.

____ Enjoy myself.

____ Recall my journey.

Figure 6.7: Visualizing—An example guiding rubric.

*Visit **go.SolutionTree.com/instruction** for a free reproducible version of this figure.*

concrete facts to abstract thoughts. Students start by producing concrete, factual ideas about people, places, things, actions, and events. As they become intellectually more flexible and fluent, they develop a capacity to generate more abstract and elaborate ideas. For example, from the moment a child connects a label or word to an object, creative thinking starts to develop the vocabulary. As that vocabulary expands, children become more fluent in expressing what they see, hear, feel, and touch. The more connections they can make, the more fluent they become in their expressions, not only in spoken words, but also in written words and visual images. Although you may start ideation with concrete examples you feel are important to the class, you might want to consider starting with individuals visualizing how they might improve concrete objects they use every day: bookbags, smartphones, school rules, and more. Later, ask them to brainstorm topics relevant to their everyday lives or topics of interest.

How Do I Construct a Personalized Learning Plan That Promotes Ideation Skills?

The playbook in figure 6.8 presents a project from a U.S. history class. Note how the plan combines development of student ideation and the concept of women's roles. Within the playbook, you will also find evidence-based strategies including graphic organizer production by cooperative learning teams, opportunities for two-way feedback, a student playbook, reflection prompts, and transfer.

Figure 6.9 (page 134) shows the start of a concept map for this project. Figure 6.10 (page 134) sequences the tasks for students in a student playbook.

1. Organize teams, identify the outcomes, and review formal team roles, expectations, guidelines, and norms.
2. Project a blank image of a tree with the personalized learning plan's title written on the trunk.
3. Provide major category names so that teams can copy the tree organizer on chart paper and label the larger limbs with selections such as these: Supreme Court justices, on currency, cited in national or state education standards, African Americans, activists, Latinas, scientists, visual artists, musicians, or others the students brainstorm.
4. Explain how each team will research a woman who fits in a category and then add further branches to show her contributions. Each team will make and post its own map with four or more branches.
5. Brainstorm names of famous American women. (Encourage inclusion from all walks of life or focus on a single group, such as authors or athletes.) Prime the pump with examples from the following list.

Maya Angelou	Marsha P. Johnson	Betsy Ross
Joan Baez	Dolley Madison	Lakshmi Singh
Margaret Cho	Margaret Mead	Sonya Sotomayor
Tammy Duckworth	Sandra Day O'Connor	Harriet B. Stowe
Amelia Earhart	Annie Oakley	Harriet Tubman
Ruth Bader Ginsburg	Michelle Obama	Serena Williams
Dolores Huerta	Rosa Parks	

6. Invite teams to complete maps (figure 6.9, page 134) for the selected person. After teams complete maps, create a new tree map showing the connections among the women that occur in addition to time and physical location.
7. As a follow-up, organize future investigations with outcomes connecting women to the times or places in which they lived. Invite teams to construct and illustrate a timeline based on what they discovered about American women in history. You can widen the focus to include women from any time period or from around the world.
8. Conclude with a reflection on creative thinking. Prompt with questions such as, "How did the map help you generate more ideas, make connections, or have new insights?"

Figure 6.8: Teacher playbook—Promoting ideation example.

Visit go.SolutionTree.com/instruction for a free reproducible version of this figure.

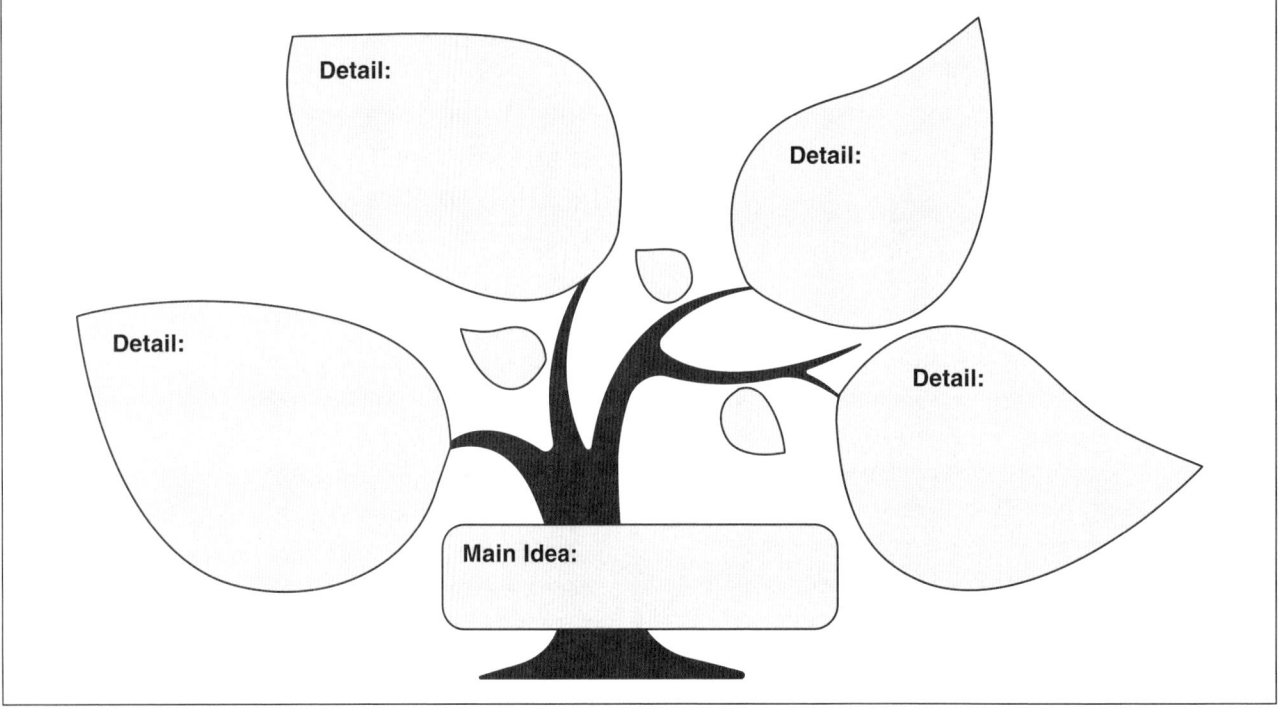

Figure 6.9: Women in American history—Starter map example.

*Visit **go.SolutionTree.com/instruction** for a free reproducible version of this figure.*

1. Agree on team roles and responsibilities.
2. Select a category of American women in history. Research and list the names in the selected category. Be prepared to explain why you made that choice.
3. Select one woman your team will study in depth. Identify sources and brainstorm questions that will help you understand why she is important. Questions might be something like, What characteristics, incidents, or contributions made her important?
4. At the agreed-on time, with your team, construct your concept map.
5. When invited by your teacher, add your team's map to the class tree. Join the class discussion your teacher will lead to find the commonalties among individuals who contributed to American history.
6. After the map is complete, invite teams to reflect and share. Ask questions such as the following.
    - "What did you learn about making connections?"
    - "What was hard to do during this task?"
    - "What was easy?"
    - "What information did you have to synthesize?"
    - "Where in the past have you had to synthesize?"
    - "How can what you learned about being innovative and making connections help you academically? Socially?"
    - "What criteria did you use to evaluate your performance as a connection maker?"
7. Focus on the concept map as a tool for connecting ideas. Prepare a personalized learning plan guiding rubric for one map-making activity per quarter. In the next quarters, attend to characters, places, or events, concepts, rules, ideas, and standards studied in the units.

Figure 6.10: Student playbook—American women in history concept map.

*Visit **go.SolutionTree.com/instruction** for a free reproducible version of this figure.*

What Strategies and Activities Promote Ideation?

Brainstorming is a key technique for promoting ideation at any age, in any content area, by any student. However, it is important to remember that brainstorming is a multifaceted *method*, not a skill. With the brainstorming method, your aim is to help students develop their ability for thinking divergently. There are other divergent thinking methods as well.

Divergent thinking methods ask students, without setting limits, to generate multiple ideas or examples. A divergent thinking method, like brainstorming, will create many ideas for what a jazz fan includes in a playlist. (*Who should I consider to put on my favorite jazz players list?*) Contrast *divergent* thinking methods with *convergent* thinking methods. A convergent method, like sequencing, asks that multiple objects be placed in an order by time. When a jazz fan wants to provide instructions for his children to play his favorite musician, he makes a sequenced playbook. (*When you want to listen to Miles Davis, please follow the instructions step by step.*)

As students expand basic creative-thinking skills, teachers can prompt them in different ways, the foremost of which may be via informal and formal brainstorming techniques.

Brainstorming Techniques

Think about both formal and informal brainstorming. *Informal brainstorming* starts with prompts and questions that encourage flexible and fluent thinking. Remember that flexibility reveals variations, and fluency reveals an amount. Figure 6.11 has prompts, stems, and questions that attend to these characteristics.

Formal brainstorming, unlike its informal sibling, follows explicit group norms and procedures in response to a driving question with an implied but desired outcome. Most often, outcomes from formal brainstorming are assessed with an innovative criterion. Innovative may include novel ideas or novel variations brought about by varying key attributes or qualities of the target such as the possibilities that follow. "Shall we make it bigger, better, smaller, heavier, or lighter? A different color? A different flavor? Upside-down?" and on and on to produce variations that may be outlandish but always novel in some way.

Although one student might brainstorm alone, the formal tool is most productive when it involves three to seven persons building random responses off each other's ideas. The opportunity for multiple heads to build off each other's ideas together can make it easier to expand a list with more variety (AlMutairi, 2015). Before initiating a group brainstorm, it is productive to identify norms. Group brainstorming norms are a key element for any environment that fosters creativity (Covey, 2004). By reviewing the norms of brainstorming with a group or the whole class, you establish the needed climate of safety, which can reassure hesitant students that it is emotionally safe to join in and add their divergent responses. In practice, positive norms are meant to dissuade negative comments, put-downs, and mean behaviors. Brainstorming norms encourage positive acceptance of the wildest ideas.

- **There are no dumb ideas in a brainstorm.** This is absolute. The goal is as many connected ideas on the topic selected as anyone can add. The more the merrier. The crazier and further outside the box, the better.
- **There is no criticism of any idea.** Just keep the flow going as fast as the recorder can write. Don't judge an idea by saying one is good or bad. Don't stop to discuss. Only give more ideas.
- **There are always ways to add to others' ideas.** Make any idea bigger or smaller, fuller or thinner. Think of close and far cousins. Have fun with words; visualize synonyms.

Flexibility	Fluency
Encourage flexibility with questions or prompts like the following. • "What's another way to . . . ?" • "What is a different way to . . . ?" • "What else can you tell me about . . . ?" • "A different way might be . . ."	Encourage fluency with open-ended starter stems such as the following. • "Tell me three . . ." • "List as many . . ." • "How many more examples will show . . . ?"

Figure 6.11: Flexibility and fluency questions, prompts, and stems.

Formal brainstorming is the most common technique for helping students prepare personalized learning plans. When guiding students through the plans, call on group brainstorming to facilitate all-class lists of possible outcomes, possible steps to take, resources or tools to use, obstacles, and criteria for rubrics. To encourage more divergent and innovative thinking, you can ask students to combine, modify, double, or divide ideas as they collaborate to make group lists.

For equipment, you need a flat surface all can see, such as chart paper or an interactive whiteboard, and markers or sticky notes. For small-group or whole-class instruction, an interactive whiteboard works well, especially if you can network it with digital devices. Remember the following tips for managing formal brainstorming.

- Large sheets of chart paper or sticky notes to post on a bulletin board are non-digital substitutes.
- Networked computers allow each small group to brainstorm its list before you connect as a whole group to show the lists on the interactive whiteboard.
- Call on student volunteers to facilitate, keep time, and record the activity.
- For assessment, focus first personalized learning plans on fluency—sheer numbers. Later rubrics can guide fluency, flexibility, or both qualities together.

To facilitate group brainstormed lists, follow the playbook in figure 6.12.

After students are familiar with formal brainstorming, consider advanced variations that further stimulate fluency, flexibility, and novelty. When you plan units in a subject area such as chemistry, world history, or a world language, encourage development of this skill. Encourage students to brainstorm outcomes, strategies, and applications that will help their learning in your classroom. Align individual plans, ideation activities, and rubrics to focus on student ideation about a lesson or unit's big idea.

Elementary School

The following activities promote ideation skills in elementary school students but are adaptable to all grades.

My Neighborhood Web

Follow these two steps to promote ideation.

1. Show student pairs how to make a graphic web design using the SmartArt option in Word.
2. Invite pairs to draw pictures or write single words for the many different people they could meet in their neighborhood: a grocer, a mail deliverer, or a neighbor walking her dog. Make quantity the lead criterion in a guiding rubric. The multiple rays from a web challenge students to produce more ideas, practicing fluency.

How Many Uses? Stars in the Sky

Follow these four steps to promote ideation.

1. From a whole-class circle, record how many uses the class can brainstorm for a common item.
2. Pair students. Let each pair cut out a star pattern and write or show one use on its front.
3. Each week, after selecting a prompt to change one use in some way, hang the stars.

1. Select a fast-writing recorder and a student facilitator who encourages more ideas from everyone in the room. You observe from the side. A student timer is optional.
2. Identify the outcome. For example, it might sound like "as long a list as possible to identify . . . in three minutes."
3. Show and review a guiding rubric with the various ways to think divergently.
4. If you want, add your ideas when student flow slows. Invite all to build on your ideas by adding, dividing, expanding, and more.
5. Determine to what degree the brainstorm effort achieved the outcome.
6. Review the rubric and ask, "What was done well?" and "How can we improve our brainstorming?"

Figure 6.12: Brainstorm playbook.

Visit go.SolutionTree.com/instruction for a free reproducible version of this figure.

4. Structure personalized learning plans to improve brainstorming skills. Outcomes can focus on flexibility (different ideas) or fluency (many new ideas).

What I've Learned

Ideation is the focus of this activity's steps.

1. In a whole-class circle, invite students to give an example of one idea learned in your class.
2. Discuss classroom norms and brainstorm norms.
3. On the whiteboard, record new responses. Keep the time short but repeat every few days and add new ideas. Reassess the norms.
4. Make a personalized learning plan about what students learn from this activity. For example, they might elect as an outcome that they give more specific ideas or add an example to an idea.

Middle School

The following activities promote ideation skills in middle school students.

Hero Mindstorming

Try these four steps with students for brainstorming practice.

1. Review brainstorm norms.
2. Invite the class to brainstorm characteristics of people they admire. Record them on the whiteboard. Link this to the social-emotional skills discussed in chapter 7 (page 149). You might work on a personalized learning plan cultivating a characteristic a lot of the class admired.
3. Set up formal trios, provide a guiding rubric for teamwork, and ask teams to create a hero with a costume and a storyboard showing the hero's characteristics in action.
4. Teams present boards before self-assessing teamwork (figure 7.8, page 166).

Pieces of Junk

Follow these five steps for brainstorming practice.

1. Group students in formal cooperative trios.
2. Develop individual plans with a guiding rubric for brainstorming (page 139). Do a whole-class brainstorm and select the criteria for this rubric.
3. Each trio collects ten pieces of junk they find at home or in the neighborhood. After brainstorming what they can make with these pieces, they sketch the best idea and then make it.
4. In a presentation, each trio self-assesses their brainstorming and explains their products.
5. End with a follow-up personalized learning plan for each student's brainstorming improvement. Ask each student to pick one way he or she would like to improve brainstorming. For example, that might be *making more contributions to the team list*. Frame the choices as their outcomes. You may have a vote and just pick one for the class.

Person, Place, Thing Review

Follow these four steps for brainstorming practice.

1. The class brainstorms names of people, places, or things learned about in your class and arranges them in three columns.
2. Set trios to select one name from a hat and build a concept map about it. The map will show all information they can recall or find in a text or notes and show on a concept map (like the one in figure 6.13, page 138).
3. Host a gallery walk and discuss how ideation helped while making the maps.
4. Make a personalized learning plan for individual ideation skill improvement with flexibility, teamwork, or fluency as an outcome.

High School

The following activities promote ideation skills in high school students.

The Matrix Generator

Follow these five steps for brainstorming practice.

1. From the topics in a lesson or unit for your course, list between four and six headers in a matrix of between six and eight rows. For example, in science, you could include attributes of a genus. In a world language class, you could include verb forms.
2. Invite the class to fill in columns with random examples of headers. After filling in each column, teams throw dice to select one item in each column.

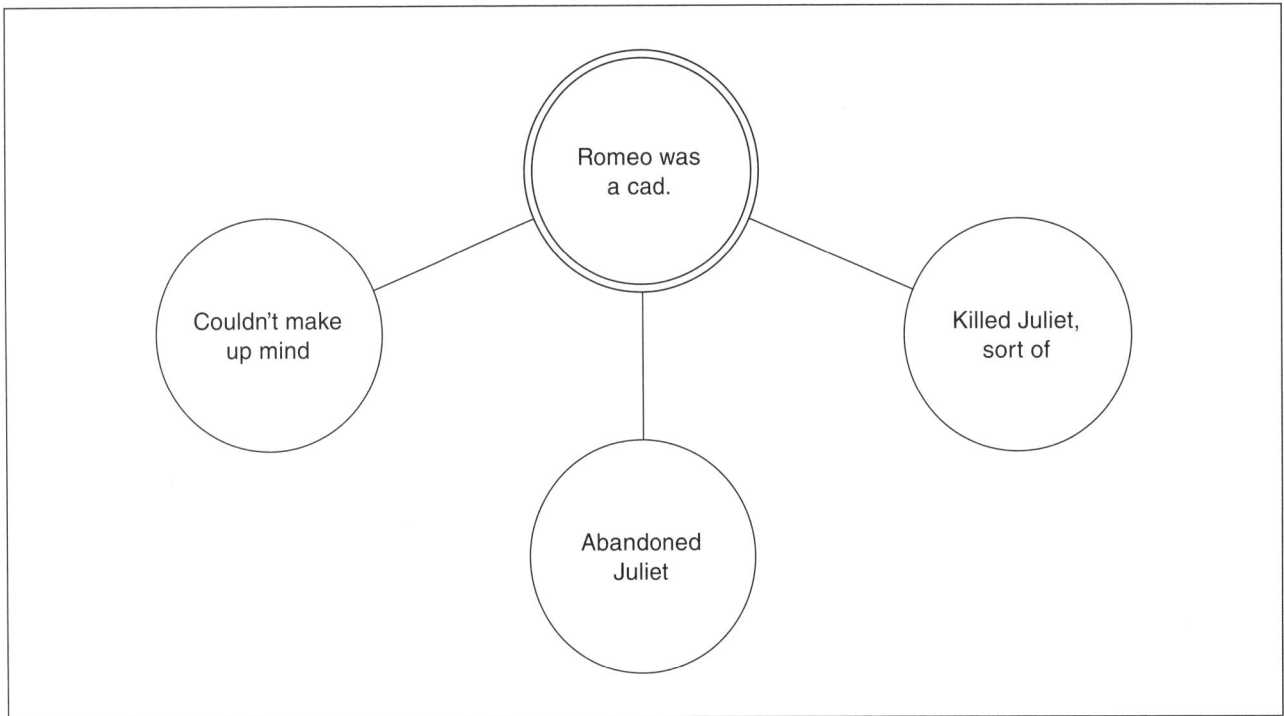

Figure 6.13: Concept map.

3. Students sketch the result, name it, and share with the class.
4. The whole class discusses how the matrix stretched ideation.
5. Students self-assess ideation and make a personalized learning plan for the next ideation outcome.

Digital Brain Netting

This five-step strategy helps students benefit from digital networks. By coupling the interactive whiteboard and networking with student teams on a single digital device per team, you enhance their digital facility with a sharing tool.

1. Select a brainstorm activity to spread over multiple periods or outside the classroom as a homework activity.
2. Teams of five review brainstorm norms and brainstorm a topic related to the unit they have just studied. Start with a think-pair-share with the driving question *What do we think are the five most important ideas we have studied in this unit?* For each item, the pair constructs a *why*.
3. Show how digital brain netting works with the Google Share function. Each pair in turn adds one item to the shared list. If an item is already on the list, it should not be duplicated. Continue in turn until all items from pairs are listed.
4. Review the process with an *I learned* stem about digital brain netting. Have a student record the responses to share with all.
5. Optional: Have each student identify a skill to improve on digital netting.

My Career

Follow these four steps for brainstorming practice. This activity works well when you want to clarify or practice forward transfer (page 107) with students.

1. Pairs brainstorm career ideas related to your course's competencies, and then the whole class brainstorms a complete career list.
2. With digital sticky notes or paper notes on a wall, students post competencies they think are needed to work in this career.
3. Assign each pair to a group. Pairs research and create a digital ad via Google, Canva (www.canva.com), or a similar website for a job that requires those competencies.
4. Host a gallery walk and ask students to sign up for any career they find interesting. Arrange for a counselor to speak, or arrange for speakers to discuss each career with interested students.

How Do I Create a Guiding Rubric for Formal Brainstorming?

Figure 6.14 is a sample rubric ready for adoption or adaption with a different format or different criteria. See the reproducibles "Single-Point Guiding Rubric—Grades 3–12" and "Multi-Point Guiding Rubric—Grades 3–12" (pages 226 and 228) for blank templates. Single-point rubrics are most user friendly when students are novice self-assessors and you want to focus on two-way feedback. Multi-point rubrics are more detailed and therefore work better when you are relying on the criteria to show students more explicitly what it takes for high performance. It also makes it easier for you to tabulate points if you turn the guiding rubric into a grading rubric.

What Is Synthesizing?

Synthesizing is the cognitive process of joining ideas together to make a new idea which combines elements of the original two. When synthesizing, the mind looks to find commonalities or relationships even among apparently opposing ideas so that it can join different parts to make a whole new object. As with the other creative-thinking skills, you can insert the skill into a personalized learning plan.

What features do flowers, friends, book characters, famous battles, or number sequences have in common? How are the objects in this group linked?

- In literature, you ask students to analyze an idea, character, or situation, but then invite them to see how the parts or the whole link to ideas with similar characteristics or ways of behaving.

- In social studies, you ask two opposing political parties with different views on climate change to agree to a workable solution.

- In a project-based interdisciplinary unit, you ask students in what ways a historic figure such as Queen Victoria is linked to late 19th century literature and the development of large urban slums.

Name:		Date:		Grade:
Class:		Period:		Topic:
Teammates:				
Criterion	**Not Yet**	**Somewhat**	**Mostly**	**Top Notch**
Set up our cooperative team.	No roles or designated responsibility agreement No norms No rubric	One from Not Yet column	Two from Not Yet column	Three from Not Yet column
Review our norms.	No norms created	Read norms and asked a clarifying question	Read norms, clarified, and expressed agreement	Discussed and signed norms agreement
Generate many ideas.	No ideas generated	Between ten and fifteen ideas generated	Between sixteen and twenty ideas generated	Over twenty-one ideas generated
Generate many different ideas.	No different ideas generated	4–5	6–8	9+
Generate many novel ideas.	No novel ideas generated	2–3	4–6	7+

Figure 6.14: A multi-point guiding rubric—Synthesizing example.

*Visit **go.SolutionTree.com/instruction** for a free reproducible version of this figure.*

In the fifth stage, synthesizing, Bloom's revised taxonomy verbs associated with synthesizing reveal the many mental processes that students might set as outcome statements for developing how they make connections which end as performances, products, and outcomes (Anderson & Krathwohl, 2001). Synthesis in action might look like a student originating, integrating, and combining ideas into a new product, plan, or proposal. When synthesizing, a student may perform the following.

- Arrange
- Assemble
- Compose
- Connect
- Construct
- Create
- Design
- Develop
- Devise
- Formulate
- Generate a plan
- Invent
- Join together
- Rearrange
- Relate
- Reorganize
- Set up

When a teacher is synthesizing, he or she may design a classification scheme for writing educational objectives that combines three 21st century skill sets: (1) complex cognitive, (2) social-emotional, and (3) digital.

Examples of student synthesizing include writing and drawing a picture story about a pet; a class revitalizing a pond so it is environmentally balanced; painting a public mural with images of historic interest to the community; and a chemistry student finding an acid-metal combination that extends car battery life. When making a synthesis, students may need a formal lesson about the skill plus your coaching to capture the nuances of the process and see how connections are made. You certainly can initiate a series of personalized learning plans centered on this skill from an introductory lesson to its transfer into other lessons. For instance, the public mural would have a guiding rubric with criteria that focus on the synthesizing shown.

How Do I Construct a Lesson or Project That Promotes Synthesis Skills?

When you read about ideation earlier in this chapter, you analyzed the what, why, and how to answer a similar guiding question about the complex thinking skill of generating ideas in a sample project about American women in history. For that example, a concept map organized how to facilitate students' learning to *generate* multiple facts and ideas. The map relied on the secondary skills *making connections* and *synthesizing*. A synthesis statement for that process would discuss how the two skills—generating ideas and connecting ideas—were themselves connected. It would also identify how the organizer helped synthesize ideas that didn't appear to be connected at first glance.

If you go back and look at that project's playbook (figure 6.10, page 134) through the lens of a different outcome and rubric, you will see one way to answer the question, How do I construct a lesson or project that promotes students' synthesizing skills? Instead of planning for ideation, you will plan and assess *synthesizing* as the featured skill. After you modify the outcome and guiding rubric in figure 6.14 (page 139), you need only make minor tweaks among the strategies. Table 6.2 outlines the differences and similarities of these two skills in the same project.

What Strategies and Activities Promote Synthesis?

In addition to adapting other activities from ideation and visualization included in this chapter, pick from the following as age-appropriate synthesis-enhancing activities. As you review, think how you can integrate synthesizing into personalized learning plans.

Table 6.2: Ideating and Synthesizing

	Ideating	Synthesizing
Outcome	Produce five groups of ideas about an important woman's role.	Find ten connections in an important woman's life experiences.
Rubric	Focus on generating many different ideas.	Focus on finding connections among ideas.
Organizer	Concept map	Concept map

Elementary School

The following activities promote synthesis skills in elementary school students but are adaptable to all grades.

Math Simile

A simile is a figure of speech that connects two different things in a different, interesting way. It will include the phrases *is like, same as*, or *similar to*. An example is, "A numerator is like the top half of an Oreo cookie." The following two steps promote practice of similes.

1. Pairs brainstorm all terms they can recall from the lesson.
2. Pairs select two terms and brainstorm the ways they can connect each in an analogy.

Random Word Links

Follow these four steps to promote synthesis skills.

1. Students start by connecting a collection of items that don't seem to go together (such as *Harry, mystery,* and *broomstick*).
2. Pairs go online to search for any key word in a book title or by opening a book to any page at random and sticking a finger on a word. If it is a noun, they write it and someone else points to another random page and noun. If the word is not a noun, they continue down the page to the first noun.
3. Teams find and write the third and fifth nouns they have found. Ask students, alone or in pairs, to draw a picture with the two connected words as an animal they name. You can see an example in figure 6.15.
4. Display and discuss the idea of synthesis. You might say that students can use the skill in the future and ask them when they think they will use it.

Middle School

The following activities promote synthesis skills in middle school students.

A Computer Science Metaphor

A metaphor is a figure of speech that connects two objects in a way not easily perceived. It does not include the phrases you find with similes, such as *like* ("My brother is like a giraffe"). Instead, a metaphor would read something like "My giraffe brother has a long neck."

1. Students go online and search a list of nouns that start with the same letter as their last name.
2. Students then select a noun with the same number on the list as the month they were born, and select a second to correspond with the first number of the year. They will then make metaphors with the two words selected and then bridge them into vocabulary words from computer science.

Source: Adapted from Rowling, 1998.

Figure 6.15: Random word links.

3. Students ID key words from their noun lists.

4. The teacher checks for understanding of the concept *metaphor* by asking student pairs to make a metaphor from the selected nouns and giving corrective feedback as needed when they share.

5. The teacher announces that the class is going to transfer metaphor making to computer science as a way to reinforce what they have learned about that subject.

6. With the whole class, brainstorm a list of key computer science words they know.

7. Pairs select and create a metaphor to share.

8. Collect and assess the metaphors. Provide whole-class feedback and share examples (without using names) of those you enjoyed.

9. Discuss the value of metaphors and invite the class to repeat the strategy in future lessons. If you teach elementary students, you can insert the strategy into one different subject each week and make a personalized learning plan for their metaphor making. For instance, one week could cover mathematics, the second week social studies, and so on.

10. Optional: Use personalized learning plans on metaphor making after the first or second round of personalized learning plans. With the class, brainstorm the criteria they think are most important when making metaphors. Their inclusion makes this activity very high agency.

Random Webs

Follow along with these seven steps for synthesis practice.

1. Share an image, such as a spiderweb, that a student pair sharing a computer can create in Word by inserting SmartArt.

2. Paired students name their web and find ten random, dissimilar emojis to place around the web graphic.

3. Two pairs exchange their webs and give each other a random number from one to ten.

4. After you read aloud a story, each pair adds the random number emoji to that story as its new main character.

5. Pairs storyboard and then share the new story with each other or the class.

6. The whole class discusses how and why the synthesis makes the story unique.

7. Focus the story's personalized learning plan on the synthesis of the emoji with the original story. Start with an outcome aimed at the skill of synthesizing. Each will produce a storyboard based on a character created synthesizing his or her persona via ten randomly selected words.

High School

The following activities promote synthesis skills in high school students.

A U.S. Constitution Analogy

Analogies are figures of speech which connect two ideas, topics, people, and so on by identifying hidden relationships. Metaphors and similes are figures of speech used to make analogies. *The Constitution is the pillar of our democracy* is an example. Use the following three steps.

1. Focus a personalized learning plan on this skill.

2. After teaching with examples, check for understanding.

3. Embed analogy making into a content lesson.

That's a Good Connection Because . . .

Promote synthesis with these five steps.

1. Make teams of five, review roles and norms, and give each team a set of colored markers and three sheets of chart paper.

2. Recorders divide a sheet of chart paper into two columns. One column is titled *An improvement*, and the other column is titled *That's a good connection because . . . .*

3. Give each team a topic from a lesson just finished. The recorder starts a round-robin by saying, "A real-world connection I make to this topic is . . ." and writes the connection in the corresponding column. The next person clockwise says, "That's a good connection because . . ." and states why; the recorder writes the response on the chart paper in the corresponding column.

4. That same person adds the next connection, and the person clockwise says, "That's a connection because . . ." and so on around the group. Watch the teams to see when the chart paper is filling up. Decide when to end the round-robin.

5. Each team discusses the ideas and picks the three best connections. Star these and then post the charts for a gallery walk.

How Do I Create a Guiding Rubric for Synthesis?

End with a personalized learning plan assessment on how each student can improve connection making, as illustrated in figure 6.16. Adapt the rubric for assessing the synthesizing skill. Note the call for a synthesis of feedback.

What Is Accessing the Future?

Accessing the future is a creative-thinking process that enables accurate and precise predictions. This skill is essential for helping students do many things, including the following.

- When reading fiction, the student looks for textual clues, such as in what a character says or does and what others may say about her or him. He then makes informed guesses about what the character will do next.

- In a science experiment, the student applies the prediction-making skill to the proposed outcome. She relies on evidence she observes about a process to predict the result. She will not have all the evidence to be 100 percent certain but will strive to find as much evidence as possible for the prediction.

- In mathematics, the student calls on as many facts as possible for estimating (the mathematical equivalent of predicting) a more complex relationship. For instance, using the knowledge of how many marbles fill one cup, the student relies on prior knowledge to estimate how many marbles will fill a two-inch by two-inch container. In advanced mathematics, students develop their estimation skills as they study probability and statistics.

- Art students must estimate canvas size matched with estimates of the painted figure size.

Name:	Date:	
Class:	Grade:	Period:

Feedback is by:
- ☐ Self
- ☐ Teacher
- ☐ Peers: _____
- ☐ Other: _____

Things Done Well	Criteria	Ideas for Improvement
	I took notes on two or more opposing points of view.	
	I considered similarities and differences.	
	I combined differences.	
	I explained why for my combination.	
	I defined the synthesized idea.	

I synthesized feedback by:

Figure 6.16: A guiding rubric—Synthesizing.

*Visit **go.SolutionTree.com/instruction** for a free reproducible version of this figure.*

Predicting may be the most repeated creative-thinking skill in the K–12 curriculum. It is the beating heart of reading comprehension in both literature and informational text. It is a cousin to estimating in mathematics. It appears first when kindergarten students recall what they know about letters and sounds and predict how these help with words they have not yet seen. It continues through times when high school seniors must call on prior knowledge gained in middle school to complete a capstone project. Over the years, strong readers make predictions whenever they read new material, calling on clues to understand novel text.

How Do I Construct a Lesson or Project That Promotes Predicting Skills?

Directed reading is a well-researched, widely practiced strategy that has passed the test of time and spawned at least two derivations that focus teachers' directed questions to maximize student thinking: directed reading thinking activity (DRTA; Stauffer, 1969) and reciprocal teaching (Palincsar & Brown, 1984). DRTA is a comprehension strategy that guides students in asking questions about a text, making predictions, and then reading to confirm or refute their predictions (Kurniaman et al., 2018). Reciprocal teaching means the student and teacher take turns leading a discussion about a text (Palincsar & Brown, 1984). This approach allows teachers to spotlight the creative-thinking skill of predicting. Instead of the factual questions that guide the standard-directed reading interaction, students are asked to make predictions about the text and then to read on to confirm what they proposed. In reciprocal teaching, students learn to use four reading strategies: summarizing, question generating, clarifying, and *predicting* (Pilten, 2016).

For elementary students, DRTA begins with a teacher reading a story. In the midst of the book, the teacher asks students, "What do you think will happen next?" They predict. As the story progresses, each checks to see whether the prediction was accurate. As students move into middle and high school, the teacher looks for students to transfer the procedures and take control of the process.

This creative-thinking skill is one of the easiest to adapt into a personalized learning plan instructional model. It is especially valuable when students are struggling to read. Prior to introducing a prediction-centric personalized learning plan, introduce the skill with a prediction chart like the one in figure 6.17.

The story, remember, is the medium for developing the skill. (For DRTA, adjust the chart's vocabulary to students' grade or reading levels) The chart readies the students to make predictions and draw conclusions about activities in the story. No matter what content area or grade, it is important to review the three key terms in the chart—*predict, clues, accurate*—and to fill in any missing prior knowledge of each term's meaning. By repeating their reading task with this chart, you have another tool for guiding instruction. Through repeated use, look to see the three questions becoming second

Names: Ronaldo, Estevan, Stephanie		**Date:** 9/10
Teacher: Mr. Gregory		**Grade:** 8
Story and author: "The Most Dangerous Game" by Richard Connell (1924)		
What do I (we) predict?	**What clues make us think this?**	**Was the prediction accurate?**
Zaroff eaten by animals Zaroff killed by Rainsford Rainsford loses	No sailors escape Zaroff is great hunter, not challenged by animals anymore Zaroff says "life is for the strong" (survival of the fittest) Zaroff finds Rainsford easy prey The traps fail A matter of time	No

Figure 6.17: Prediction chart—Middle school example.

Visit go.SolutionTree.com/instruction for a free reproducible version of this figure.

nature. Watch for evidence that each can read to make predictions without the chart.

When you repeat prediction making in subsequent directed reading lessons, adding a personalized learning plan makes clear your expectation that each student internalize the questions. The prediction chart in figure 6.18 works for elementary students who are making predictions that the teacher fills in on the board for all to see. The teacher reads a big book and asks a prediction question ("What will happen next?") and a reason question ("Why do you think so?").

With your playbook (figure 6.19, page 146), you can adjust the tool so students learn how to use it no matter what material they read or what their age. It works as well with prewriting and prereading first-grade students' science predictions—such as, Which objects will float, and which will sink?—as it does with twelfth-grade AP history students—Given Malcolm X's ideas about racism, what do you predict he would do?

What Strategies and Activities Promote Predicting Skills?

The following ideas suggest other grade-appropriate strategies for engaging students with prediction making. By wrapping the predicting skill in a personalized learning plan, you increase student focus on the skill and spotlight its importance in the lesson.

Elementary School

The following activities promote predicting skills in elementary school students.

Prediction Pail

Use these five steps to help improve prediction skills.

1. Provide each student an index card. This is an exit ticket to deposit in a bucket posted by the door.
2. Ask each to write on one side of the card what he or she predicts will happen in the next page (or chapter or at the end). On the other side, students write what happened on the current page (or chapter) that is a clue to their predictions.
3. Tabulate and share results after you collect them.
4. Make a second list from the answers on the other side of the card—how they made their predictions. Add ideas and refine the list.
5. Set up plans for future stories (read aloud or individually). Some elementary-level stories that facilitate making predictions follow.
   - *Chester's Way* by Kevin Henkes (1988)
   - *Doctor De Soto* by William Steig (1982)
   - *Duck on a Bike* by David Shannon (2002)
   - *Enemy Pie* by Derek Munson (2000)
   - *Hungry Hen* by Richard Waring (2001)
   - *Ruby the Copycat* by Peggy Rathmann (1991)
   - *Over in the Meadow* by John Langstaff (1957)
   - *I Read Signs* by Tana Hoban (1987)
   - *What Do You Do With a Tail Like This?* by Steve Jenkins and Robin Page (2003)

The Weather Project

The following five steps help improve prediction skills.

1. Invite a local weather person to class (in person or via Skype or Zoom).

Prediction	Reasons	Float 😊 ☹
[Teacher enters student predictions]	[Teacher enters student response]	[Student adds smiley face for an accurate prediction and a sad face for an inaccurate prediction]

Figure 6.18: Prediction chart—Elementary example.

Visit go.SolutionTree.com/instruction for a free reproducible version of this figure.

1. Determine your age-appropriate driving question and outcome for making predictions (such as, *Students will increase the number of accurate predictions by 10 percent per short story*).
2. Set up trios of heterogeneous readers with one strong, one average, and one struggling reader per team. Review roles, norms, and expectations.
3. Pep talk the value of predicting for now and future readings.
4. Define key words for making predictions and check prior knowledge.
5. Pep talk a current news story and show a prediction chart like the one in figure 6.17 (page 144). Ask volunteers to make a prediction about what will follow this news event and tell what clues they picked. Chart responses on your interactive whiteboard as shown here.
6. Introduce a story with an appropriate reading level (for example, elementary school: "Rikki-Tikki-Tavi" [Kipling, 1894]; middle school: "The Most Dangerous Game" [Connell, 1924]; high school: "The Lottery" [Jackson, 1948]).
7. Instruct teams to use the chart as follows.
    a. Read the first page.
    b. Make three predictions about the story's outcome.
    c. Make three more predictions about what will happen next (and give a number of pages).
    d. Continue reading and finding clues. Change predictions so each is two or three pages.
    e. Check the outcome versus the prediction.
    f. Chart the number of accurate predictions (including pages and whole story).
    g. Review to see what you missed or what helped.
8. In the program Word, show students how they will choose Insert, then Chart, then Line Graphs. When a line graph appears, show how they will use it to chart their progress up or down making predictions. The line graph will remind students that the skill is what is most important in this unit and its improvement is theirs to control as they learn from doing now and for the future.
9. Have teams assess how well they made predictions with this story. Use open-ended prompts like the following.
    - "Tell me what you did well making predictions."
    - "What would you do differently in the next story?"
    - "What pleased you about your predictions? What displeased you?"
    - "How can you improve this skill?"
10. After teams discuss, hold a whole-class discussion about teams' answers. Make a list on the interactive whiteboard of all good ideas for making more accurate predictions.
11. For the first near transfer, ask each student to select one idea that will help make predictions more accurate. Make this an outcome for a personalized learning plan. Over an eight-week unit, keep the focus on making predictions with other short stories or novels. When the class graduates to novels, set up the short activity for each chapter. Have students reflect on how they are improving in prediction making. For far transfer, add prompts about how to use predicting in instructional text, science labs, current events, and success in future education.
12. Invite teams to keep a record of accurate versus inaccurate predictions per story.
13. After the plan is achieved, assess progress.

Figure 6.19: Teacher playbook—Making predictions with close reading example.

*Visit **go.SolutionTree.com/instruction** for a free reproducible version of this figure.*

2. Prior to the visit, brainstorm a list of questions about predicting the weather.

3. If possible, pair students and give each pair a question. One asks and the other responds.

4. Discuss resulting ideas and then invite pairs to build simple weather machines to place in the school yard.

5. Using what they learned from the weather person, let the class predict the weather for one week and use the simple machines to gather evidence. Make a teamwork guiding rubric for a personalized learning plan (like the one in figure 6.20, page 148).

Middle School

The following activities promote predicting skills in middle school students.

Dream Job Letter

Follow these four steps for prediction practice.

1. Each student thinks of a dream job and writes a letter of inquiry to a company that might hire someone for the job. In this letter, the student should ask about job requirements.

2. After proofreading, students mail their letters.

3. After responses come in, hold a discussion about what applicants can do to prepare for a job.

4. Students prepare personalized learning plans to polish one of the skills needed for their dream job.

Our STEM Museum

Follow these six steps for prediction practice.

1. Group students in trios for a class project to create a STEM career museum.

2. The whole class brainstorms items they think involve at least two science, technology, engineering, and mathematics (STEM) fields and could be displayed in a museum. Those might include truss bridges, catapults, robots, drones, race cars, a house of cards, or other engineering challenges.

3. Each team researches an object to learn what STEM skills are required.

4. Trios build the objects and attach lists of required skills.

5. Host a gallery walk.

6. Make personalized learning plans for each student to investigate and report on a possible future career.

High School

The following activities promote predicting skills in high school students.

Estimation Games

Follow these six steps to help students make predictions.

1. Set students in groups of five.

2. Calling on VISA skills (page 129), each team creates an estimating game for a third-grade class.

3. Have the team's pair predict how well the game will do.

4. Each team matches with a third-grade class to test the game. Have a common guiding rubric ready for assessing the success.

5. After testing and assessing, discuss the results with a spotlight on how well a game helped the third graders learn about estimation.

6. Make a personalized learning plan with each student selecting a prediction application that he or she thinks would provide academic benefit.

Fishbone for the Future

Follow these three steps to help students make predictions.

1. Teams of five survey parents and other adults in the community to identify a problem such as, for example, homelessness, bus pollution, or noise pollution.

2. Teams analyze the causes of the community-identified problem and suggest a solution. Each team's solution must focus on the causes of the problem by employing the fishbone graphic organizer (figure 6.6, page 129). The solution must satisfy the community's needs.

3. Make team personalized learning plans for planning and assessing the solution's effectiveness.

How Do I Create a Guiding Rubric for Predicting?

Adjust this rubric's language, criteria, and format to your students' ages and reading levels. Attach your modified figure 6.20 (page 148) to your students' personalized learning plans.

Name:	**Date:**
Teacher:	**Period:**
Book title and author:	
Focus: ☐ Main character ☐ Plot	
Feedback is by: ☐ Self ☐ Teacher ☐ Peers: _____ ☐ Other: _____ ☐ Summative grade	
Rating scale: 0 = No accurate predictions yet 1 = One or two accurate predictions 2 = Three or four accurate predictions 3 = All predictions accurate	
To what degree did I (you) do the following? ____ Make accurate predictions. ____ Show evidence for each prediction. ____ Describe my prediction precisely. What I (you) do well when making predictions: What I (you) could improve: What help I (you) need:	

Figure 6.20: Guiding rubric for predicting—Example.

*Visit **go.SolutionTree.com/instruction** for a free reproducible version of this figure.*

TAKEAWAYS

What have you learned about the complex cognitive skill set? What will you do to increase attention to these skills in future lessons and projects?

CHAPTER 7
THE SOCIAL-EMOTIONAL SKILL SET

> If your emotional abilities aren't in hand, if you don't have self-awareness, if you are not able to manage your distressing emotions, if you can't have empathy and have effective relationships, then no matter how smart you are, you are not going to get very far.
>
> —Daniel Goleman

Once, a student revealed to me that she was pregnant. I was silent. I was confused. I could feel upset starting in my stomach, but I knew better than to ask her lots of questions. She admitted being scared and explained what she thought her choices were. I listened. I nodded my head and handed her tissues. When she finished sharing her story, I acknowledged her pain and her predicament. I was an English teacher in no way prepared for this, yet as an important adult in this student's life, I needed to do something.

I said, "I'm going to do what I can to help. The way I can best help you right now is to connect you with a friend, a social worker who has the skills to support you as you make tough decisions."

Many believe that a teacher's job is to teach classes, grade papers and tests, and do lunchroom or bus duty—that's it. Veteran educators know that the reality of what a teacher's work encompasses is often more than that. In addition to the daily decisions teachers make about how to teach, and sometimes what to teach, a teacher's job also involves social-emotional support of and guidance for students. In the words of author Dean Koontz (as cited in Younger, 2016), "Some people think only intellect counts: knowing how to solve problems, knowing how to get by, knowing how to identify an advantage and seize it. But the functions of intellect are insufficient without courage, love, friendship, compassion, and empathy." Empathy is critical to successful teaching and learning.

Later in the school year, I asked my friend, the social worker, for feedback. Without breaking the student's confidence, my friend shared the pluses and minuses on my response at that time. As part of her feedback, she introduced me to Daniel Goleman's (2005) writing, including the quote that begins this chapter. Responding to this student, getting feedback on how I responded, and reading Goleman's work helped me understand the nature of self-awareness, empathy, and emotion management more fully, especially the roles these elements play in making decisions. I learned to appreciate the importance of preparing teachers with the *how* for teaching for social-emotional learning, both for their own benefit and for the benefit of their students.

In chapter 2 (page 35) you read about the classroom climate needed to foster students' growth with the 21st century skill sets. A healthy classroom climate is the social-emotional condition that solidifies a foundation of mutual trust and respect in which students feel psychologically safe to engage in healthy conversations with their peers and with you. When in place, that foundation supports development of social-emotional skills needed by students to engage in meaningful, constructive relationships with peers and to initiate lifelong habits for applying what they have learned. Chapter 2 offers multiple tools that furnish options for promoting collaboration and interpersonal communication while later chapters integrate these two skills into other key deeper learning skill sets. In this chapter, after defining social-emotional learning and the four skills included in this set, you will receive specific suggestions for additional adaptations of the plan tools to each of these skills. When you finish the chapter, you will have gained a deeper understanding of what you can do tomorrow and further in the future to enrich the necessary SEL trust culture.

> **Driving question:** How do I develop social-emotional skills with personalized learning plans?

What Is Social-Emotional Learning?

Per CASEL (n.d.a), *social-emotional learning* (SEL):

> is the process through which children and adults acquire and effectively apply the knowledge, attitudes, and skills necessary to understand and manage emotions, set and achieve positive goals, feel and show empathy for others, establish and maintain positive relationships, and make responsible decisions.

With complex cognition as the head, SEL is the heart of what and how young people learn. CASEL (n.d.b) and other organizations have codified social-emotional theory, and for good reason: "Emotions are not add-ons that are distinct from cognitive skills, but rather become a dimension of the cognitive skill itself" (Immordino-Yang, 2016, p. 21, as cited in Schmidt, 2019.). However, it is important that social-emotional skills don't become a denying set of school codes that are culturally negative for ethnic minorities.

What Skills Make Up the Social-Emotional Skill Set?

CASEL's (n.d.a) theory extends Goleman's (2005) practices of emotional intelligence in the classroom. Four social-emotional skills are the theory's beating heart. *Emotional intelligence* is the ability to understand, use, and manage one's own emotions in positive ways. Positive ways can include empathizing with others, effectively communicating and collaborating, solving inter- and intrapersonal problems, resolving conflicts, and being aware of one's social environment.

Four skills—(1) managing one's emotions, (2) empathizing, (3) establishing positive interpersonal relations, and (4) setting personal goals—are vital for decision making in a social situation inside or outside the classroom. Figure 7.1 illustrates the social-emotional skill set—an intertwined, cyclical improvement pattern with constant opportunity for cross-fertilization. Keeping this image in mind enables the exposition of each social-emotional skill, starting with managing emotions as a distinct, but always connected, element in the self-improvement process.

How does goal setting fit in this cycle? Goal setting and decision making do not occur without an emotional dimension (Lerner et al., 2015). Sometimes emotion helps with setting goals, such as when a student is passionate about the outcome. Sometimes emotion hinders the process, such as when anger occurs. Finally, this skill applies as much to mastering one's emotions and decision making as it does to solving a complex problem.

What Is Emotion Self-Management?

On any given day, students experience many emotions during school. These emotions, including anxiety, "enjoyment, anger, hope, pride and boredom, can each affect students and learning in a variety of ways" (Pekrun, Goetz, & Perry, 2010, as cited in Trezise, Bourgeois, & Luck, 2017). Often, those emotions do not interfere substantially with the class's work or the student's learning. However, in many cases, they are disruptive—to the student, if to no one else. This

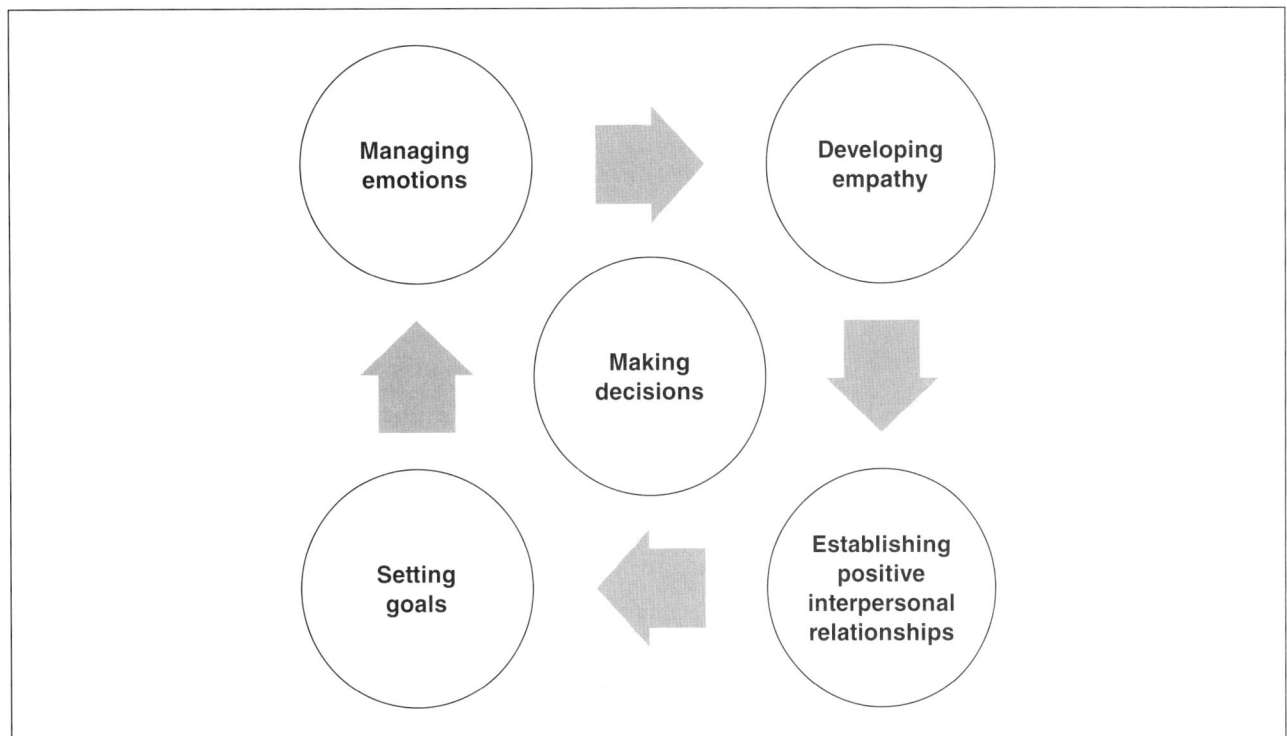

Source: Adapted from Goleman, 2005.

Figure 7.1: Social-emotional skill set.

disruption can stem from frustration at struggling with an academic concept, anxiety about an upcoming assessment, or distress at not meeting a goal. In extreme cases, an entire classroom or hallway of classrooms can become victims of a student's volatility and inability to control his or her emotions, as that student lashes out physically or verbally.

Self-awareness, monitoring our emotions, "is arguably the most crucial academic skill and a building block of self-regulation" (Kamath, 2019). Managing one's emotion's is the next step in that social-emotional proficiency. Students benefit when they manage their frustration with a game referee, screaming coach, unkind peers, a parent who says no, or about what they perceive as an unfair grade. For those who are overwhelmed with anxiety or fear of failure, emotional self-management may be a survival skill.

The cool-down guideline in table 7.1 (page 152) is an easy personalized learning plan fit. Instead of you or a counselor implementing the guidelines each time a student's emotions run high (or indicate they are getting to that point), step back and switch the responsibility to the student to follow the guideline. Invite the student to pick specific personalized learning plan outcome strategies.

How Do I Construct a Lesson or Project That Promotes Emotion Self-Management?

As with any of the skills in the major skill set, you can design one or more lessons or projects around this skill. Attending explicitly to social-emotional skills throughout the school year decreases the chances you will lose time with a student (or the class as a whole) to behavioral remediation. With social-emotional skills that build self-management in your personalized learning plans, you help your students build a climate of trust and mutual respect (chapter 2, page 35; Gregory & Fergus, 2017). Personalized learning plans can help build social-emotional skills in many ways. Consider the full range of outcomes possible by including learning how to give and receive warm and cold feedback, which requires reading another's cues, showing empathy and diplomacy, and all sorts of conflict management.

Start the first social-emotional personalized learning plan with one skill. In some plans, that skill will intersect with critical or creative thinking or digital skills. The social-emotional skill might be *monitoring my emotions*. You and students prepare a SMART outcome statement followed by strategies and rubrics that allow

Table 7.1: Cool-Down Guideline

What to Do	What to Say
1. Give the student time to get calm.	"I notice you're really upset. Let's work together on breathing slowly for one minute in order to manage your impulses."
2. Direct the student to be aware of thoughts and feelings.	"What's going on in your brain and body right now? Tell me how you feel and what you're thinking, and if you're ready to focus on moving forward on calming down."
3. Have the student redirect his or her thoughts.	"Take a minute, close your eyes, breathe slowly, and think about something that makes you happy. I know you told me how much you love your grandma's cookies. Think about walking into grandma's house in a calm state of mind as you smell the cookies, taste the cookies, and feel the warmth of them right out of the oven."
4. Give the student positive feedback on becoming calm.	"Now open your eyes. How are you feeling? If you need more time to settle down, let me know. You should feel happy and excited about your work in getting to this point."
5. Give the student a little more time to refocus.	"Take a minute and do something for you. Go for a walk and get some air or tell me about your game the other night."
6. Have the student reflect for the future.	"The next time you're feeling this way and I'm not with you, can you tell yourself to take charge of your behavior and get yourself to a regulated place?"
7. Guide the student to make a plan in which he or she sets goals, includes strategies to control anger, and sets criteria. Set a time for daily self-assessment and a fixed report time no more than a week away. Highlight the benefits but don't ignore a set of consequences listed in the plan. Be sure the student and the teacher each get a copy of the plan.	"This is really going to help you stay calm when someone tries to get under your skin. Let's meet at lunchtime this week so you can share the experience and see what you can do the next time if it doesn't work."
8. Speak encouraging words as you walk with the student to the classroom. Review the agreement with the teacher and student.	"I'm pleased that we made this agreement. I am looking forward to meeting so you can tell me how well you did. I think you will do as well as you told me. If you do have a bump, please come see me."

each student to monitor and guide his or her behavior and assess results. Remember, you are measuring how the student manages the emotion. If the rubric details criteria for what the *management* (not the *emotion*) looks and sounds like, you make it possible to measure specific signs of improvement. Consider anger management as an example. Ask the student to share what it will look like and sound like when controlling the anger. Examples could be *I will walk away, I will focus on my breathing, I will envision myself in a calm place, I will play a game, I will count to one hundred,* or *I will listen to music.* Other research-based anger-management strategies include reframing the problem or conflict (rather than being angered by a mean comment because it feels like a personal attack, a student might reinterpret the comment as a sign of the friend's exhaustion; Bushman, 2013). Students can prepare improved response outcomes such as distracting themselves by thinking of a pleasant topic or doing other activities that remove the focus on angry feelings (such as play ball with a pet dog, feed the goldfish, do chores, or daydream about a vacation spot [Bushman, 2013]).

Helping students with strategies for diffusion of anger is a first step. By conducting follow-up personalized learning plans, you can maximize agency (chapter 4, page 87) with self-assessment and opportunities for two-way feedback. You can adjust the plan to differentiate students' needs. Even as you focus a plan on anger control for one student, you can allow peers confidentially to respond to their fears and concerns about sitting near an angry or otherwise disruptive student.

What Prompts Encourage Emotion Self-Management?

It is important that you model social-emotional skills during your daily interactions. The following open-ended PACTS prompt model makes it easy to adopt communication skills for personalized learning plans. Figure 7.2 showcases *paraphrase*, *affirm*, *clarify*, *try options*, and *share feelings* prompts that are helpful when calming an upset student. Delivering *I* messages in a warm tone with matching warm and compassionate body language is essential. Think how you can add these prompts to your instructional and relational repertoire.

Try the following with the PACTS model.

- Model these steps when talking calmly in emotional situations such as a meltdown or a lockdown practice.
- Make a bulletin board with this matrix and discuss how and when to use it.
- Lead a make-and-take workshop for teams to make posters to display around the room.
- Role-play starting with your demonstration of the skills in an emotionally charged moment, followed by student pair-practices.
- Discuss how the figure 7.2 skills help self-manage feelings.
- Incorporate a PACTS skill in a personalized learning plan. Pinpoint one of the PACTS as the outcome and provide a guiding rubric so

students can develop it to competency over a month or a semester. To choose, listen to student interactions for a week and chart what you hear and don't hear. Which of the five do you think need most immediate attention?

What Strategies and Activities Promote Emotion Self-Management?

Helping students practice emotional self-management can play a significant role in helping them feel safe with volatile peers. But it does more. By managing their emotions, they expand their sense of self-worth and build their sense of belonging and self-esteem so that they can feel confident about the choices they make in their daily lives (Jones Barnes, Bailey, & Doolittle, 2017). In a classroom, self-management skills contribute to a better work environment as they enable students to persist, show resilience, and be patient as they work with others (Suess, 2015).

To facilitate students' development of this social-emotional skill, you can select from a treasure chest of helpful strategies. However, a single activity done once is a waste of time. It is important to schedule time to practice these skills so students can internalize ways to control their own emotions. For you, the payoff comes with fewer meltdowns and increased trust. By adding personalized learning plans with self-assessment rubrics, you communicate to students the importance of self-management in the classroom and beyond. As with other skill sets, the more agency you structure into personalized learning plan planning, conducting, and assessing, it stands to reason that students will reap benefits.

Elementary School

The following activities promote emotion self-management skills in elementary school students.

P	Paraphrase	"Did I hear you say . . . ?"	"This is what I heard you say . . . ."
A	Affirm	"I appreciate how you . . ."	"I am pleased that you . . ."
C	Clarify	"My example is . . ."	"To be specific, I . . ."
T	Try options.	"I'd like you to try to . . ."	"I think you can . . ."
S	Share feelings.	"I feel that . . ."	"I'm concerned that . . ."

Figure 7.2: Communication skills to manage conflict.

Visit go.SolutionTree.com/instruction for a free reproducible version of this figure.

The following activities help students learn to self-manage.

Classroom Calm Center

Set up a center so students can prevent or calm out-of-control emotions. Encourage students to go to the center when an upset is coming on. Provide materials so students can try the following.

- Squeeze a stress ball.
- Read a book for pleasure.
- Play a computer game.
- Stop and think.
- Draw a web with ideas to control emotions.
- Fill a fishbone graphic organizer showing cause of upset.
- Pick a fun solo game like pick-up sticks or solitaire.
- Invite a share buddy to talk.
- Draw an *I am good at . . .* web.
- Write an *I appreciate . . .* note to a friend.
- Do breathing exercises.
- Journal about a trigger situation.
- Sketch themselves doing what they need to gain control.
- Rehearse how they want to address an emotional trigger the next time.
- Write a *What I did well when . . .* reflection.
- Write a personalized learning plan with an outcome that shows a way to take control of a bad emotion.

Pick a Story

The following three steps help students learn to self-manage.

1. Read a story to the class about a *bad* emotion. Some possibilities follow.
    - *Alexander and the Terrible, Horrible, No Good, Very Bad Day* (Viorst, 2014)
    - *The Feeling Flower* (Dakroub, 2018)
    - *Grumpy Monkey* (Lang, 2018)
    - *When Sophie Gets Angry—Really, Really Angry* (Bang, 1999)

2. Guide a discussion about how the characters feel, how they control their emotions, and so on.

3. Introduce a plan for the character and discuss how the plan might help. For example, Sophie needs to learn anger control. What help could her friends give? What would result from that help? Ask students to make a plan that helps Sophie stay calm. Students pilot the plan, measuring the result with a rubric that fits the outcome. For instance, Sophie's outcome will be a journal she keeps. A chart in the journal will show a percentage improvement over a certain number of weeks of her using a strategy she calls *just leave it*. For the rubric criteria, she can use these five strategies: (1) I walk away at once and don't look back, (2) I count to myself, (3) I take deep breaths, (4) I do push-ups, and (5) I go for a run. She rates those on a 1–4 scale for how effectively they help her, with 1 being not at all helpful and 4 being the best idea ever because she felt better. She might try each if she has a lot of anger, and could end with a rating scale comparing results.

ABC Book

The following three steps help students learn to manage their emotions.

1. Read books focused on feelings and talk about feelings.

2. Brainstorm how students can make their own ABC book about managing emotions. (Visit www.readwritethink.org for detailed help.)

3. Consider an all-class personalized learning plan focused on *sharing my feelings*. For assessment, offer two stems: *what I found easy* and *what I found hard*. After a round-robin responding to the stems, guide an open-ended discussion where students respond to, "What method from this discussion would you like to add to make talking about feelings easier?"

Emoji Card Trading

The following four steps help students learn to manage their emotions.

1. The class brainstorms the names of emotions they feel.

2. Provide materials for paired partners to make sets of trading cards with emojis on one side and key words that match the emoji emotions

on the other. Show a model of happy faces being glad and sad faces frowning or crying to prime the pump.

3. Hold weekly conventions so pairs can share and trade cards. Stand the class together in an open space. Tell them to mingle until they hear a bell. At the bell, they find a partner with whom they have not chatted and share their cards. Go through several rounds with a new partner each bell.

4. Initiate personalized learning plans with selected communication skills such as introducing oneself, taking turns, or showing appreciation.

Middle School

The following activities promote emotion self-management skills in middle school students.

Teach Self-Monitoring Questions

Try this strategy's two steps to instruct on managing emotions.

1. Students watch a video or read a short story that involves an emotion, such as fear.

2. Teach self-monitoring questions in paired partner prompts. Share one of the following prompts with students after they read or watch the video.

    - What emotion would I feel in this situation?
    - What do I think I should do to control my feelings?
    - What effect would that strategy have for other people and for me?
    - Does this action fit with who I want to be?
    - If not, what else could I do that might fit better?
    - Is there anyone else I could ask about this who might help me?

PACTS

Use PACTS in the following two steps to extend conversations about managing emotions.

1. After sharing figure 7.2 (page 153) with students and modeling PACTS, invite each student to make a personalized learning plan focused on controlling an emotion that sometimes unsettles them.

2. Each student selects one PACT skill for a personalized learning plan focus.

Me Journals

Follow these two steps to help students learn to manage their emotions.

1. As a class, brainstorm guiding stem statements like those that follow.
    - When I feel (*emotion*), I am trying to . . .
    - It is helpful if . . .
    - I am pleased that . . .
    - . . . is what I'm doing well when I feel . . .
    - I need help to . . .

2. Provide time each week so students can choose a stem and reflect in a journal how they are controlling their emotions. If a student wishes to sketch or make her own self-directed entry, that's a higher-agency option. Never read entries without a student's request.

Podcasts

Follow these three steps for an emotion-management activity.

1. Read a story about a character struggling to maintain self-control.

2. Teams make a five-minute podcast about lessons learned from the main character's emotion management.

3. Turn one lesson into a personalized learning plan with an outcome, such as *By the end of this month, our team will produce a five-minute podcast in which we role-play our own story of someone struggling to control an emotion.*

Support Groups

Follow these three steps for an emotion-management activity.

1. Engage in trust-building activities (chapter 2, page 35) for twenty minutes once a week.

2. When bonded, let groups decide what emotional trigger issues they want to share. Be sure groups focus on emotion management. Leave personalities out of the discussion. Trigger issues might include *my little brother tells my parents when I'm on Snapchat after lights out; my best friend bugs me to do her homework; my boss at*

my part-time job makes inappropriate comments; and *the mean girls in our advisory pick on us*.

3. End with personalized learning plans that focus on self-control when someone pushes a personal button.

High School

The following activities promote emotion self-management skills in high school students.

Board Game Invention

Self-management skills are the focus of this four-step activity.

1. Teams brainstorm board games built around the theme of controlling emotions.
2. Teams select their own focus and gather materials. One-word prompts for a potential board game focus follow.
   - Benefits
   - Drawbacks
   - Management at home
   - Management in school
   - Management with friends
   - Management in sports
   - Specific emotions
   - Skills
3. After games are complete, hold a tournament.
4. Reflect on what students learned about emotion control—including while brainstorming, creating, and playing the games—and a list of ways to do that for a guiding rubric.

Children's Book

Follow these four steps for self-management help with middle school students.

1. After brainstorming a list of themes, structure teams to write and illustrate big books about controlling emotions.
2. After searching online for picture books and grade stories, each team makes a book to read to a primary-level class. Arrange with primary teachers so each team can visit and read its story.
3. Back in their own class, discuss what they learned about managing emotions from the selected stories and for the stress they experienced (if any) of reading to the younger students.
4. Make personalized learning plans about managing emotions.

Dig Their Feelings

After analyzing a character in a short story or a historic or scientific figure, teams make a list of objects they imagine would be favorites in the character's daily life. Teams pick one object that, if lost or damaged, could prompt a strong emotional reaction. Make the object and bury it where designated. Other teams go on a dig, find an object, find its makers, listen to their description of the character, and guess the emotion. After explaining why they chose the emotion, the teams compare notes and write a rubric that assesses emotion self-management. The criteria they select should call on their own experience managing emotions well.

How Do I Create a Rubric for Monitoring Emotions?

Figure 7.3 shows an example guiding rubric for responding with feedback about a peer's emotions. Obviously, the classroom would have to be a high-trust environment where psychological safety is well established. If students are not yet ready, change this example to self-feedback or feedback from the teacher.

What Is Empathy?

Empathy is putting yourself in another's shoes, listening with caring ears, and feeling the other's feelings—or at least trying to. It differs from sympathy, because empathy is about feeling another's feelings and communicating what you are feeling in that situation, instead of simply feeling sorry for the other person. When students feel or share empathy, they figuratively step inside another's shoes. When they see a classmate or sibling suffering, they can envision themselves in the other person's place, feel for what they are going through, and do what they can to assuage the other's pain.

Students come to your classroom able to feel empathy in different degrees. Some are highly attuned to the feelings of others. They may show their empathy with animals, especially pets, as well as peers, parents, and teachers. At the other extreme are those who are

Name:	Date:
Teacher:	Class:

Feedback is by:
☐ Self
☐ Teacher
☐ Peers: _____
☐ Other: _____

My emotion:

What I (You) Did Well	Criteria	Areas for Improvement
	I know the signals that tell me I am getting out of control.	
	I practice _____ strategies to keep control of my _____.	
	I practice _____ strategies to regain control.	
	I monitor this feeling when I am in control.	

Source: Adapted from Field, 2017.

Figure 7.3: Self-monitoring emotions—Single-point guiding rubric.

Visit go.SolutionTree.com/instruction for a free reproducible version of this figure.

Table 7.2: What Empathy Looks and Sounds Like

Looks Like	Sounds Like (With Matching Tone)
• Helping someone in distress • Listening attentively to another's problems without interruption • Picking up on another's discomfort, concern, or injury • Responding gently to another person's sad tone • Mirroring down emotions with a concerned facial expression • Inquiring about feelings when helping others • Responding visually to pain in a person's troubled feeling words • Looking for ways to alleviate another's pain • Giving a hug	• "How can I help?" • "Oh. That's a big problem." • "I'm sorry that you feel . . . ." • "I sense you are feeling . . . . Is that true?" • "I am really sorry that happened. How can I help you feel better?" • "I sense you are feeling . . . . When I have experienced that, I try to . . . . ." • "I do get it. You are really . . . . . I can see why. I too . . . ." • "Would it help you feel better if I . . . .?" • "What else can I do to make it easier?" • "I can't say how sorry I am . . . ." • "Will it help if I give you a hug?" • "How else can I help you?"

indifferent to others' difficulties and will say so. How do you recognize empathy? What are its more subtle signs? Table 7.2 (page 157) lists some examples of what empathy looks and sounds like. This is a skill that translates readily when assessing to what degree a student is empathetic.

The actions and words that project empathy cannot stand alone. The person receiving the support needs to sense a sincere, warm, comforting feeling under the words and deeds. Consider this example of an expression of empathy during an encounter between two friends, one of whom confides in her best friend Sharon about her bad grades.

"My mom's going to kill me," Mia whispered. "I can't have these grades. I'll be grounded for the semester. What am I going to do?"

Sharon hugged Mia and said, "You sound terrified. I think I know how you feel. I skipped hockey practice last week. My dad got really mad. He said I had to stop playing. That was the last thing I wanted. I don't like it when he's mad. I'll help you figure this out."

In this example, Sharon shows empathy by not only saying she cares about her friend's experience but by describing how she was and could be feeling in a similar situation, in essence, sharing her friend's feelings. What teacher who wants to promote deep learning through social-emotional skill development wouldn't benefit from more students ready to empathize with their peers in such a way?

Astrophysicist Neil deGrasse Tyson (as cited in Newkirk, n.d.) sees the skill of empathy as just as important to teach as traditional academic subjects:

> Humans aren't as good as we should be in our capacity to empathize with feelings and thoughts of others, be they humans or other animals on Earth. So maybe part of our formal education should be training in empathy. Imagine how different the world would be if, in fact, that were 'reading, writing, arithmetic, empathy.'

Don't forget, however, that empathy can take its toll. Evan as you promote empathy among students in your classroom, you want to be wary of downsides. Social worker Amy Morin (as cited in Agarwal & Avella, 2016) reminds us it is not healthy for a student to "rescue peers, refuse to say no to peers, let peers take advantage, all because the student fears he/she will hurt their friend's feelings." If you hear a student constantly saying, "You won't be mad at me if *X*, will you?", this student's empathy personalized learning plan will have to focus on worrying less about others and developing comfort saying no (Morin, as cited in Agarwal & Avella, 2016). Tell students what problems they should take to an adult, such as another student mentioning abuse or thoughts of hurting him- or herself.

How Do I Construct a Lesson or Project That Promotes Empathy?

You can design a lesson or project around empathy with the same templates you use for anger control, fractions, a Maya Angelou novel, or any other topic. A short template would indicate the lesson's driving question, outcome, vocabulary strategies, guiding rubric, and a reflection prompt. Determine the time allowed, as well as materials and equipment needed, and voilà! You are off and running. Determine what follow-up you will design to help students build confidence and competence (Eikenberry, 2012).

What Prompts Encourage Empathy?

Prompts, anywhere, anytime in a lesson can encourage empathy. You can call on empathy prompts to start a lesson in the middle and at the end. Even when addressing other skills or content through the year, you can drop empathy prompts to start or end the week, in lulls, or at the end of each day. When students are working on personalized learning plans, build prompts formally into their plans as a strategy or as a reflection. When working one-on-one with a student about a personalized learning plan, start or end your coaching with a prompt.

Figure 7.4 offers prompts that model empathy based on the acronym PIES: *problem solve, invite, encourage,* and *share similar feelings*. Share this acronym and figure with students and remind them (and yourself while modeling) of the following.

- A prompt is only a set of words. The empathic feeling behind the prompt is essential so that you are seen as practicing what you preach.

- Encouragement is not a reward. Encouragement occurs before the act; rewards come after. Encouragement prompts push the student to try.

- Avoid saying "I know how you feel."

- Body language, including facial expressions and movements, must reflect a prompt's words.

P	Problem solve.	"Let's solve this together."
		"Let's figure this out together."
I	Invite.	"Will you sit with me?"
		"Will you join our table for lunch?"
E	Encourage.	"I think you can . . . ."
		"I feel you are ready to . . . ."
S	Share similar feelings.	"I felt . . . when I . . ."
		"When . . . , I feel . . . ."

Figure 7.4: PIES.

Visit go.SolutionTree.com/instruction for a free reproducible version of this figure.

What Strategies and Activities Promote Empathy?

Engaging, age-appropriate activities stimulate interest and deeper learning involving empathy. Coupled with the goal setting inherent in a personalized learning plan, you can help students learn from planning, doing, and assessing your selection of activities.

Elementary School

The following activities promote empathy in elementary school students.

Our New Word List

Empathy in elementary school students is the focus in this five-step activity.

1. In a whole-class meeting, prompt a list of emotions for display. Encourage students to sketch a face showing that emotion.

2. Pairs pick one emotion to sketch onto art paper and tell a personal story about the selected emotion. Repeat the show-and-tell once weekly for four weeks, with each pair picking a different emotion each time. Set up paper pair portfolios so each pair can store its sketches.

3. In the fifth week, read a story about empathy and discuss how people show empathy.

4. Pairs pick an emotion sketch where empathy is needed and make a short story or explanation of how empathy would help.

5. In the end, make two lists of helpful and unhelpful emotions based on these mini projects. Discuss what criteria the students use to define *helpful* and *unhelpful*.

Story Role Play

Follow these three steps for an empathy exercise.

1. Groups of three write and perform a role play about a time when a friend was nice to them. How did you know the person was being nice? What did the friend say or do?

2. After all performances, students make a T-chart showing what being nice looks and sounds like.

3. Write a personalized learning plan with behaviors as outcomes from this chart for students to select and assess.

Posters

Follow these three steps for an empathy exercise.

1. The class brainstorms attributes that signal being a real friend.

2. Students, alone or in pairs, paint a 16 inch by 24 inch or larger poster advertising being a real friend or one of its attributes, such as listening or standing in another's shoes.

3. Make personalized learning plans to include the poster attribute.

Middle School

The following activities promote empathy in middle school students.

Make a Mobile

Follow these three steps for an empathy exercise.

1. After reading *Where the Red Fern Grows* (Rawls, 1961), *Wonder* (Palacio, 2012), or another

story in which empathy is a theme, the whole class contributes to a concept map.

2. Provide materials to groups of three for making mobiles. Model how and invite each team to build a mobile with key words from the list.

3. Hang the mobiles. Once per day, one team explains its word choices.

Cook a Meal for Someone Who Needs It

Follow these five steps for an exercise in empathy.

1. Invite the operators of a community homeless shelter to discuss the costs and issues involved in feeding their clientele (or ask students to research or interview this expert online).

2. With the expert's help, make a budget and menu for one dinner for thirty people.

3. Plan how the class can raise funds, prepare, serve, and clean up after the meal.

4. When done, students reflect on what they learned and the role empathy played in their learning and experience.

5. Discuss pity and contrast it to empathy.

Give Seniors Help

Empathy can increase when students follow these three steps.

1. As a class, students brainstorm survey questions asking about senior citizens' needs.

2. With the help of a community agency serving senior citizens, the students conduct the survey with SurveyMonkey (www.surveymonkey.com) or an equivalent polling website or application.

3. Make personalized learning plans for empathic responses (such as those in table 7.2, page 157).

High School

The following activities promote empathy in high school students.

Just Doodle It

Students will practice empathy as they follow these four steps.

1. Students download the fee-based program Doodly (www.doodly.com) or free Prezi software (www.prezi.com) and familiarize themselves with it.

2. Teams of three decide on a situation and determine what empathy should look and sound like in that situation.

3. Using Doodly or Prezi, teams create an empathy superhero and draw an adventure story about that hero. A plan will guide the inclusion of empathy outcomes in the story.

4. Include a guiding rubric about empathy as students practice their skill.

No More Noise

Solve a community problem with the following four-step activity.

1. Each team creates personalized learning plans to develop empathy in the team as they work through the project.

2. Using SurveyMonkey or a similar site to poll specific community members who are affected, teams of five identify a local community problem, determine a need, brainstorm solutions, and test a prototype to address the need.

3. Each team prepares visuals to explain how it addressed the need, the solution, and a plan to measure results.

4. In a reflective discussion, each team addresses the value of planning for resolving a *need*, versus planning a solution to a *problem*. Round-robin each team's report before a whole-class final reflection on what was learned about the distinction.

Quotes

Students will practice empathy as they follow these four steps.

1. Share the quotes in figure 7.5, or any quotes you find applicable, with students.

2. Teams of three select one quote and plan a smartphone video ad around it, storyboarding the quote's message.

3. They photograph real-life scenes, role plays, sketches, and more to match the storyboard.

4. When done, each team shares with the class before writing personalized learning plans on empathy.

> - "You can only understand people if you feel them in yourself." —John Steinbeck (Goodreads, n.d.)
> - "If you judge people you have no time to love them." —Mother Teresa (Crossroads Initiative, n.d.)
> - "When you start to develop your powers of empathy and imagination, the whole world opens up to you." —Susan Sarandon (Beliefnet, n.d.)
> - "The great gift of human beings is that we have the power of empathy, we can all sense a mysterious connection to each other." —Meryl Streep (Center for Building a Culture of Empathy, n.d.)
> - "Learning to stand in somebody else's shoes to see through their eyes, that's how peace begins. And it's up to you to make that happen." —Barack Obama (2009)

Figure 7.5: Playlist of quotes about empathy.

*Visit **go.SolutionTree.com/instruction** for a free reproducible version of this figure.*

How Do I Create a Rubric for Building Empathy?

As with other 21st century deeper learning skills, you have several rubric formats from which to choose. Refer back to chapter 3 (page 53) for guidance. After you select between three and seven criteria and fill in the rubric, add the logistics and ask a colleague or team member for feedback via the SMART criteria.

What Are Interpersonal Relationship Skills?

Interpersonal relationship skills are those which promote positive relationships between two persons or among a group. Followers of Howard Gardner (1983, as cited in University of Tennessee, n.d.) will recognize these skills as part and parcel of intelligence, since he explains that intelligence is the ability "to understand and interact effectively with others. It involves effective verbal and nonverbal communication, the ability to note distinctions among others, sensitivity to the moods and temperaments of others, and the ability to entertain multiple perspectives." In this subset of skills, you will find both interpersonal communication and leadership; they fit in when two or more individuals interact as they listen to each other, set shared goals, make and assess plans, discuss disagreements, resolve conflicts, think critically and creatively, solve complex problems, and complete tasks in collaboration with each other. The skills apply at home, at school, at work, and at play.

Interpersonal relationship skills are the heart skills often ignored in formal instruction. Attention is given almost fully to the head skills. Because the heart skills were deemed too soft and too difficult to measure, the hard skills received preferential treatment. Thanks mainly to Gardner's (1983) and Goleman's (2005) popularizing the interpersonal skills as essential in almost every area of life, learning, and work, corporations and some state offices of education have seen the light. The value of head *and* heart—the whole child—is now much more balanced; acknowledging the role of how students interact with each other has to be front and center in helping all achieve their academic goals.

As discussed in chapter 2 (page 35), positive interpersonal communication skills promote the positive relationships, helping build and keep a culture of mutual trust and respectful interactions for all. The stronger the interpersonal bonds among individuals in a classroom, the higher their personal satisfaction and productivity (Reis da Luz, 2015).

One of the most effective ways students can develop their interpersonal skills is via cooperative learning (Reis da Luz, 2015). Johnson and Johnson's (1999) groundbreaking research touts that development as one of five key attributes of productive classrooms. Although some students may feel they can accomplish more by themselves—team members don't pull their weight, they don't like the other students—a desire to go it alone is short-sighted. Smooth, productive classrooms depend on how well each student gets along with the teacher and peers. Students learn how to get along and work with each other. Being uncomfortable working in a group doesn't mean we aren't learning from others or from working with others. Few jobs exist where teamwork—collaboration, cooperation—is not required. Not having these skills can be detrimental to a career: emotional intelligence, "rather than the individual's personality type, is the decisive factor in assigning a person for a certain job or position" (Dumbravă, 2011, p. 87) and the skill "accounts for 15%–45% of one's job success, whereas the IQ accounts for less than 6%" (p. 88).

How Do I Construct a Lesson or Project That Promotes Interpersonal Skills?

As the world-renowned Center for Creative Leadership (n.d.) advocates, leaders, of which you are one, place high value on collaboration. Chapter 2 introduced basic methods for creating a trusting, respectful climate so that every student feels emotionally safe. Beyond the basic skills taught through cooperative learning, students benefit by developing advanced skills that go beyond teamwork and foster collaboration. That collaboration occurs "when two or more people (often groups) work together through idea sharing and thinking to accomplish a common goal. It is simply teamwork taken to a higher level" (Hill, n.d.). The quality of collaboration is advanced by team members' interpersonal skills. Through the school year, it is helpful when you stimulate team building and help students maintain their focus on its outcomes. In addition to a diet of high-energy team-building activities for strengthening positive relationships among classmates, don't neglect ongoing assessments of those skills.

Select starter activities from table 7.3 and start the work early in the year, creating teams of between two and five students that meet once weekly. These teams stay together, bonding and making fun products with a different activity each time even as they develop the interpersonal skills that will help all reach a personalized learning plan or lesson outcome.

One example from this list clarifies the role of interpersonal skills in these informal activities. The popular science experiment where students drop an egg asks teammates to agree on one goal—the hallmark of collaborative work. The team members problem solve together as they design a way to drop an egg from a height and ensure it does not break. Although there are not formal roles or rubrics instructing the team how to work together, the excitement of the task engages all. After the drop, the team has to identify what worked or didn't work. A teacher leading the debrief asks guiding questions like the following about the interpersonal skills they had to use (or lacked) and poses hypotheses for change.

- "When you were planning your design, how did you include ideas from everyone?"
- "How well did you work together?"
- "What didn't work so well?"
- "How equally were team tasks dispersed?"
- "What options did you include?"
- "What would you do differently with the task and with your team?"

Table 7.3: Informal Team-Building Activities

Elementary School	Middle School	High School
• Team name • Team flag • Team motto • Team cheer • Team banner • Team poem • Team snack • Team timeline for accomplishing a task	Any from elementary school, plus the following: • Team shield • Team song • Team theme • Team license plate • Team word cloud • Team poster • Team mobile • Team portfolio • Team playlist of bonding ideas	Any from middle school, plus the following: • Team blog • Team newspaper • Team autobiography • Team movie about members • Team concept map • Team ad • Team app • Team Facebook page • Team Instagram account • Team Twitter account • Team playbook • Team journal • Team egg drop

What Prompts Encourage Interpersonal Skills?

Prompts from guiding questions and stem statements are more than cues and clues. They are attempts to motivate students to think more deeply about the skills they are cultivating or have used in a personalized learning plan or lesson.

Prior to a personalized learning plan, consider these prompts to set students' anticipation of what's about to happen.

- What has happened in past courses or lessons when you had to work with team members?
- What are the characteristics of good teammates?
- Why did you find it easy or hard to work with others?
- How did you learn to work with others?
- How would you feel about working with teammates you didn't know well?

During a personalized learning plan, include these stems.

- Right now I like (dislike) working with my team because . . .
- My team is helping (not helping) with my goal by . . .
- I am helping (not helping) with my team's goal by . . .
- What I am bringing most to this team so far is . . .
- My biggest hope for the team is . . .

After a personalized learning plan, include these stems.

- What I learned about teamwork is . . .
- What I discovered about teamwork is . . .
- A way to improve my teamwork is . . .
- Help I need to be a better teammate is . . .

There are two things to keep in mind. The first is to make sure the class's level of trust and respect is well established before introducing critiques. If you must ask for critiques, be sure students take responsibility for any negatives, avoiding blaming others. The second is to ask for clarification as often as needed.

What Strategies and Activities Promote Interpersonal Skills?

In addition to your choices for fun, informal team activities, there are many others you can embed in formal cooperative learning structures with norms, roles, and rubrics. Each is designed for increasing interpersonal communication in a collaborative format.

Elementary School

The following activities promote interpersonal skills in elementary school students.

People Search

Students will practice interpersonal skills as they follow these three steps.

1. Make a list of between four and six special characteristics for each student.
2. Start every morning with "Find the person who . . ." and five minutes every morning, students match the characteristic with a person in the room and ask that person to sign the sheet.
3. Continue for as many mornings as needed to find everyone.

About Us Scavenger Hunt

Follow these six steps to practice interpersonal skills; this activity gets students up and moving.

1. Post each student's photo on the bulletin board.
2. Students take turns bringing three items that show something about their family.
3. Mark the items *clue 1*, *clue 2*, and *clue 3* and hide them around the classroom.
4. Post guiding questions such as *What did you learn about* (name)? and *What were your clues?*, and have students search the room for clues. As students find them, post the clues with the picture on the bulletin board.
5. Discuss what everyone discovered about the student. Start with the guiding questions and then ask the following.
    - "How is (*student*) like you?"
    - "How is that person different from you?"
    - "What is special about this student?"
    - "What did you learn about the talents that people in the classroom have?"

6. Make a personalized learning plan for students to learn added insights about a peer.

"Who Am I?" Show and Tell

This four-step activity promotes interpersonal skills, helps students feel special, and highlights positive experiences with different cultures.

1. Students bring in something that represents them—something about their culture, for instance—or they describe an activity they enjoy doing.
2. Plan between five and ten minutes each day for a few students to share what they brought or want to describe until everyone has shared.
3. Repeat each eight weeks with a new focal point that will help students know more about one another. Other focal points may spotlight siblings, talents, dreams, or parents. Customize the template to fit each new focal point.
4. Follow with a personalized learning plan for interviews to add to their appreciation of others' cultures.

Middle School

The following activities promote interpersonal skills in middle school students.

Class Collaboration Contract

This four-step activity promotes interpersonal skills.

1. On sticky notes, students write ideas for how, when, where, and why they want everyone in the class to collaborate (such as *so we can all be friends when we are in teams*). Prime the pump with a first example for each prompt.
2. Record each participant's suggestion in the mind map in figure 7.6. For each suggestion, ensure that all participants have the same understanding of the idea. If not, change the suggestion until there is consensus from all participants.
3. Share the mind map to all digital devices, make hard copies, or post on the classroom wall.
4. Each person selects one behavior (*How*) for a personalized learning plan outcome.

Name Game

These five steps help students work on interpersonal skills. Before you begin, remind students that no put-downs or ridicule are allowed.

1. Sit in a class circle on the first day of school. Introduce yourself: "I am Mrs. Smith. I love vanilla swirl ice cream."
2. The student to your right repeats what *you* said and adds his or her name and favorite ice cream.
3. Continue as each recalls all names and ice creams.
4. When one student can't recall, others can offer clues but must stay seated.
5. End when the complete list is given. Don't forget your ice cream!

High School

The following activities promote interpersonal skills in high school students.

Back to Back

Follow these seven steps.

1. Pair students back to back and give one copy of the diagram in figure 7.7 to one person in each pair. The other person in the pair can't see the diagram!

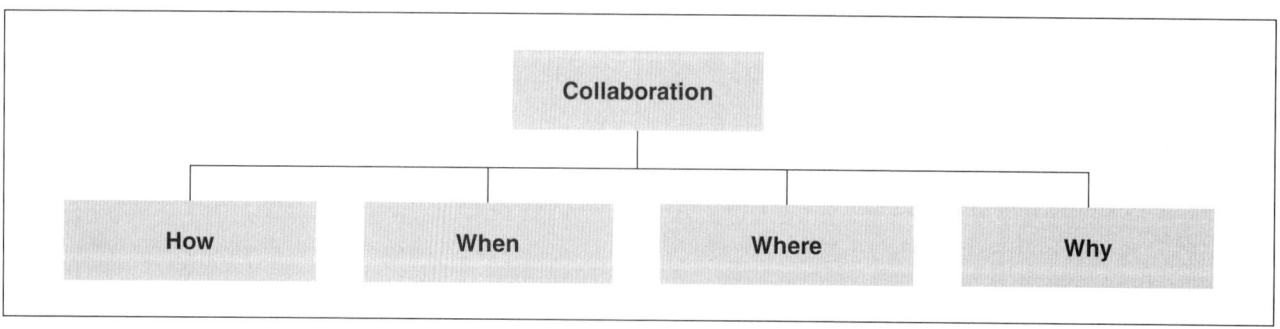

Figure 7.6: Class Collaboration Contract mind map.

Visit go.SolutionTree.com/instruction for a free reproducible version of this figure.

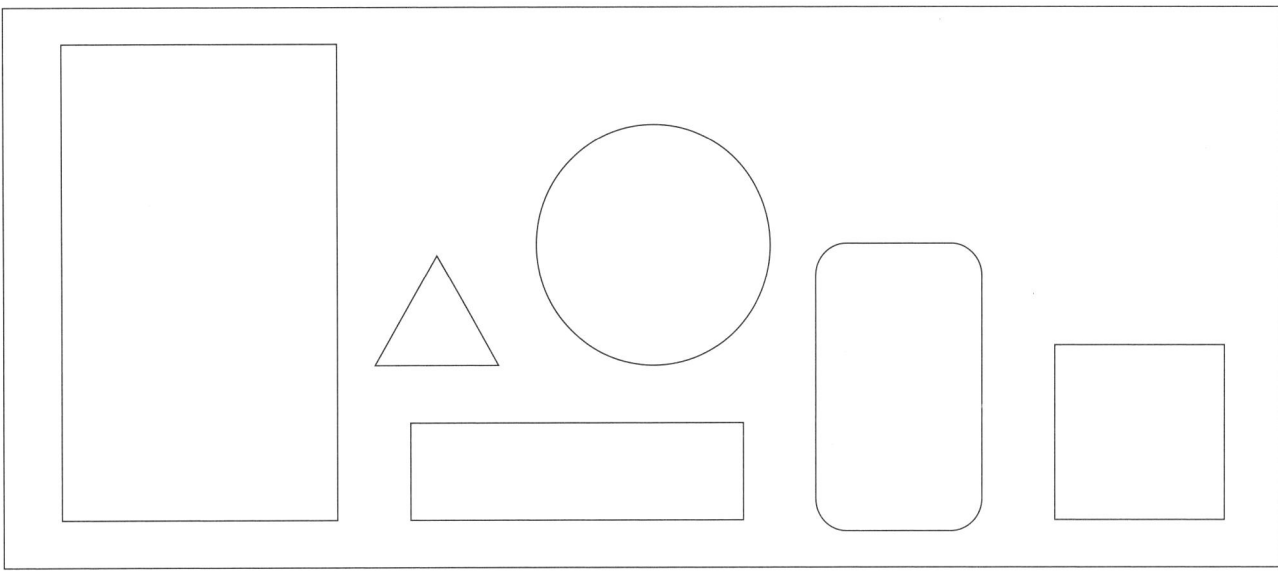

Figure 7.7: Diagram for Back to Back activity.

*Visit **go.SolutionTree.com/instruction** for a free reproducible version of this figure.*

2. The person holding the diagram explains the shapes to the partner, who must draw them based on his or her partner's directions.

3. After the drawing is done, the describer shows the drawer the diagram and notes the result.

4. Reverse the process.

5. After the students are done drawing and have done the second results check, the pair makes a guiding rubric with at least four ways to improve the describing.

6. Repeat the process and assess with the rubric.

7. The whole class agrees on five rubric criteria and makes a communication personalized learning plan.

Make a Magazine Cover

This five-step activity results in students creating a magazine cover story about the class. The players don't have to write the complete story; they only have to write the headlines and create images, quotes, and sidebars. Follow these steps.

1. Create teams of between three and five students and give teams markers, pens, and anything else they'll need to create a cover. Share a few different magazine covers to prime the pump.

2. Distribute a personalized learning plan for interpersonal relationships. Outcomes might address active listening, empathy statements, random acts of kindness, conflict management, and so on.

3. Create several templates for different elements of the magazine story and include the following.
    - Magazine cover dimensions
    - Cover story headline
    - Quotes from team members
    - Sidebars about talent after peer interviews
    - Images, including baby pictures and short biographies

4. Each team gets weekly time to assemble its unique magazine cover.

5. Share all magazines, perhaps with a gallery walk, and then assess with the plan's rubric.

How Do I Create a Rubric for Interpersonal Relationship Skills?

For teamwork through the year, schedule time at least once monthly for formative teamwork assessment with a guiding rubric like the one in figure 7.8 (page 166). Adjust the criteria and language to adapt the rubric, which is designed for secondary students, to fit any grade.

Name:	**Date:**
Teacher:	**Class:**
Feedback is by: ☐ Self ☐ Teacher ☐ Peers: _____ ☐ Other: _____	

Rating scale:

0 = Not yet
1 = Once or twice
2 = Sometimes
3 = Frequently
4 = Always

____ Followed norms for conversations

____ Monitored staying on task

____ Kept focus on the common goal

____ Expressed empathy

____ Listened to different points of view

____ Encouraged others

____ Attempted to resolve conflicts

____ Included others' ideas

____ Communicated with PACT skills

____ Gave and received specific, warm feedback

____ Gave and received specific, cool feedback

What I did well as a _____:
       role

What I can improve:

I need help to:

Figure 7.8: Teamwork guiding rubric.

*Visit **go.SolutionTree.com/instruction** for a free reproducible version of this figure.*

What Is Goal Setting?

Goal setting is like the direction sign at a busy intersection. It helps people who are trying to get to a specific place find it. Aided by the complex cognitive skills of critical thinking and creative thinking (such as creative problem solving), students learn how to achieve goals with their built-in emotional content. When you integrate personalized learning plans into your weekly instruction, you can make goal setting the preferred skill, which noted cognitive psychologists name a prerequisite to learning (Feuerstein et al., 2015). Whatever the skill set, a personalized learning plan provides the opportunity for goal setting to lead student learning. Critical thinking, creative thinking, and social-emotional skills infused, the plan becomes the hub for advancing all students' learning.

Research says why this skill should lead the learning parade: it is linked with motivation, autonomy, and self-efficacy (Midwest Comprehensive Center, 2018). A study by psychologist Gail Matthews (as cited in Economy, 2018) shows that when people write down their goals, they are 42 percent more successful achieving them than people who only formulated outcomes in their heads. Brain research explains how goal setting restructures the brain:

> While that process sounds as straightforward as a computer program, what's actually happening is much more complex. Because your brain has something called neuroplasticity, goal-setting literally changes the structure of your brain so that it's optimized to achieve that goal. (James, 2020)

In chapter 3 (page 53), you reviewed the what, how, and why of helping students make their personalized learning plan goals SMART. In this next section, activities to engage students with goal setting give you options for helping students develop their goal-setting capabilities from a social-emotional perspective.

How Do I Construct a Lesson or Project That Promotes Goal Setting?

Although you can construct a lesson on goal setting from the complex cognitive perspective, doing so combined with social-emotional skills can enrich lessons or projects. The list in figure 7.9 shows both head and heart in a high school project in which students apply goal-setting skills. Each time you construct a lesson or project plan, return to this checklist.

What Prompts Promote Goal Setting?

In the response to this question asked in the previous social-emotional skill, interpersonal relations, you read that prompts at the start, middle, and end of a personalized learning plan are made at your discretion. Prompts

1. Check prior knowledge and experience with goal setting via a need-to-know graphic organizer.
2. Share the outcome and the driving question so students can set post–high school SMART goals.
3. Engage students with an entry activity.
4. Share the guiding rubric focused on SMART criteria.
5. Initiate individual personalized learning plans focused on goal-setting outcomes.
6. Form teams of three and check for collaboration readiness.
7. Schedule need-to-know labs as appropriate or requested.
8. Provide student playbooks you have prepared (figure 7.10, page 168).
9. Set schedule for work, including formative assessments.
10. Monitor teams and engage in two-way feedback.
11. Plan and present products.
12. Conduct the summative assessment and end reflection.

Figure 7.9: Teacher playbook—Goal setting.

*Visit **go.SolutionTree.com/instruction** for a free reproducible version of this figure.*

Tasks

1. Identify resource persons.
2. Make a survey with the following questions.
   - What are your current career goals?
   - What is the importance of goals in your career?
   - What methods did you use to select your goals?
   - What methods did you use to assess your goals?
   - What samples can you provide?
   - What advice would you give regarding this goal?
3. Teams summarize data from the survey.
4. Teams prepare data for a digital medium of their choice.
5. Teams prepare their chosen digital medium.
6. Teams plan how to present the medium.
7. Students make presentations.
8. Perform a formative assessment on the selected medium.

Product

- Multimedia selection by each team

Resources

- Computers, apps, and websites
- Survey tool
- Mathematics teacher as guest expert discussing data analysis

Assessments

- Outcome: Multimedia format of choice (such as a slide, podcast, or blog) providing statistics from the survey and illustrated with graphics
- Criteria: To be created before assessing the digital presentation of choice; teams can research sample assessments online.

Figure 7.10: Student playbook—Goal setting.

*Visit **go.SolutionTree.com/instruction** for a free reproducible version of this figure.*

are two-ended methods available to you wearing your coaching hat. You are the determiner when a prompt will advance the target skill, be it goal setting, interpersonal relations, analysis, or generating ideas on a digital device. You pick when and where in the lesson.

For goal setting, starter prompts might say or ask the following.

- "What goals would motivate you?"
- "What others might you consider?"
- "How do you feel about the goals given to you?"
- "How will you measure your goal?" (For example, *I will count the days in my seat at the bell each week.*)
- "How can you be more specific?" (For example, *Can you change the word* more *to something specific, such as* in my seat?)
- "How will you make your goal attainable?"
- "Can you give me some steps you will take?"
- "How important is this goal for you?"

- "How invested are you in being on time?"
- "How much time will it take to show progress?"

In the middle of a lesson, adjust these prompts by shifting to the present tense. At the end, shift to the past tense.

You may also wish to vary the medium that you and students use when sharing a prompt. Obviously, voice sharing is the most common. You ask the prompt and signal how students individually, in a group, or as a whole class respond aloud. You can call on students who have their hands up, or, to attain equal distribution, do a round-robin, pull names from a jar, or throw dice.

What Strategies and Activities Encourage Goal Setting?

Select activities which promote interest and develop skills in making SMART goals. Couple these activities with personalized learning plans so that students see the process and not just a single fun activity.

Elementary School

The following activities promote goal setting in elementary school students.

My Future Self

Try this five-step activity to get students thinking about setting goals.

1. Students sketch pictures of themselves five years in the future. You can provide the following prompts if they need them.
    - Who would they like to be, and where?
    - Who would they be friends with?
    - What would they like to be doing?
2. Do a pair-share.
3. New pairs repeat the drawing the following week.
4. End with a third draw-pair-share for thirty years out. Post the sketches with each student's name.
5. Make goal-setting personalized learning plans based on the selves students see at their next schooling level (middle or high school, college or vocational school) all the way to a career. As personalized learning plan sample outcomes, think about students using different digital media (such as a blog, a public service announcement, or an Instagram post) to show dreams for the future.

Levi's Great and Wonderful Life

The following three-step activity promotes goal setting.

1. Read *Levi's Great and Wonderful Life* (Vannoy, 2018) about overcoming fears, setting goals, and achieving success through visualization.
2. Follow the advice and teach the students how to visualize goals.
3. Invite goal visualization plans to enrich this skill. (See page 130 for visualization activities.)

Three Stars and a Wish

Follow these five steps for a goal-setting activity.

1. Each student cuts three stars from colored sheets of paper. On one side of each, they write or sketch one thing they do well or one talent they have.
2. On the other side of each star, the students write or sketch a wish for improving the thing they already do well or developing the talent.
3. In the days after they finish the stars, each student shares with the class the sides of one star. Be sure that all follow norms for listening.
4. At the end of each presentation, call for a silent round of applause and hang the stars above the room.
5. Later, introduce personalized learning plans as a way to turn the wishes into goals.

Middle School

The following activities promote goal setting in middle school students.

Wheel of Fortune

Follow these six steps to encourage students setting goals in different areas of their lives.

1. Show students a wheel and give each student the materials to copy your model.
2. Slice the wheel into the following segments.
    - Activities
    - Fun
    - Friends
    - Family
    - Health
    - School and Work
    - Hobbies

3. Give examples of each category and have students write goals they would like to accomplish this year in each.

4. Groups of three share with each other, pick one category, and ask "How would you do that?" After the student answers, the other members respond with, "I think that's a good idea because . . . "

5. Repeat the activity with ten-minute weekly share sessions until all categories are covered.

6. Structure personalized learning plans on student-selected dream *dos* as outcomes.

Goal Ladders

Help students break their goals down into manageable chunks with the following six steps.

1. Show or digitally share the stepladder graphic organizer in figure 7.11.

2. Students think about dreams they would like to fulfill and write the word *dream* at the top of the ladder.

3. Students write a first goal for getting to the dream on the bottom rung. That is the first action toward that dream. Follow with added steps up the ladder.

4. Do a pair-share. At the end of each share, the partner says, "What I like about your dream is . . . " Say something about the goals they are setting to get to the dream.

5. After they finish, they tell the whole class what they liked about the activity and how it helped them become goal setters. List multiple responses to each question on the whiteboard so that all can review the ideas and see new ideas.

6. Add personalized learning plans for specific first steps for each dream.

High School

The following activities promote goal setting in high school students.

Interest Maps

Follow this five-step playbook to facilitate personal goal setting.

1. Display the concept map in figure 7.12. The My Interests circle should answer, "What do I like to do? What are my interests or favorite activities?" Fill the first question with your own answers.

Figure 7.11: Graphic for Goal Ladders activity.

*Visit **go.SolutionTree.com/instruction** for a free reproducible version of this figure.*

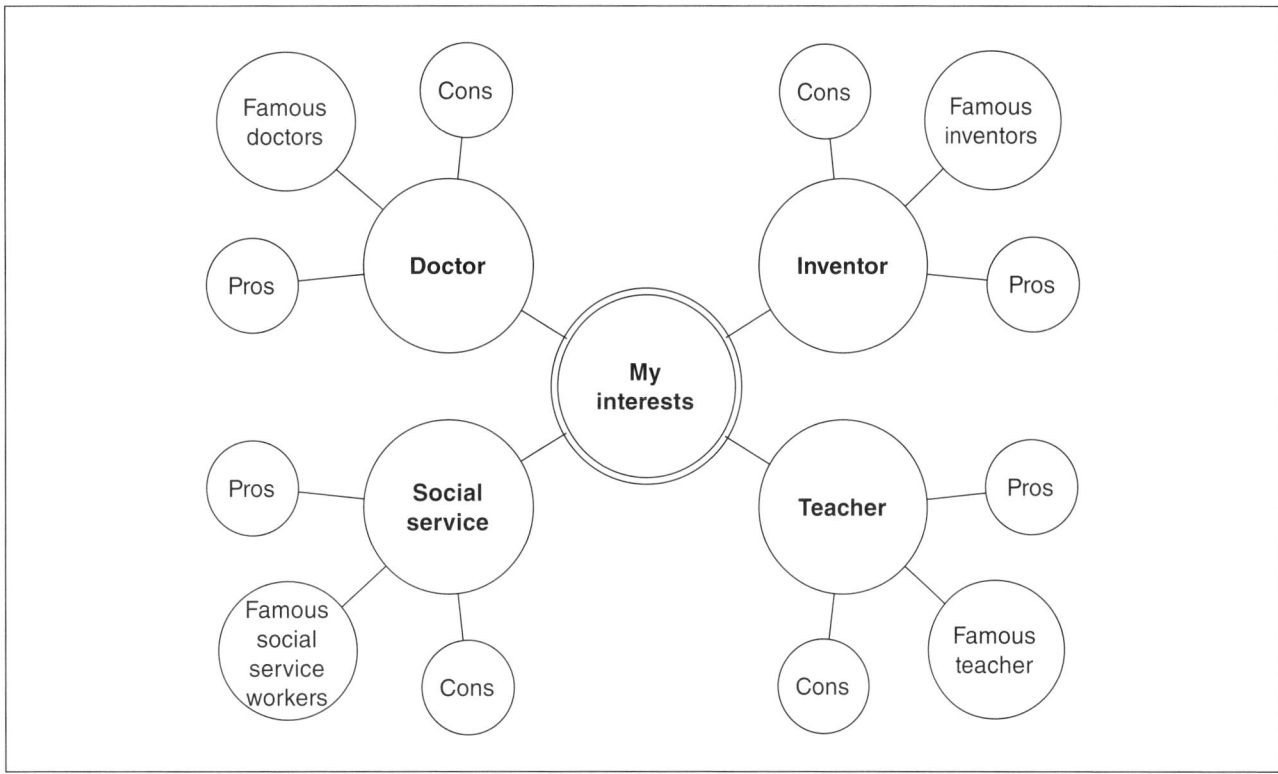

Figure 7.12: Image and teacher playbook—Concept map for Interest Maps activity.

*Visit **go.SolutionTree.com/instruction** for a free reproducible version of this figure.*

2. Ask students to think about what they like to do. What are *their* interests and favorite things to do?

3. Create an interest map by grouping ideas with bubbles or boxes in groupings that make sense.

4. Facilitate the picking of an interest to turn into a SMART goal (page 57).

5. Extend the activity into a goal-setting personalized learning plan.

Vision Boards

Vision boards are a helpful tool to plan long-range goals. Follow these five steps.

1. Students gather old magazines and cut out pictures that represent hopes and dreams for the future.

2. On poster boards, students arrange the pictures and glue them into place. Provide glitter, stickers, ribbons, markers, and more for them to decorate their vision boards.

3. In groups of five, each student describes their vision, what each picture represents, and how to work toward the vision.

4. Invite students to make a personalized learning plan with an important SMART goal toward their visions.

5. You can do a small-group or whole-class round-robin share where each student says, "My vision is . . . and my starter goal is . . . ."

World of Dreams

Follow these five steps.

1. Show a map with all continents as a graphic organizer, as in figure 7.13 (page 172).

2. Each student fills in the characteristics of his or her dream job, writing one characteristic per continent.

3. All students say why the characteristics they chose are important to them and what they have to do to develop each characteristic.

4. Each student selects the one characteristic most important to develop and prepares a plan to facilitate development.

5. Set a timeline for the personalized learning plan and schedule a class period for a round-robin sharing (four per group, ten minutes, with a guiding rubric).

Figure 7.13: Continents map for World of Dreams activity.

*Visit **go.SolutionTree.com/instruction** for a free reproducible version of this figure.*

How Do I Create a Rubric for Goal Setting?

Figure 7.14 shows a sample rubric for goal setting. The outcome is a résumé for a dream job. As shown in the last section of the sample, this rubric allows for two-way feedback between the student and an adult expert in the student's field of interest.

How Do I Best Develop Students' Social-Emotional Skills During Remote Learning?

Personalized learning plans are a good way to focus on social-emotional needs. Many schools turned their attention to SEL when the COVID-19 pandemic forced many students to learn from home or severely different classrooms.

Collaboration

This includes two-way peer feedback. There is a deep need for higher-level interpersonal communication, especially during remote learning. Because students may be casual about engagement and effort during remote learning, including using their phones and simply not being as alert as they might be in person, it is to everyone's benefit to accentuate sharp listening. That helps ensure that instructions, points of view, and feedback are accurately spoken and heard. In a remote conversation, communication can fall apart not only on technical merits as simple as insufficient voice volume, but also on grasping more complex nuances of meaning. Leaving interpersonal nuances such as facial expressions, voice inflections, body language, and so forth out of the communication equation (or simply being tougher to detect on video) can have disastrous consequences. Teachers who managed the first semester of COVID-19 remote learning say students did not pick up on the look teachers can give that puts students back on task or the slight nod that signals approval. More of a concern, they report, is the trouble remote students can have perceiving when teachers underscore important directions with a change of tone, and misinterpreting (K. Tummins, B. Jiminez, & N. Kim, personal communication, June 9, 2020).

You will benefit by mediating the social skills needed for effective dialogue and constructive feedback. Whenever you do so, you also address the English language arts speaking and listening skills as you show students how to speak with a video screen voice and facial expressions, take turns listening to each other during virtual discussions, and hear meaning in instructions and feedback.

Name: Al Caponelli	Date: 3/28	
Period: 6	Class: Marketing	Teacher: Mr. Blume

My goal: To prepare a résumé according to five criteria I found online for my dream job as a mergers and acquisitions officer in a food service company

Feedback is by:
- ☐ Self
- ☐ Teacher
- ☐ Peers: _____
- ☒ Other: family friend in the field, Mrs. Schneider—manager of M&A Smithson Partners

This Is Done Well	Criteria	Ways to Improve
Your summary is well organized with relevant examples. This list is strong. This is a SMART résumé.	Has a strong, succinct summary paragraph of my school experience for this field I include education credentials showing what I accomplished in addition to schoolwork. Is easy to skim I include quantifiable accomplishments and results. Shows my relevant technical and business skills	Proofread for punctuation and spelling. What about your accounting internship? Do you have any other job experience? Use more headers and subheaders in bold so they stand out. Please spell out each skill with examples.

Help I need: I'm not sure about the last criterion. I need to know how to identify skills that fit.

Notes: I will be happy to discuss the skills. I am available by FaceTime Saturday before 10 p.m. You have my phone number. —Sue Schneider

Figure 7.14: Guiding rubric for goal setting.

Visit go.SolutionTree.com/instruction for a free reproducible version of this figure.

Student Agency, Self-Direction, and Self-Management

Personalized learning increases student agency because students are doing assignments individually or with peers. Self-directed learning research shows that such students might be likelier to take the initiative diagnosing their learning needs (with or without help from others), formulating learning goals, identifying resources, and assessing their own skill development (Guglielmino, 1977). Especially during asynchronous time slots (with online learning, for example), there is increased need for most students to learn how to self-direct. The students follow their lesson and personalized learning plan playbooks so they can prepare for the next day's class. As noted in the discussion of student agency (page 87), because remote students must spend more time completing tasks and accomplishing goals away from a teacher's presence, there is more need for intrinsic motivation and self-direction.

Personalized learning plans that spotlight the skills that lead to increased self-direction and help ensure that students learn how to productively use their time are essential, especially in remote classrooms. Each time you trust students to self-manage their learning, you are bringing SEL development into your classroom. Remote learning demands much more trust from teachers in students, who are learning and working elsewhere. Your trust immediately creates the quality of learning culture called for in SEL research. You don't have to schedule additional time for SEL lessons. As you rely on personalized learning plans to undergird their learning time, especially the asynchronous times, you encourage students to self-manage their time. If you focus a personalized learning plan on any one of the self-directed learning behaviors such as goal setting or self-assessment, you do even more to promote SEL.

TAKEAWAYS

Once again, you are invited to record key ideas you gleaned from the chapter.

CHAPTER 8
THE DIGITAL SKILL SET

Most jobs today require a cell phone— not a pencil . . . but we know how that goes in most classrooms.

—Ted Fujimoto

Digital skills are a basic competency every student needs. Technology "is the pen and paper of our time, and it is the lens through which we experience much of our world," says teacher David Warlick (as cited in Keogh, 2015). Author Heidi Hayes Jacobs (as cited in Sastri, 2019) adds, "Teachers need to integrate technology seamlessly into the curriculum instead of viewing it as an add-on, an afterthought, or an event." Why? Career recruiters note that "technology is the primary job creator" (Anderson, 2018). Mozilla Foundation is an organization that advocates for accessibility of the internet (as opposed to privatizing parts of it). Its executive director, Mark Surman (as cited in Read, 2013), says, "Becoming literate in how the technical world works is equivalent to reading, writing and maths. We need to look at this fourth literacy as mainstream."

The world is one of a digital-democratic society; citizenship is about voting, interacting with social media, communicating, and collaborating in social venues, interacting online with government services, and conducting business. Developing students into capable, responsible digital citizens requires an understanding of this.

> Students need to be educated on how to be good citizens of their country and what their rights and responsibilities are as members of society. The same issues need to be addressed with regard to the emerging digital society, so that students can learn how to be responsible and productive members of that society. (Ribble, 2011, p. 109)

This chapter will answer driving questions about the most ignored skill set among those promoting 21st century deeper learning outcomes. This chapter invites you to place digital skill development for all students at the forefront of the desired skills list. It explains how and why personalized learning plans make possible the inclusion of digital skills to drive instructional practice, and what they do to ensure this inclusion. It provides guidance on the use of personalized learning plan templates, playbooks, and playlists of ideas for targeting digital skills and shows how these tools are both ends and means for making this skill set central to all instruction. Thus, as you face the challenge of learning how to integrate this unfamiliar skill set across your curriculum, it will be far more beneficial to learn the process. If you learn the *process* for planning, implementing, and assessing whatever skill emerges as a need, for your students, you can engage their digital development integrated in your content over the entire year.

> **Driving question:** How do I develop students' digital skills through personalized learning plans?

What Are Digital Skills?

From an overarching viewpoint, digital skills are those that enable people "to effectively and critically navigate, evaluate and create information using a range of digital technology tools" and use technology strategically to find, evaluate, and create information, connect and collaborate with others, produce and share original content, and use the internet and technology tools to achieve academic, professional, and personal goals (Grech, 2016).

In addition to helping students attain fluency with general skills on tools like smartphones, tablets, ereaders, video games, and other common digital devices, teachers need a more specific curriculum of explicit skills available equitably in a K–12 scope and sequence. With that, every learner can develop the competencies that apply no matter what new devices emerge. A well-articulated, systemically implemented scope and sequence of digital skills should receive a daily treatment equivalent, says the OECD (n.d.a), to the three Rs—reading, writing, and arithmetic.

What Skills Make Up the Digital Skill Set?

Although it is the responsibility of a school district or charter management organization to set forward systemic curricula, individual teachers working without a provided curriculum can do well by drawing from the European Union's Digital Competence Framework for Citizens (Vuorikari, Punie, Carretero, & Van den Brande, 2016). The framework allows a district, school, or individual teacher to identify which digital skills to incorporate when creating a year-long curriculum.

Consider the following resources.

- **DigComp 2.0:** The Digital Competence Framework for Citizens (Vuorikari et al., 2016; https://bit.ly/39ostss) gives an overview of the framework and related work.
- **DigComp 2.1:** The Digital Competence Framework for Citizens (Carretero, Vuorikari, & Punie, 2017; https://bit.ly/2CFArld) details the eight proficiency levels and includes examples.
- **DigCompEdu:** The European Framework for the Digital Competence of Educators: DigCompEdu (Redecker & Punie, 2017; https://bit.ly/3huno4V) is separate from the other frameworks, and "directed towards educators at all levels of education, from early childhood to higher and adult education, including general and vocational training [and] special needs education." This version helps educators assess their proficiency teaching about separate pieces of digital literacy, including accessibility and self-regulated learning.

The EU's Digital Competence Framework for Citizens (DigComp 2.0; Vuorikari et al., 2016) consists of five areas and twenty-one competencies detailed in eight proficiency levels. The set is available online. The five subsets that follow do overlap with the complex cognitive and social-emotional skill sets.

1. **Managing information:** Identifying, locating, retrieving, storing, organizing, and analyzing digital information and judging its relevance and purpose (Remember that teachers "are more important than ever in preparing students for an ever-changing world with infinite access to all types of information" [Olson, 2017].)

2. **Communicating in digital environments:** Sharing resources through online tools, linking with others to collaborate through digital tools, interacting with and participating in communities and networks, and building cross-cultural awareness

3. **Creating digital content:** Creating and editing new content (from word processing to images and video), integrating and re-elaborating knowledge, producing creative expression, programming, and dealing with and applying intellectual property rights and licenses

4. **Managing safety:** Protecting data and one's digital identity, establishing security measures, and using technology safely and sustainably

5. **Problem solving:** Identifying digital needs and resources, making informed decisions on most-appropriate digital tools according to the purpose or need, solving conceptual problems through digital means, creatively using technologies, solving technical problems, solving loose and tight problems, making decisions, and updating one another's competencies

With this list, you can take a deeper dive and select even more specific skills that lead to these competencies. Do so by either analyzing your own digital experience or by searching online for the competencies needed. For example, you might drill down to the following tasks for yourself in preparation for teaching students about communicating in digital environments ("sharing through digital technologies" per Vuorikari et al., 2016).

- Determine the tools your students have for sharing digital information.
- Plan a lesson that introduces your class to this tool.
- Prepare a guiding rubric for infusing the lesson in your other content (such as writing an essay and sharing it with a peer partner and you for feedback).
- Facilitate the lesson by assessing how well students share with the targeted tool.
- Add follow-up lessons for added sharing practices until students are competent.

Another example is developing content ("copyright and licenses" per Vuorikari et al., 2016). You might drill down and see that you need to do the following tasks in order to teach students those skills.

- Read the article "14 Copyright Essentials Teachers and Students Must Know" (Ed Tech, 2016; https://bit.ly/3hl8Y74)
- Determine what your students need to know and select what information you will infuse into your daily instruction.
- Determine how students will learn the information they need to know and include the information as they approach copyright information.
- Prepare a guiding rubric to assess how they consider this information in any copyright material they take from online sources.

In addition to its multi-grade outcome-based curriculum, the European Commission (n.d.) framework provides self-assessments, tools, support materials, and implementation models. Modified frameworks address specific groups such as teachers, lifelong learners, and employers in different sectors. The following list is a snapshot of specific, expected internet skills (European Commission, n.d.).

- Connect to a WiFi network.
- Download apps to a mobile device.
- Keep track of the costs of mobile app use.
- Install apps on a mobile device.
- Open a new tab in a browser.
- Go to the previous page when browsing the internet.
- Bookmark a website.
- Adjust privacy settings.
- Determine which apps or software are safe to download.
- Make pop-up ads disappear and stay blocked.
- Avoid computer viruses and malware.
- Open a website directly without using a search engine like Google.
- Complete online forms.
- Find a previously visited website.

Other sources include Learning.com, which offers fee-based K–8 courses (https://bit.ly/30SCPgK) organized by specific topics ranging from word processing to coding and visual mapping. The Harvard Graduate School of Education's Project Zero (https://bit.ly/2WWY5R3) shares a free K–12 curriculum in a series of grade-specific lessons that highlight digital citizenship and a downloadable scope and sequence.

After choosing a skill or skills and drilling down, you are ready to complete each skill's task analysis based on your own digital experiences. If you intend to use partner activities (chapter 2, page 35), follow a similar sequence as shown in those activities when the selection is communicating in digital environments and managing safety (Vuorikari et al., 2016). From there, you can make lessons accompanied by whole-class or individual personalized learning plans. As shown in the Digital Competence Framework for Citizens (Vuorikari et al., 2016), specifics about the following are organized in a grade-level scope and sequence.

- Competencies
- Proficiency levels
- Knowledge, skills, and attitudes associated with each competency

As you review planning, guiding, and assessing processes, observe how the processes aim to ready you to apply the steps and strategies to any specific skill you choose in any of the five categories or a combination of them. When you see these skills through the lens of 21st century skills—complex cognition, collaboration, communication, and transference—organizing tools such as playbooks and personalized learning plans help you make the stronger decision about which roads to travel with each of your students.

How Do I Determine What Digital Skills Students Need to Learn?

Even if your district has adopted a curriculum, it is best to start with a needs assessment of your students' digital competence. Rather than plan a complete year-long scope and sequence, you may find it practical to highlight the topics or competence in one or two categories that best align with your curriculum. Most students with little formal digital experience, no matter their grade level, will benefit from focusing on the basic skills outlined in the Digital Competence Framework for Citizens (Vuorikari et al., 2016) before looking at the intermediate and advanced skills.

- **Basic digital skills** ready students to function at a minimum level in a digital society. These skills align with learning traditional literacy and numeracy and introduce the 21st century deeper learning's complex thinking skill set. Basic digital skills include keyboarding and touch-screen technology, managing files, managing privacy, emailing, searching the internet, completing online forms, and procuring government, commercial, and financial services.
- **Intermediate skills** ready students to evaluate technology and create content. Here students will apply the fundamentals applied to learning how to code, program, design, and publish. These skills are generic, meaning their mastery prepares students for a wide range of digital tasks needed to participate as engaged citizens and productive workers.
- **Advanced skills** are those needed by specialists in information and communications technology professions such as computer programming and network management, including artificial intelligence, big-data management, robotics, advanced coding, cybersecurity, Internet of Things (IoT), and mobile apps. Although modified introduction for some of these applications (such as robotics, apps, and coding) may appear in advanced science, technology, engineering, and mathematics (STEM) electives with selected students, K–8 teachers will do more for all students by ensuring that they are fluent with the fundamentals at the end of grade 8 and generally leave the intermediate and advanced skills for grades 9–12 (International Telecommunication Union, 2018).

If you teach preK, kindergarten, first grade, students with special needs, EL students, or older students who have minimum computer experience, start from scratch. Sequence skills from the first set in one category, such as browsing the internet, to looking for and sorting through content and data (Vuorikari et al., 2016).

If your students have access to digital devices (with a minimum 1:3 ratio), your first step is to assess their readiness to use digital devices to complete work in your classroom. If you are a middle school or high school teacher, determine what experience your students have with the skills listed in the five categories: (1) managing information, (2) communicating in digital environments, (3) creating digital content, (4) managing safety, and (5) problem solving (Vuorikari et al., 2016).

1. For a single-class assessment, share a KNM graphic organizer (figure 8.1) on your whiteboard or on chart paper to identify the following.

    - *Know*–What they already know and can do with a skill
    - *Need to Know*–What they think they need to know
    - *Must Know*—What they must know (which you add after they complete the graphic organizer)

Know	Need to Know	Must Know

Figure 8.1: KNM graphic organizer for assessing digital skill needs.

2. Start with one skill set from (1) managing information, (2) creating digital content, or (3) managing safety (Vuorikari et al., 2016).

3. Show the organizer to the entire class as you guide them through the columns.

4. In the Know column, start with the category's skills. For example, that might be you asking the class, "What have you learned about browsing, searching, and filtering data, information, and digital content?" Show grade-level examples so students have a model to check.

5. Record unduplicated responses in that column before attending to the Need to Know column. You might ask, for example, "If I require you to turn in all written homework assignments through your laptops, what do you think you will need to know?"

6. Finally, fill in the Must Know column with tasks students must do.

With this information, you have what you need to include in your pacing chart so all will have the digital readiness needed to complete homework assignments on the computer. Do you start with keyboarding, or can you skip it and have students set up a Word document and search for online information? If your students are reading at grade level, go immediately after the KNM organizer is finished to a hands-on test. In five-minute slots, ask students to complete tasks: open the computer screen, find letters on the keyboard, and so on. Document what you observe.

If you are creating your own curriculum with the EU framework as guidance, you can select the outcomes you will emphasize in your grade or course and focus on specific digital skills as SMART outcomes. If you are building a semester- or year-long curriculum, you can determine which categories you want as each semester's outcomes. With those, you can select the more specific skills as lessons or project outcomes and pace them over shorter times. For instance, by the end of grade 5, you might want students to interact with teammates and parents using a personal email account on a phone to organize a scavenger hunt. Leading up to this end-of-year outcome, you will have shown through prior projects that you can select options available in an email suite to organize the event, such as sending calendar invitations; you can fix problems (such as an incorrect email address); you can use a chat function on a phone (such as the one in Facebook) to organize group work; you can choose other digital communication methods on the classroom tablet; and you can fix problems (such as adding or deleting group chat members).

To structure student learning through a semester-long sequence, you can rely on a series of personalized learning plans, one for each lesson with an appropriate outcome. In this example, one of those outcomes might be *All my teammates will confirm reception of my calendar invitation.*

How Do I Construct a Lesson or Project That Promotes Digital Skills?

The following sections walk you through examples for elementary school, middle school, and high school. Each grade-level plan has abbreviated personalized teaching plans, pacing guides, and rubrics, as well as ideas for variations. These three grade-level targeted examples are built on plans specific to grade levels, but adaptable to other grades and other skills.

Elementary School

Keyboarding is a starter digital skill in the elementary example in figure 8.2, which has an abbreviated personalized teaching plan. It is a skill whose hands-on nature lets kindergarten teachers adopt keyboarding (typing) in concert with students' early phonics reading and first numeracy lessons. Thus, teachers avoid trying to find time each day to add a new skill set. Instead, they call on the keyboard skills to introduce two of the Rs—reading and arithmetic. Students' prior knowledge is assessed and includes experience opening and closing the device, opening a Word document, and keying letters in keyboard order and then in alpha sequence. The following example is an elementary starter lesson. For students just starting this set, teachers can change the reading text. Elementary teachers too may wish to select a different story or informational text.

Skill Set
Digital Keyboarding
Teaching Plan *Enter your response in the blanks.*
What is my improvement outcome for students? In thirty class periods over fifteen class days, teams of three or four students on the eighth-grade team will research cyberbullying, design a product, test it, assess, and report on the product's impact on cyberbullying in this school.
Who will I teach with this plan? ☐ One student: _____ ☐ Small group: _____ ☒ Whole class
What SMART goals do I want my students or student to achieve? Students will demonstrate, with 100 percent accuracy, the ability to name numbers 1–10 as shown on a keyboard and print a list of those numbers from a digital device. Goals: connect with numeracy outcomes, introduce number awareness and number value
What people or resources will I call on? Computers in class
What strategies will I use to reach my goal? Paired partners, keyboard practice, feedback, need-to-know lab, guided assessments Use this activities playlist. • Read-aloud story: *One Is a Snail, Ten Is a Crab* (Sayre, Sayre, & Cecil, 2003). Highlight the numbers. • Write and show: Provide crayons and ask students to copy and name each number. Add drawings to show each number. • Pair partners: Discuss and demonstrate how to take turns showing and saying each number and tracing with fingers. • Digital tool: Have each pair open keyboards and locate numbers 1–10. Each partner takes turns picking out each number. In a second round, review how to open a blank document. • Number search: Invite pairs to search the room for objects I placed around the room identified by a number. Pairs can divide the objects or numbers found, draw images with the number, and share with each other. Post the drawings on the bulletin board. End with keyboarding practice of the numbers. Let pairs count on the keyboard with each other's help.

- Number value: Teach the value of each number (how many single objects make the number). Start with a read-aloud of *Spaghetti and Meatballs for All!* (Burns & Tilley, 1997).
- Activity: Follow reading with pairs doing hands-on number-value activities with materials and objects from the classroom. (I might set up one chair labeled 1, one book, one pencil, one computer, and so on. The next day, I'd add another item to make sets of two, and so on. Assign different pairs to make the next numbers. After students complete a number-value activity, show them how to do the same on the keyboard. Whenever the activity involves making a product, hold a show-and-tell by pairs).

What materials and equipment will I need?

Digital devices to share in pairs, printers, crayons, paper, various objects for identifying numbers, rubric copies; SMART Board, read-aloud books

How much time will we need?

Twenty minutes, two days per goal

What are my criteria for success?

For each keyboarding goal, I want 80 percent minimum proficiency shown.

What measurable evidence of learning will I look for?

I will look for 80 percent accuracy in one minute per skill; saved samples of numbers identified; sketches of numbers and figures, final rubric.

What other things do I want to note here?

First run through. I want to see how smoothly assessments go.

☒ Attached pacing chart
☒ Attached rubric

Pacing Chart

Start and end dates: 12.1 and 12.14

	Mon	Tues	Wed	Thurs	Fri
Week one	Introduce numbers with story. Set up pairs.	Show guiding rubric. Write and show.	Review prior digital knowledge. Demonstrate numbers on keyboard.	Do number search activity.	Show and tell numbers. Guiding rubric review. Hold hurrahs.
Week two	Read aloud number value book. Practice.	Do labeled items number-value activity. Practice.	Continue labeled items number-value activity. Practice. Hold need-to-know lab.	Hold keyboard assessment and use rubric. Pair students (optional). Hold activity and need-to-know labs.	Hold final assessment and hurrahs.

Rubric

Name: June **Date:** 10/12

Teacher: Mrs. Henderson

Digital skill: Identifying keyboard numbers

Figure 8.2: Abbreviated personalized teaching plan—Kindergarten example.

continued →

Draw the number of stars for each skill. 0 = I do not do it yet. 1 = I can do some of it. 2 = I can do most of it. 3 = I can do all of it.	**My comments:**
Skills	**Stars**
I open my laptop.	
I see 1–9 and 0 on the keyboard.	
I enter 1–10.	
I print 1–10 from the printer.	
I can show the differences among numbers 1–10.	
I am pleased with what I can do.	

*Visit **go.SolutionTree.com/instruction** for a free reproducible version of this figure.*

Variations for different grades could include the following. Review chapters 6 (page 119) and 7 (page 149) for more strategies and activities.

Elementary school variations follow.

- **Activities to introduce lessons:** Many read-aloud stories will prompt student interest in early numeracy and literacy. This lesson's format works the same with literacy stories. You can find the print and audiobooks with a fast internet search of *read-aloud*.
- **Activities to reinforce:** Many engaging activities pair digital tools with numbers, helping students build each set in one swoop. Search online for the following and allow twenty minutes for most of them. That time can include time to process the skills so that young minds connect the skill sets.
  - *Number mazes*
  - *Trace a number*
  - *Match-a-number cards*
  - *Make number blocks*
  - *Guess my number*
  - *Find the numbers* (around school, at home, on the bus)
  - *Find-a-number race*

Middle and high school variations follow. Schedule each over two or three class periods.

- **Activities to introduce lessons:** Go directly to keyboards, inviting students to note numbers and complete a task making a list of items (such as their ten favorite songs). Let students brainstorm, individually or in teams of three, a random list and request they sequence the items.
- **Activity to reinforce:** Use challenges to calculate with numbers from grade-level mathematics problems or science formulas.

Middle School

Knowing how to maintain safety is an essential digital competence. The Digital Competence Framework for Citizens (Vuorikari et al., 2016) calls for students to know how to:

> be able to avoid health-risks and threats to physical and psychological well-being while using digital technologies. To be able to protect oneself and others from possible dangers in digital environments (e.g. cyber bullying). To be aware of digital technologies for social wellbeing and social inclusion. (p. 9)

The document defines *well-being* as "a state of complete physical, social and mental well-being, and not merely the absence of disease or infirmity" (Vuorikari et al., 2016, p. 9). Because many students believe casually, "It never will happen to me," paired with how little neuroscience knows yet about screen-time effects on young brains (Paulus et al., 2019), safety concerns springing from their lack of experience with the world, including online, and the fragility of their developing brains (Annenberg Public Policy Center, 2017) requires that adults stop and think carefully about the increased risk the digital world poses to their well-being.

Research like the following reinforces the importance of educators' paying attention to the effects of living and learning in a digital environment.

- Early literature on the brain effects of technology on young students' cognitive, social-emotional, and physical development is sparse, sometimes ominous, and sometimes auspicious (OECD, 2019).

- What seems clearest is that technology is rewiring young brains, and there are more questions than answers as to how and to what benefits there are (Taylor, 2012).

- Attention from educators will need to focus on how time on-screen is impacting how students are learning, how they are feeling, and how they are developing the social-emotional readiness to deal with the risks (Ehmke, n.d.).

In addition to mental health issues, the digital world has become saturated with issues that infringe on teachers planning authentic online learning experiences. It becomes increasingly more important for schools to ensure that online safety and security are not only introduced to elementary students, but continuously scaffolded through the entirety of their in-school experience. With parents often less savvy than their children about the hacks and trolls roving social media, other risks such as cyberbullying, propaganda purported to be news, disguised ads seeking personal information, plagiarism, and adult predators, along with the addictive quality of social media, educators cannot ignore the responsibility of including well-being in the annual course of study (Walton, 2017).

The interdisciplinary project in the example in figure 8.3 (page 184) integrates one digital well-being topic of high interest to middle school students with a state-mandated social-emotional outcome (Illinois Anti-bullying Statute, 2017). The issue is an authentic learning topic relevant in middle school (and high school) classrooms. By addressing it in an interdisciplinary project, middle school teachers and teacher teams can allot the time needed more easily. This plan assumes that students have prior knowledge about cooperative learning, how to brainstorm, digital tools, and presentation options. The teacher would make and share a guiding rubric for teams and review research guidelines before beginning the plan.

The following variations suggest options for adapting this plan as a pilot lesson and including other grades.

Elementary school variations follow.

- Adapt the project to one class and one teacher.

- Use pairs for a team activity. Pair students for any of the activities listed in the "What strategies will I use to reach my goal?" section. Adapt circle time for whole-class discussions online.

- Integrate guided reading that allows differentiated meetings with teams to review progress and set goals while others read or work independently on other project activities.

- Replace surveys with stories and videos about bullying, online sharing of staying safe, and equipment security settings and available elementary-appropriate experts.
  - Champions Against Bullying has resources for students, parents, and teachers: www.championsagainstbullying.org.
  - WeAreTeachers has over twenty popular books on bullying: https://bit.ly/39nY3qD.
  - Childhood101 recommends a dozen videos appropriate in elementary and middle school: https://childhood101.com/bullying-videos-kids.

- Limit activity online to twenty or thirty minutes twice a day and enter it in your pacing schedule.

- Don't forget to add time to introduce the digital skills *before* teams start to work. You may schedule all activities in synchronous time. When teams are working, schedule digital round-robin observations and need-to-know lab check-ups to ensure all teams stay on task.

Skill Set
Digital
Protecting oneself and others from possible dangers in a digital environment
Teaching Plan   *Enter your response in the blanks.*
What is my improvement outcome for students?
In thirty class periods over fifteen class days, teams of three or four students on the eighth-grade team will research cyberbullying, design a product, test it, and assess and report on the product's impact on cyberbullying in this school.
Who will I teach with this plan?   ☐ One student: _____   ☐ Small group: _____   ☒ Whole class
What SMART goals do I want my students or student to achieve?
Over fifteen class periods, each student will complete a personalized learning plan for self-protection and protection of classmates from cyberbullies, do the plan, and assess what happened. (Students needing added time will have prescheduled studio access during study periods and Monday, Wednesday, and Thursday after school.)
What people or resources will I call on?
Invite students to go online and identify an expert to invite for an online interview (for instance, Theresa Payton, former White House CIO, CEO of Fortalice, and team member on the TV show *Hunted*).   Ad production digital tools and materials, SMART Board, Canva or Google Docs, Schoology LMS
What strategies will I use to reach my goal?
Collaborative teams, online research, digital design, digital products, asking an expert, two-way feedback, student copy of pacing chart (student playbook substitution) <ul><li>Role play: Introduce the project in an all-team assembly with a roleplay by four teachers showing one or more cyberbullying scenarios. Divide presentation responsibilities among faculty members.<ul><li>Form teams of four or five (each member from a different advisory) and review contracts and guiding rubrics for (a) collaboration, (b) understanding of cyberbullying effects, and (c) problem-solving or presentation skills.</li><li>Distribute a student pacing chart, one per team.</li><li>Prepare interview questions (below).</li><li>Review the pacing chart with all teams. Share a copy to digital devices (one per team, and highlight required meeting times).</li></ul></li><li>Brainstorm: Ask the whole class, "What are the components of an ad that motivates you to act? What are the ways or media to communicate a message that motivates? Which of these allows you to use your digital skills?"</li><li>Team vote: Each team uses the whole-class list to vote on which digital tool they are familiar with so they can develop a product for an anti-cyberbullying campaign.</li><li>Guiding rubrics: At least once a week, the team's advisor will meet for formative assessments with the guiding rubric.</li><li>Research: Teams will collaborate to research online and, based on at least four online articles, make a definition and identify the social-emotional effects of cyberbullying on adolescents; they will prepare a survey to go to at least four persons from three audience groups (parents, peers, teachers, siblings). With the mathematics teacher's help, the teams will analyze the data and make at least two charts representing their data.</li><li>Ask an expert: Students search, select, invite, interview, and thank an expert to interview about cyberbullying.</li><li>Need-to-know labs: Faculty team members will conduct labs or conferences as requested by students (like what interview questions to ask, how to find experts, what protocols to follow for interviews, and so on).</li></ul>

- Coaches: Advisors will coach teams as they work. Once weekly they will have conferences, ask how it's going, and give feedback. They may also hold solo conferences.
- Product labs: Teams will gather materials and make their final products. In the digital medium selected and with appropriate digital tools, each team will create its ad to make and distribute in their school.
- Check-in conference: Each team will have a faculty advisor who will coach and give feedback as the students work through the process.
- Product: Student teams create ads during asynchronous time.
- Presentation: Each team will determine how and where it will distribute its ad, subject to the advisor's OK. Audiences may include parents, guardians, other classes, school officials, or other appropriate groups. I have a print; they must secure location permission.
- Final grades and assessments: See pacing chart. Each team will provide self-assessments and peer assessments; the audience will assess, and the coach will give feedback. Students compile that feedback and assessments in a digital folder for the team advisor. Team advisors will grade the final addition of the grading rubric, with half of the final grade based on progress shown in interim assessments and half based on the final assessment. The team will agree on the scale prior to the start of the project.
- Reflection: Allow the final period for each advisor's teams gathered together to reflect on what and how they learned in this project. Advisors ask What did you learn? What did you like and dislike? How will the digital skills you learned in this project transfer in your other courses? Projects?" Volunteer students will keep digital notes of the responses. Faculty advisors will collate the results and share a digital document with students and parents.

What materials and equipment will I need?

A digital device per team, interview questions and protocols, student pacing chart, Canva or Google Docs, plus social media as approved

How much time will we need?

We need four weeks with whole-class synchronous and asynchronous times, including teams working together as they schedule team synchronous and asynchronous times. Teams are allowed one optional day. Teams will schedule their own synchronous and asynchronous time.

What are my criteria for success?

See the rubric below and outcome above.

What measurable evidence of learning will I show?

A collaborative ad on cyberbullying, research notes, interview notes, and completed assessments

What other things do I want to note here?

The interviews will be trickiest. My plan B, if can't get an expert, is to have them get parent or guardian interviews or to call on our district tech staff. I have made the pacing schedule student playbook. I have found that the pacing chart is better for my students.

- ☒ Attached pacing chart
- ☒ Attached rubric

Pacing Chart

Start and end dates: 10/1 and 10/29

	Monday	Tuesday	Wednesday	Thursday	Friday
Week one	Introduce project with outcomes and check prior knowledge.	Make teams. Review prior knowledge check by teams.	Teams plan research refinements.	Conduct research labs. Offer need-to-know labs.	Students conduct interviews (through second week to schedule and complete).

Figure 8.3: Abbreviated personalized teaching plan—Middle school example.

continued →

Week one	Review guiding rubric. Hold whole-class brainstorm.	Discuss requirements by team. Conduct whole-class need-to-know labs.	Continue research.	Perform formative assessment one. Explain initial contact with expert and interview time, method, team responsibilities, questions, and interview strategy. Set interview protocols.	Offer need-to-know lab. Conduct, analyze, and research data need-to-know lab.
Week two	Hold advisor weekly rubric review and goal setting. Offer need-to-know lab. Continue research lab analysis.	Continue offering need-to-know labs. Advisory teams create research reports. Give feedback on research for each team.	Prepare interview labs by team. Advisors coach. Offer choice between advisor coaching or need-to-know lab.	Students conduct interviews. Hold need-to-know lab. Advisors coach. Offer a choice between advisor coaching or need-to-know lab.	Students continue research. Continue holding interview labs. Offer need-to-know lab.
Week three	Hold advisor weekly rubric review and goal setting. Hold open need-to-know lab.	Conduct need-to-know labs for interviews. Teams write explanation essay. Coach. Ready students for interviews. Review and approve interview plans.	Review need-to-know team labs. Teams continue research and interviews on own time.	Collect surveys. Coach and give feedback. Students collect and analyze data with outside help. Conduct data analysis need-to-know lab. Introduce final product (digital ad) with criteria and presentation expectations.	Teams prepare ads and practice presentations. Conduct need-to-know lab on products and presentations.
Week four	Students present. Peers and other audience members give feedback. Teams review feedback, assess themselves, and share with me.	Personalized learning plans are completed. Students complete and turn over personalized learning plan assessments to me.	Students reflect by team, saying what they learned, and listing four digital skills they used or learned and their research, interview, data analysis, teamwork, ad creation, and presentations.	Reflection continues as needed. I give feedback to whole class on their digital skill development. Hold round-robin team summaries of "I learned" selections with sticky note feedback from other classmates ("I appreciate how . . .").	This is an overflow day or transition to the next lesson.

The Digital Skill Set

Name: Sergio Protoofsky	**Date:** 10/2
Teacher: Mrs. Johanson	**Period:** 4
Partners: Madeline Alstar, Alison Orlibeck, Reggie Jackson, Maya Bloethner	

Completed by:
- ☒ Self
- ☒ Teacher
- ☒ Peers: Madeline, Alison, Reggie, and Maya
- ☒ Other: _____

Digital skill: researching, using social media, graphics program

Need to Improve	Criterion	Doing Well
You forgot dates.	Our team set a SMART goal for an anti-bullying product for our school.	
It was when Alison and Reggie were late getting online for team meetings. Alison wasn't finished with her job, and I had to figure out how to get her on time because she is my bestie.	I did my fair share in making our plan.	Yes. I was the product manager, and I had to make sure everyone got done on time. I finally did at the end.
See above.	I did my fair share in designing the product.	I was recorder for the brainstorm.
Yes, but I have to speak up more when I see it.	I have increased what I know about how cyberbullying affects my peers.	Yes, and I am getting better at speaking out.
Doing the online research was hard. The sites you sent me helped.	I have increased my skill using digital communication tools to prepare a message.	I feel I am now really, really good at research and at sharing with my team online. I can really manage Zoom and Facebook.
I need to come up with better examples.	I did my fair share in assessing the impact of our product.	
I need more ideas for our brainstorm and I didn't always agree on what we picked.	I can make a storyboard for our campaign.	I know all the steps and they really fit with what I learned in visual arts class. My team let me do lots of cartoons and they liked my style.
I was not the best presenter. I should use notes.	I am proud of the product our team made.	I am really proud of what I added with my sketches.
I would say I have become a 4 out of 5 teammate.	I am proud of my contribution.	I always did my part and more. My sketches were a hit and my team told me I was a good timer person.

continued →

Summative Remarks	
Remarks made by: Mrs. Johanson	**Date:** 10/10
I like how you finished your personalized learning plan on teamwork. I see you getting your say more and more. I always knew you were conscientious about your team jobs. Finally, I was happy to discover your artistic talent. The cartoons were not only funny, they really made the point. Most importantly, how you adapted your art talent to making the storyboard and the final ad to share with the school showed your flexible thinking. Digital art and design may be a future to consider.	
What needs to improve:	
I would like to see you continue to work on speaking your voice in your team. I would also like to see you speaking up more in class. Your progress in the team has been really good, so keep at it!	
What help you need:	
In your next personalized learning plans, I suggest continuing with more specific outcomes that push you to ask more clarifying questions. You also might volunteer to be the team summarizer.	

Visit **go.SolutionTree.com/instruction** *for a free reproducible version of this figure.*

Middle and high school variations follow.

- Adjust the time when a faculty team leads the project. For example, you could conduct this in four periods over eight days.
- Use a different safety topic for projects such as protecting personal data online and safe etiquette.
- Vary the team size.
- Keep teams in the same home advisory. If your school has no advisory, form pairs or other teams among different departments. In high school, include specialties such as world languages or other electives. Consider pairing special needs, English learners, or other specialists with mainstream classroom teachers.
- If your students are in the classroom, adapt what activities appear online to the classroom with your physical presence, learning with teams prepared to meet online without advisors for team events.

Ideally, older students will arrive with fluent mastery of Word and the other prior-knowledge skills for creating written text, which includes opening a program on a laptop; using Word to type, copy, and paste text; reading and manipulating a toolbar, menu bar, and a toolbox; opening and filling in a template; collaborating with a partner, photographing with a digital tool such as a smartphone or notebook; making and sharing a document; and making a folder and saving files to it. More likely, you will have to assess students' text-creation skills. Prior to starting this lesson, you will have filled in any gaps.

GIMP (www.gimp.org) is a free (*open-source*) photo-editing program and just one example of a program that allows high school students to apply the basic-level skills designated in the Digital Competence Framework for Citizens (Vuorikari et al., 2016). The skills ask them to call on problem solving, ready them to polish future reports for your and other classes, and open new career vistas in marketing, architecture, art conservancy, and digital design. Teachers in diverse disciplines such as science, mathematics, world languages, and English language arts can connect this plan to careers in their fields. If done as an interdisciplinary study, teacher subject-area teams could co-teach this project with you. For instance, social studies and English teachers could add copyright and licensing features to the career mix even as they ready students to sort through and select content from the internet. Figure 8.4 is an integrated plan that connects problem solving in two or more disciplines.

These variations suggest options for adapting this plan as your pilot lesson in other grades.

- **Elementary school:** Select a grade-level application that requires students to transfer prior skills so they know how to use digital programs with proficiency. For example, first graders could type an ABC book (see https://bit.ly/2Jxne1r) so they have to apply not only what they know about the alphabet, but also their keyboarding skills; second graders could

Skill Set
Digital: digital editing, photo editing, problem solving
Teaching Playbook *Enter your response in the blanks.*
Who will I teach with this plan? ☐ One student: _____ ☐ Small group: _____ ☒ Whole class
What is my improvement outcome for students? In twenty-five class periods, teams of three tenth-grade visual arts students will create, present, and assess a digital ad showing proficiency ratings for all digital editing and problem-solving criteria in their personalized learning plans.
What SMART goals do I want my students or student to achieve? • Produce notes from one photo-editing program from an online tutorial (during time shown in the class pacing schedule). • Partner to create a visual ad for a sculpture using editing knowledge. • Include the ad and the unused photographs in an online portfolio. • Explain the selection of three photographs and text in the ad. • Share a document online to explain how the editing program helped them complete the project. • Explain how a partner helped complete the project. • Assess by criteria for quality of work (ad for a sculpture). • Assess by criteria for skill proficiency (problem solving).
What people or resources will they call on? GIMP (or a similar app) and its tutorial, digital portfolios in Google Docs folders
What strategies will they use to reach the outcome? Paired partners, make-a-photostory, make a visual ad, make digital portfolios, tutorials Follow this playbook. • Display: Approve completed sculptures for the school display. • Program selection: Select a program, review it, and complete the key activities for my own sample portfolio. • Pairs: Set up pairs that will help each other create the ads. • Prior-knowledge check: Conduct a class discussion. Who has used the program to publish an image? To publish multiple images? What do they know? What can they share about their experience? What more do they need to know? Survey the entire class with a brainstormed list or with a survey each completes. • Art portfolio: Show a completed digital portfolio with your work or the work of a known artist such as Leonardo da Vinci or Jackson Pollock and check students' prior experience with portfolios. • Keyword search: Designate Photoshop and instruct pairs to search for the program. Coach as needed. • Online tutorial: Select a tutorial for beginners. Preview a variety or let each pair select one or more tutorials. Highlight the tools they select. Pairs already proficient with the program can skip this step. • Class norms: Review guidelines for teamwork. • Photographs: Pairs help each other photograph their sculptures and explain the goal of the lesson as well as the reason for making a portfolio. They will use their smartphones. (Check for know-how.)

Figure 8.4: Abbreviated personalized teaching plan—High school example.

continued →

- App review: Pairs divide the jobs, choosing between device operator and recorder and switch jobs each day. With the tutorials on the pair's devices, the recorder will make, share, and store in a folder the key points the pair will need to recall about using the program. Using a variation of KWL, let each pair record and save on its device what they know and need to know about using this app. Pairs ready to advance can start with the app which I have shared to their devices. Guide others by answering quick questions first and then by walking the remainder of students with a need-to-know through the menu. Check for readiness to use.
- Coach: Coach and give feedback as needed when students are learning the tool.
- Assessments: At least once weekly, require each pair to follow the guiding rubric and give each other feedback. Completed rubrics are stored in the portfolio and should progress through to the summative rubric. It will help that I schedule time each week to observe and give pairs feedback guided by the rubric's criteria.
- Show and tell: Each pair will show its completed ad on the SMART Board and share their final self-assessments in a five-minute presentation. If time allows, I can give brief feedback and encourage peer feedback.
- Final reflection: Allow the last twenty minutes for the class to reflect on what and how it learned in this project. Ask "What did we like and dislike? How will the digital skills you learned in this project transfer in your other courses?" Ask for specific examples.

What materials and equipment will I need?

Digital photo device, photo-editing program, production supplies, portfolio, selected tutorials

How much time will we need?

Five weeks

What are my criteria for success?

See the rubric and outcome below.

What measurable evidence of learning will I show?

Each student will show the finished product, work artifacts, and personalized learning plan placed in a portfolio. The personalized learning plan rubric will show feedback and my final product evaluation. Each student will take twelve photographs and choose three for an ad campaign about the public sculpture with a written explanation of why the three were chosen, an explanation of how the program helped prepare the final three, accompanying text for the ad, and a final rubric with self-assessment and my feedback.

What other things do I want to note here?

I am ready to go.

- ☒ Attached pacing chart. Post and share with the playbook above.
- ☒ Attached rubric

Pacing Chart

Start and end dates: 10/1 and 10/22

	Mon	Tues	Wed	Thurs	Fri
Week one	Introduce project with outcomes and check prior knowledge. Review guiding rubric.	Make pairs. Introduce the portfolios and tutorials. Conduct keyword search.	Teams select tutorials. Review roles and procedures. Review class and teamwork norms.	Offer tutorials with coaching.	Offer tutorials with coaching. Provide guiding rubric one.
Week two	Host photo-editing need-to-know labs. Coach.	Host photo-editing need-to-know labs. Coach.	Host photo-editing need-to-know labs. Coach.	Host photo-editing need-to-know labs. Coach. Introduce rubric two.	Host ad need-to-know lab. Coach. Go over rubric two again.

Week three	Host ad lab about text. Coach.	Host ad lab. Detail the explanation essay. Coach. Introduce rubric three.	Explain presentation procedures. Host presentations. Prepare for presentations. Introduce rubric three.	Host presentations. Check portfolios.	Provide the final rubric. Reflect.

Guiding Rubric
Name: Reggie Hathale　　　　　　　　　　**Date:** 9/5
Teacher: Mr. Erickson　　　　　　　　　　**Period:** 3
Check-up dates: 9/12, 9/19, 9/26
Partners: Mary Eagle, Thomos Jones
Feedback is by: ☐ Self   ☐ Teacher   ☒ Peer: Teams   ☐ Other: _____
Digital skill: Editing in a digital photo-editing program

Need to Improve	Criterion	Doing Well
	I identified my need-to-knows from the tutorial.	Your examples were clear.
	I asked questions.	Yours were right on target.
	I helped my partner.	You took charge of the team.
The criteria weren't specific enough. Review models and show me new ones.	I made criteria for judging photos I altered in Photoshop.	
	I listened to feedback and made adjustments.	You were direct and specific here.
	I made a storyboard for preparing photos with the program.	Your drawings were very clear.
	I produced three images altered in GIMP for the ad.	You did this.
	I produced text for the ad.	Your ideas were creative and funny. I loved the cartoons, too!
Again, be more specific when explaining and give examples.	I produced and included the final ad with explanations in my portfolio.	
	My work shows pride.	

continued →

Need to Improve	Criterion	Doing Well
	I am pleased with my proficiency in using GIMP.	
	My final product shows pride.	
Summative Remarks		

Remarks made by: T. Erickson   **Date:** 10/2

You did this well:

I liked how you took a leadership role on your team, especially with specific feedback. The text for your ad was very creative. The humor was great.

What needs to improve:

The explanations in your portfolio seemed rushed. I would like more detail in your second and third explanations and more detail in your criteria.

What help you need:

I don't see anything with which you need help. Bravo!

Visit *go.SolutionTree.com/instruction* for a free reproducible version of this figure.

draft an email message to a senior to share a seasonal greeting so they have to apply Outlook skills and develop the skills to compose an email communication. Adapt the rubric and the playbook to this age.

- **Middle and high school:** Transfer basic digital skills into other programs or apps as you work through the curriculum such as photo essays, spreadsheets, video production, shareware visuals, and others found in Google's suite of creativity tools. Couple these with your content curriculum to increase student engagement while simultaneously developing digital acumen. Cross-curricular skills could include storyboarding historic events, concept mapping a Shakespeare play, graphing interest surveys, and charting cost of living, for example.

What Strategies and Activities Promote Digital Skills?

First, you can adapt strategies and activities from other skill lessons in this book, including the following.

- **Brainstorming:** This strategy, which you can read more about in chapter 6 (page 119), will help primary students make lists of places they have seen numbers and letters or ideas to make up their own number stories.

- **Informal and formal cooperative learning:** Try think-pair-share when the skill is introduced; formal cooperative teams (chapter 2, page 35) will enrich discussion about online readings.

- **Two-way feedback:** This strategy, discussed in chapter 4 (page 87), is one you can integrate into any lesson several times. The more often you include it in a lesson, the more this strategy benefits students. Consider calling on it formally in your pacing chart to stimulate discussion of guided assessments each week.

- **Design project:** Design the use of a new digital tool and its applied skills in group-guided projects. Invite students to generate a list of digital tools they would like to access. Guide students in a brainstorm of technology questions that they might want to answer such as "How do I . . .

    - . . . connect to a WiFi network?"
    - . . . download apps to a mobile device?"
    - . . . keep track of the costs of mobile app use?"
    - . . . bookmark a website?"
    - . . . avoid computer viruses?"
    - . . . open a website directly without using a search engine like Google?"
    - . . . complete online forms?"

- **Team investigation:** Teams investigate to determine what digital skills they will need to complete the project. This investigation, enriched within a formal cooperative learning framework, asks each group to plan, complete, and assess the project with digital skill outcomes in mind. For instance, after the class brainstorms local environmental issues, each team selects a community issue such as chemical waste, air pollution, COVID-19, or garbage disposal. Each plan includes a digital skills rubric related to the project. You highlight the criteria each time you sit down with a group.

Second, in addition to these previously mentioned strategies, you can try and adapt the following to various grades.

- **Make it a problem:** When primary students are learning word-processing and email skills, challenge them to engage their parents with an email campaign. Students brainstorm ideas for letters that they will then write. Middle schoolers could address the city council about a local problem. They could include spreadsheets showing the results of a poll or collected data. High school students could make a local public service announcement using storyboarding as well as media tools. In all instances, determine the digital skills they need to know and make those skills the outcome of your unit. If you aren't ready to go into authentic real-world PBL, simulate problems that require online research.

- **Simulate it:** You can assign each online learner working alone or on a team to solve a problem with new online skills. For example, assume you want students to learn how to summarize articles they read online and report results on a timeline about a specific scientific breakthrough (such as the polio vaccine or the first transatlantic flight). They will apply online skills to research online articles, videos, or other internet resources to find the information they require and then summarize key points.

- **Blog it or podcast it:** While teachers can draw blanks about topics that will excite student interest in communicating, their digital world provides not only a plethora of hot topics they want to know more about, it also provides digital communication tools that they rely on and which can turn them from being passive adopters to proactive creators of their learning. To take advantage, for example, social studies and ELA teachers can ask students to write their own blogs or create podcasts on topics relevant to their lives in a digital world and extend their digital skills. For instance, consider student blogs about online safety and security. Rather than lecture about stranger danger, set assignments that allow preadolescents and adolescents to choose topics for blogging and podcasting. Since the popularization of the term *fake news*, the challenges of discerning not only what is real and fake online but real or fake in the multitude of all media fields, as well as the marketing capabilities to collect and disseminate personal information, provide more than enough fodder for students to investigate and share their ideas. Media literacy is paramount.

How Do I Create a Guiding Rubric for Digital Skills?

These steps capture the generic instructions for creating any rubric similar to the example in figure 8.4 (page 189).

1. Select the format.
2. Narrow the subsets to digital skills or whatever you are emphasizing and fill in the desired outcomes. (For digital skills, go to the EU curriculum, page 176). For instance, if you are teaching social studies, your outcomes might dictate skills for developing ethical online behavior and relevant digital skills. If you prioritize tight problem solving in mathematics, you may select a digital outcome for making charts and graphs to explain a solution.
3. Determine the criteria that will instruct the students and give specifics.
4. Add a student playbook.
5. Ask students to review the rubric at the start of the lesson, again during the middle of the lesson, and prior to the summative assessment at the end of the lesson. Word the criteria so students rate progress or improvement.
6. Determine who gives feedback, if a grade is required, and who determines the final grade and how.
7. Instruct students to follow the student playbook.
8. If you are using a personalized learning plan aligned to the key skills, you can choose one rubric for the entire class, or rubrics by groups or individuals. You might have a case where you have a guiding rubric that isn't aligned to the thinking or content in a particular standard, or a different outcome for a specific skill that doesn't show up in the content standard but that you or a student want to develop. Be sure to build in time for the all-important feedback.

How Do I Assess My Implementation Plan?

Your plans will result in guiding rubrics that not only assess digital skill development, but also serve as a powerful instructional strategy that teaches students about the skill they are developing. You can vary the guiding rubric format to be a single-rater list or single-point feedback, or add other formats. (See the appendix, page 211, for single-point and multi-point templates.) Consider the following elements as well.

- **Students are the primary assessors:** Whether you (for students in grades K–2) or students (grades 3 and later) determine what students need to know and do with this skill or establish the proficiency criteria, the student is the first assessor. If you must, you can do the final number tabulation for scores.

- **Peer feedback is number one:** When students collaborate, it is beneficial that they give and get feedback. Remember that Hattie's (2012) research ranks two-way feedback as the most effective on student achievement. Collaboration adds to the impact (Johnson & Johnson, 2018).

- **Teacher feedback is crucial:** During formative assessments, the guiding rubric is a goal-setting tool when you present it at the start of a lesson, and it helps students focus on what's important to learn. Equally important, it structures your use of the most powerful tool in your repertoire—feedback (chapter 4, page 87). At the end, your formative comments on the same template capture what tells you and the students how far each has traveled toward grade-level fluent use of the skill.

- **List specific criteria:** These are the benchmarks that identify the skill.

- **Use a developmental rating scale:** This allows ratings to focus on the process of getting to proficiency overtime. What progress is being made week to week? How is the student using feedback to improve?

- **Include space for comments:** Criteria guide to a measurable score. Comment spaces allow the teacher or student to write more, especially emphasizing improvements to make and those that were made.

- **Please don't use grades while assessing formatively:** The emphasis is on self-assessment supported by helpful feedback. Although you can score criteria and scale it for a grade, it is more important for student motivation that you resist bean counting. If parents, guardians, or next year's teachers want to know how a particular student is doing, you can share evidence from the student's portfolio, and discuss it digitally (via email, for example) or face to face. If parents ask for a comparison, you can talk about how their child's work fits with the others' in the class. You will have a ton of specific examples. If you need to translate a student's scores into grades or provide a comparison between others, you can maintain a folder of work that redacts student information.

What Are the Most Helpful Digital Tools for Enhancing Personalized Learning Plans?

Following recommendations from the Erikson Institute (Herdzina & Lauricella, 2020) and other early childhood learning organizations such as the International Literacy Association (2019), teachers ideally thread early digital skill development into as many daily learning experiences as possible. At what age could it be more important to establish the safety basics and initiate other digital skills as essential tools for learning than in the elementary years?

In the basic skills, your district almost certainly provides a scope and sequence to follow in the early grades. In middle and high school, each course has its own scope and sequence. If not, you may informally make the textbook your curriculum. There is a good chance that you do not have a grade-level scope and sequence for digital skills that anywhere nears approaches the thoroughness of your school's mathematics and English language arts curricula. At best, your school may make digital skills an elective. As you read earlier in this chapter, you must make your own scope and sequence if this is the case.

In a district without a digital curriculum with a clarified scope and sequence, you may also find a very wide range of digital expertise. There is a likelihood that some students will show proficiency far beyond their grade level (perhaps even making their own apps, for instance). It is even likelier that some students will arrive with minimum digital skills. You may have a mix. When you have a mix, go to heterogeneous grouping. Let your high-flying techies help. As many as possible can lead cooperative teams as the majority are learning the digital skills. Peer coaching and other formal and informal cooperative learning strategies (detailed in chapter 2, page 35) will go a long way in moving all forward. When teaching a lesson or project, personalized learning plans can focus on the digital skills students will practice during completion. Thus, if one student arrives with the minimum keyboarding ability, he can work on a mixed digital-ability team and take responsibilities appropriate to his starter level. As the team progresses, it is their job to coach his digital advance. And of course, there is always the need-to-know lab. In a given day (in elementary school) or week (in middle or high school), you and one or more techies can differentiate need-to know labs so the students who are struggling can reach grade-level competency.

Highlighting a digital skill–focused personalized learning plan is a way of engaging students in learning how to learn with a focus on technology skills. You can ask students to target other digital skill outcomes which help them use the multitude of digital tools available to them. As they work through digital personalized learning plans, students experience technology as an organizing tool and as an agency producer and developer of new communication skills. By using hardware as basic as smartphones, you foster agency and help students learn how to set goals, design strategies, evaluate what and how they want to learn, research, collaborate, communicate about setting up a coaching and conferencing schedule, and assess themselves with feedback to and from you and their peers. By adopting personalized learning plans, technology helps you bolster students' learning with familiar tools. The idea is to decrease your workload even as you teach students how to become *masters of their own fate, the captains of their own ships* (Henley, 1888). Engaging students in adapting love for or familiarity with technological tools and enhancing their skills with new tools advance their academic know-how and develop 21st century digital skills.

Another plus of using digital tools and making sure your students know how to use them is that this helps you avoid piles of paper and logistical nightmares regarding communicating due dates, stacks of projects in various forms, and feedback turnover. Instead, you can call on a variety of digital tools to organize the plans and the multiple artifacts students generate. To start, it will help to set up a digital system for managing plans, artifacts, and rubrics. If you are not already using an LMS, here are the modifiable components that work best. If you already have an LMS in place, make sure it includes all components that you decide are necessary to give your students the fullest engagement: plan management, artifact storage, rubrics, scheduling, feedback depository, grades, and parent and guardian communication.

As you begin preparing the digital aspect of your classroom's personalized learning plans, consider the two tool categories you can tap into, as well as the following tools, which you will find most helpful.

- Google Docs
- Digital portfolios
- Playlists
- Playbooks
- Rubric banks
- Templates
- Reflection journals
- Social media networks
- Free websites

Tool Categories

Technology offers a cornucopia of learning tools that can make students more effective. Two categories of tools shape the digital character of classroom activity. Category one simply doesn't meet the need for digital literacy. Category two offers what you need to focus on digital skills.

Category One

Category one includes programmed or machine learning tools that focus on traditional content skill mastery in reading, mathematics, and science, as well as the factual information of advanced content-area courses. This *computer-assisted instruction* (CAI) delivers measurable results derived from single answers.

The CAI format serves the following needs.

- Basic skill practices in reading and mathematics
- High school credit recovery
- Distance learning
- Adult training courses

Although often touted as the magic tool that produces agency, the claim is disingenuous. As discussed in chapter 4 (page 87), agency comes from students' ability to choose. Agency is most likely to develop from student choices about authentic learning experiences—What do I want to learn? How do I want to learn? With whom do I want to learn? These are the essential questions students are allowed to ask and answer. CAI allows students to choose a program at a time each day and to answer preset questions in an order prescribed by the machine. Bells and whistles celebrate selection of each correct answer, award points, readjust the difficulty level, and may let the student shut down the program.

Preset algorithms in the digital machine determine choices that allow a student to select one answer from many, to receive corrective information when she or he chooses a wrong answer, and to see instant progress charts. Advanced versions automatically vary pace, difficulty, corrective information, and rewards; basic algorithms automatically adjust levels of difficulty. Single-answer questions, however, are limited to bite-size pieces of information in a course's content. In the basic skills, students practice and re-practice each isolated skill until the program allows movement to a new skill. Small, recallable chunks are preferred. The same small-bites method holds true for high school and adult learning courses which allow information to be chunked and easily recalled. Courses that cover an automatic sequence of steps (how to operate a crane or write a program, for instance) and lead to a grade or a certificate fit well with machine-delivered learning. CAI is not yet close to delivering coursework that ends in deeper learning outcomes. If, however, the aim of a course is to cover specific information with correct answer scores, the only SMART results will be a count of correct answers.

Demands for *digital literacy*—being able to create, understand, and communicate meaning and knowledge—suggest that CAI is inadequate. This definition and other studies favor deeper learning's bias for thinking and problem-solving proficiencies. Matthew Lynch (2017) writes:

> One of the most important components of digital literacy is the ability to not just find, but also to evaluate, information. This means finding the answer to a question or a bit of needed information and then judging whether the source is reliable. Educators can, and should, teach students how to tell whether information on the internet is true. The ability to weed out false information and find reliable sources is a key part of digital literacy and a crucial life skill in the 21st century.

In short, deeper learning outcomes are not going to arrive via CAI. At best, CAI may help some students practice or review basic skills.

Category Two

Category two offers an abundance of tools for enhancing deeper learning outcomes in lessons, projects, courses, personalized learning plans, or other formats teachers select. Teachers working within category two strive to expand their skills. They also take advantage of every available digital tool with the goal of preparing all students to become competent digital learners and 21st century digital citizens.

> Many people think that when we start talking about 21st century learning and education we are talking about technology and the infrastructure. We are not. When we talk about problem solving, critical thinking, communication, collaboration, creativity or any of the other competences we are talking about the cognitive and not about the hardware. These 21st century competences are thinking skills and have been nicknamed by some as "headware" (not hardware) competences. (Department of eLearning, 2015, p. 12)

Teachers must be ready to adopt basic tools, such as smartphones, earphones, game consoles, and social media as classroom aid to advance deeper learning by digital citizens but must understand the difference between *headware* and hardware. To further promote digital learning, teachers must learn to integrate lessons that employ hardware such as the following.

- 3-D printers
- Calendars
- Computers
- Education websites
- Ereaders
- Global libraries accessible online from anywhere at anytime
- Interactive whiteboards
- Plug-ins (which add features to programs)
- Programmed learning (CAI)
- Learning management systems
- Music and video playlists
- News feeds
- Notebooks and tablets
- Online games
- Video projectors
- Voice over Internet Protocol (VoIP) technology such as Skype and FaceTime

The supermarket of available digital tools that can enhance personalized learning grows daily. You can ignore as many devices as you choose or elect as many as you desire to adapt for your students' personalized learning plans. Be assured that students of whatever age, economic status, sexual preference, religion, language, or special needs may be more comfortable with technology than you. In addition to filling students' digital toolkits, teachers must grow their own skills as they prepare their students to generate deeper understandings and solve increasingly complex, authentic problems. Teachers can prepare personal playlists with instructions for use, in and outside a personalized learning plan, as they and their students expand their toolkits.

Of course, teaching with technology forces one to look forward, since the evolution is constant and quick. Despite that evolution, teachers are necessary and will be many more decades into the future, and not just as grade recorders or tech repair persons. According to artificial intelligence expert Kai-Fu Lee (2018):

> AI will be a great tool for teachers and educational institutions, as it will help educators figure out how to personalize curriculum based on each student's competence, progress, aptitude, and temperament. However, teaching will still need to be oriented around helping students figure out their interests, teaching students to learn independently, and providing one-on-one mentorship. These are tasks that can only be done by a human teacher. As such, there will still be a great need for human educators in the future.

Learning Management System

The commonly called-on Google Docs, or an equivalent LMS, will help you organize and share personal learning plans. To utilize an LMS, follow these six steps.

1. Provide each student with a personal identification number and a personal folder, and also create a whole-class folder.

2. Share and discuss security, safety, and confidentiality in the personalized learning plan context. Guidance by teachers around these guidelines is crucial for personalized learning plan success. It is likely that your students have heard much about safety online. It is also crucial that you keep them attuned to the absolute importance of psychological security. Everyone must feel that whatever

information they share with you and their peers will be stored and shared in the boundaries of absolute confidentiality. As discussed earlier, violations not only damage the classroom trust and positive climate, they can cause severe damage to the self-worth of the peers violated. As a teacher, consider it a serious offense to allow anyone access to a student's portfolio, the content of your personalized learning plan dialogues, or other personal information in a personalized learning plan without the express permission of those under sixteen (or their parent or guardian). When you structure personalized learning plans as part of your students' learning lives, it is important that your administrators understand that you cannot respond to pressure to reveal any personalized learning plan information. Your firmness is similar to a journalist's protection of information sources.

3. Prepare students for two-way sharing. They will share their entries with you and, if you allow, with approved peers. Those who hear will learn about the others' personal learning goals and plans via personalized learning plan templates and feedback via rubrics. Check that all students can share from whatever *approved* digital devices they will be using—desktop or laptop computer, notebook, or smartphones, and be sure all sign a confidentiality pledge. For instance, *I promise to keep private any conversation I have with a classmate about . . .* Discuss what this means and why it is important. The guided discussion, following SEL best practice, would do well to address any concerns anyone in class might have, including using information to bully.

4. Electronically distribute the personalized learning plan template and guide students to complete it with a technology-inclusive lesson. During the first template, model and walk students, item by item, through the template. After each field in the template, give students time to save and, if appropriate, submit. With experience, move from teacher-directed to student-centered high-agency completion.

5. Monitor students as they share the first completed personalized learning plan with you and place it into the proper folders. While they're preparing their first plans, stop by student workstations, observe, and engage in two-way feedback as needed. Focus this first warm feedback (page 101) on their learning how to complete the template.

6. Encourage each student to target a personal outcome (chapter 3, page 53) that will enrich their digital learning. Do not ignore how digital skills could be included.

Digital Portfolios

Digital portfolios (also known as *electronic* or *e-portfolios*) are one of the easiest ways to organize personalized learning plans even as you promote fluent digital skills. As soon as possible, prepare students to access their portfolios on their own and upload their personalized learning plan templates, guiding rubrics with your feedback, artifacts, and reflections. You can use Macintosh Finder or Windows Explorer programs, and you can call on cloud services like Google Drive (www.google.com/drive), Microsoft OneDrive (https://bit.ly/3eSdn0s), or Dropbox (www.dropbox.com/?landing=dbv2). Cloud service allows you to work on the internet instead of on a private network, so students can access their work anywhere that has an accessible internet connection.

If your students have limited access to the equipment or the internet, you can create an online schedule for accessing the class portfolio in one master desktop device. Each student will have a time to sign into his or her portfolio. If your students want to make their own artistic, personalized portfolios, have them seek out an online site such as Weebly (www.weebly.com) or download a portfolio app you have selected. TeachThought (https://bit.ly/2ABF6DV) offers a dozen education portfolio apps.

There is no reason students should not carry a digital portfolio on their smartphones. This would allow each to download a scanner app such as Tiny Scanner (https://apple.co/2VsFE6b), Office Lens (for Apple devices; https://bit.ly/3ifRb2o), or Genius Scan (for Android devices; https://bit.ly/2YJGrBA). The scanner and the phone's camera ensure students can share quick copies of homework and artifacts directly to a folder as well as share with you or team peers.

To help students set up and maintain basic digital portfolios, start with the playbook in figure 8.5, which you can adapt. You will want to guide elementary students step by step through the creation. Once they demonstrate they can follow the process, step back and leave the playbook for them to manage. Tech-savvy students will jump right in with the playbook as a checklist. For those who need more detailed instruction, send them to https://bit.ly/3cIJLCn and hold a need-to-know lab.

If your students lack digital tools or internet access to keep digital portfolios, stay with portfolios but put items in manila folders. Figure 8.6 is a playbook for creating these portfolios.

Playlists

Like the music or podcast playlists students keep on their personal music systems, you can set up playlists with ideas for outcomes, strategies, guiding rubrics, and reflection prompts to guide individual students or teams as they develop proficiency with their plans. You can also make student playlists to post at learning stations or to store on student devices. To help students with their personalized learning plans, construct playlists in different ways or provide space for their personal preferences.

- To increase student agency, avoid setting the elements of a plan for them. Let them choose from playlists.

- As students create outcome statements, go to the grade-level standard and identify those that are most appropriate for your students. Make each statement an outcome in the playlist and clarify language as needed so that each student can select an outcome.

- As students develop strategies for their personalized learning plans, guide a brainstorm or provide tools, activities, or instructional strategies. You do not have to brainstorm each

1. Invite each student to open Google Drive.
2. Open a folder and name it.
3. Add your first and last name, class, period, and other details on the first page.
4. Make a new page with a blank table of contents.
5. Set up following pages for each personalized learning plan or lesson.
6. Upload artifacts and rubrics to this page or link to documents online.
7. Write reflections about how the artifacts demonstrate goal achievement.
8. Add each new personalized learning plan and lesson on a new page.
9. Publish portfolios online and set up sharing with access codes.
10. Discuss confidentiality expectations.

Figure 8.5: Teacher playbook—Digital portfolio creation example.

1. Provide each student with a manila folder.
2. Add first and last name, class, period, and other identifiers.
3. Encourage students to personalize their covers.
4. Set up a blank table of contents.
5. Set up one section for each personalized learning plan or lesson.
6. Include artifacts and rubrics for each personalized learning plan with a section divider.
7. Include reflections.
8. Discuss confidentiality expectations.
9. Identify a secure site and procedures for taking out and returning portfolios.

Figure 8.6: Teacher playbook—Paper portfolios example.

*Visit **go.SolutionTree.com/instruction** for a free reproducible version of this figure.*

part of the plan with the whole class; encourage teams to jigsaw the subsections (one team per element) and then share responsibility for relaying to the class.

- Predict what playlists you want to create. Start with playlists for major writing tasks, science lab experiments, mathematics problem solving, or team project procedures. Keep these handy in your playbook.
- Share your playlists with students on their devices.
- Store playlists online.

Figures 8.7–8.9 show example grade-level playlists with ideas for students to pursue as they develop proficiency with digital skills. When students become more comfortable choosing from options, increase their agency by helping them develop their own playlists.

Playbooks

When students need more detailed instructions to complete a task or project, or if some are ready to complete a learning task with less oversight, distribute playbooks to selected individuals or teams or the whole class. You can differentiate playbook instructions for tasks due from each student or each group. For those needing more detailed instructions, put them in groups so you can coach, allowing others to move ahead. You can display these charts in class and send them into student playbooks. The Google site (https://bit.ly/2FYyF0l) will give you easily adaptable tutorials, including those that more explicitly delineate steps for completing a Google e-portfolio. Middle and high school students may well go directly to the tutorial to set up.

What you are doing as you prepare a playbook is called *task analysis*. Set a goal and then break the task into sequenced steps. You might use a graphic organizer such as the ladder to assist. Once you have listed all the subtasks students must do to complete the task, review them and think about what's missing, unnecessary, duplicated, or in the wrong order. Ask someone else, maybe a grade-level partner, to review the list. Refine the statement and add helpful details or examples. When you present the analysis to students, watch and listen for any confusion. Since this guide on the side is your voice answering the question, "What do I (we) do?", check for understanding before they launch into the task. Review sample teacher and grade-appropriate playbooks in other chapters. Once familiar with playbooks you provide, encourage middle and high school students to complete their own searches for how-to task analyses, especially for digital tools they may be unfamiliar with.

Figures 8.10–8.12 (pages 202 and 204) illustrate how easy it is to adopt a task analysis as a playbook to store in student folders. Rather than repeat instructions over and over, communicate procedures on a playlist. In this way, you shift the responsibility for following task procedures to students and halt (or decrease) "I don't know what I

Instructions: You may select one of the ideas to write your personalized learning plan outcome. If you don't understand a word, ask me for help. Copy the statement you pick into your plan for the story you have chosen.

I want to improve how I:
- ☐ "Ask and answer such questions as who, what, where, when, why, and how to show I understand key details in a story."
- ☐ "Tell stories, including fables and folktales from diverse cultures."
- ☐ "Retell a story's central message, lesson, or moral."
- ☐ "Describe how characters in a story I pick respond to major events and challenges."
- ☐ "Describe how words and phrases (e.g., regular beats, alliteration, rhymes, repeated lines) supply rhythm and meaning in a story, poem, or song."
- ☐ "Describe how the beginning introduces a story and the ending finishes the action."
- ☐ "Read words the characters use to talk to each other just like they would say the words."
- ☐ "Use information gained from the pictures and words in a print or digital story to show that I understand characters, setting, or plot."

Source for standards: NGA & CCSSO, 2010a.

Figure 8.7: Reading comprehension ideas—Elementary example.

> **Instructions:** You and your team can select one option as the digital medium for communicating your ideas. If you have another idea, check with me to explain your choice. Please access the website and make your list of strategies.

Pick one option.
- ☐ Digital picture book
- ☐ Brochure via Canva or Google
- ☐ Poster via Canva or Google
- ☐ Newsletter
- ☐ PowerPoint slides or another shareware
- ☐ Blog
- ☐ Podcast
- ☐ Video
- ☐ Comic strip
- ☐ Website

Figure 8.8: Digital project ideas—Middle school example.

> **Instructions:** "How to make a better . . ." is your challenge. Review this list of ideas from previous entries by students at this school. You may select one of these by describing in one paragraph how you will call on your science know-how or research to improve this product. Or you can come up with your own ideas and explanation. After your selection, you will design a team personalized learning plan.

Pick one of the following.
- ☐ Car battery
- ☐ Lavender hand soap
- ☐ Clothes dye
- ☐ Solar house garden heater
- ☐ Dog or door
- ☐ Small vegetable garden
- ☐ Xeriscape garden
- ☐ Rainfall predictor
- ☐ Plastic bag masher
- ☐ Boxcar racer
- ☐ Comfortable desk chair
- ☐ Beehive protection

Figure 8.9: Science project ideas—High school example.

am supposed to do." As needed, any student can access a playbook anytime, anyplace if it's online. The example in figure 8.10 (page 202) has instructions for collecting data on a spreadsheet to create a bar chart.

Now consider this middle school intermediate unit studying the history of Chicago. The example in figure 8.11 (page 202), which functions as a rubric and a playbook, asks students to submit each task to the teacher, get feedback, and store feedback. With five computer stations, the teacher shares her feedback to each student's protected online portfolio.

In a high school project-based learning unit, the teacher identifies students who chose online research skills. He or she groups these students with the same chart. In a different class, because the PBL is for the whole class, the teacher provides the list to every student's notebook. Figure 8.12 (page 204) shows the teacher's playbook for online research.

1. Open the Excel program. Find the spreadsheet you will use to make a bar chart, and open it.
2. Choose all the data you want to put in the bar chart. Make sure to include the column and row headers. Those will be the labels in the bar chart. If you want different labels, type them in the appropriate header cells.
3. Click the Insert tab and then click the Insert Column or Bar Chart key (in the Charts group). Choose 2-D Columns from the choices. You'll see the chart and bars with the names of your headers (at the bottom of your graph).
4. Click on the Chart Title section (at the top of the graph) and type in a title for your bar chart.
5. Decide whether to put the bar chart on a separate sheet or embedded in the spreadsheet. Save it.
6. If you need to start over, move the mouse so the cursor is on the edge of the chart. You will see something titled Chart Area come up. Press the Delete key.

Figure 8.10: Bar chart playbook—Elementary example.

Name: Anthony	**Date:** 11/30	**Grade:** 5
Teacher: Mrs. Jenkins-Lopez	**Class:** Social studies	**Product:** Digital story
Start date: 10/22	**Final date:** 11/30	**Project topic:** Fort Dearborn
Outcome: A digital story about an event in Chicago history		

Playbook:
1. Share your work after each step to my computer desktop.
2. Attach and share your final story to your portfolio folder.
3. Clean up each day. Keep your materials in your box behind my desk.

Task	Teacher Feedback	Due	Done
Pick your event from the playlist posted on class bulletin board			
Make sequence chart telling what happened in order			
Decide what you want to say; review elements for telling a historic story			
Find and scan images online for story; fill in with your own sketches if needed			
Load scanned images onto your notebook and add written comment for each image			
Add title page and credit page			
Add music or narration			
Prepare presentation plan			
Share story in class network			
Describe best element of your digital story			

Figure 8.11: Playbook for digital stories—Middle school example.

*Visit **go.SolutionTree.com/instruction** for a free reproducible version of this figure.*

Middle and high school students may also add a self-management rubric if you want them to call on the playbook as a strategy promoting their self-organizing skill or categorizing skill.

Rubrics Bank

Rubrics come in many forms (chapter 3, page 53) with which students can read and assess their work with your feedback. They are a key personalized learning plan component. Whether you make your own, co-create them with students, or adopt them, you can store your favorite selections in a rubric bank. You can keep your bank of rubrics and rubric templates in a folder to share on a classroom network. When you make team subfolders in which you store each member's rubrics, you can add their personal plans, artifacts, and notes. A rubric bank also allows you to invite parents and guardians to review their child's progress. If parents and guardians wish to see student work, invite them to confer with you in person or online with Skype or FaceTime during your office hours online.

Templates

When you scan reproducibles from the appendix (page 211) or download them from **go.SolutionTree.com/instruction**, they are sharable to digital devices. This ensures that students produce documents that follow a consistent format. The format not only guides students to include all key components in a product they will hand in, it also makes it easier for you to give consistent feedback on all submissions.

Reflection Journals

Reflection journals are valuable tools to extend students' deeper learning from their plans. Students reflect on what and how they are moving forward to reach their personal outcomes. Formal moments for looking back, scheduled during and at a plan's close, or a student's decision to informally reflect, enrich the self-assessment process and encourage metacognition (Cavilla, 2017). You can share prompts electronically as the means for starting reflections. The following prompts work well in a write-pair-share.

- "This plan has helped me . . ."
- "I am pleased that I . . ."
- "In the future, I need to . . ."
- "While completing my personalized learning plan, I discovered . . ."

After writing a reflection, ask each student to share the response on the class network or with another student, a team, or the whole class. For teams and the whole class, conduct a non-digital round-robin so that everyone has a chance to share or pass. The following clarifying probes may get students to reflect further.

- "Say more about . . ."
- "Why do you say that?"
- "Where do you think you can use what you learned?"

After a few rounds of successful reflection, and when your professional judgment discerns that the climate is sufficiently safe, invite students to guide the reflection. Ask for volunteers to take on this leadership role. Ideally early in the school year, start with volunteers and then go to the class list until everyone has had a turn as leader. Repeat as time allows. You can fine-tune reflections by asking students to reflect on what individuals have shared that gives them ideas for the whole class.

- "What are some common ideas we have shared that tell us about learning?"
- "What can we learn from ideas we shared today?"

Social Media Networks

Just as home is where Dorothy prefers to be (Baum, 1899), there's no place like social media to engage students as they design, implement, and assess their plans. As digital natives, middle and high school students are ready to get onto their smartphones, notebooks, or laptops to interact and collaborate with peers. By taking advantage of their love for online socializing, you have built-in engagement, especially when it comes time to reflect on the progress they are making to achieve the outcomes they are striving to reach. When you invite inclusion of social media, you do engage them with a tool they love. However, watch out for confidentiality by asking them to do two things: (1) give permission to view what's posted and (2) watch what they say. The first could lead to discussions about how to allow others to safely see what they share without breaking confidence, and to a whole lesson that starts with brainstorming about *loose lips sinking ships* and the need to raise self-management up several notches.

Name: Chanelle Floyd	Date: 11/30	Period: 4
Class: English	Grade: 12	Teacher: Stan Moore
Start date: 12/1	End date: 1/11	Check-up dates: 12/7, 12/14, 12/21
Team members: Jane Snethen, Eric DeLong, Jada Brown		
Topic: Propaganda (also known as fake news)		
Outcome: Identification of seven sources that pass the Currency, Relevance, Authority, Accuracy, and Purpose (CRAAP) test (by Sarah Blakeslee, 2004)		
Driving question: How do I distinguish fake news from real news?		Digital skill: Finding online information

Feedback from:
- ☐ Self
- ☐ Teacher
- ☐ Peers: _____
- ☐ Other: _____

Instructions:
1. Review the tasks listed in the Tasks column.
2. Enter summary data in the Notes column and add dates in the Date column.
3. Attach documents and share them to each team member's portfolio.
4. Attach and share your final essay to your portfolio folder.
5. Use the material to prepare for your final test for this outcome. Prepare for the outcome, skill proficiency, or both in the summative assessment.

Tasks	Your Notes	Date Completed
Copy and save this playbook to the laptop (each team member).		12/1
Search online sources for your topic. Make a website list.		12/3
Teams preview the assigned articles for assessing online or other assigned informational text via CRAAP. Find CRAAP guiding questions at California State University, Chico.	Steps taken to find CRAAP Name each letter. ID the website address.	12/7
Make notes as you assess the articles via CRAAP.	Article Reader	12/12
Agree on five articles that meet criteria for unbiased news with CRAAP criteria.	Article 1–5 compliance score	
Add citations.	Attach.	
Add or write reasons for selecting each article as unbiased.	Attach.	
Share and agree on the final list of articles.	List titles 1–4. List titles 5–7.	
Present and defend selections with another team as assigned.	Partner team members. Rate 0–5 on CRAAP criteria.	
Each prepare a seven-page essay explaining how to distinguish unbiased news from propaganda (fake news). Include citations. Attach and share.		

Figure 8.12: Online research personal competence playbook—High school example.

Visit go.SolutionTree.com/instruction for a free reproducible version of this figure.

Select one social platform as a starter for students to share reflections with you and with peers. Expand from there. Brainstorm ideas with the class to build playlists for Facebook, Instagram, or other social media sites. Establish norms for safe and secure use, and be advised that most social media allow no one under age thirteen.

- Connect the class to fee-based Kidblog (www.kidblog.org) and extend their reflections from the personalized learning plans with individual or team blogs shared with the whole class.
- Set up a private class Twitter account so students can tweet their reflections with each other and engage in two-way feedback with you about their progress—even daily— toward their goals.
- Start a podcast project, a YouTube video on your own channel, or a digital pamphlet so students can embed their personal goals, self-assessments, and reflections in a project that excites them.
- Help students set up a Facebook page or Instagram account on which they can post reflections, photos, and comments about their goals, strategies, and reflections.

Gaining parental consent will be important.

Free Websites

You can connect every subject area and student interests to at least one easy-to-use, grade-appropriate website with engaging activities, video materials, and learning tools all aligned with your standards. There is little reason to pay for access to similar tools. Investigate these examples.

Elementary School Websites

If you are an elementary teacher, start with your own personalized teaching plan to bring one digital site into your classroom. That might include PhET (https://phet.colorado.edu), Kidblog, or Khan Academy, as examples. Don't make it an add-on! Instead, once you have learned what you want to do with the digital site, save by filing now-redundant worksheets and textbooks in the trash, and spend the savings for new digital equipment. If you can't go all the way yet, set up three or four digital learning stations, each dedicated to a subject area. Students can gear their plans to the options you provide at these stations. They can connect their online portfolios and add guiding rubrics and personalized learning plans set up at each station.

Middle and High School Websites

If you are a middle or high school teacher, you need only worry about free sites for your single content area. Determine how you want to integrate personalized learning plans into your lessons or projects. One option is to set up a home base on a content site that will allow you to differentiate your current lessons or schedule need-to-know labs for students who need more background. For example, in physics, introduce a PhET lab to a group of students who are struggling with kinetic energy. As students progress, they communicate with you via Google and end by storing key documents in their personal online portfolios. Investigate your content site. Khan Academy (www.khanacademy.org), National Geographic Education (www.nationalgeographic.org/education), and CK–12 (www.ck12.org/student) work for any of these topics and more. Some vetted websites are in table 8.1 (page 206).

If you offer PBL to students, you might wonder how to individualize instruction within cooperative learning frameworks and include technology. These interactive programs integrate personalized learning plans as a tool for solving that dilemma.

- **Foundry** (https://bit.ly/2XG4Zde) provides free kits for teachers to plan, implement, and assess PBL.
- **Science A–Z** (https://bit.ly/2Xfs0Vd) provides resources that encourage students to use creativity, critical thinking, communication, and collaboration skills.

What Digital Tools Facilitate Remote Learning?

Remote learners are physically removed from a teacher's sight and sound. Limited (or no) eye contact. No more proximity observations. A potential lag in feedback. An array of digital tools enables entry into digital learning. Once in the door, your big job will be adding tools and adapting some you already have in your toolkit. The new tools will let you connect and communicate with students, parents, guardians, and your collaborative teams about operational logistics of remote learning and enhance communication related to instruction.

Table 8.1: Middle and High School Subject Websites

Subject	Website and URL	Description
Science	• PhET (https://phet.colorado.edu)	Provides simulations for physics, earth science, chemistry, biology, and mathematics. You can run them online or download them (to Chromebooks, notebooks, and iPads).
Mathematics	• Math Science Music (https://mathsciencemusic.org) • PhET (https://phet.colorado.edu)	See Science.
English language arts	• Quill (www.quill.org) • Read-Write-Think (www.readwritethink.org)	Read-Write-Think provides interactives and ready-to-use lesson plans searchable by grade, theme, 21st century skills, and topic.
Social studies	• iCivics (www.icivics.org) • Google Earth (www.google.com/earth/index.html) • Digital History (www.digitalhistory.uh.edu) • Utah Education Network (www.uen.org/3−6interactives/social_studies.shtml)	These are content-centered sites. Many can replace a textbook for the content area or serve as a rich online alternative.

The playlists in figure 8.13, which sometimes overlap, provide examples gathered from *this-tool-was-helpful-to-me* declarations from students, parents, and teachers.

Selecting and assigning the proper digital tools for managing remote communication can feel like uncharted territory to even experienced classroom teachers. For productive learning, decide on digital documents for personalizing learning (including personalized learning plans, guiding rubric templates, playbooks, and playlists). In your pacing chart, decide how much time to spend preparing students to use these tools. Following this, there will be your full lesson plans, which detail events for synchronous and asynchronous instruction. Finally, you can plan, conduct, and assess classroom and remote tasks using the necessary tools.

Remember that most of the switch to remote learning is the selection and preparation to use digital tools that are not required when you are physically present with students, and you are setting up for multiple remote lessons. Also, remembering that these are only *adjustments* to your prior planning and assessments—you are not reinventing the wheel—you will soon move beyond most discomfort. Jigsawing how you make these changes with your colleagues and pacing how quickly you adapt tools can make things manageable.

To manage communication, use the following.

- **Canvas:** This LMS has separate parent and student accounts and instructional features to create, share, story, coach, and assess results; it hosts recorded lessons as well.
- **Eventlink:** This calendar app sends smartphone reminders for scheduled events.
- **GroupMe:** This free messaging app lets parents, teachers, and students share solo messages as reminders, allows two-way feedback, and more.
- **Remind:** This smartphone app allows instant two-way messaging, including reminders about projects due and more.
- **Skyward:** This LMS allows students and parents to have separate accounts for access to forms, grades, attendance records, schedules, discipline, and other records.

To facilitate instruction, use the following.

- **Google Meet:** Students use this browser-activated tool to share desktop essays, slides, videos, and other presentations.
- **Google Share for Google Docs:** This program helps teams post and edit assignments.
- **Kahoot!:** This gamification learning platform makes it easy to create, share, and play learning games.
- **Padlet:** This online portfolio program allows posting and storing reports and other projects.
- **Zoom:** Video conferencing for synchronous instruction can work with the whole class, small groups, or one-to-one meetings, and the program allows asynchronous messaging collaboration among offline teams.

Figure 8.13: Helpful digital tools playlist.

TAKEAWAYS

What have you learned in this chapter? Select the ideas that are new or most reinforcing for what you already believe.

CONCLUSION
PERSONALIZED DEEPER LEARNING FOR A LIFETIME

> Learning is a lifelong process of keeping abreast of change. And the most pressing task is to teach people how to learn.
>
> —Peter Drucker

Technology is disrupting every aspect of our lives. Artificial intelligence is a digital force that futurists claim will eliminate 50 percent of jobs by 2035. Developments are accelerating the pace, promising to dissolve industries with the largest number of routine jobs—manufacturing, call centers, banks, retail, fast food, mining, basic construction, and so on. Anyone prepared only for rote work will find themselves displaced.

It's been popular on TED Talks (Robinson, 2010), in surveys from business groups (American Management Association, 2019), and in articles from academia (Bellanca & Brandt, 2010) to plead for elimination of assembly line schools prepping students with rote-learned facts on single-answer standardized tests. Instead of preparing students to live, learn, work, and compete for jobs high on the soon-to-be-eliminated list, an increasing number of these voices calls for schools to educate with the future in mind, with updated curriculum and instruction.

As this book postulates, deeper learning outcomes enrich instruction with the new competencies today's students will need as compassionate citizens, productive employees, and inspiring leaders in their future world. In order to master core academic content, tomorrow's successful workers, citizens, and leaders must show they can think critically and creatively, collaborate, and communicate in solving complex problems, learning how to learn with digital tools, and transferring deeper learning competencies across an expanding curriculum.

Deeper learning is not for the faint of heart. It is for educators and students willing to accept the challenge of advancing their complex thinking and problem solving, social-emotional decision making, and digital designing skills to address lifelong learning and living challenges in old and new coursework.

Technology, empowered by innovative discoveries, plays a pivotal role in what, how, and even when learning happens. AI's ability to refine existing products (such as Apple Watches), design solutions for complex problems (like a coronavirus vaccine), and even correct serious technological errors (like Boeing's 737 MAX) holds promise for future enhancements of the personalized learning process. AI's affinity for innovation already feeds the drive to imbue personalized learning with more agency-stimulating digital tools than ever before. As digitally enabled personalization that ensures complex cognition with the social-emotional skills necessary for collaboration and self-discipline sinks its roots deeper below the learning garden's surface, it will become clearer how substantive student agency can enhance individual learning experiences resulting in deeper learning outcomes. But teaching is not an obsolete profession; in future years, educators will be the engines of learning more than ever. This view trusts responsibility for learning leadership to stay in teachers' hands. Technology's machines may someday provide more and better tools for supporting students' walks to deeper learning, but they are far from prepared to take over the job in the near future.

In these chapters, you have examined answers to key questions about how to feature deeper learning competencies in your classroom through new tools for agency-rich personalized learning plans. These chapters introduce a blueprint as a versatile tool to help you meet the deeper learning challenges in diverse ways suitable to your students' diverse, personal learning needs. Because this book's main tool—the personalized learning plan blueprint—presents a solution that requires little risk, it allows any teacher with any teaching style, any content, and students in any place to take one small step (or a giant leap) into the deeper learning waters with no more investment than a simple, inexpensive template. You have seen how to adapt this tool to any skill, content, method, or situation—including the pandemic, which blew through like a swarm of locusts to destroy the effort and beauty of many growing plants—while always keeping the processes of planning and assessing as the foundation. The personalized learning plan and its process give you a practical tool for keeping your garden growing abundantly. The blueprint empowers you to grow single specimens and to construct multicolored beds, each with its personal characteristics. You have seen how you, as a guide on the side, adjust the blueprint any time with any content, but also with any skills that students can transfer, aimed to personalize deeper learning. The template and variations you have examined will enable you to turn evidence-based deeper learning practices into viable deeper learning outcomes. Its companion blueprint—the personalized teaching plan template—allows you to engage with colleagues to construct an inexpensive schoolwide model.

For you and every colleague who shares the challenge of teaching, the vision for enriching students' lives and learning with the capability to control what they do and how they do it is now sharper. New seeds planted in your mind are now ready to break the soil's surface. It becomes imperative that you fertilize and water the seedlings and watch your deeper learning flowers bloom. Enjoy the results for a lifetime.

APPENDIX

TEMPLATES

Visit **go.SolutionTree.com/instruction** for free versions of these templates. Along with playbooks and acronyms, you can display these reproducibles in class, share them to students' digital devices, or make print copies.

Personalized Learning Plan

Name:	Grade:	Teacher:
Start date:	**End date:**	**Check-up dates:**

Content Focus

- ☐ English language arts
  - **Strand:**
    - ☐ Reading
    - ☐ Writing
    - ☐ Speaking and listening
    - ☐ Language
- ☐ Mathematics
- ☐ Performing or visual art
- ☐ Science
- ☐ Social studies
- ☐ World language
- ☐ Other: _____

Skill Set

Basic Cognitive	**Digital**	**Complex Cognitive**	**Social-Emotional**
☐ Decoding	☐ Basic	☐ Critical thinking	☐ Collaboration
☐ Fluency	☐ Applied	☐ Creative thinking	☐ Communication
☐ Numbers	☐ Other: _____	☐ Problem solving	☐ Self-direction
☐ Operations		☐ Design thinking	
☐ Phonics		☐ Cognitive function	
☐ Vocabulary			
☐ Other: _____			

Feedback

Feedback is by:
- ☐ Self
- ☐ Teacher
- ☐ Peers: _____
- ☐ Other: _____

| **Plans** |
| *Enter your response in the blank after each request.* |
| The improvement outcome I want: |
| What do I need to know for this learning plan? |
| What people or resources will I call on? |
| What materials and equipment will I use? |
| What strategies will I use to reach my goal? |

What skills and talents will I apply?

What are my criteria for measurable success?

What evidence of learning will I show?

How much time will I need?

Notes:

Starter Personalized Learning Plan

Name:	Grade:	Teacher:
Start date:	**End date:**	**Check-up dates:**

Content Focus

- ☐ English language arts _____
  - **Strand:**
    - ☐ Reading
    - ☐ Writing
    - ☐ Speaking and listening
    - ☐ Language
- ☐ Mathematics
- ☐ Performing or visual art
- ☐ Science
- ☐ Social studies
- ☐ World language
- ☐ Other: _____

Skill Set

- ☐ Basic cognitive
- ☐ Digital
- ☐ Complex cognitive
- ☐ Social-emotional

Specific skill

Plans
Enter your response in the blank after each request.

The improvement outcome I want:

Who can help?

What materials do I need?

How much time do I need?

How will I know I have made progress?

Other thoughts or ideas:

Personalized Deeper Learning © 2021 Solution Tree Press • SolutionTree.com
Visit **go.SolutionTree.com/instruction** to download this page.

Interview Questions

My Name:	Grade:	Teacher:
My School:	Date:	Subject:

Peer Interviewers:

A partner will interview you. Your partner will record what you say in the blank spaces. Spaces will expand. Spell check when finished and check for accuracy of your recorded answers. Be specific with your response and honor the *respect* guidelines your class lists.

I learn best when I . . .

I am interested in . . .

Talents I have include . . .

In this class, what do I want to accomplish most in the following.
- ☐ Semester: _____
- ☐ School year: _____

What are my dreams for after the following. ☐ elementary ☐ middle ☐ high school

What are my school goals?

What are my current learning strengths?

What learning areas do I need to improve?

How can the teacher help me succeed?

How can peers help?

What else would I like to say about myself?

Personalized Teaching Plan

Name:	Grade:	Teacher:
Start date:	End date:	Check-up dates:

Content Focus

- ☐ English language arts
    - **Strand:**
        - ☐ Reading
        - ☐ Writing
        - ☐ Speaking and listening
        - ☐ Language
- ☐ Mathematics
- ☐ Performing or visual art
- ☐ Science
- ☐ Social studies
- ☐ World language
- ☐ Other: _____

Skill Set

Basic Cognitive
- ☐ Decoding
- ☐ Fluency
- ☐ Measurement
- ☐ Numbers
- ☐ Operations
- ☐ Phonics
- ☐ Vocabulary
- ☐ Other: _____

Digital
- ☐ Basic
- ☐ Applied
- ☐ Other: _____

Complex Cognitive
- ☐ Critical thinking
- ☐ Creative thinking
- ☐ Problem solving
- ☐ Design thinking
- ☐ Cognitive function
- ☐ Specific skill: _____

Social-Emotional
- ☐ Collaboration
- ☐ Communication
- ☐ Self-direction
- ☐ Specific skill: _____

Feedback

Feedback is by:
- ☐ Self: _____
- ☐ Teacher: _____
- ☐ Peers: _____
- ☐ Other: _____

Personalized Deeper Learning © 2021 Solution Tree Press • SolutionTree.com
Visit **go.SolutionTree.com/instruction** to download this page.

Teaching Plan
Enter your response in the blanks.

What is my improvement goal?

Whom will I teach with this plan?
- ☐ One student: _____
- ☐ Small group: _____
- ☐ Whole class

What SMART goals do I want my students or student to achieve?

What people or resources will I call on?

What strategies will I use to reach my goal?

What materials and equipment will I need?

How much time will we need?

What are my criteria for success?

What measurable evidence of learning will I show?

What other things do I want to note here?
☐ I have attached my pacing chart. ☐ I have attached the rubric.

Rated Checklist—PreK–3

Student Name:	Date:
Grade:	Teacher Name:

Skill Outcome:

Criterion:	🙂	☹️
Criterion:	🙂	☹️
Criterion:	🙂	☹️
Criterion:	🙂	☹️

Peer Feedback:

Teacher Feedback:

Playbook

1. For youngest students not yet ready to read or write, fill in demographic information. Otherwise, students complete with your step-by-step guidance as you share the template on the whiteboard.
2. Enter the skill outcome in SMART terms. Review the procedures and confidentiality agreement in age-appropriate words.
3. Select between two and six criteria that indicate what the skill looks or sounds like.
4. Give each student a paper copy. If in remote learning, snail mail a copy to each or share to each student's or parent's digital device. Invite an at-home sibling or adult to help in synchronous time and to return completed templates.
5. For student self-assessment, read the criteria aloud and ask each student to circle the appropriate face. Complete this item with an individual student, small group, or the whole class.
6. Add your own assessment after, using a different color or mark. Thank students and parents with an emoji or warm note.
7. Place templates in the lesson subfolder with other lesson artifacts. Place the folder in the portfolio.

Improvement Rating Scale—Grades 3–12

Student Name:	**Grade:**	**Date:**
Period:	**Teacher Name:**	

Skill Outcome:
Date: _____ Content: _____ Skill: _____

Feedback
Feedback is by: ☐ Self ☐ Teacher: _____ ☐ Peers: _____ ☐ Other: _____ ☐ Summative grade: _____
To what degree did you improve? Use this rating scale. 0 = I have not started to improve at all. 1 = I am a novice. 2 = I am working toward mastering the skill. 3 = I've mastered it. 4 = I've gone beyond mastery.

Rate how much better you (or the feedback receiver) did	Criteria	Feedback

Rate how much better you (or the feedback receiver) did	Criteria	Feedback
Total points:		Summative grade (optional):

Playbook

See the example (figure 3.14, page 76) in chapter 3.

1. Share a copy of the template to each student via snail mail or electronically.
2. Guide each student to fill in demographic information. Show a visual model.
3. Enter the skill outcome in SMART terms. Review procedures, trust, and the confidentiality agreement in age-appropriate words.
4. Select between two and six criteria that indicate what proficient skill performance looks or sounds like.
5. Clarify each criterion and ask each to score their most recent performance with consideration of feedback received. Remember this is a high-agency activity, dependent on honest, accurate assessments and feedback.
6. Encourage honest, warm feedback or adviser students to say nothing.
7. If feedback is provided, provide each giver with a blank copy. The peer giver scores (or you score the receiver) and gives examples to explain the score.
8. Givers return the finished document to receivers. Repeat as formative assessments without grades per the lesson or project schedule. Remember this is a high-agency activity. Honor accuracy balanced with encouragement for those who may be struggling.
9. Complete each item with an individual student, small group, or the whole class with set due dates.
10. Add your own assessment after all others. Thank students with an emoji for their contribution.
11. Students place all documents in the lesson folder with other lesson artifacts, including personalized learning plans. All folders should be organized in the student's portfolio according to the model you share with students.
12. Vary templates as necessary for students (especially if students must complete templates asynchronously as remote learners). Make appropriate adjustments based on student feedback. Include parents in the process after getting the OK from students.
13. After the summative assessment process is complete and folders are filed, guide the final reflection.

Single-Point Guiding Rubric—Grades 3–12

Name:	Date:	Assessment Number:

Skill:

Content:

Feedback

Feedback done by:

☐ Peer: _____

☐ Teacher: _____

☐ Other: _____

What Was Done Well	Criteria	Suggestions to Improve

What Was Done Well	Criteria	Suggestions to Improve

Playbook

See the example in figure 3.15 (page 78).

1. Share a copy of the template with each student via hard copy or electronically.
2. Each student fills in demographic information as you share a model.
3. Enter the outcome in SMART, age-appropriate terms. Review procedures, trust, and the confidentiality agreement in age-appropriate words.
4. Select between two and six criteria that indicate what proficient skill performance looks or sounds like.
5. Clarify each criterion and ask each to rate or give feedback on most recent performance. Remember this is a high-agency activity, dependent on honest, accurate assessment with specifics.
6. Encourage honest, warm feedback or advise students to say nothing.
7. If feedback is given, provide each giver with a blank copy of the template. The peer giver provides (or you provide) specific examples in the What Was Done Well and Suggestions to Improve columns addressed to the person getting feedback. Self-assessors should be equally specific.
8. Givers return the completed document to receivers. Repeat as formative assessments without grades per lesson or project schedule. Remember, this is a high-agency activity. Honor accuracy balanced with encouragement for those who may be struggling.
9. Complete each item with an individual student, small group, or the whole class with set due dates.
10. Add your own assessment after all others. Thank students with an emoji for their contribution.
11. Students place all documents in the lesson folder with other lesson artifacts, including personalized learning plans. All folders should be organized in the student's portfolio according to the model you share with students.
12. Vary templates as necessary for students (especially if students must complete templates asynchronously as remote learners). Make appropriate adjustments based on student feedback. Include parents in the process after getting the OK from students.
13. After the summative assessment process is complete and folders are filed, guide the final reflection.

Multi-Point Guiding Rubric—Grades 3–12

Name:	Date:	Grade:
Period:	Teacher:	Topic:

Skill:

Start date:	End date:	Check-up dates:

Feedback is by:
- ☐ Self
- ☐ Teacher
- ☐ Peers: _____
- ☐ Other: _____

Student instructions: If you are giving feedback, *what you give is private*. If you are self-assessing, do so *before* you review the others' scores and comments.

Below, select the statement you think is most accurate. Write your initials in the block. Add specific reasons for each choice you make.

Scores				
5	4	3	2	1

My score total:

Student Initials	Reason for Rating

Pick which rating scale number was your best effort and explain why.

What was your most important learning result?

Teacher feedback:

Place your completed form in your portfolio.

Playbook

See the example in figure 3.14 (page 76) for the completed template.

1. Prepare this template with the high performance in the first column and low performance in the last column.
2. Use one, three, or five rating columns. The middle score shows average performance or improvement.
3. Share a copy of the template with each student via hard copy or electronically.
4. Guide each to fill in demographic information with your visual model.
5. Enter the skill outcome in SMART, age-appropriate terms.
6. Review procedures, trust, and the confidentiality agreement in age-appropriate words.
7. Select between two and six criteria that indicate what proficient skill performance looks or sounds like in a range of indicators. A rubric-making site can help you generate descriptive indicators.
8. Clarify each criterion with students and ask each to rate or give feedback on most recent performance. Remind all that this rubric is a way of learning about the skill. (See the high-performance column.)
9. Remember this is a high-agency activity dependent on honest, accurate assessment.
10. Encourage honest, warm feedback or say nothing.
11. If feedback is given, provide each giver with a blank copy.
12. Givers share the finished document with receivers. Repeat as formative assessments without grades as per lesson or project schedule. Remember that because this is a high-agency activity, accuracy should be honored and balanced with encouragement for those who may be struggling. The summary section allows space for specific warm feedback.
13. Complete each item with an individual student, small group, or the whole class with set due dates.
14. Add your own assessment after all others. If grades are required, this system makes it easier for you to fit points to your grading scale.
15. Thank students with an emoji for their contributions. Encourage them to consider what needs to improve in future lessons.
16. Students place all documents in their own lesson folders with other lesson artifacts, including the personalized learning plan. All folders should be organized in the student's portfolio. If helpful, use portfolio organization as a categorization lesson.
17. Vary template elements as necessary for your students. Make appropriate adjustments based on student feedback. Include parents in the process after getting the OK from students.
18. After the summative assessment process is complete and folders are filed, guide students in the final reflection.

Open-Ended Self-Assessment Rubric—Grades 3–12

Grade:	Period:	Teacher:
Topic:	Skill:	

Feedback is by:
- ☐ Self
- ☐ Teacher
- ☐ Peer: _____
- ☐ Other: _____

What I (you) did well:

What I (you) can improve:

What help I (you) need:

Playbook

See the example in figure 3.15 (page 78) for the completed template.

1. Share a copy of the template with each student via snail mail or electronically.

2. Guide each student to fill in demographic information; show your visual model.

3. This model works well as a response to specific open-ended guiding questions presented at the lesson start or as an open response to the three questions shown. The three open questions allow the most agency for students versed in responding with reasons and specifics.

4. Review procedures, trust, and the confidentiality agreement in age-appropriate words.

5. The student defines criteria based on guiding questions and responds with evidence to back performance claims and may ask others to give feedback on most recent performance. Remember this is an extremely high-agency activity, dependent on honest, accurate assessment with specifics.

6. Encourage honest, warm feedback or say nothing.

7. If feedback is given, provide each giver with a blank copy. The peer giver (or you) provides specific examples in What I (You) Did Well and What I (You) Can Improve boxes addressed to the person getting feedback. Self-assessors must be equally specific and honest about strengths and improvements. The help question is difficult for many; your nonjudgmental, warm feedback will help.

8. Feedback givers share the finished document with receivers. Repeat as formative assessments without grades per lesson or project schedule, or save this as the summative template after students have used point rubrics for formative assessment. Remember that this is a high-agency activity. It is not recommended for students who are struggling with the lesson or project.

9. Complete each item with an individual student, small group, or the whole class with set due dates.

10. Add your own assessment after all others. It is not recommended for students who fear the open-endedness, have to have a grade, have below-grade-level writing skills, or who are struggling to reach the outcomes.

11. Encourage students to articulate specific improvement needs feedback in future lessons.

12. Students place all documents in their own lesson folders with other lesson artifacts, including the personalized learning plan. All folders should be organized in the student's portfolio. If helpful, use portfolio organization as a categorization teaching lesson.

13. Vary template elements as necessary for your students. Make appropriate adjustments based on student feedback. Include parents in the process after getting the OK from students.

14. After the summative assessment process is complete and folders are filed, guide students through the final reflection.

REFERENCES AND RESOURCES

Achieve. (2017). *Strong standards: A review of changes to state standards since the Common Core.* Accessed at www.achieve.org/files/StrongStandards_032919.pdf on June 29, 2019.

AchieveIt. (n.d.). *The history and evolution of smart goals.* Accessed at www.achieveit.com/resources/blog/the-history-and-evolution-of-smart-goals on March 24, 2020.

Agarwal, R., & Avella, J. (2016, February 8). *Here is why you should learn to say no* [Video file]. Accessed at www.businessinsider.com.au/you-should-learn-to-say-no-2016-2 on November 12, 2020.

Aguilar, E. (2013, March 25). How coaching can impact teachers, principals, and students [Blog post]. *Edutopia.* Accessed at www.edutopia.org/blog/coaching-impact-teachers-principals-students-elena-aguilar#:~:text=Coaching%20allows%20teachers%20to%20apply,their%20work%20with%20each%20other. on June 12, 2020.

Aleccia, V. A. (2011). Taming the crammed curriculum: Selective abandonment as a strategy in professional learning communities. *Northwest Journal of Teacher Education, 9*(1), 89–93.

Alioon, Y., & Delialioğlu, Ö. (2019). The effect of authentic m-learning activities on student engagement and motivation. *British Journal of Educational Technology, 50*(2), 655–668.

Alliance for Excellent Education. (2017, August 23). *Building competencies for careers: Preparing students for twenty-first-century jobs* [Webinar]. Accessed at https://all4ed.org/webinar-event/aug-23-2017 on March 24, 2020.

Alliance for Excellent Education. (2020, February 18). *Hearts and minds: Building capacity around social and emotional learning* [Webinar]. Accessed at https://all4ed.org/webinar-event/hearts-and-minds-building-capacity-around-social-and-emotional-learning on March 24, 2020.

AlMutairi, A. N. M. (2015). The effect of using brainstorming strategy in developing creative problem solving skills among male students in Kuwait: A field study on Saud Al-Kharji School in Kuwait City. *Journal of Education and Practice, 6*(3), 136–145.

American Management Association Staff. (2019, January 24). AMA critical skills survey: Workers need higher-level skills to succeed in the 21st century [Blog post]. *American Management Association.* Accessed at www.amanet.org/articles/ama-critical-skills-survey-workers-need-higher-level-skills-to-succeed-in-the-21st-century on March 24, 2020.

Anderson, B. (2018, November 29). Twelve jobs you'll be recruiting for in 2030 [Blog post]. *Linkedin Talent Blog.* Accessed at https://business.linkedin.com/talent-solutions/blog/future-of-recruiting/2018/12-jobs-you-will-be-recruiting-for-in-2030 on May 29, 2020.

Anderson, L. W., & Krathwohl, D. (Eds.). (2001). *A taxonomy for learning, teaching, and assessing: A revision of Bloom's taxonomy of educational objectives.* New York: Pearson Education.

Ankucic, M. (2020, January 30). Here's what the science says about building trust with new students [Blog post]. *3P Learning.* Accessed at www.3plearning.com/blog/building-trust-with-students/ed August 2020 on October 5, 2020.

Annenberg Public Policy Center. (2017). *Why teens take risks: It's not a deficit in brain development.* Accessed at www.sciencedaily.com/releases/2017/08/170816122345.htm on July 23, 2020.

Archer, S., Eyster, J. P., Kelly, J. J., Kowalski, T., & Shanahan, C. F. (2014). *Reaching backward and stretching forward: Teaching for transfer in law school clinics*. Accessed at https://scholarship.law.nd.edu/law_faculty_scholarship/1131 on August 17, 2020.

Armstrong, T. (2012). *Neurodiversity in the classroom: Strength-based strategies to help students with special needs succeed in school and life*. Alexandria, VA: Association for Supervision and Curriculum Development.

Augustine, C. H., Engberg, J., Grimm, G. E., Lee, E., Wang, E. L., Christianson, K., et al. (2018). *Can restorative practices improve school climate and curb suspensions? An evaluation of the impact of restorative practices in a mid-sized urban school district*. Santa Monica, CA: RAND.

Bailey, K., & Jakicic, C. (2012). *Common formative assessment: A toolkit for Professional Learning Communities at Work*. Bloomington, IN: Solution Tree Press.

Baldwin, T. T., Ford, J. K., & Blume, B. D. (2017). The state of transfer of training research: Moving toward more consumer-centric inquiry. *Human Resource Development Quarterly, 28*(1), 17–28.

Bang, M. (1999). *When Sophie gets angry—really, really angry*. New York: Blue Sky Press.

Barone, R. (2019, September 18). Coding for kids: Reasons kids should get started, and how they can find success [Blog post]. *iD Tech*. Accessed at www.idtech.com/blog/5-reasons-your-child-should-learn-to-code on September 7, 2020.

Barrett, L., & Krauss, S. (2018). *Ending the testing debate: New report is advancing the case for ways to measure the hard-to-measure*. Accessed at https://measuringsel.casel.org/ending-testing-debate-new-report-advancing-case-ways-measure-hard-measure on February 5, 2020.

Bartleby Research. (2020). *Essay on Common Core State Standards and its impact on curriculum*. Accessed at www.bartleby.com/essay/Common-Core-State-Standards-and-Its-Impact-F32WYLYVJ on August 15, 2020.

Baum, L. F. (1899). *The wonderful Wizard of Oz*. New York: G.M. Hill.

Beck, J. (2017). *Imagining the future is just another form of memory*. Accessed at www.theatlantic.com/science/archive/2017/10/imagining-the-future-is-just-another-form-of-memory/542832 on September 5, 2020.

Beliefnet. (n.d.). *'The power of one': Interview with Susan Sarandon*. Accessed at www.beliefnet.com/love-family/charity-service/2005/07/the-power-of-one-interview-with-susan-sarandon.aspx on October 4, 2020.

Bellanca, J. A. (Ed.). (2015). *Deeper learning: Beyond 21st century skills*. Bloomington, IN: Solution Tree Press.

Bellanca, J. A., & Brandt, R. (Eds.). (2010). *21st century skills: Rethinking how students learn*. Bloomington, IN: Solution Tree Press.

Bellanca, J. A., & Fogarty, R. (1993). *Catch them thinking: A handbook of classroom strategies, grades 4–12* (2nd ed.). Glenview, IL: Skylight Professional Development.

Bellanca, J. A., & Fogarty, R. (2003). *Blueprints for achievement in the cooperative classroom* (3rd ed.). Glenview, IL: Pearson.

Bellanca, J. A., Fogarty, R. J., & Pete, B. M. (2020). *How to teach thinking skills: Seven key student proficiencies for college and career readiness* (2nd ed.). Bloomington, IN: Solution Tree Press.

Berg, C. (2017). *Teaching website evaluation: The CRAAP test and the evolution of an approach*. Accessed at www.internetatschools.com/Articles/Editorial/Features/Teaching-Website-Evaluation-The-CRAAP-Test-and-the-Evolution-of-an-Approach-116769.aspx on March 24, 2020.

Berger, R. (2013, January 3). *Deeper learning: Highlighting student work* [Blog post]. Accessed at www.edutopia.org/blog/deeper-learning-student-work-ron-berger on January 10, 2020.

Bersin, J. (2016). *Predictions for 2017: Everything is becoming digital*. Accessed at www2.deloitte.com/content/dam/Deloitte/at/Documents/about-deloitte/predictions-for-2017-final.pdf on March 24, 2019.

Betts, E. A. (1946). *Foundations of reading instruction*. New York: American Book Company.

Bitter, C., & Loney, E. (2015). *Deeper learning: Improving student outcomes for college, career, and civic life*. Accessed at www.air.org/resource/deeper-learning-improving-student-outcomes-college-career-and-civic-life on March 24, 2020.

BlackPast. (2007, October 15). *Malcolm X's speech at the founding rally of the Organization of Afro-American Unity*. Accessed at www.blackpast.org/african-american-history/1964-malcolm-x-s-speech-founding-rally-organization-afro-american-unity on September 28, 2020.

Blakeslee, S. (2004). *Evaluating information—Applying the CRAAP test.* Accessed at https://library.csuchico.edu/sites/default/files/craap-test.pdf on June 30, 2020.

Blankert, T., & Hamstra, M. R. W. (2016). *Imagining success: Multiple achievement goals and the effectiveness of imagery.* Accessed at www.ncbi.nlm.nih.gov/pmc/articles on September 5, 2020.

Bloom, B. S. (Ed.). (1956). *Taxonomy of educational objectives: Handbook I—Cognitive domain.* New York: David McKay.

Bradley, L. (2014, October 2). Student agency: Voice, choice and making [Blog post]. *Edutopia.* Accessed at www.edutopia.org/discussion/student-agency-voice-choice-and-making on August 15, 2020.

BrainyQuote. (n.d.). *Eleanor Roosevelt quotes: It takes as much energy to wish as it does to plan.* Accessed at www.brainyquote.com/quotes/eleanor_roosevelt_379411 on September 28, 2020.

Bransford, J., Brown, A., & Cocking, R. (1999). *How people learn: Brain, mind, experience, and school.* Washington, DC: National Academies Press.

Broadwell, M. M. (1969). *Teaching for learning.* Accessed at https://edbatista.typepad.com/files/teaching-for-learning-martin-broadwell-1969-conscious-competence-model.pdf on March 24, 2020.

Bruce-Lockhart, A. (2020). *Davos 2020: Here's what you need to know about the future of work.* Accessed at www.weforum.org/agenda/2020/01/davos-2020-future-work-jobs-skills-what-to-know on June 15, 2020.

Bryant, K. N. (2017). *Engaging 21st century writers with social media.* Hershey, PA: IGI Global.

Bucholz, J. L., & Sheffler, J. L. (2009). Creating a warm and inclusive classroom environment: Planning for all children to feel welcome. *Electronic Journal for Inclusive Education, 2*(4).

Bughin, J., Hazan, E., Lund, S., Dahlström, P., Wiesinger, A., & Subramaniam, A. (2018). *Skill shift: Automation and the future of the workforce.* Accessed at www.mckinsey.com/featured-insights/future-of-work/skill-shift-automation-and-the-future-of-the-workforce on October 6, 2020.

Burns, R. (1786). *Poems, chiefly in the Scottish dialect.* Kilmarnock, Scotland: John Wilson.

Bushman, B. J. (2013, September 25). Anger management: What works and what doesn't [Blog post]. *Psychology Today.* Accessed at www.psychologytoday.com/us/blog/get-psyched/201309/anger-management-what-works-and-what-doesnt on September 5, 2020.

Business Dictionary. (n.d.). *Creative thinking.* Accessed at www.businessdictionary.com/definition/creative-thinking.html on September 5, 2020.

Caffarella, R. S. (2002). *Planning programs for adult learners: A practical guide for educators, trainers, and staff developers* (2nd ed.). San Francisco: Jossey-Bass.

Carlin, G. (Writer), & Urbisci, R. (Producer) (2005). *George Carlin: Life is worth losing* [Television special]. United States: Cable Stuff Productions.

Cavilla, D. (2017). *The effects of student reflection on academic performance and motivation.* Accessed at https://journals.sagepub.com/doi/full/10.1177/2158244017733790 on June 30, 2020.

Center for Building a Culture of Empathy. (n.d.). *The great gift.* Accessed at http://cultureofempathy.com/References/Experts/Meryl-Streep.htm on October 4, 2020.

Center for Creative Leadership. (n.d.). *How to lead a collaborative team.* Accessed at www.ccl.org/articles/leading-effectively-articles/how-to-lead-a-collaborative-team on October 29, 2020.

Center for Educational Innovation. (n.d.). *Constructivism.* Accessed at www.buffalo.edu/ubcei/enhance/learning/constructivism.html on September 5, 2020.

Champions Against Bullying. (n.d.). *The #1 source of bullying prevention solutions and resources for families and schools.* Accessed at www.championsagainstbullying.org on September 5, 2020.

Cherry, K. (2020). *What is empathy?* Accessed at www.verywellmind.com/what-is-empathy-2795562 on September 5, 2020.

Chow, B. (2010). *The quest for 'deeper learning'.* Accessed at www.edweek.org/ew/articles/2010/10/06/06chow_ep.h30.html on March 13, 2020.

Collaborative for Academic, Social, and Emotional Learning. (n.d.a). *Overview of SEL*. Accessed at https://casel.org/overview-sel on April 1, 2020.

Collaborative for Academic, Social, and Emotional Learning. (n.d.b). *What is SEL?* Accessed at https://casel.org/what-is-sel on June 22, 2020.

Collaborative for Academic, Social, and Emotional Learning. (n.d.c). *Core SEL competencies*. Accessed at https://casel.org/core-competencies on June 3, 2020.

Commonwealth of Pennsylvania. (n.d.). *Standards detail*. Accessed at www.pdesas.org/Standard/Detail?linkStandardId=0&standardId=162527 on June 1, 2020.

Connell, R. (1924, January 24). The most dangerous game. *Collier's Weekly*.

Conzemius, A. E., & O'Neill, J. (2014). *The handbook for SMART school teams: Revitalizing best practices for collaboration* (2nd ed.). Bloomington, IN: Solution Tree Press.

Cook, C. R., Coco, S., Zhang, Y., Fiat, A. E., Duong, M. T., Renshaw, T. L., et al. (2018). Cultivating positive teacher–student relationships: Preliminary evaluation of the establish–maintain–restore (EMR) method. *School Psychology Review*, *47*(3), 226–243.

Costa, A. L., & Kallick, B. (1993). Through the lens of a critical friend. *Educational Leadership*, *51*(2), 49–51.

Costa, A. L., & Kallick, B. (2004). Launching self-directed learners. *Educational Leadership*, *62*(1), 51–57.

Costin, F. (1972). Lecturing versus other methods of teaching: A review of research. *British Journal of Educational Technology*, *3*(1), 4–31.

Covey, S. R. (2004). *The seven habits of highly effective people: Powerful lessons in personal change*. New York: Free Press.

Crosby, H. (1931). *Transit of Venus: Poems*. Paris: Black Sun Press.

Crossroads Initiative. *Mother Teresa of Calcutta: Quotes and stories*. Accessed at www.crossroadsinitiative.com/saints/quotes-from-blessed-mother-teresa-of-calcutta on October 4, 2020.

Crown. (2018). *Essential digital skills: Framework*. Accessed at https://assets.publishing.service.gov.uk/government/uploads/system/uploads/attachment_data/file/738922/Essential_digital_skills_framework.pdf on July 21, 2020.

Dakroub, L. (2018). *The feeling flower*. Scotts Valley, CA: CreateSpace.

Daniels, K. (2019). Notions of agency in early literacy classrooms: Assemblages and productive intersections. *Journal of Early Childhood Literacy*, *3*(3), 223–247.

Danielson, C. (2019). *A vision of excellence*. Accessed at https://danielsongroup.org/framework on June 23, 2020.

Darling-Hammond, L. (1997). *The right to learn: A blueprint for creating schools that work*. San Francisco: Jossey-Bass.

Darling-Hammond, L. (2017). *Developing and measuring higher order skills: Models for state performance assessment systems*. Palo Alto, CA: Learning Policy Institute.

Darling-Hammond, L., & Adamson, F. (2013). *Developing assessments of deeper learning: The costs and benefits of using tests that help students learn*. Stanford, CA: Stanford Center for Opportunity Policy in Education.

Darling-Hammond, L., & Oakes, J. (2019). *Preparing teachers for deeper learning*. Cambridge, MA: Harvard Education Press.

Darling-Hammond, L., & Pecheone, R. L. (2010). *Developing an internationally comparable balanced assessment system that supports high-quality learning*. Princeton, NJ: Educational Testing Service.

Davenport, M. (2018, August 16). *Using circle practice in the classroom*. Accessed at www.edutopia.org/article/using-circle-practice-classroom on September 5, 2020.

de Boer, H., Timmermans, A. C., & van der Werf, M. P. C. (2018). The effects of teacher expectation interventions on teachers' expectations and student achievement: Narrative review and meta-analysis. *Educational Research and Evaluation*, *24*(3–5), 180–200.

De Fruyt, F., Wille, B., & John, O. P. (2015). Employability in the 21st century: Complex (interactive) problem solving and other essential skills. *Industrial and Organizational Psychology*, *8*(2), 276–281.

de Jager, A., Fogarty, A., Tewson, A., Lenette, C., & Boydell, K. M. (2017). Digital storytelling in research: A systematic review. *The Qualitative Report, 22*(10), 2548–2582. Accessed at https://nsuworks.nova.edu/tqr/vol22/iss10/3 on March 24, 2020.

Dede, C. (2010). Comparing frameworks for 21st century skills. In J. Bellanca and R. Brandt (Eds.), 21st century skills: Rethinking how students learn (pp. 51–75). Bloomington, IN: Solution Tree Press.

Department for Children, Schools and Families. (2008). *Developing critical and creative thinking: In science.* Accessed at www.stem.org.uk/resources/elibrary/resource/33481/developing-critical-and-creative-thinking-science on November 12, 2020.

Department for Education. (2013). *The national curriculum in England: Key stages 1 and 2 framework document.* Accessed at https://assets.publishing.service.gov.uk/government/uploads/system/uploads/attachment_data/file/425601/PRIMARY_national_curriculum.pdf on October 6, 2020.

Department of Defense Education Activity. (n.d.). *DoDEA College and Career Ready Standards for Arts (CCRSA): General music, grades K–8.* Accessed at www.dodea.edu/Curriculum/FineArts/upload/CCRSA_only_music_general_k8_v2.pdf on June 3, 2020.

Department of eLearning. (2015). *Digital literacy: 21st century competencies for our age.* Accessed at https://manuelzammit.files.wordpress.com/2016/08/digital-literacy.pdf on July 21, 2020.

Design Thinking for Educators. (n.d.). *What is in the toolkit?* Accessed at https://designthinkingforeducators.com/about-toolkit on September 5, 2020.

Desjardins, J. (2018, July 2). *10 skills you'll need to survive the rise of automation.* Accessed at www.weforum.org/agenda/2018/07/the-skills-needed-to-survive-the-robot-invasion-of-the-workplace on August 15, 2020.

Di Giacomo, D., Vittorini, P., & Lacasa, P. (Eds.). (2019). *Editorial: Digital skills and life-long learning—Digital learning as a new insight of enhanced learning by the innovative approach joining technology and cognition.* Accessed at www.frontiersin.org/research-topics/5377/pdf on March 24, 2020.

Dignath-van Ewijk, C., & van der Werf, G. (2012). *What teachers think about self-regulated learning: Investigating teacher beliefs and teacher behavior of enhancing students' self-regulation.* Accessed at www.hindawi.com/journals/edri/2012/741713 on October 15, 2020.

Dogra, A. (2017). *Deeper learning, deep learning and user innovation.* Accessed at https://edtechreview.in/trends-insights/trends/2775-deep-learning-and-user-innovation on February 5, 2020.

Domingue, B. W., Belsky, D. W., Fletcher, J. M., Conley, D., Boardman, J. D., & Harris, K. M. (2018). The social genome of friends and schoolmates in the National Longitudinal Study of Adolescent to Adult Health. *Proceedings of the National Academy of Sciences, 115*(4), 702–707.

Donahue, W. A. (1992). *Managing interpersonal conflict.* Newbury Park, CA: SAGE.

Doran, G. T. (1981). There's a S.M.A.R.T. way to write management's goals and objectives. *Management Review, 70*(11), 35–36.

Dorman, J. P., Aldridge, J. M., & Fraser, B. J. (2006). Using students' assessment of classroom environment to develop a typology of secondary school classrooms. *International Education Journal, 7*(7), 906–915.

Double, K. S., McGrane, J. A., & Hopfenbeck, T. N. (2019). *The impact of peer assessment on academic performance: A meta-analysis of control group studies.* Accessed at https://link.springer.com/article/10.1007/s10648-019-09510-3 on December 9, 2020.

Doyle, C. C., Mieder, W., & Shapiro, F. R. (2012). *The dictionary of modern proverbs.* New Haven, CT: Yale University Press.

Duckworth, A. (2016). *Grit: The power of passion and perseverance.* New York: Scribner.

DuFour, R., DuFour, R., Eaker, R., Many, T. W., & Mattos, M. (2016). *Learning by doing: A handbook for Professional Learning Communities at Work* (3rd ed.). Bloomington, IN: Solution Tree Press.

Dumbravă, G. (2011). *Workplace relations and emotional intelligence.* Accessed at http://ns1.upet.ro/annals/economics/pdf/2011/part3/Dumbrava.pdf on October 1, 2020.

Dweck, C. S. (2006). *Mindset: The new psychology of success.* New York: Random House.

Eastern Connecticut State University. (n.d.). *Project-based learning.* Accessed at www.easternct.edu/center-for-early-childhood-education/teaching-strategies/project-based-learning.html on April 1, 2020.

Economy, P. (2018). *This is the way you need to write down your goals for faster success.* Accessed at www.inc.com/peter-economy/this-is-way-you-need-to-write-down-your-goals-for-faster-success.html on October 2, 2020.

Ed Tech. (2016). *14 copyright essentials teachers and students must know.* Accessed at https://ditchthattextbook.com/14-copyright-essentials-teachers-and-students-must-know on December 7, 2020.

Ehmke, R. (n.d.). *How using social media affects teenagers.* Accessed at https://childmind.org/article/how-using-social-media-affects-teenagers on July 23, 2020.

Eikenberry, K. (2012, October 15). The confidence/competence loop [Blog post]. *Leadership and Learning With Kevin Eikenberry.* Accessed at https://Blog.Kevineikenberry.Com/Leadership-Supervisory-Skills/The-Confidencecompetence-Loop on September 5, 2020.

Ellis, S., & Moss, G. (2013). Ethics, education policy and research: The phonics question reconsidered. *British Educational Research Journal, 40*(2), 241–260.

ePortfolio Resource Center. (n.d.). *Using Google sites for creating an ePortfolio.* Accessed at https://sites.google.com/site/resourcecentereportfolio/how-to-use-google-sites on April 24, 2019.

European Commission. (n.d.). *Digital education action plan (2021–2027).* Accessed at https://ec.europa.eu/education/education-in-the-eu/digital-education-action-plan_en on March 24, 2020.

Evans, K. M., & King, J. A. (1994). Research on OBE: What we know and don't know. *Educational Leadership, 51*(6), 12–17.

Faust. (n.d.). *Johann Wolfgang von Goethe.* Accessed at www.faust.com/books/authors/johann-wolfgang-von-goethe on May 29, 2020.

Feuerstein, R., Feuerstein, R. S., & Falik, L. H. (2010). *Beyond smarter: Mediated learning and the brain's capacity for change.* New York: Teachers College Press.

Feuerstein, R., Falik, L. H., & Feuerstein, R. S. (2015). *Changing minds and brains—The legacy of Reuven Feuerstein.* New York: Teachers College Press.

Feuerstein, R., Rand, Y., Hoffman, M. B., & Miller, R. (1980). *Instrumental enrichment: An intervention program for cognitive modifiability.* Baltimore: University Park Press.

Field, S. P. (2017). *Evaluating the effects of a self-management program with a peer-mediated praise procedure.* Doctoral dissertation, Western Michigan University, Kalamazoo. Accessed at https://scholarworks.wmich.edu/dissertations/3134 on September 6, 2020.

Florida Department of Education. (2014). *Mathematics Florida standards (MAFS)—Grade 1.* Accessed at www.fldoe.org/core/fileparse.php/12087/urlt/G1_Mathematics_Florida_Standards.pdf on June 3, 2020.

Fogarty, R. (1999, March). *Architects of the intellect.* Paper presented at the annual conference and exhibit show of the Association for Supervision and Curriculum Development, San Francisco. Accessed at https://files.eric.ed.gov/fulltext/ED430683.pdf on June 3, 2020.

Foley, J. M., & Kaiser, L. M. R. (2013). *Learning transfer and its intentionality in adult and continuing education.* Accessed at https://doi.org/10.1002/ace.20040 on June 23, 2020.

Forbes. (n.d.). *Thoughts on the business of life.* Accessed at www.forbes.com/quotes/7932 on September 28, 2020.

Fujimoto, T. [tedfujimoto]. (2015, May 25). Most jobs, today, req a cell phone-not a pencil . . . but we know how that goes in most classrooms [Twitter moment]. Accessed at https://twitter.com/tedfujimoto/status/60295 0447993729024 on June 30, 2020.

Furman, N., & Sibthorp, J. (2013). Leveraging experiential learning techniques for transfer. *New Directions for Adult and Continuing Education, 137,* 17–26. Accessed at https://onlinelibrary.wiley.com/doi/abs/10.1002/ace.20041 on June 23, 2020.

Gage, G. J. (2019). The case for neuroscience research in the classroom. *Neuron, 102*(5), 914–917. Accessed at www.sciencedirect.com/science/article/abs/pii/S0896627319303423 on March 24, 2020.

Gardner, H. (1983). *Frames of mind: The theory of multiple intelligences.* New York: Basic Books.

Georgia Department of Education. (2017). *Course standards template.* Accessed at www.gadoe.org/Curriculum-Instruction-and-Assessment/CTAE/Documents/Course-Standards-Template.docx on Dcember 6, 2020.

Gleeson, B. (2019, August). *How Navy SEALs plan, lead and learn*. Accessed at www.forbes.com/sites/brentgleeson/2019/08/27/how-navy-seals-plan-lead-and-learn/#51dad6273087 on September 5, 2020.

Goddard, R., Hoy, R., & Hoy, A. W. (2000). Collective teacher efficacy: Its meaning, measure, and impact on student achievement. *American Education Research Journal, 37*(2), 479–507.

Goleman, D. (2005). *Emotional intelligence*. New York: Bantam Books.

Gomez, S. C., Vuorikari, R., & Punie, Y. (2017). *DigComp 2.1: The digital competence framework for citizens*. Luxembourg: Publications Office of the European Union. Accessed at https://publications.jrc.ec.europa.eu/repository/bitstream/JRC106281/web-digcomp2.1pdf_(online).pdf on December 9, 2020.

Goodreads. (n.d.). *John Steinbeck quotes*. Accessed at www.goodreads.com/quotes/33268-you-can-only-understand-people-if-you-feel-them-in on October 4, 2020.

Gottschalk, F. (2019). *Impacts of technology use on children: Exploring literature on the brain, cognition and well-being*. Accessed at www.oecd.org/officialdocuments/publicdisplaydocumentpdf/?cote=EDU/WKP%282019%293&docLanguage=En on July 23, 2020.

Grech, A. (2016). *Skills to navigate the digital world*. Accessed at www.strategyworks.net/skills-navigate-digital-world on December 7, 2020.

Gregory, A. & Fergus, E. (2017). Social-emotional learning and equity in school discipline. In S. M. Jones, E. Doolittle, & S. McLanahan (Eds.) *The future of children, 27*(1), 117–136.

Guglielmino, L. M. (1977). *Development of the self-directed learning readiness scale*. Dissertation, University of Georgia, Athens. *Dissertation Abstracts International, 38*(11-A), 6467.

Harding, S. M., de Barba, P. G., & Goh, F. (2016, October). *Teaching self-regulated learning skills*. Accessed at www.teachermagazine.com.au/articles/teaching-self-regulated-learning-skills on March 24, 2020.

Hasso Plattner Institute of Design at Stanford University. (2018). *Design thinking bootleg*. Accessed at https://static1.squarespace.com/static/57c6b79629687fde090a0fdd/t/5b19b2f2aa4a99e99b26b6bb/1528410876119/dschool_bootleg_deck_2018_final_sm+%282%29.pdf on December 3, 2020.

Hattie, J. (2009). *Visible learning: A synthesis of over 800 meta-analyses relating to achievement*. New York: Routledge.

Hattie, J. (2012). *Visible learning for teachers: Maximizing impact on learning*. New York: Routledge.

Hattie, J., & Clarke, S. (2019). *Visible learning: Feedback*. New York: Routledge.

Hattie, J., & Timperley, H. (2007). *The power of feedback*. Accessed at www.columbia.edu/~mvp19/ETF/Feedback.pdf on October 6, 2020.

Henderson, P., & Karr-Kidwell, P. J. (1998). *Authentic assessment: An extensive literary review and recommendations for administrators*. Accessed at https://files.eric.ed.gov/fulltext/ED418140.pdf on March 24, 2020.

Henkes, K. (1988). *Chester's way*. New York: Greenwillow Books.

Henley, W. E. (1888). *A book of verses*. London: D. Nutt.

Henschke, J. A. (2012). *Research on the use of learning and degree contracts within university and other settings in Italy and the USA*. Accessed at https://trace.tennessee.edu/cgi/viewcontent.cgi?article=1421&context=utk_IACE-browseall on October 6, 2020.

Herdzina, J, & Lauricella, A. R. (2020). *Media Literacy in Early Childhood Report*. Accessed at http://teccenter.erikson.edu/wp-content/uploads/2020/06/TEC-MediaLiteracy-Report.pdf on December 7, 2020.

Hernandez, L. E., Hammond, L. D., Adams, J., Bradley, K., Grand, D. D., Roc, M., et al. (2019, October). *Deeper learning networks: Taking student-centered learning and equity to scale*. Accessed at https://learningpolicyinstitute.org/product/deeper-learning-networks-report on September 5, 2020.

Hewlett Foundation. (2013). *Deeper learning competencies*. Accessed at https://hewlett.org/wp-content/uploads/2016/08/Deeper_Learning_Defined__April_2013.pdf. on June 10, 2020.

Hill, A. (n.d.). *Collaboration in the workplace.* Accessed at https://study.com/academy/lesson/what-is-collaboration-in-the-workplace-definition-benefits-examples.html#:~:text=Collaboration%20in%20the%20workplace%20is%20when%20two%20or%20more%20people,group%20to%20accomplish%20a%20task on September 5, 2020.

Hill, C. (2009, July 29). *Top ten criteria that make or break a resume.* Accessed at www.nydailynews.com/news/money/top-ten-criteria-break-resume-article-1.367914 on September 5, 2020.

Hilliard, C. (2006). Using structured reflection on a critical incident to develop a professional portfolio. *Nursing Standard, 21*(2), 35–40.

Hoban, T. (1987). *I read signs.* New York: Scholastic.

Hohensee, C. (2014). Backward transfer: An investigation of the influence of quadratic functions instruction on students' prior ways of reasoning about linear functions. *Mathematical Thinking and Learning, 16*(2), 135–174.

Hokanson, B., Clinton, G., & Tracey, M. W. (Eds.). (2015). *The design of learning experience: Creating the future of educational technology.* New York: Springer.

Hoy, W. K., & Sabo, D. J. (1998). *Quality middle schools: Open and healthy.* Thousand Oaks, CA: Corwin.

Huberman, M., Bitter, C., Anthony, J., & O'Day, J. (2014, September). *The shape of deeper learning: Strategies, structures, and cultures in deeper learning network high schools.* Accessed at www.air.org/resource/shape-deeper-learning-strategies-structures-and-cultures-deeper-learning-network-high on March 24, 2020.

Huberman, M., Duffy, H., Mason, J., Zeiser, K., & O'Day, J. (2016). *School features and student opportunities for deeper learning: What makes a difference?* Accessed at www.air.org/resource/school-features-and-student-opportunities-deeper-learning-what-makes-difference on March 24, 2020.

Hughes, K. (2018). *25 of the best planning quotes.* Accessed at www.projectmanager.com/blog/planning-quotes on September 28, 2020.

Hung, W. (2013). *Problem-based learning: A learning environment for enhancing learning transfer.* Accessed at https://doi.org/10.1002/ace.20042 on June 23, 2020.

Illinois Anti-Bullying Statute, Pub. L. No. 105 ILCS 5/27-23.7 Sec. 27–23.7 (2017).

Illinois Early Learning Project. (n.d.). *Helping children sketch and draw from observation.* Accessed at https://illinoisearlylearning.org/pa/project-planning/children-sketch on May 31, 2020.

Illinois State Board of Education. (2017). *Illinois learning standards for social science–2nd grade.* Accessed at www.isbe.net/Documents/ss-stds-grade2-012716.pdf on December 6, 2020.

Indeed. (n.d.). *How to write an IT technician job description sample.* Accessed at www.indeed.com/hire/job-description"/it-technician?hl=en&co=US on September 7, 2020.

Indiana Department of Education. (n.d.). *Grade 4-Reading literature 3.1.* Accessed at www.doe.in.gov/literacy/framework/4rl31 on December 6, 2020.

International Literacy Association. (2019). *Digital resources in early childhood literacy development: Position statement and research brief.* Accessed at https://literacyworldwide.org/docs/default-source/where-we-stand/ila-digital-resources-early-childhood-literacy-development.pdf?_ga=2.253219085.527633822.1607356313-1475106223.1605494585 on December 7, 2020.

International Society for Technology in Education. (n.d.). *ISTE standards for students.* Accessed at www.iste.org/standards/for-students on March 24, 2020.

International Telecommunication Union. (2018). *Digital skills toolkit.* Accessed at www.itu.int/en/ITU-D/Digital-Inclusion/Documents/ITU%20Digital%20Skills%20Toolkit.pdf on July 21, 2020.

Jackson, S. (1948). *The lottery.* Accessed at www.newyorker.com/magazine/1948/06/26/the-lottery on December 6, 2020.

Jacobs, H. H. (2010). *Curriculum 21: Essential education for a changing world.* Alexandria, VA: Association for Supervision and Curriculum Development.

James, G. (2020). *What goal-setting does to your brain and why it's spectacularly effective.* Accessed at www.inc.com/geoffrey-james/what-goal-setting-does-to-your-brain-why-its-spectacularly-effective.html on September 5, 2020.

Jenkins, S., & Page, R. (2003). *What do you do with a tail like this?* Boston: Houghton Mifflin.

Jezard, A. (2018, June). *The 3 key skill sets for the workers of 2030.* Accessed at www.weforum.org/agenda/2018/06/the-3-skill-sets-workers-need-to-develop-between-now-and-2030 on March 31, 2020.

Jigsaw Classroom. (n.d.). *Overview.* Accessed at www.jigsaw.org on September 1, 2020.

Johnson, D. W., & Johnson, R. T. (1999). *Learning together and alone: Cooperative, competitive, and individualistic learning* (5th ed.). Englewood Cliffs, NJ: Prentice Hall.

Johnson, D. W., & Johnson, R. T. (2018). *Cooperative learning: The foundation for active learning.* Accessed at www.intechopen.com/books/active-learning-beyond-the-future/cooperative-learning-the-foundation-for-active-learning on July 21, 2020.

Johnson, D. W., Johnson, R. T., & Holubec, E. J. (2008). *Cooperation in the classroom* (8th ed.). Edina, MN: Interaction Book.

Johnson, R. T., & Johnson, D. W. (n.d.). *An overview of cooperative learning.* Accessed at www.co-operation.org/what-is-cooperative-learning on August 16, 2020.

Johnston, P. H. (2004). *Choice words: How our language affects children's learning.* Portland, ME: Stenhouse.

Jones, S. M., Barnes, S. P., Bailey, R., & Doolittle, E. J. (2017). *Promoting social and emotional competencies in elementary school.* Accessed at www.wallacefoundation.org/knowledge-center/Documents/FOC-Spring-Vol27-No1-Compiled-Future-of-Children-spring-2017.pdf on December 7, 2020.

Kanning, R. G. (1994). What multimedia can do in our classrooms. *Educational Leadership, 51*(7), 40–44. Accessed at www.ascd.org/publications/educational-leadership/apr94/vol51/num07/What-Multimedia-Can-Do-in-Our-Classrooms.aspx on March 31, 2020.

Keogh, M. (2015, September 11). Technology empowering education [Blog post]. *Huffington Post.* Accessed at www.huffingtonpost.co.uk/maria-keogh/technology-empowering-edu_b_8488130.html?guccounter=1&guce_referrer=aHR0cHM6Ly93d3cuZ29vZ2xlLmNvbS8&guce_referrer_sig=AQAAAD7lr5fqHrz27-kWqxP1xteSO-rvLrglOhYAiY43DyP0mZ5Sj9G46xpaJiRmYLR8AH2EZmEs-eegu-BQNdlPN36daa4I_4Oz5UHb61PWNoHH71E-4oCCYInhKOAOWm6zPWxKyr8VNNBz01JQQ9qCkuzM-0IoU8iaLkOGL2krja-5 on June 29, 2020.

Khattri, N., Reeve, A. L., & Kane, M. B. (1998). *Principles and practices of performance assessment.* Mahwah, NJ: Erlbaum.

King, M. L. Jr. (1963). *Martin Luther King Jr.'s "Letter from Birmingham jail."* Accessed at www.theatlantic.com/magazine/archive/2018/02/letter-from-a-birmingham-jail/552461 on June 2, 2020.

Kipling, R. (1894). *The jungle book.* London: Macmillan & Co.

Klein, A. (2019, November 5). International study finds major inequities in computer literacy [Blog post]. *Education Week.* Accessed at http://blogs.edweek.org/edweek/DigitalEducation/2019/11/international-comparison-computer-literacy-teacher.html on March 10, 2020.

Klemenčič, M. (2015). What is student agency? An ontological exploration in the context of research on student engagement. In M. Klemenčič, S. Bergan, & R. Primožič (Eds.), *Student Engagement in Europe: Society, Higher Education and Student Governance* (pp. 11–29). Strasbourg Cedex, France: Council of Europe.

Knight, S. (2018, September 4). Building background knowledge to make learning impactful [Blog post]. *GCU Blogs.* Accessed at www.gcu.edu/blog/teaching-school-administration/building-background-knowledge-make-learning-impactful on August 15, 2020.

Knowles, M. S. (1975). *Self-directed learning: A guide for learners and teachers.* Chicago: Association Press.

Kohn, A. (2016, March 13). The overselling of ed tech [Blog post]. *Psychology Today.* Accessed at www.psychologytoday.com/us/blog/the-homework-myth/201603/the-overselling-ed-tech on April 1, 2020.

Kratochwill, T. R., Cook, J. L., Travers, J. F., & Elliott, S. N. (2000). *Educational psychology: Effective teaching, effective learning* (3rd ed.). Boston: McGraw-Hill.

Krause, J. (n.d.). The history and evolution of SMART goals [Blog post]. *achieveit.* Accessed at www.achieveit.com/resources/blog/the-history-and-evolution-of-smart-goals on March 24, 2020.

Krishna, A., & Strack, F. (2017). *Reflection and impulse as determinants of human behavior.* Accessed at https://link.springer.com/chapter/10.1007/978-3-319-44588-5_9 on December 9, 2020.

Kurniaman, O., Noviana, E., Charlina, C., Simulyasih, S. B. N., Handayani, N. D., Sofyan, N. S., et al. (2018). Why should primary teachers develop learning material by directed reading thinking activity (DRTA) strategy? 4-D model. *Advanced Science Letters, 24*(11), 8389–8391.

Kurshan, B., & McManus, C. (2017). *Teaching 21st century skills for 21st century success requires an ecosystem approach.* Accessed at www.forbes.com/sites/barbarakurshan/2017/07/18/teaching-21st-century-skills-for-21st-century-success-requires-an-ecosystem-approach/#1b6ff8e83fe6 on March 24, 2020.

Kyōkai, B. D. (2008). *The teaching of Buddha.* Tokyo, Japan: Kosaido Printing.

Lakhani, C. M., Tierney, B. T., Manrai, A. K., Yang, J., Visscher, P. M., & Patel, C. J. (2019). Repurposing large health insurance claims data to estimate genetic and environmental contributions in 560 phenotypes. *Nature Genetics, 51*(2), 327–334. Accessed at www.nature.com on August 16, 2020.

Lang, S. (2018). *Grumpy monkey.* New York: Random House.

Langlois, S. (2018, June). *Billionaire investor Ray Dalio has three words of advice for kids headed to college—and parents may not like them.* Accessed at https://marketwatch.com/story/billionaire-investor-ray-dalio-has-3-words-of-advice-for-kids-headed-to-college----and-parents-may-not-like-them-2018-06-14 on April 1, 2020.

Langstaff, J., & Rojankovsky, F. (1957). *Over in the meadow.* New York: Harcourt, Brace.

Lee, K-F. (2018, October 1). Ten jobs that are safe in an AI world [Blog post]. *LinkedIn.* Accessed at www.linkedin.com/pulse/10-jobs-safe-ai-world-kai-fu-lee on March 31, 2020.

Lee, S., & Carpenter, R. (2015). *Creative thinking for 21st century composing practices: Creativity pedagogies across disciplines.* Accessed at https://wac.colostate.edu/docs/atd/arts/lee_carpenter2015.pdf on March 31, 2020.

Lennon, J., & Ono, Y. (1971). Imagine [Recorded by J. Lennon]. On *Imagine* [Album]. Berkshire, England: Ascot Sound.

Lerner, J. S., Li, Y., Valdesolo, P., & Kassam, K. S. (2015). *Emotion and decision making.* Accessed at www.annualreviews.org/doi/full/10.1146/annurev-psych-010213-115043 on December 6, 2020.

Liedtka, J. (2018). *Why design thinking works.* Accessed at https://hbr.org/2018/09/why-design-thinking-works on September 2, 2020.

Locke, E. A., Shaw, K. N., Saari, L. M., & Latham, G. P. (1981). *Goal setting and task performance: 1969–1980.* Accessed at https://doi.org/10.1037/0033-2909.90.1.125 on September 5, 2020.

Long, H. B., & Agyekum, S. K. (1983). Guglielmino's self-directed learning readiness scale: A validation study. *Higher Education, 12,* 77–87.

Longobardi, C., Prino, L. E., Marengo, D., & Settanni, M. (2016). *Student-teacher relationships as a protective factor for school adjustment during the transition from middle to high school.* Accessed at www.ncbi.nlm.nih.gov/pmc/articles/PMC5179523 on December 6, 2020.

Los Angeles County Department of Education. (2019). *TESA teacher handbook.* Los Angeles: Author.

Lynch, M. (2017). *What is digital literacy?* Accessed at www.thetechedvocate.org/what-is-digital-literacy on March 15, 2015.

Mader, M. (2020). *More coding instruction would be helpful.* Accessed at www.wsj.com/articles/more-coding-instruction-would-be-helpful-11583275634?mod=searchresults&page=1&pos=1 on March 31, 2020.

Manyika, J., Lund, S., Chui, M., Bughin, J., Woetzel, J., Batra, P., et al. (2017, November). *Jobs lost, jobs gained: What the future of work will mean for jobs, skills, and wages.* Accessed at www.mckinsey.com/featured-insights/future-of-work/jobs-lost-jobs-gained-what-the-future-of-work-will-mean-for-jobs-skills-and-wages on March 31, 2020.

Manyika, J., Mischke, J., Bughin, J., Woetzel, J., Krishnan, M., & Cudre, S. (2019, May). *A new look at the declining labor share of income in the United States.* Accessed at www.mckinsey.com/~/media/mckinsey/featured%20insights/employment%20and%20growth/a%20new%20look%20at%20the%20declining%20labor%20share%20of%20income%20in%20the%20united%20states/mgi-a-new-look-at-the-declining-labor-share-of-income-in-the-united-states.ashx on March 31, 2020.

Martin, A. J., & Collie, R. J. (2019). Teacher–student relationships and students' engagement in high school: Does the number of negative and positive relationships with teachers matter? *Journal of Educational Psychology, 111*(5), 861–876.

Marzano, R., Pickering, D., & Pollock, J. (2019). *PowerPoint summary: A handbook for classroom instruction that works—Research-based strategies for increasing student achievement.* Centennial, CO: Marzano Research.

Matthews, P. (2018, March). Near and far transfer of learning [Blog post]. *Training Journal.* Accessed at www.trainingjournal.com/blog/near-and-far-transfer-learning#:~:text=In%20the%20Near%2FFar%20model,application%20context%20and%20application%20behaviour.&text=Near%20transfer%20involves%20the%20study,a%20high%20level%20of%20automaticity on August 16, 2020.

Maxwell, S., Reynolds, K. J., Lee, E., Subasic, E., & Bromhead, D. (2017). *The impact of school climate and school identification on academic achievement: Multilevel modeling with student and teacher data.* Accessed at www.ncbi.nlm.nih.gov/pmc/articles/PMC5723344 on September 7, 2012.

McCrae, R. R., & Costa, P. T. (1989). The structure of interpersonal traits: Wiggins's circumplex and the five-factor model. *Journal of Personality and Social Psychology, 56*(4), 586–595.

McDonald's Corporation. (n.d.). *How does McDonald's promote effective team work?* Accessed at www.mcdonalds.com/gb/en-gb/help/faq/18524-how-does-mcdonalds-promote-effective-team-work.html on June 15, 2020.

McDowell, M. (2021). *Teaching for transfer: A guide for designing learning with real-world application.* Bloomington, IN: Solution Tree Press.

McKeough, A., Lupart, J., & Marini, A. (Eds.). (1995). *Teaching for transfer: Fostering generalization in learning.* Mahwah, NJ: Erlbaum.

McKinsey Global Institute. (2019). *The future of work in America: People and places, today and tomorrow.* Accessed at www.mckinsey.com/featured-insights/future-of-work/the-future-of-work-in-america-people-and-places-today-and-tomorrow on September 5, 2020.

McTighe, J., & Willis, J. (2019). *Upgrade your teaching: Understanding by design meets neuroscience.* Alexandria, VA: Association for Supervision and Curriculum Development.

Meadows, D. (2003). Digital storytelling: Research-based practice in new media. *Visual Communication, 2*(2), 189–193. Accessed at https://journals.sagepub.com/doi/10.1177/1470357203002002004 on March 24, 2020.

Meyer, M. L., Zhao, Z., & Tamir, D. I. (2019). *Simulating other people changes the self.* Accessed at https://doi.org/10.1037/xge0000565 on September 5, 2020.

Midwest Comprehensive Center. (2018). *Student goal setting: An evidence-based practice.* Accessed at https://files.eric.ed.gov/fulltext/ED589978.pdf on October 2, 2020.

Mile by Mile Running. (2020, January 14). Be stubborn about your goals, but flexible about your methods [Blog post]. *Mile by Mile Running.* Accessed at www.milebymileblog.com/be-stubborn-about-your-goals-but-flexible-about-your-methods on September 7, 2020.

Ministry for Education and Employment. (n.d.). *Malta national lifelong learning strategy 2020.* Accessed at https://education.gov.mt/en/Documents/Malta%20National%20Lifelong%20Learning%20Strategy%202020%20-%20Draft%20for%20Public%20Consultation.pdf on October 6, 2020.

Moawad, T. (2020). *It takes what it takes: How to think neutrally and gain control of your life.* New York: HarperOne.

Morin, A. (2017). *Thirteen things mentally strong people don't do: Take back your power, embrace change, face your fears, and train your brain for happiness and success.* New York: HarperCollins.

Mulvahill, E. (2019, June 14). Why teachers quit [Blog post]. *We Are Teachers.* Accessed at www.weareteachers.com/why-teachers-quit on March 24, 2020.

Munson, D. (2000). *Enemy pie.* San Francisco: Chronicle Books.

Murayama, K. (2018). *The science of motivation.* Accessed at www.apa.org/science/about/psa/2018/06/motivation on September 7, 2020.

Murtafi'ah, B., & Putro, N. H. P. S. (2019). Digital literacy in the English curriculum: Models of learning activities. *Acta Informatica Malaysia, 3*(2), 10–13.

National Council for the Social Studies. (2010). *National curriculum standards for social studies: A framework for teaching, learning, and assessment* (2nd ed.). Silver Spring, MD: Author.

National Governors Association Center for Best Practices & Council of Chief State School Officers. (2010a). *Common Core State Standards for English language arts and literacy in history/social studies, science, and technical subjects.* Accessed at www.corestandards.org/assets/CCSSI_ELA%20Standards.pdf on May 28, 2019.

National Governors Association Center for Best Practices & Council of Chief State School Officers. (2010b). *Common Core State Standards for mathematics.* Accessed at www.corestandards.org/assets/CCSSI_Math%20Standards.pdf on April 1, 2020.

New York State Department of Education. (2018). *New York state social emotional learning benchmarks.* Accessed at www.p12.nysed.gov/sss/documents/NYSSELBenchmarks.pdf on August 16, 2020.

Newkirk, I. E. (n.d.). *Dr. Neil deGrasse Tyson's interview with PETA.* Accessed at www.peta.org/features/dr-neil-degrasse-tyson-interview on December 7, 2020.

NGSS Lead States. (2013). *Next Generation Science Standards: For states, by states.* Washington, DC: National Academies Press.

Obama, B. (2009, April 7). *Remarks of President Barack Obama at student roundtable.* Accessed at https://obamawhitehouse.archives.gov/realitycheck/the-press-office/remarks-president-barack-obama-student-roundtable-istanbul on October 4, 2020.

Ogle, D. M. (1986). K-W-L: A teaching model that develops active reading of expository text. *The Reading Teacher, 39*(6), 564–570.

Ohio Department of Education. (2019, June). *Ohio's K–12 social and emotional learning standards.* Accessed at http://education.ohio.gov/getattachment/Topics/Learning-in-Ohio/Social-and-Emotional-Learning/Social-and-Emotional-Learning-Standards/SEL-Standards-K-12.pdf.aspx?lang=en-US on June 1, 2020.

Olson, A. (2017, September 27). Personalized learning: The importance of teachers in a technology-driven world [Blog post]. *Brookings.* Accessed at www.brookings.edu/blog/brown-center-chalkboard/2017/09/27/personalized-learning-the-importance-of-teachers-in-a-technology-driven-world on April 1, 2020.

O'Neill, J., & Conzemius, A. (2006). *The power of SMART goals: Using goals to improve student learning.* Bloomington, IN: Solution Tree Press.

Organisation for Economic Co-operation and Development. (n.d.a). *CERI—Digital learning resources as systemic innovation.* Accessed at www.oecd.org/education/ceri/ceri-digitallearningresourcesassystemicinnovation.htm on July 21, 2020.

Organisation for Economic Co-operation and Development. (n.d.b). *Social and emotional skills: Well-being, connectedness, and success.* Accessed at www.oecd.org/education/school/UPDATED%20Social%20and%20Emotional%20Skills%20-%20Well-being,%20connectedness%20and%20success.pdf%20(website).pdf on August 16, 2020.

Organisation for Economic Co-operation and Development. (2015). *Skills for social progress: The power of social and emotional skills.* Accessed at www.oecd.org/education/ceri/skills-for-social-progress-executive-summary.pdf on December 3, 2020.

Organisation for Economic Co-operation and Development. (2019). *OECD employment outlook: The future of work.* Accessed at www.oecd-ilibrary.org/sites/9ee00155-en/index.html?itemId=/content/publication/9ee00155-en on October 15, 2020.

Paciga, K., & Kucirkova, N. (2019). *Digital resources in early childhood literacy development.* Accessed at www.academia.edu/40661764/Digital_resources_in_early_childhood_literacy_development on April 1, 2020.

Palacio, R. J. (2012). *Wonder.* New York: Alfred A. Knopf.

Palincsar, A. S., & Brown, A. L. (1984). Reciprocal teaching of comprehension-fostering and comprehension-monitoring activities. *Cognition and Instruction, 1*(2), 117–175.

Pandolpho, B. (2020, March 10). *Simple ways to promote student voice in the classroom* [Blog post]. *Edutopia.* Accessed at www.edutopia.org/article/simple-ways-promote-student-voice-classroom on March 10, 2020.

Partnership for 21st Century Learning. (2019). *Framework for 21st century learning: A unified vision for learning to ensure student success in a world where change is constant and learning never stops.* Accessed at http://static.battelleforkids.org/documents/p21/P21_Framework_Brief.pdf on March 31, 2020.

Paulus, M. P., Squeglia, L. M., Bagot, K., Jacobus, J., Kuplick, R., Breslin, F. J., et al. (2019). Screen media activity and brain structure in youth: Evidence for diverse structural correlation networks from the ABCD study. *Neuroimage, 185,* 140–153.

Pellegrino, J. W., & Hilton, M. L. (Eds.). (2012). *Education for life and work: Developing transferable knowledge and skills in the 21st century.* Washington, DC: National Academies Press.

Perkins, D. N. (2014). *Future wise: Educating our children for a changing world*. San Francisco: Jossey-Bass.

Perkins, D. N., & Salomon, G. (1988). Teaching for transfer. *Educational Leadership, 46*(1), 22–32.

Perry, T. (2017, February). *The golden rule and the magic circle*. Accessed at https://activelearningps.com/2017/02/15/the-golden-rule-and-the-magic-circle on August 15, 2020.

Petry, A. L. (1955). *Harriet Tubman: Conductor on the Underground Railroad*. New York: Crowell.

Pilten, G. (2016). *The evaluation of effectiveness of reciprocal teaching strategies on comprehension of expository texts*. Accessed at https://files.eric.ed.gov/fulltext/EJ1114674.pdf on September 5, 2020.

Poore, B. S. (2011). *Users as essential contributors to spatial cyberinfrastructures*. Accessed at www.pnas.org/content/108/14/5510/tab-article-info on March 31, 2020.

Poore, M. (2011). *Digital literacy: Human flourishing and collective intelligence in a knowledge society*. Accessed at https://search.informit.com.au/documentSummary;dn=111308665720373;res=IELHSS>ISSN on September 30, 2020.

Promethean. (n.d.). *A quick guide to technology compliance and legislation in schools*. Accessed at https://techease.biz/wp-content/uploads/2017/11/A_Quick_Guide_to_Technology_Compliance___Legislation_in_Schools.pdf on April 1, 2020.

Quora Contributor. (2018). *How artificial intelligence job displacement will affect the worldwide economy*. Accessed at www.forbes.com/sites/quora/2018/10/09/how-artificial-intelligence-job-displacement-will-affect-the-worldwide-economy/#9e8446d1f522 on March 31, 2020.

Quotes.net. (n.d.). *Do not confine your children*. Accessed at www.quotes.net/quote/40464 on December 6, 2020.

Rathmann, P. (1991). *Ruby the copycat*. New York: Scholastic.

Rawls, W. (1961). *Where the red fern grows*. Philadelphia: The Curtis Publishing Company.

Read, J. G. (2013, November 11). Digital literacy "as important as reading and writing." *The Telegraph*. Accessed at www.telegraph.co.uk/education/educationopinion/10436444/Digital-literacy-as-important-as-reading-and-writing.html on April 1, 2020.

Redecker, C., & Punie, Y. (2017). *European framework for the digital competence of educators: DigCompEdu*. Luxembourg: Publications Office of the European Union.

Reis da Luz, F. S. D. (2015). *The relationship between teachers and students in the classroom: Communicative language teaching approach and cooperative learning strategy to improve learning*. Accessed at https://vc.bridgew.edu/cgi/viewcontent.cgi?article=1020&context=theses on October 1, 2020.

Ribble, M. (2011). *Digital citizenship in schools* (2nd ed.). Eugene, OR: International Society for Technology in Education.

Rickles, J., Zeiser, K., Mason, J., & Garet, M. S. (2016). *Deeper learning and graduation: Is there a relationship?* Accessed at www.air.org/resource/deeper-learning-and-graduation-there-relationship-4-4 on March 24, 2020.

Robinson, K. (2010, October). *Changing education paradigms* [Video file]. Accessed at www.ted.com/talks/sir_ken_robinson_changing_education_paradigms on March 31, 2020.

Root-Bernstein, M., & Root-Bernstein, R. (2010, March 31). Einstein on creative thinking: Music and the intuitive art of scientific imagination [Blog post]. *Psychology Today*. Accessed at www.psychologytoday.com/us/blog/imagine/201003/einstein-creative-thinking-music-and-the-intuitive-art-scientific-imagination on September 30, 2020.

Rosenthal, R., & Jacobson, L. (1968). *Pygmalion in the classroom*. Accessed at https://doi.org/10.1007/BF02322211 on October 5, 2020.

Rowling, J. K. (1998). *Harry Potter and the sorcerer's stone*. New York: Scholastic.

Ryan, R. M., & Deci, E. L. (2000). *Self-determination theory and the facilitation of intrinsic motivation, social development, and well-being*. Accessed at https://selfdeterminationtheory.org/SDT/documents/2000_RyanDeci_SDT.pdf on June 1, 2020.

Sackett, R. S. (1934). The influence of symbolic rehearsal upon the retention of a maze habit. *Journal of General Psychology, 10*(2), 376–398.

Salovey, P., & Mayer, J. D. (1990). Emotional intelligence. *Imagination, Cognition and Personality, 9*(3), 185–211.

Sanford, S. (2019, September 26). *Hacking democracy: Two codes for the modern world.* Accessed at https://medium.com/@ssanford_77683/hacking-democracy-two-codes-for-the-modern-world-e6561a77dc12 on September 7, 2020.

Sastri, S. (2019). *Integrating technology in classrooms: The new pedagogical mantra for an enhanced curriculum.* Accessed at http://bweducation.businessworld.in/article/Integrating-Technology-In-Classrooms-The-New-Pedagogical-Mantra-For-An-Enhanced-Curriculum/17-01-2019-166256/#:~:text=%E2%80%9CTeachers%20need%20to%20integrate%20technology,an%20internationally%20acclaimed%20educational%20consultant on December 7, 2020.

Sayre, A. P., Sayre, J., & Cecil, R. (2003). *One is a snail, ten is a crab.* Somerville, MA: Candlewick Press.

Scharton, H. (2018, August). *Putting the personal in personalized learning.* Accessed at https://edtechdigest.com/2018/08/23/putting-the-personal-in-personalized-learning on March 24, 2020.

Schmidt, S. J. (2019). Embracing and harnessing the intimate connection between emotion and cognition to help students learn. *Journal of Food Science Education, 18*(4). Accessed at https://onlinelibrary.wiley.com/doi/10.1111/1541-4329.12167 on October 5, 2020.

Schwarz, E., & Kay, K. (Eds.). (2006). *The case for twenty-first century learning: New directions for youth development.* New York: Wiley.

Seeger, P., & Hickerson, J. (1962). Where have all the flowers gone [Recorded by P. Seeger]. On *The Songs of Pete Seeger* [Album]. West Chester, PA: Appleseed Recordings.

Sepp, J. N. (2012). *Helpful tips & useful links.* Accessed at http://mssepp.blogspot.com/p/helpful-tips-useful-links.html on March 24, 2020.

Shakespeare, W. (1987). *Hamlet* (G. R. Hibbard, Ed.). New York: Oxford University Press.

Shakespeare, W. (1997). Macbeth. In G. B. Evans & J. J. M. Tobin (Eds.), *The Riverside Shakespeare* (2nd ed., Vol. 1, pp. 1306–1342). Boston: Houghton Mifflin. (Original work published 1595)

Shannon, D. (2002). *Duck on a bike.* New York: Blue Sky Press.

Shi, B., Wang, L., Yang, J., Zhang, M., & Xu, L. (2017). *Relationship between divergent thinking and intelligence: An empirical study of the threshold hypothesis with Chinese children.* Accessed at https://pubmed.ncbi.nlm.nih.gov/28275361 on September 5, 2020.

Shute, V. J. (2008). Focus on formative feedback. *Review of Educational Research, 78*(1), 153–189.

Simon, H. A. (1973). The structure of ill structured problems. *Artificial Intelligence, 4*(3-4), 181–201.

Slavin, R. E. (1995). *Cooperative learning: Theory, research, and practice* (2nd ed.). Boston: Allyn & Bacon.

Smith, M. K. (2013). *Malcolm Knowles, informal adult education, self-direction and andragogy.* Accessed at http://infed.org/mobi/malcolm-knowles-informal-adult-education-self-direction-and-andragogy on March 24, 2020.

Smith, P. A., & Hoy, W. K. (2007). Academic optimism and student achievement in urban elementary schools. *Journal of Educational Administration, 45*(5), 556–568.

Sparks, S. D. (2020). *A creativity conundrum: Can schools teach kids to innovate?* Accessed at www.edweek.org/ew/articles/2020/02/05/a-creativity-conundrum-can-schools-teach-students.html on March 24, 2020.

State of Victoria. (2020). *Feedback and reporting.* Accessed at www.education.vic.gov.au/school/teachers/teachingresources/practice/Pages/insight-feedback.aspx on August 20, 2020.

Stauffer, R. G. (1969). *Directing reading maturity as a cognitive process.* New York: Harper & Row.

Steig, W. (1982). *Doctor De Soto.* New York: Farrar, Straus, and Giroux.

Stenger, M. (2014, August 6). 5 research-based tips for providing students with meaningful feedback [Blog post]. *Edutopia.* Accessed at www.edutopia.org/blog/tips-providing-students-meaningful-feedback-marianne-stenger on September 7, 2020.

Sternberg, R. J. (2003). *Wisdom, intelligence, and creativity synthesized.* New York: Cambridge University Press.

Suess, J. (2015, September 14). *Power to the people: Why self-management is important.* Accessed at https://er.educause.edu/blogs/2015/9/power-to-the-people-why-self-management-is-important on September 2, 2020.

Tankersley, K. (2005). *Literacy strategies for grades 4-12: Reinforcing the threads of reading*. Alexandria, VA: Association for Supervision and Curriculum Development.

Taylor, J. (2012, December 4). How technology is changing the way children think and focus [Blog post]. *Psychology Today*. Accessed at www.psychologytoday.com/us/blog/the-power-prime/201212/how-technology-is-changing-the-way-children-think-and-focus on July 23, 2020.

Taylor, M. J., Hallam, P. R., Charlton, C. T., & Wall, D. G. (2013). *Formative assessment of collaborative teams (FACT): Development of a grade-level instructional team checklist*. Accessed at www.researchgate.net/publication/275010003_Formative_Assessment_of_Collaborative_Teams_FACT_Development_of_a_Grade-Level_Instructional_Team_Checklist on August 16, 2020.

TeacherVision Staff. (2007). *Directed reading-thinking activity*. Accessed at www.teachervision.com/directed-reading-thinking-activity on September 5, 2020.

Texas Education Agency. (2012). *Texas Essential Knowledge and Skills for technology applications*. Accessed at http://ritter.tea.state.tx.us/rules/tac/chapter126/ch126b.pdf on September 27, 2020.

Thalheimer, W. (2018). *The learning-transfer evaluation model: Sending messages to enable learning effectiveness*. Accessed at www.worklearning.com/wp-content/uploads/2018/02/Thalheimer-The-Learning-Transfer-Evaluation-Model-Report-for-LTEM-v11.pdf on August 15, 2020.

Thalheimer, W. (2020, January 6). Major research review on learning transfer [Blog post]. *Work-Learning Research*. Accessed at www.Worklearning.Com/2020/01/06/Major-Research-Review-On-Learning-Transfer on March 24, 2020.

Thapa, A., & Cohen, J. (2013). A review of school climate research. *Review of Educational Research, 83*(3), 357–385.

Training Express. (2020, May 3). *Critical thinking skills: A guide for problem-solving* [Blog post]. *Training Express*. Accessed at www.trainingexpress.org.uk/critical-thinking-skills-problem-solving on September 5, 2020.

Tresize, K., Bourgeois, A., & Luck, C. (2017). *Emotions in classrooms: The need to understand how emotions affect learning and education*. Accessed at https://npjscilearncommunity.nature.com/posts/18507-emotions-in-classrooms-the-need-to-understand-how-emotions-affect-learning-and-education on December 6, 2020.

Trilling, B., & Fadel, C. (2009). *21st century skills: Learning for life in our times*. San Francisco: Jossey-Bass.

UN Affairs. (2019). *UK's Johnson warns of dystopian digital future, calls on UN to set global standards for emerging technologies*. Accessed at https://news.un.org/en/story/2019/09/1047422 on March 24, 2020.

UNESCO Institute for Lifelong Learning. (n.d.). *Malta: National lifelong learning strategy—2020, issued in 2015*. Accessed at https://uil.unesco.org/document/malta-national-lifelong-learning-strategy-2020-issued-2015 on March 24, 2020.

University of Tennessee. (n.d.). *Multiple intelligence theory*. Accessed at https://uthsc.edu/tlc/intelligence-theory.php#:~:text=Interpersonal%20intelligence%20is%20the%20ability,ability%20to%20entertain%20multiple%20perspectives. On December 7, 2020.

Utami, B., Probosari, R. M., Saputro, S., Ashadi, A., & Masykuri, M. (2018). Empowering critical thinking skills with problem solving in higher education *Journal of Physics: Conference Series*.

Vander Ark, T., & Schneider, C. (2014). *Deeper learning for every student every day*. Accessed at https://hewlett.org/library/deeper-learning-for-every-student-every-day on September 7, 2020.

Vannoy, B. (2018). *Levi's great and wonderful life: A child's story about overcoming fears, setting goals, and achieving success through visualization*. Scotts Valley, CA: CreateSpace.

Vaughn, M. (2018). Making sense of agency in the early grades. *Phi Delta Kappan, 99*(7), 62–66.

Viorst, J. (2014). *Alexander and the terrible, horrible, no good, very bad day*. New York: Little Simon.

Voss, J. F. (1988). Problem solving and reasoning in ill-structured domains. In C. Antaki (Ed.), *Analysing everyday explanation: A casebook of methods* (pp. 74–93). Newbury Park, CA: SAGE.

Vuorikari, R., Punie, Y., Carretero S., & Van den Brande, L. (2016). *DigComp 2.0: The digital competence framework for citizens*. Luxembourg: Publication Office of the European Union. Accessed at https://publications.jrc.ec.europa.eu/repository/bitstream/JRC101254/jrc101254_digcomp%202.0%20the%20digital%20competence%20framework%20for%20citizens.%20update%20phase%201.pdf on July 21, 2020.

Vygotsky, L. S. (1978). *Mind in society: The development of higher psychological processes*. Cambridge, MA: Harvard University Press.

Wagner, T. (2008). *The global achievement gap: Why even our best schools don't teach the new survival skills our children need—and what we can do about it*. New York: Basic Books.

Waldman, C. (2018). *New policy briefs on increasing teachers' capacity for fostering deeper learning* [Policy updates]. Alexandra, VA: National Association of State Boards of Education. Accessed at https://deeperlearning4all.org/category/report on January 23, 2019.

Walton, M. (2017, August 31). A teacher's guide to student online safety [Blog post]. *National Cybersecurity Alliance*. Accessed at https://staysafeonline.org/blog/teachers-guide-student-online-safety on July 23, 2020.

Waring, R. (2001). *Hungry hen*. New York: HarperCollins.

Wiggins, G., & McTighe, J. (2005). *Understanding by design* (Expanded 2nd ed.). Alexandria, VA: Association for Supervision and Curriculum Development.

Wiggins, G., & McTighe, J. (2008). *Put understanding first*. Accessed at www.ascd.org/publications/educational-leadership/may08/vol65/num08/Put-Understanding-First.aspx on March 31, 2020.

Willingham, D. T. (2019). *How to teach critical thinking*. Accessed at www.danielwillingham.com/uploads/5/0/0/7/5007325/willingham_2019_nsw_critical_thinking.pdf on August 17, 2020.

Willis, J. (2007). *The neuroscience of joyful education*. Accessed at www.ascd.org/publications/educational-leadership/summer07/vol64/num09/The-Neuroscience-of-Joyful-Education.aspx on April 1, 2020.

Willis, J. (2009, April 17). Brain toxic classrooms [Blog post]. *Psychology Today*. Accessed at www.psychologytoday.com/us/blog/radical-teaching/200904/brain-toxic-classrooms on April 1, 2020.

Wisconsin Department of Public Instruction. (2018). *Wisconsin standards for social studies*. Accessed at https://dpi.wi.gov/sites/default/files/imce/standards/New%20pdfs/2018_WI_Social_Studies_Standards.pdf on September 27, 2020.

Wismath, S. L., & Orr, D. (2015). *Collaborative learning in problem solving: A case study in metacognitive learning*. Accessed at http://dx.doi.org/10.5206/cjsotl-rcacea.2015.3.10 on September 5, 2020.

Woodill, G. (2018, January 23). Rapid doubling of knowledge drives change in how we learn [Blog post]. *Float*. Accessed at https://gowithfloat.com/2018/01/rapid-doubling-knowledge-drives-change-learn on September 7, 2020.

Woods, W. D., Kemppanen, J., Turhanov, A., & Waugh, L. J. (2015). *Apollo 13: Day 3, part 2—'Houston, we've had a problem'*. Accessed at https://history.nasa.gov/afj/ap13fj/08day3-problem.html on August 16, 2020.

World-Class Instructional Design and Assessment Consortium. (2007). *English language proficiency standards' grade 6 through grade 12*. Accessed at https://wida.wisc.edu/sites/default/files/resource/2007-ELPS-Grade-6-12.pdf on June 1, 2020.

World Economic Forum. (2020). *Jobs of tomorrow: Mapping opportunity in the new economy*. Accessed at www3.weforum.org/docs/WEF_Jobs_of_Tomorrow_2020.pdf on March 24, 2020.

World Health Organization. (2020). *Transmission of SARS-CoV-2: Implications for infection prevention precautions*. Accessed at www.who.int/news-room/commentaries/detail/transmission-of-sars-cov-2-implications-for-infection-prevention-precautions on August 17, 2020.

Wüstenberg, S., Greiff, S., & Funke, J. (2012). Complex problem solving—More than reasoning? *Intelligence, 40*(1), 1–14.

Xunzi. (2014). *Xunzi: The complete works* (E. L. Hutton, Trans.). Princeton, NJ: Princeton University Press.

Younger, H. R. (2016). *#1 emotion leaders have and really should use*. Accessed at www.huffpost.com/entry/1-emotion-leaders-have-and-really-should-use_b_10137518 on September 30, 2020.

Zeiser, K., Taylor, J., Rickles, J., & Garet, M. S. (2014). *Evidence of deeper learning outcomes*. Accessed at www.air.org/resource/evidence-deeper-learning-outcomes on April 1, 2020.

Zelazo, P. D., Blair, C. B., & Willoughby, M. T. (2016). *Executive function: Implications for education*. Accessed at https://ies.ed.gov/ncer/pubs/20172000/pdf/20172000.pdf on October 5, 2020.

INDEX

#
21st century skills, 7–8, 29, 30, 31. *See also* complex cognitive skill sets; digital skill sets; social-emotional skill sets

A
ABC feedback, 98–99
accessing the future, 129, 143–144. *See also* prediction skills
activities/strategies, list of. *See* list of activities/strategies
American Institutes for Research (AIR), 3
anger management, 152
Armstrong, T., 36
ARREST coaching responses, 111
artifacts of learning, 82–83, 102, 198
artificial intelligence (AI), education and, 209–210. *See also* digital tools/technology
assessments. *See also* outcome-driven instruction and assessments
    formative assessments, 76, 194
    implementation plans and, 194–195
    learning transfer and, 115
    personalized learning and, 12–13
    personalized learning plans and, 18, 19–20, 67–68
    personalized teaching plans and, 77–78
    self-assessments, 50, 231–232
    tools for. *See* guiding rubrics
authentic problems/scenarios, 50

B
backward design, 12, 58, 60
backward transfer, 107, 108. *See also* learning transfer
base groups/base teams, 46, 100
basic cognitive skills, 67. *See also* complex cognitive skill sets
Bellanca, J., 45
Blueprints for Achievement in a Cooperative Classroom (Bellanca & Fogarty), 45

brainstorming
    activities/strategies for, 135–138
    digital skill set activities/strategies and, 192
    formal brainstorming, 135, 139
    guiding rubrics for, 139
    informal brainstorming, 135
    playbook example for, 136
Buddha, 101
bullying/cyberbullying, 183

C
Carlin, G., 122
Champions Against Bullying, 183
checklists. *See* scorable checklists
Childhood101, 183
classrooms
    agency in the classroom, 88, 89
    classroom calm centers, 154
    interpersonal relationship skills and, 161
    looks and sounds of healthy classrooms, 39
    personalized learning in the classroom, 23–24
    personalized learning, readying for, 25–26
    respect and trust in, 37–39
coaching. *See also* teachers
    ARREST coaching responses, 111
    peer coaching, 58, 195
    personalized learning plan processes and, 20
    teacher playbook example and, 64
collaboration. *See also* social-emotional skill sets
    class collaboration contract activity, 164
    collaborative class puzzle activity, 44
    engagement and trust and, 36–37
    four Cs and, 2
    interpersonal relationship skills and, 162

personalized learning plans and, 13, 21
remote learning and, 172
Collaborative for Academic, Social, and Emotional Learning (CASEL), 29, 32, 150
Common Core State Standards, 29
communication
- assessing personalized learning plans and, 80–81
- conflict management and, 153
- digital skill sets and, 176, 178
- engagement and trust and, 36–37
- four Cs and, 2
- interpersonal relationship skills and, 161
- personalized learning plans and, 21

complex cognitive skill sets
- 21st century three-story intellect and, 31
- about, 119–120
- complex cognition, 120
- content and thinking skills and, 122–123
- deeper learning skills example and, 67
- job skills and, 2
- in pyramid goals with outcome and goal examples, 55
- and responding to need for students to know how to think, 123
- skill set-based competencies and, 59
- skill sets for teaching, 30–31
- skills included in, 121
- standards and, 29
- teacher playbook example for, 121

complex thinking skills, 29, 106, 120, 121
computer-assisted instruction (CAI), 196. *See also* digital tools/technology
concept maps, example of, 134, 138, 171
cooperative contracts, 164
cooperative learning
- about, 45
- digital skill set activities/strategies and, 192
- digital tools and, 195
- formal cooperative learning, 46
- informal and formal cooperative learning activity, 192
- informal cooperative learning, 45
- playbook example for, 47, 48
- social-emotional skill sets and, 32
- teamwork and, 44

Covey, S., 57
COVID-19, 24, 88, 172
creative thinking
- about, 128–129
- accessing the future, what is. *See* accessing the future; prediction skills
- four Cs and, 2
- ideating, what is. *See* ideation skills
- job skills and, 2
- synthesizing, what is. *See* synthesis
- verbs for, 121
- visualizing, what is. *See* visualizing

critical thinking
- about, 122
- activities/strategies for, 126–128
- four Cs and, 2
- guiding rubrics for, 123, 124, 125
- job skills and, 2
- teacher playbook example for, 124
- verbs for, 121

critical-friend teams, 100
Curriculum21, 122
Cushing, R., 57
cyberbullying, 183

D

Dalio, R., 129
Danielson, C., 41
Darling-Hammond, L., 58
Deci, E., 88
decision making
- activities/strategies for, 46–51
- social-emotional skill sets and, 150

deeper learning
- about, 3–4
- computer-assisted instruction (CAI) and, 196
- deeper learning competencies, prioritizing, 58–60
- example of deeper learning skills, 67
- learning transfer and, 106
- planning for deeper learning outcomes, 57–58
- pyramid of deeper learning outcomes, 4
- student-centered deeper learning outcomes, 7

Department for Children, Schools and Families, 29
depth transfer, 107. *See also* learning transfer
design thinking, 31, 57
developmental rating scale, 194
DigComp 2.0, 176
DigComp 2.1, 176
DigCompEdu, 176
digital citizens/digital citizenship, 32, 175, 197
Digital Competence Framework for Citizens, 175, 176, 177, 178, 182, 188
digital devices. *See* digital tools/technology
digital identity/safety, 177, 183, 188, 203
digital literacy, 176, 196
digital portfolios, 196, 198–199
digital skill sets
- 21st century three-story intellect and, 31
- about, 175–176
- activities/strategies for, 192–193

assessments and, 68
deeper learning skills example and, 67
digital skills, what are, 176
digital tools and, 195–200, 203, 205
guiding rubrics and, 193–194
implementation plans, assessing, 194–195
job skills and, 2
promoting with lessons/projects, 179–180, 182–183, 188, 192
in pyramid goals with outcome and goal examples, 55
remote learning and, 205–206
skill set-based competencies and, 59
skill sets for teaching, 32–33
skills included in, 176–178
skills students need, determining, 178–179
digital thinkers, 33
digital tools/technology
about, 195–196
access to, 178
computer-assisted instruction (CAI) and, 196
digital portfolios and, 198–199
education and, 209–210
learning management systems (LMS) and, 197–198
personalized learning plans and, 7, 8, 13
playbooks and, 200–201, 203
playlists and, 199–200, 206–207
reflection journals and, 203
rubrics banks and, 203
social media networks and, 203, 205
templates and, 203
Texas technology standards and, 29
tool categories, 196–197
websites and, 205
direct instruction, 67. *See also* outcome-driven instruction and assessments
directed reading, 144, 145
directed reading thinking activity (DRTA), 144
divergent thinking, 135
Dulin, M., 48

E

Einstein, A., 128
elementary school
activities for problem solving, 49, 50
activities/strategies for complex cognitive skill sets, 126, 130, 136–137, 141, 145, 147
activities/strategies for social-emotional skill sets, 154–155, 159, 163–164, 169
digital skill sets and, 180, 182, 205
guiding rubric examples for, 73, 115
leveled outcome statements developed with SMART criteria for, 70

online safety and, 183
outcome ideas, 22
personalized teaching plan example for, 180–182
planning for transfer example for, 112
playbook examples for, 47, 200, 202
prediction chart example for, 145
SMART outcomes and, 8
tight word problems for, 48
emotion self-management
about, 150–151
activities/strategies for, 153–156
conflict management and, 153
cool-down guidelines and, 152
guiding rubrics for, 156, 157
promoting with lessons/projects, 151–153
prompts and, 153
remote learning and, 173
social-emotional skill sets and, 150
emotional intelligence, 150, 161
empathy
about, 156, 158
activities/strategies for, 159–160
looks and sounds of, 157
playlist of quotes about, 161
promoting with lessons/projects, 158
prompts and, 158
rubrics and, 161
social-emotional skill sets and, 150
engagement
about, 35–36
deep engagement, 36
social-emotional engagement, 59
surface engagement, 35
engagement and trust
about, 35
activities/strategies for decision-making scenarios, 46, 48–51
activities/strategies for trust, 41–44
communication and collaboration and, 36–37
cooperative learning, about, 45–46
cooperative learning and team problem solving and, 44–45
engagement, about, 35–36
peer interviews and, 39
promoting deeper engagement, 36
reflection and, 39, 41
respect and trust, gauging, 37–39
environment
and engagement and trust, 36
and looks and sounds of healthy classrooms, 39
and toxicity in classrooms, 37–39
evidence-based practices, 8

F

far transfer. *See also* learning transfer
  look and sounds of, 113, 114, 115
  proximity transfer and, 106, 107
feedback. *See also* two-way feedback
  ABC feedback, 98–99
  assessing impact on student agency, 98–99
  assessments
    personalized learning plans and, 80, 81
  cool (versus warm) feedback, 101
  criteria for, 99
  developing feedback skills, 101–102
  guiding feedback process, 100–101
  hard feedback, 101–102
  implementation plans and, 194
  peer feedback, 100
  record-keeping systems and, 102
  teamwork skills and, 100
  warm (versus cool) feedback, 101
Feuerstein, R., 1–2, 4–5, 32
Fogarty, R., 45
formative assessments, 76, 194. *See also* assessments
forward transfer, 109, 110. *See also* learning transfer
Foundry, 205
four Cs, 2, 30
Framework for Teaching Evaluation Instrument (Danielson), 41

G

goal setting
  about, 167
  activities/strategies for, 169–171
  assessments and, 68
  digital skill sets and, 195
  promoting with lessons/projects, 167
  prompts and, 167–169
  rubrics for, 172, 173
  social-emotional skill sets and, 150
  student playbook example for, 168
  teacher playbook example for, 167
goals. *See also* SMART goals/outcomes
  example pyramid goals with outcomes and, 55
  goal ladders activity, 170
  my goal activity, 130
  outcome-driven instruction and, 53–54
  outcomes and, 12
  personalized learning and, 13
  standards for, 98–99
  vision boards activity, 171
grading rubrics, 71–72. *See also* guiding rubrics
graphic organizers
  data-analysis KNHWL, 128
  fishbone graphic organizer, 129
  for forward transfer, 109
  KNM graphic organizers, 178–179
  KWL organizers, 97
  what we know organizer, 108
grouping
  base groups/base teams, 46, 100
  brainstorming techniques and, 135–136
  cooperative learning and, 45
  feedback and, 103
  heterogeneous grouping, 195
  interpersonal relationship skills and, 161
  personalized learning plans and, 26
  support groups activity, 155–156
Guglielmino, L., 89, 92
guiding rubrics. *See also* multi-point guiding rubrics; open-ended guiding rubrics; scorable checklists; single-point guiding rubrics
  about, 8, 70–71
  assessing personalized learning plans and, 80
  critical-thinking skills and, 123, 124, 125
  digital skill sets and, 33, 193–194
  emotion self-management and, 156
  empathy and, 161
  example of, 56
  feedback process and, 100–101
  formal brainstorming and, 139
  goal setting and, 172, 173
  grading rubrics and, 71–72
  interpersonal relationship skills and, 165–166
  outcome-driven assessment and, 66
  personalized learning plan processes and, 20
  personalized teaching plans and, 61, 79
  prediction skills and, 147–148
  synthesis and, 143
  types of, 72–73, 75–77
  visualizing and, 132

H

Hattie, J., 32
Henley, W., 87
Hewlett Foundation, 3
high school
  activities/strategies for complex cognitive skill sets, 127–128, 131–132, 137–138, 142–143, 147
  activities/strategies for social-emotional skill sets, 156, 160, 164–165, 170–171
  digital identity/safety and, 188
  guiding rubric examples for, 73–74, 117, 124
  leveled outcome statements developed with SMART criteria for, 70
  outcome ideas, 22

personalized teaching plan example for, 189–192
planning for transfer example, 112–113
playbook example for, 48, 204
playlist example for, 201
problem-solving activities for, 49, 50–51
and promoting digital skill sets, 192
SMART outcomes and, 9
tight word problems for, 48
websites for middle and high school, 205, 206
higher-order-thinking skills, 30. See also complex cognitive skill sets
Hoffman, M., 32
Holubec, E., 32

I

ideation skills
about, 132–133
activities/strategies for, 135–138
creative thinking and, 129
guiding rubrics for, 139
personalized learning plans and, 133
synthesizing and, 140
teacher playbook example for, 133
implementation, 19, 194–195
information management/digital skill sets, 176, 178
inquiry lessons, 68
instructional practices, 12–13. See also outcome-driven instruction and assessments
International Literacy Association, 195
interpersonal relationship skills
about, 161
activities/strategies for, 163–165
assessments and, 68
promoting with lessons/projects, 162
prompts and, 163
rubrics and, 165
social-emotional skill sets and, 150
interviews
peer interviews, 39
playbook example for, 40
reproducibles for, 217–218
"Invictus" (Henley), 87

J

Jacobs, H. H., 122, 175
Jezard, A., 32
job skills, 2, 37
Johnson, D., 32, 45, 100
Johnson, R., 32, 45, 100

K

Knowles, M., 32, 93

L

learning management systems (LMS), 197–198
learning transfer
about, 105–106
assessments and, 68
depth transfer, 107
directional transfer, 107, 109
focus and, 110
guiding rubric examples for, 116, 117
look and sounds of, 113–115
planning for, 110–113
proximity transfer, 106–107, 113, 115
lectures and notetaking, 67
Lee, K., 197
list of activities/strategies
ABC book, 154
about us scavenger hunt, 163–164
all hands on deck, 50–51
analogy central, 131
back to back, 164–165
blog it or podcast it, 193
board game invention, 156
brainstorming for digital skill sets, 192
brainstorming techniques, 135–138
build it better, 127–128
building block toy, 130
by any other name, 44
children's book, 156
class collaboration contract, 164
classroom calm centers, 154
collaborative class puzzle, 44
computer science metaphor, 141–142
cook a meal for someone who needs it, 160
design project, 193
dig their feelings, 156
digital brain netting, 138
dream job letter, 147
emoji card trading, 154–155
engineering feats, 44
estimation games, 147
fishbone for the future, 147
give seniors help, 160
goal ladders, 170
hero mindstorming, 137
how many uses/stars in the sky, 136–137
informal and formal cooperative learning, 192
informal team-building activities, 162
interest maps, 170–171
invent a dinosaur, 126
invent it my way, 131
journey: a story board, 131
just doodle it, 160

Levi's Great and Wonderful Life, 169
loose problem solving, 50–51
magic circle, 43
make a magazine cover, 165
make a mobile, 159–160
make it a problem, 193
math simile, 141
matrix generator, 137–138
me collage, 130
me journals, 155
model interview, 132
my career, 138
my future self, 169
my goal, 130
my neighborhood web, 136
my story, 130–131
name game, 164
need-to-know on the go, 127
need-to-know survey, 127
no more noise, 160
our new word list, 159
our STEM museum, 147
PACTS, 155
peer interviews, 39
people search, 163
perseverance, 49
person, place, thing review, 137
pick a story, 154
picture book, 130
pieces of junk, 137
podcasts, 155
posters, 159
precision and accuracy, 49
prediction pail, 145
problem-solving procedures, 49
prompt circle, 43
public sculpture, 131–132
quotes, 160
random webs, 142
random word links, 141
science scavenger search, 43–44
shapes made perfect, 43
simulate it, 193
story role play, 159
support groups, 155–156
survive, 50
tangrams, 126
teach self-monitoring questions, 155
team cup pyramid, 50
team investigation, 193
that's a good connection because, 142–143

three stars and a wish, 169
tight problem solving, 46, 48–49
two-way feedback, 192–193
U.S. Constitution analogy, 142
vision boards, 171
weather project, 145, 147
what I've learned, 137
wheel of fortune, 169–170
"Who am I?" show-and-tell, 164
word clouds, 127
world of dreams, 171
loosely structured problems, 28
Lynch, M., 196

M

Mader, M., 33
Maki, C., 38
Malcolm X, 57
Mandela, N., 87
manual skills, 6, 31, 67
Matthews, G., 167
McDowell, M., 106
McTighe, J., 57
mediated learning experiences, 32
memorization, 48, 120
metacognition, 29
middle school
    activities/strategies for complex cognitive skill sets, 127, 130–131, 137, 141–142, 147
    activities/strategies for social-emotional skill sets, 155–156, 159–160, 164, 169–170
    digital identity/safety and, 188
    guiding rubric examples for, 73–74, 116
    leveled outcome statements developed with SMART criteria for, 70
    outcome ideas, 22
    personalized teaching plan example for, 184–188
    playbook example for, 47, 110, 202
    playlist example for, 201
    problem-solving activities for, 49, 50
    and promoting digital skill sets, 182–183, 188, 192, 205
    SMART outcomes and, 9
    tight word problems for, 48
    websites for middle and high school, 205, 206
Miller, R., 32
mindsets, 67–68
"More Coding Instruction Would Be Helpful" (Stanford), 32
Morin, A., 158
multi-point guiding rubrics. *See also* guiding rubrics
    about, 75–76
    examples of, 76–77, 117, 139
    reproducibles for, 228–230

N

near transfer. *See also* learning transfer
    look and sounds of, 113, 114, 115
    proximity transfer and, 106–107
need-to-know labs, 97
need-to-know statements, 95, 96, 97
need-to-know teachable moments, 80–81
New York State Department of Education, 21
Next Generation Science Standards, 29

O

Ogle, D., 97
online safety, 177, 183, 188, 203. *See also* digital skill sets
open-ended guiding rubrics. *See also* guiding rubrics
    about, 77
    example of, 78
    reproducibles for, 231–232
open-ended questions, 45
Organisation for Economic Co-operation and Development (OECD), 21, 29, 36–37
outcome-driven instruction and assessments
    about, 53
    assessing personalized teaching plans and, 77–78
    authentic outcomes and, 65
    deeper learning competencies, prioritizing, 58–60
    deeper learning outcomes, planning for, 57–58
    design thinking and personalized learning plans and, 57
    logistics for a personalized learning plan assessment, 83–84
    organizing playbooks, playlists, rubrics, and artifacts and, 82–83
    outcome-driven assessments, about, 65–66
    outcome-driven instruction, about, 53–55
    outcomes, assessing with a personalized learning plan, 67–68
    outcomes-driving assessments, looks and sounds of, 68–69
    personalized learning plan assessments, responsibilities in, 78–82
    personalized teaching plan, creating, 60–61
    tools for assessing personalized learning plan outcomes. *See* guiding rubrics
    two-way feedback, time and place for, 103–104
outcomes. *See also* SMART goals/outcomes
    assessing personalized learning plans and, 79–80
    assessing with a personalized learning plan, 67–68
    authentic outcomes, constructing, 65
    leveled outcome statements, 70
    outcome ideas, 22
    personalized learning plans and, 7, 12, 20
    personalized teaching plans and, 54

    planning for deeper learning outcomes, 57–58
    pyramid goals with outcome and goal examples, 55

P

Partnership for 21st Century Learning, 2, 30
peers
    empathy and, 158
    peer coaching, 58, 195
    peer feedback, 100, 194
    peer interviews, 39
personalized learning plans
    about, 11–12
    addressing what students need to know with, 27
    design thinking and, 57
    evidence supporting, 13
    examples of, 14–15, 16–17
    launching, 20–23
    looks and sounds of, 23
    potential for, 23–24
    preparing class for, 25–26
    processes of, 18–20
    remote learning and, 24–25
    reproducibles for, 212–214, 215–216
    skill sets for, 30–33
    standards, covering, 27–30
    student agency and, 95
    tools, results, and guide-on-the-side diagram, 7
    what it looks like, 13–14, 16–17
personalized teaching plans
    assessing, 77–78, 79
    creating, 60–61
    digital skill sets example for, 180–182, 184–188, 189–192
    example of, 62–63
    outcomes and, 54
    reproducibles for, 219–221
planning process, 13, 18–19
playbooks. *See also* student playbooks; teacher playbooks
    about, 5
    assessing personalized learning plans and, 81
    for brainstorming, 136
    category-style, 84
    for cooperative learning, 47, 48
    digital tools and, 200–201, 202, 203, 204
    example of, 40
    organizing playbooks, playlists, rubrics, and artifacts and, 82–83
    playbook and playlist ideas, 83
    for portfolios, 84
    for skill transfer, 110
    for teamwork, 42

playlists
- assessing personalized learning plans and, 81–82
- digital tools and, 196, 199–200
- digital tools example for, 206–207
- examples of, 103, 200, 201
- organizing playbooks, playlists, rubrics, and artifacts and, 82–83
- playbook and playlist ideas, 83
- playlist of quotes about empathy, 161

PLC (professional learning communities), 5

portfolios
- digital portfolios, 196, 198–199
- personalized learning plans and, 22

prediction skills
- about, 143–144
- activities/strategies for, 145, 147
- guiding rubrics for, 147–148
- prediction chart example, 144, 145
- promoting with lessons/projects, 144–145
- teacher playbook example for, 146

prior knowledge, 27, 107

problem solving
- content and thinking skills and, 122
- digital skill sets and, 177
- loose problem-solving activities, 50–51
- problem-solving procedures activity, 49
- tight problem-solving activities, 46, 48–49

professional learning communities (PLC), 5
project-based learning (PBL), 3, 4, 68, 92, 205
Project Zero, 177

prompts
- backward transfer and, 108
- emotion self-management and, 153
- empathy and, 158
- flexibility and fluency questions, prompts, and stems, 135
- forward transfer and, 109
- goal setting and, 167–169
- interpersonal relationship skills and, 163
- open-ended prompts, 98
- PACTS prompt model, 153, 155
- PIES prompt model, 158, 159
- prompt circle activity, 43
- reflection journals and, 203

Q

questioning/questions
- flexibility and fluency questions, prompts, and stems, 135
- teach self-monitoring questions activity, 155
- think-pair-share and, 45

R

Rand, Y., 32
rated checklists. *See* scorable checklists

recall
- complex cognitive skill sets and, 30
- learning transfer and, 107
- standards and, 28, 120
- use of, 48

reciprocal learning strategies, 71, 144

record-keeping systems
- assessing personalized learning plans and, 80
- feedback and, 102
- learning management systems and, 197–198
- organizing playbooks, playlists, rubrics, and artifacts and, 82–83

reflection
- example reflection questions, 41, 51
- promoting reflection, 39, 41
- reflection journals, 196, 203

relationships. *See* interpersonal relationship skills

remote learning
- digital tools and, 205–206
- personalized learning plans and, 24–25
- social-emotional skills and, 172–173

reproducibles for
- improvement rating scale, 224–225
- interview questions, 217–218
- multi-point guiding rubric, 228–230
- open-ended self-assessment rubric, 231–232
- personalized learning plan, 212–214
- personalized teaching plan, 219–221
- rated checklist, 222–223
- single-point guiding rubric, 226–228
- starter personalized learning plan, 215–216

Roosevelt, E., 57
round-robin responses, 41, 42

rubrics. *See also* guiding rubrics
- digital tools and, 203
- goal setting and, 172
- for persistence in learning, 90
- rubrics banks, 203

Ryan, R., 88

S

scaffolding, 95
scope and sequence, 28
scorable checklists. *See also* guiding rubrics
- about, 73
- example of, 73–74
- reproducibles for, 222–223, 224–225

self-assessments. *See also* assessments
    loose problem-solving activities and, 50
    reproducibles for, 231–232
self-directed learning, 12, 89, 93, 173
Self-Directed Learning Readiness Scale (SDLRS), 89, 92
self-management. *See also* emotion self-management
    looks and sounds of self-management, 37, 38
    remote learning and, 173
shallow transfer, 107. *See also* learning transfer
SHARE, 39
single-point guiding rubrics. *See also* guiding rubrics
    about, 73, 75
    example of, 75, 102, 115, 116, 157
    reproducibles for, 226–227
skill transfer
    about, 105
    assessing transfer, 115
    assessments and, 68
    learning transfer, about, 105–107, 109
    learning transfer, focus on, 110
    look and sounds of proximity transfer, 113, 115
    planning for, 110–113
skills/skill sets
    complex cognitive skill sets. *See* complex cognitive skill sets
    deeper learning skills example, 67
    digital skill sets. *See* digital skill sets
    foundational skills, 27
    job skills, 2, 37
    manual skills, 6, 31, 67
    personalized learning plan processes and, 20
    skill set-based competencies, 59
    social-emotional skill sets. *See* social-emotional skill sets
SMART goals/outcomes
    assessing personalized learning plans and, 79–80
    in the classroom, 8–9
    critical thinking and, 123
    feedback and student agency and, 98
    guiding rubrics example for, 66
    leveled outcome statements developed with SMART criteria, 70
    outcome-driven instruction and, 53–54
    personalized learning plan processes and, 18
    personalized learning plans and, 7
    planning for deeper learning outcomes, 57–58
social media networks, 196, 203, 205. *See also* websites/applications
social-emotional skill sets
    21st century three-story intellect and, 31
    about, 149–150
    assessments and, 68
    CASEL and, 29

    communication and collaboration and, 36–37
    deeper learning skills example and, 67
    empathy. *See* empathy
    goal setting. *See* goal setting
    interpersonal relationship skills. *See* interpersonal relationship skills
    job skills and, 2
    personalized learning plans and, 21
    in pyramid goals with outcome and goal examples, 55
    reflection and, 41
    remote learning and, 172–173
    skill set-based competencies and, 59
    skill sets for teaching, 32
    skills included in, 150
    social-emotional learning, what is, 150
standards
    critical-thinking skills and, 120
    personalized learning plans and, 27–30
    proximity transfer and, 113
    unwrapping/unpacking standards, 120
Stanford, S., 32
student agency
    about, 87–88
    agency from two perspectives, 90–91
    degrees of agency, determining, 91–93, 95
    digital skill sets and, 195
    encouraging and developing agency, 95–97
    feedback, agency-enhancing, 99–102
    feedback, assessing, 98–99
    levels of agency, 93–94
    look and sounds of, 89
    research on, 88
    student agency continuum, 92
    two-way feedback and, 173
    two-way feedback, promoting with, 97–98
student playbooks. *See also* playbooks; teacher playbooks
    about, 5
    examples of, 61, 82, 103, 134, 168
student self-efficacy, 13
students
    and agency from two perspectives, 90–91
    authentic outcomes and, 65
    fears and, 26
    and looks and sounds of personalized learning, 24
    responding to need for students to know how to think, 123
Surman, M., 175
synthesis
    about, 139–140
    activities/strategies for, 140–143
    creative thinking and, 129
    guiding rubrics for, 139, 143

ideating and, 140
promoting with lessons/projects, 140

T
task analysis, 200
teacher playbooks. *See also* playbooks; student playbooks
    about, 5
    for complex cognitive skills, 121
    for critical thinking, 124
    for deeper learning competencies, 60
    examples of, 18, 19
    for getting started, 21
    for goal setting, 167
    for ideation skills, 133
    image teacher playbook concept map, 171
    personalized learning plans and, 16–17
    for portfolios, 199
    for predicting, 146
    for round-robin responses, 42
    for SHARE, 82
teachers
    agency from two perspectives, 90–91
    assessing personalized learning plans and, 78–82
    as guide on the side, 8
    looks and sounds of personalized learning, 24
    peer coaching and, 58
    SMART outcomes and, 9
teamwork/team skills
    activities/strategies for, 46–51
    assessments and, 165
    cooperative learning and team problem solving and, 44–45
    formal cooperative learning and, 46
    guiding rubrics for, 166
    informal team-building activities, 162
    interpersonal relationship skills and, 162
    team cup pyramid activity, 50
    team investigation activity, 193
technology. *See* digital tools/technology
Texas technology standards, 29
Thalheimer, W., 123
thinking skills, 123. *See also* complex cognitive skill sets
think-pair-share, 45, 46, 77, 109
tightly structured problems, 28
trust, activities/strategies for, 43–44. *See also* engagement and trust
two-way feedback
    digital skill sets activities/strategies and, 192–193
    establish norms for, 99–100
    guiding rubrics and, 76, 100–101
    peer feedback and, 100
    promoting agency with, 97–98
    student agency and, 173
    time and place for, 103–104
    two-way feedback activity, 192–193
Tyson, N., 158

V
visualizing
    about, 129–130
    activities/strategies for, 130–132
    guiding rubrics for, 132
    vision boards activity, 171
Vygotsky, L., 95

W
Warlick, D., 175
WeAreTeachers, 183
websites/applications. *See also* digital tools/technology
    Classkick, 25
    digital tools and, 196, 205
    Dropbox, 198
    Facebook, 205
    Foundry, 205
    GIMP, 188
    Google, 198
    Khan Academy, 205
    Kidblog, 205
    Macintosh Finder, 198
    Microsoft OneDrive, 198
    National Geographic Education, 205
    Nearpod, 25
    Office Lens, 198
    PhET, 205, 206
    Science A–Z, 205
    TeachThought, 198
    Tiny Scanner, 198
    Twitter, 205
    Weebly, 198
    Windows Explorer, 198
    YouTube, 205
Wiggins, G., 57
Williams, H., 57
Wisconsin state standards, 29
write-pair-share, 45, 109, 203

X
Xunzi, 78

Z
Zipkes, S., 97

Deeper Learning
Edited by James A. Bellanca
Education authorities from around the globe explore deeper learning, a process that promotes higher-order thinking, reasoning, and problem solving to better educate students and prepare them for college and careers. Relying on research as well as their own experience, the authors show how to use intensive curriculum, instruction, assessment, and leadership practices to meet the needs of 21st century learners.
BKF622

Connecting the Dots
Edited by James A. Bellanca
Confront the issues that profoundly affect teachers, administrators, and students. From cover to cover, this collection is packed with examples of effective strategies for 21st century classrooms. Discover the shift in day-to-day practice that must occur to prepare students for college and careers, and look forward to what exemplary professional practices will be crucial in deepening student learning as the 21st century progresses.
BKF659

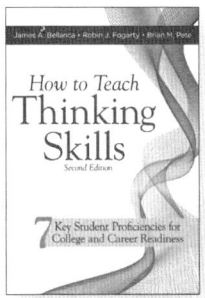

How to Teach Thinking Skills
James A. Bellanca, Robin J. Fogarty, and Brian M. Pete
Ensure your students develop the higher-order, complex thinking skills they need to not just survive but thrive in a 21st century world. The latest edition of this best-selling guide details a three-phase teaching model and dives deep into how to teach seven key student proficiencies: critical thinking, creative thinking, complex thinking, comprehensive thinking, collaborative thinking, communicative thinking, and cognitive transfer.
BKF900

Teaching for Transfer
Michael McDowell
Empower students to become creative, well-rounded citizens who are prepared to meet and overcome real-world challenges. With *Teaching for Transfer*, you'll discover a road map for reconfiguring K–12 classroom instruction to ensure learners can expertly apply their knowledge and skills to new contexts. The resource includes ample practices and protocols you can begin using today to cultivate essential transfer-level skills in students.
BKF950

Metacognition
Robin J. Fogarty and Brian M. Pete
Empower your students to become mindful, reflective, and proficient thinkers and problem solvers. In *Metacognition*, authors Robin J. Fogarty and Brian M. Pete provide a practical framework to nurture these essential skills in every learner. Research-based and classroom-approved, this resource is a must-read for educators committed to strengthening student self-awareness, self-assessment, and self-confidence for school and life.
BKB008

Visit solution-tree.com or call 800.733.6786 to order.

Wait! Your professional development journey doesn't have to end with the last pages of this book.

We realize improving student learning doesn't happen overnight. And your school or district shouldn't be left to puzzle out all the details of this process alone.

No matter where you are on the journey, we're committed to helping you get to the next stage.

Take advantage of everything from **custom workshops** to **keynote presentations** and **interactive web and video conferencing**. We can even help you develop an action plan tailored to fit your specific needs.

Let's get the conversation started.

Call 888.763.9045 today.

SolutionTree.com